UNIVERSITY PRESS OF FLORIDA

Florida A&M University, Tallahassee
Florida Atlantic University, Boca Raton
Florida Gulf Coast University, Ft. Myers
Florida International University, Miami
Florida State University, Tallahassee
New College of Florida, Sarasota
University of Central Florida, Orlando
University of Florida, Gainesville
University of North Florida, Jacksonville
University of South Florida, Tampa
University of West Florida, Pensacola

University Press of Florida

GAINESVILLE · TALLAHASSEE · TAMPA · BOCA RATON

PENSACOLA · ORLANDO · MIAMI · JACKSONVILLE · FT. MYERS · SARASOTA

CATEGORY

5

THE 1935 LABOR DAY HURRICANE

Thomas Neil Knowles

14   13   12   11   10   09   6   5   4   3   2   1

LIBRARY OF CONGRESS CATALOGING-IN-PUBLICATION DATA
Knowles, Thomas Neil.
Category 5 : the 1935 Labor Day hurricane / Thomas Neil Knowles.
p. cm.
Includes bibliographical references and index.
ISBN 978-0-8130-3310-5 (alk. paper)
1. Labor Day Hurricane, 1935. 2. Hurricanes—Florida—Florida Keys—
History—20th century. 3. Hurricanes—United States—History—20th century.
4. Florida Keys (Fla.)—History—20th century. I. Title.
QC945.K62   2009
975.9'41—dc22
2008039345

The University Press of Florida is the scholarly publishing agency for the State
University System of Florida, comprising Florida A&M University, Florida At-
lantic University, Florida Gulf Coast University, Florida International University,
Florida State University, New College of Florida, University of Central Florida,
University of Florida, University of North Florida, University of South Florida,
and University of West Florida.

University Press of Florida
15 Northwest 15th Street
Gainesville, FL 32611-2079
www.upf.com

To the survivors and others who generously shared
their experiences, and to my wife, Barbara, whose help
and patience enabled me to write this book

Contents

Preface and Acknowledgments

This book is a true account of the destruction of the Upper Florida Keys by the first Category 5 hurricane known to have made landfall in the United States. The description of events contained herein was derived from historical records and from the firsthand recollections of people who were there and lived to tell about it.

Due to space constraints, the bibliography at the end of the book is an abbreviated selection of the materials researched. A complete list of sources is available in hard copy and in electronic (pdf) form in the Florida History Department of the Monroe County May Hill Russell Library, 700 Fleming Street, Key West, FL, 33040.

Many people provided information, materials, photographs, and/or assistance to me during the twelve years it took to research and write the book. Especially important are the recollections of and materials provided by seven survivors of the hurricane: Leone Carter Carey, Elizabeth Williams Chance, Evelyn Williams Clifton, Markelle Law Hightower, Wilbur Jones, Carolyn Lowe, and Fay Parker Marrotte. Bascom Grooms (Rosalind Groom's brother), Frank Pepper (Senator Claude Pepper's brother and George Pepper's first cousin), Woodrow Pepper Clark (George Pepper's sister), Charles Carter (brother of Leone Carey and Betty King), Norma Yates Dopp, Alce Curry Maurer, and Helen Muir also provided firsthand recollections of people and events involved with the hurricane.

The following current and former employees of the Weather Bureau and its successor, the National Weather Service, and of the National Oceanic and Atmospheric Administration (NOAA) were very helpful: Roger Plaster, Steve Letro, Paul Duval, Chris Landsea, and Hugh Willoughby. Additional help with weather and storm surge topics was provided by members of the Florida State University faculty.

The description in Chapter 13 and the portrayal in the related exhibit of the Florida Bay resurgence and its dynamics appear to be a plausible explanation for the differences in the times and directions of the surging water as reported by witnesses. To my knowledge this specific aspect of the surge has not been confirmed by computer modeling or other research.

The following people provided information and materials important to the book: Mary Louisa Porter Grooms; Janet Reno; Maggy Reno Hurchalla; George Hurchalla; Jim Servies; Max Carraway, former registrar at Florida State University; Susan Abbott, archivist at the National Archives and Records Administration; Joan and Wright Langley of the Wright Langley Archives; the staff of the Strozier Library at Florida State University with special thanks to Charles Miller, former director of FSU Libraries; Tom Hambright, curator of the Florida History Department of the Monroe County May Hill Russell Library; Jerry Wilkinson, president of the Historical Preservation Society of the Upper Keys; Horace Rudisill, director of the Darlington County Historical Commission; John Shipley of the Miami-Dade Public Library; Dawn Hugh of the Historical Museum of South Florida; and Karen Furnweger, editor and content manager, Shedd Aquarium.

Talbot D'Alemberte, C. Lawrence "Larry" Carter, Frank Almyda, Penny Scruggs, Connie Phillips, and Rick Damron, M.D., also provided information and/or support that was helpful.

Larry Abele, Rodney Dillon Jr., Joe Knetsch, John Viele, and Jerry Wilkinson reviewed drafts; their constructive comments were invaluable. Special thanks to Dave Tranchand, who reviewed drafts and also assisted with the tedious work of proofreading. Finally, I want to thank the staff of the University Press of Florida for their courtesy and guidance throughout the publication process.

Tom Knowles

Maps

The following maps show the indicated areas as they existed prior to the 1935 Labor Day Hurricane. The map of South Florida and the Florida Keys was adapted from a drawing by George Mangos, circa 1927. The maps of specific islands were developed from U.S. Coast and Geodetic Survey chart 1250, issued November 1933; Topographic Map T-5540; aerial photographs taken on January 26, 1935; and information provided by people who lived on the Florida Keys in 1935.

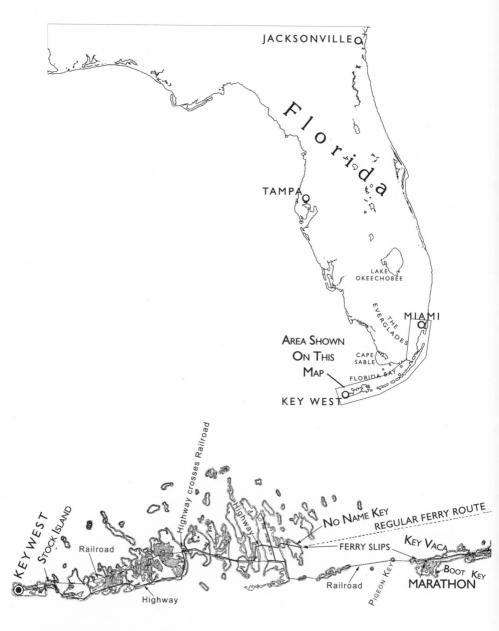

South Florida and the Florida Keys, 1935. (Adapted from a map by George Mangos, ca. 1927)

THE FLORIDA KEYS
1935

MILEAGE TO SOUTH FLORIDA DESTINATIONS		
FEC Rail Miles	Destination	Highway Miles
0	Miami	0
5.3	Coconut Grove	5.4
8.2	South Miami	9
10.7	Kendall	11.5
16	Perrine	17
20.2	Goulds	23
22.1	Princeton	25
23.8	Naranja	26.7
25.9	Modello	28.6
28.3	Homestead	30.4
30	Florida City	32
51.7	Key Largo	58
58.8	Rock Harbor	65
65.4	Tavernier	72
74.5	Islamorada	81
85.7	Lower Matecumbe Key*	95
91.7	Long Key Fish Camp	-----
108.5	Marathon	-----
-----	No Name Key*	135
156.4	Key West	176

* = Ferry Slip
Sources: 1928 Road Map and FECR schedule.

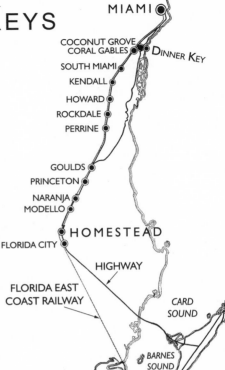

MIAMI

COCONUT GROVE
CORAL GABLES
DINNER KEY
SOUTH MIAMI
KENDALL
HOWARD
ROCKDALE
PERRINE

GOULDS
PRINCETON
NARANJA
MODELLO

HOMESTEAD
FLORIDA CITY

HIGHWAY

FLORIDA EAST
COAST RAILWAY

CARD SOUND

BARNES SOUND

KEY LARGO
KEY LARGO

ROCK HARBOR

Railroad — Highway
TAVERNIER

WINDLEY KEY
PLANTATION KEY
ISLAMORADA
SNAKE CREEK
WHALE HARBOR
UPPER MATECUMBE KEY
Highway crosses Railroad

FLORIDA BAY

LIGNUMVITAE KEY
FERRY SLIP
INDIAN KEY
LOWER MATECUMBE KEY

40 Miles

FERRY SLIP
CRAIG KEY
LONG KEY
GRASSY KEY Fish Camp

ATLANTIC OCEAN

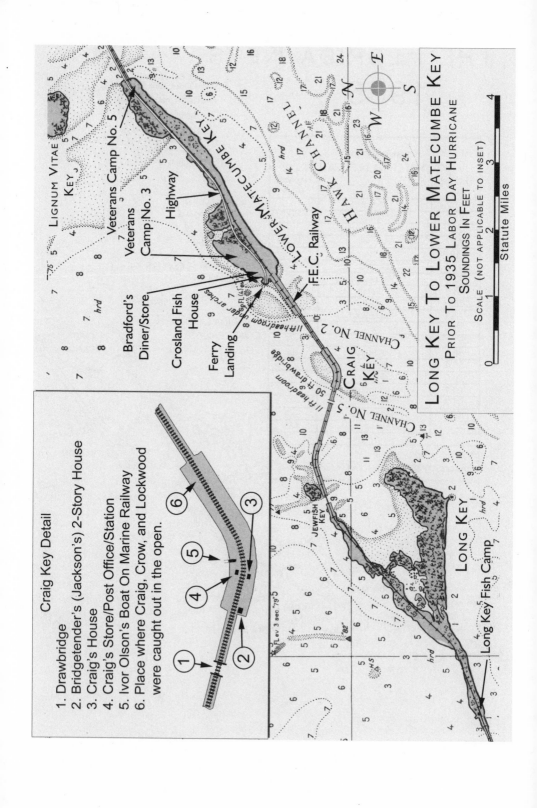

LONG KEY TO LOWER MATECUMBE KEY

PRIOR TO 1935 LABOR DAY HURRICANE

SOUNDINGS IN FEET

SCALE (NOT APPLICABLE TO INSET)

Statute Miles

Craig Key Detail

1. Drawbridge
2. Bridgetender's (Jackson's) 2-Story House
3. Craig's House
4. Craig's Store/Post Office/Station
5. Ivor Olson's Boat On Marine Railway
6. Place where Craig, Crow, and Lockwood were caught out in the open.

LIGNUM VITAE KEY

Veterans Camp No. 5

Veterans Camp No. 3

Highway

Veterans Camp No. 3

Bradford's Diner/Store

Crosland Fish House

Ferry Landing

LOWER MATECUMBE KEY

F.E.C. Railway

HAWK CHANNEL

CRAIG KEY

CHANNEL No. 2

CHANNEL No. 5

JEWFISH KEY

LONG KEY

Long Key Fish Camp

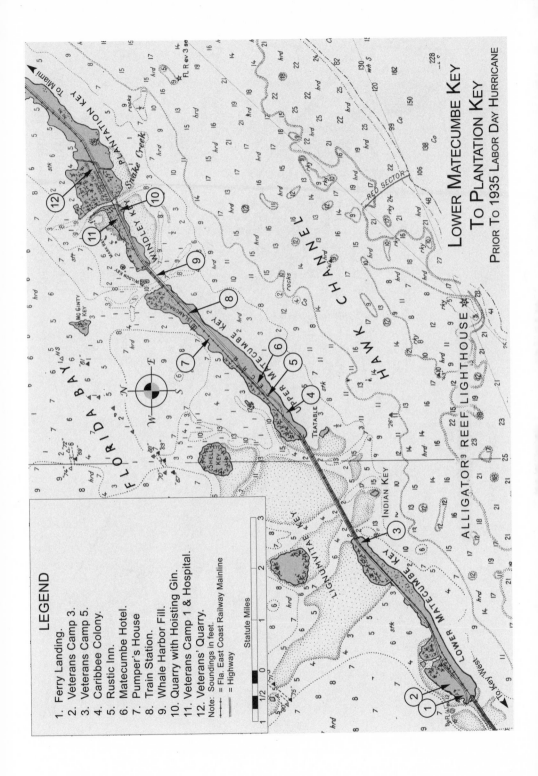

LEGEND

1. Ferry Landing.
2. Veterans Camp 3.
3. Veterans Camp 5.
4. Caribbee Colony.
5. Rustic Inn.
6. Matecumbe Hotel.
7. Pumper's House.
8. Train Station.
9. Whale Harbor Fill.
10. Quarry with Hoisting Gin.
11. Veterans Camp 1 & Hospital.
12. Veterans' Quarry.

Note: Soundings in feet.
━━━ = Fla. East Coast Railway Mainline
━━━ = Highway

Statute Miles
1   1/2   0   1   2   3

LOWER MATECUMBE KEY
TO PLANTATION KEY
PRIOR TO 1935 LABOR DAY HURRICANE

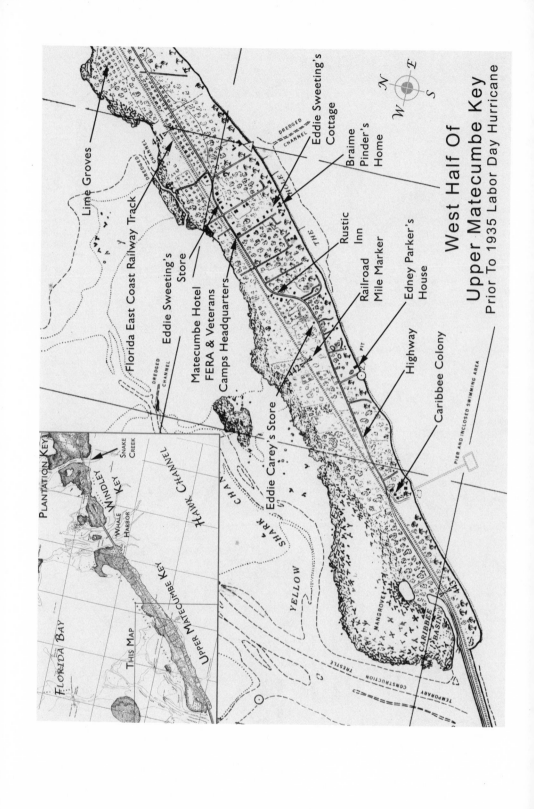

West Half Of
Upper Matecumbe Key
Prior To 1935 Labor Day Hurricane

Lime Groves

Florida East Coast Railway Track

Eddie Sweeting's Store

Matecumbe Hotel
FERA & Veterans
Camps Headquarters

Eddie Sweeting's
Cottage

Braime
Pinder's
Home

Rustic
Inn

Railroad
Mile Marker

Edney Parker's
House

Highway

Caribbee Colony

Eddie Carey's Store

THE HOUSE

DREDGED CHANNEL

DREDGED CHANNEL

411

412

PIT

PIER AND INCLOSED SWIMMING AREA

SHARK CHANNEL

YELLOW

MANGROVES

CARIBBEE
BASIN

CONSTRUCTION TRESTLE

TEMPORARY TRESTLE

N
W   E
S

PLANTATION KEY

SNAKE
CREEK

WINDLEY
KEY

WHALE
HARBOR

HAWK CHANNEL

FLORIDA BAY

THIS MAP

UPPER MATECUMBE KEY

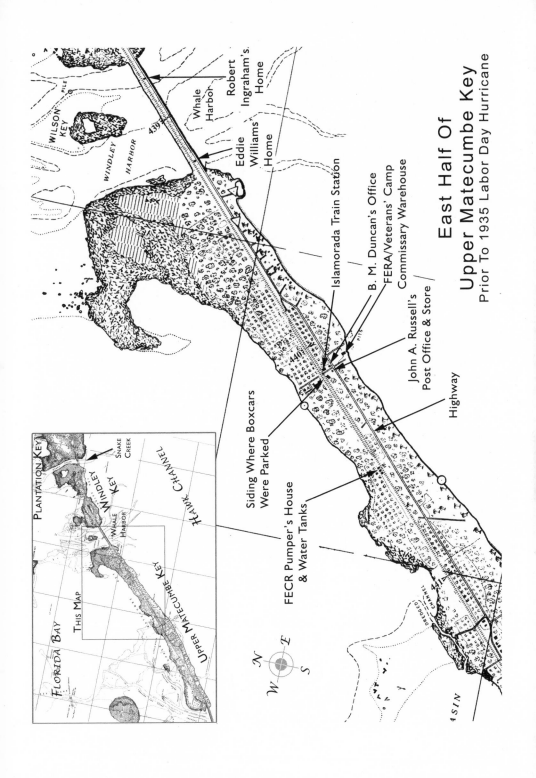

East Half Of
Upper Matecumbe Key
Prior To 1935 Labor Day Hurricane

Robert Ingraham's Home

Whale Harbor

Eddie Williams' Home

Islamorada Train Station

B. M. Duncan's Office

FERA/Veterans' Camp Commissary Warehouse

John A. Russell's Post Office & Store

Highway

Siding Where Boxcars Were Parked

FECR Pumper's House & Water Tanks

WILSON KEY

PILE

WINDLEY HARBOR

439

440

PITS

441

DREDGED CHANNEL

BASIN

PLANTATION KEY

SNAKE CREEK

WINDLEY KEY

WHALE HARBOR

HAWK CHANNEL

THIS MAP

FLORIDA BAY

UPPER MATECUMBE KEY

N
W E
S

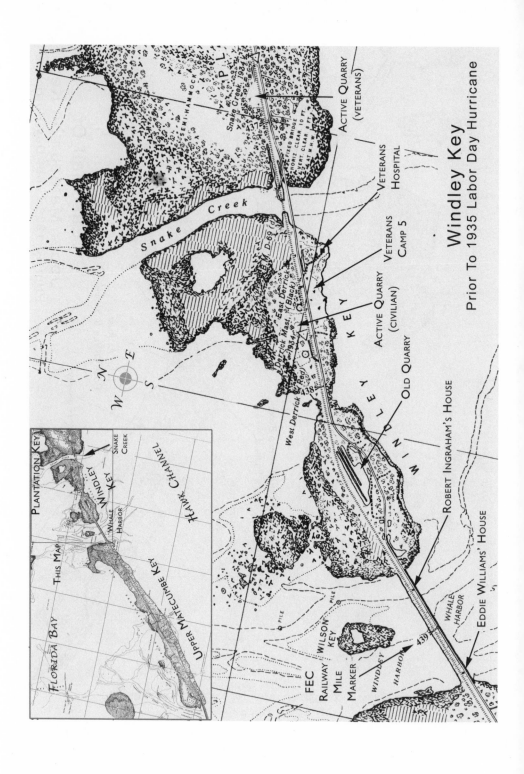

Windley Key
Prior To 1935 Labor Day Hurricane

Prologue

Liz sat on the overstuffed sofa next to her sister Evelyn, their eyes glistening with tears. Her head tilted down as if to look at her lap, where her hands alternately grasped each other and then relaxed. Her sister gazed straight ahead toward their husbands, who sat on the far side of the room; her eyes were not focused on them, but on something much farther away.

Liz's home is located next to a small creek near Jacksonville, Florida. The area is prone to flooding so the house was built high up on pilings and nestles among the leafy limbs of the tall trees that shade the entire lot. Of an unpretentious, functional design, it is a comfortable, homey house endowed with a natural serenity by the trees that envelop it and by the pleasant twitter of the birds that do not seem to mind this intrusion into their habitat. On this summer day, rays of sunlight filtered through the dome of leaves producing a diffused light that filled the living room with soft, even illumination.

The husbands were involved in their own conversation, discussing cars and other matters of interest to them, but not long after the sisters started to talk, their spouses became quiet as they heard things they had not known until that moment about the women they had married. Their expressions turned from mild curiosity to awe, and eventually to quiet respect for what their wives had endured and overcome.

Liz and Evelyn were recounting their experiences from decades ago in a place five hundred miles away. It was during the Great Depression, when their family lived in the Florida Keys and Liz was nine and Evelyn was eight. At first they conversed in a light, lilting way as they talked of their childhood and pleasant times with their family and friends, but when they moved into the events of that fateful day in 1935 they became somber, and deep emotions began to stir.

Reaching over to a box on the end table, Liz pulled out a tissue and pressed it into Evelyn's hand. Both struggled to control their tears and maintain their voices while describing the death of their father and the fearful trek among the dead as their mother led them out of an alien landscape of horror and devastation that had once been their home.

With their house—and, indeed, their community—destroyed, Liz and Evelyn were taken to their grandparents' home in Miami near Woodlawn Cemetery. "For a while, before the bodies bloated and would not fit into coffins," Evelyn explained, "they could bring the dead up to Woodlawn for burial." Slowly, in a cracking voice, Liz said: "They would have the services late in the afternoon and we could sit on the steps at Granny's house and we could hear them play 'Taps.' It would be late in the afternoon and they would play that—I still can't take it now. And it hurt, and it still does."

Both women fell quiet as the sorrow of those painful times was visited upon them once again. Their sadness was made more profound by the cheerfulness of the birds chirping outside. A passing cloud dimmed the natural light; the yellow glow from the table lamp became predominant, and golden teardrops slowly migrated down the fair skin of their faces. Liz looked at her sister and said quietly, "Our lives were so changed in just a matter of hours."

Liz and Evelyn were recalling the hurricane that struck the Florida Keys during the late afternoon and evening of Labor Day 1935. The occurrence of a hurricane at that time of year and in that location was not unusual. Many of the residents were accustomed to such events. The storm had been detected five days earlier and was expected to pass to the south of the Florida Keys. No one had an inkling that this tropical cyclone was to become the first Category 5 hurricane to strike the United States. According to the National Oceanographic and Atmospheric Administration (NOAA), "The simplest characterization of hurricane intensity is embodied in the Saffir-Simpson scale: from Category 1, barely a hurricane, to Category 5, the worst imaginable."

An unusual mix of people was on the islands of the Upper Florida Keys that Labor Day weekend: longtime residents familiar with the vagaries of the sea and hurricanes; newcomers filled with optimism and totally ignorant of tropical storms; several camps of war veterans; administrators and staff of the veterans camps; railroad employees and their families; lighthouse keepers; ferryboat personnel; visiting family and friends of the preceding groups; tourists; and sports fishermen. Many were to share a common fate.

For almost three decades, the iron rails of the Florida East Coast Railway stretched across the islands and over the intervening waterways, becoming a major economic lifeline to the mainland. Named the "oversea railroad" by the New York Times, it was considered one of man's great achievements, and had successfully withstood many storms and hurricanes. In the late afternoon and evening of September 2, 1935, a special train rode the rails in a desperate attempt to evacuate as many people off the Keys as possible; it was the last train to go to Matecumbe.

Offshore several large ships skirted the Gulf Stream heading south, while others bound for northern ports rode in the middle of the powerful current to aid their progress. The sleek liner *Dixie*, the pride of the Southern Pacific–Morgan Line fleet, was loaded with cargo and carrying passengers ranging from the very wealthy to schoolteachers, all bound for New York City. When the lines were cast off in New Orleans, none of the 375 people on board were aware they were beginning a race with a killer hurricane.

By late afternoon on Labor Day 1935, when barometers on the Upper Keys began to indicate the approach of a very powerful hurricane, it was too late for people ashore to evacuate or for those at sea to take evasive action. Soon winds of vicious velocity were upon them, and all they could do was take cover, pray, and ride it out.

A very compact tropical cyclone, the hurricane seemed to defy detection. It was as if the Mayan storm god Hurakan had grown tired of man's tampering with the islands and decided to use this storm to vent his wrath, nourishing and guiding the hurricane so that it would wreak maximum havoc. If Hurakan was at the helm, he must have been very pleased with his handiwork.

The first line of defense against hurricanes was the U.S. Department of Agriculture's Weather Bureau. In the early decades of the twentieth century, there were no weather satellites, radar, hurricane-hunter airplanes, computers, or sophisticated instrument telemetry. Meteorology was still a mixture of art and science with high reliance on the observational, analytical, and interpretive skills of individual forecasters. When it came to hurricanes, Harry Boyer was one of the best.

Key West's Reluctant Weatherman

Early on the first day of November 1870 in one of the rooms of the large, three-story, cupola-topped Russell House in Key West, a Signal Corps observer-sergeant closely watched the minute hand of a clock. Outside the hotel, muffled noises rose from Duval Street as people headed toward the waterfront and the shops and offices in the commercial district. To them it was just another Tuesday; they were unaware that a historic event was about to take place.

At precisely 7:35 a.m. Eastern Standard Time, the sergeant began reading the barometer, thermometer, and other weather instruments installed for this occasion. After making his observations, the soldier went straight to the nearby telegraph office and had the data transmitted to Washington, D.C. The same routine occurred simultaneously at twenty-three other sites around the country. In Washington, four sergeants at the headquarters of the Division of Telegrams and Reports for the Benefit of Commerce received the two dozen messages and began immediately to plot and analyze the data. The result of their labor was a report they referred to as a forecast. For the first time, weather observations had been made simultaneously across the United States and transmitted within minutes to a central office for analysis; the term "forecast" would henceforth be a part of the meteorological lexicon.

Congress established the federal weather service in 1870 as a division of the U.S. Army Signal Corps. By law it carried the cumbersome and misleading name "The Division of Telegrams and Reports for the Benefit of Commerce." Originally staffed by regular army personnel aided by a few academicians, the division struggled for a decade until General W. B. Hazen became head of the Signal Corps and made upgrading the personnel of the weather service a priority. He believed that to effectively fulfill its mission, the division should be manned by a cadre of professionals possessing formal training in meteorology and communications. The program he set in motion dramatically improved the quality of weather forecasting.

For many young men, especially those with a scientific bent, the prospect of becoming a weatherman was exciting; meteorology was developing into a science all its own, and there was great appeal in being at the forefront of a new technological era. The timing could not have been better for Harry Bright Boyer of Sunbury, Pennsylvania. As he noted years later in a National Weather Service publication, "General Hazen, recognizing that the meteorological work of the Corps demanded men of higher educational attainments, began reaching out into high schools, universities, and colleges. The glittering bate [sic] was commissions." On May 25, 1881, fresh out of high school, Boyer took the bait and joined the army. He was sent to Fort Myer in Virginia, near Washington, D.C., for basic military training and technical instruction in meteorology and communications. Only seventeen years old and away from home for the first time, he would have been homesick except that the rigorous training schedule did not allow time for such luxuries.

A fellow trainee, H. C. Frankenfield, wrote that the routine was "eight hours for work, six hours for more work, two hours for recreation, and eight hours for sleep, the latter not guaranteed." The course of instruction was as diverse as it was intense: "We had mastered the military details, mounted and dismounted and kept guard. We also had studied meteorology, physics, telegraphy, mathematics and military signaling by wand, flag and torch. We had constructed telegraph and telephone lines, spliced marine cables and learned how to ride a horse, wait at table, clean a carbine, act as valets de chambre and wield a saber. . . . [W]e soon became sufficiently versed in the theory and care of meteorological instruments and in the taking and reduction of observations to qualify us as assistant observers."

Completing his training in March 1882, Harry Boyer went to his first assignment at Nashville, where he served as an assistant for ten months. He was then sent to New Orleans, and after three months was assigned as the official-in-charge of the remote Port Eads station located on the southern tip of the Mississippi Delta. When that station was closed in July 1883, Harry returned to New Orleans and was told he was being sent to Key West.

He had heard rumors that yellow fever was endemic in the Florida Keys and especially at Key West. His friends did not help the situation by telling him that newcomers, not being acclimated to the tropical environment, were certain to come down with the fever and die an untimely and horrible death. Entries in Harry's diary indicate he was genuinely traumatized:

"On learning of my probable assignment, my friends gathered around me with lugubrious and sympathetic faces, and recounted the most horrifying tales of the great 1878 epidemic—stories that congealed my blood, and at night, made me spring up in bed and cry out in terror with nightmare. And they denounced in unstinted terms a Government that would heartlessly and cold-bloodedly and brutally send its servants to certain death!"

Harry Boyer had reason to be fearful of Yellow Jack. Yellow fever is caused by a virus that attacks the liver, kidneys, lungs, and heart with horrific effect, including bleeding from the eyes, nostrils and anus, and the production of vile, black-colored vomit having the texture of coffee grounds. As the liver begins to fail and bile accumulates, the skin acquires a yellow cast, which, along with recurring fever, gave the disease its name. About 20 percent of the people who became infected died, usually between four and eight days after they first showed symptoms. Those who were spared had to withstand the emotional devastation of watching family and friends succumb. In severe epidemics, the only people who had regular work were caregivers and undertakers. Such was the stuff that fed Harry's nightmares.

Boyer requested his orders be changed so that he could remain at New Orleans or go to a duty station other than Key West. He apparently did not know that New Orleans had far more yellow fever epidemics than any other city in the United States, including the duty station he was trying to avoid.

When his request for a different assignment was denied, Harry sent his father a long telegram and told him of the situation and the impending sentence of death. His father contacted Senator Don Cameron of Pennsylvania, who intervened. The orders were cancelled, and Harry remained in New Orleans for twenty-three more months—then he was sent to Key West!

In June 1885, Harry Boyer walked with great trepidation down the steamer's gangway onto the dock at Key West. Instead of a dreary land of the dead and dying, the twenty-two-year-old soldier found himself in a thriving city of more than ten thousand very-much-alive people—the largest city in Florida, according to the 1880 census. Teeming with wreckers, spongers, fishermen, cigar makers, and merchants, the waterfront was a clatter of dialects as Cubans, Bahamians, Asians, Yankees, and southerners went about their business at the busy port. They were part of an eclectic populace that was growing larger each day.

The Island City, with its brilliant sunshine and lush tropical plants, had none of the aspects of the dark, disease-ridden place that had frequented the weatherman's nightmares. In fact, Key West had something, or rather someone, who made for much more pleasant dreams. Beulah Williams was the daughter of Cortland and Druscilla Williams. Of sturdy stock, her good figure, wit, and charms soon captivated young Harry. Although Beulah was four years his senior, he knew she was the girl for him, and it was not long before they wed.

When he arrived in Key West, the army's weather service office was in the Wall Building on the north side of Front Street. Nine months later, a major conflagration consumed most of the business district of Key West including the Wall Building. The weather service was relocated to the U.S. Naval Depot building for the remainder of 1886. In January 1887, Harry's office moved a third time to the Waite Building at the corner of Duval and Front streets.

Weeks later, as spring arrived, a Cuban family with a sick child immigrated to Key West from Havana. Not long after they had moved into an apartment above a restaurant, the owner of the restaurant became ill and died. The disease began to spread, and a yellow fever epidemic was declared. The number of cases grew steadily into the summer. Harry Boyer's worst fears were on the verge of becoming reality, and it was not only his own life at risk, but also the lives of his family for Beulah was pregnant with their first child.

The epidemic peaked during the summer; by the time it was over in early September, a total of 282 people had become infected, resulting in sixty-three deaths. The Boyer family and most of the people on the island were spared thanks to a thirty-nine-year-old doctor who had established a solid reputation as an expert in the management of yellow fever epidemics. Dr. J. Y. Porter, a native of Key West and a captain in the U.S. Navy, was attached to the Marine Hospital and also served as the city's public health officer. Under his skillful direction, the effects of the outbreak were minimized. In 1889, in recognition of his services and expertise in managing epidemics throughout the state, Dr. Porter was appointed the first state health officer of Florida, a post he would hold for twenty-eight years.

On March 13, 1888, Beulah and Harry became the proud parents of a daughter, Viola Antoinette Boyer. Being a father did not diminish Harry's interest in his work. With access to telegraph facilities and his writing skills, Boyer began to build a network of public and private sector weather professionals throughout the Caribbean. He maintained these collegial contacts when Congress transferred the weather service from the Army Signal Corps to the U.S. Department of Agriculture on July 1, 1891. At that time, Harry became a civilian employee of the U.S. government. Three months later his second daughter, Rosalie, was born.

In the late 1890s, American newspapers carried dramatic accounts of atrocities occurring in Cuba under Spanish rule. Relations between Spain and the United States began to deteriorate. With Cuba located only ninety miles away, the townspeople of Key West began to fear that a powerful Spanish armada would be sent to capture the island. Half of the seventeen thousand people living in Key West were Cubans, most of whom had fled the cruelty of the Spaniards ruling their homeland; the perceived threat was great enough that many of them moved their families to Tampa. By the end of 1897, it appeared that war with Spain was imminent. Harry did not want his wife and two young daughters living in the middle of a war zone, so when an opportunity arose to transfer to Savannah, he moved his family to the safety of Georgia. The Boyer family arrived in Savannah in February 1898, the same month the USS *Maine* exploded and sank in Havana harbor.

Savannah was a bustling metropolis with five times as many people as Key West. There were many interesting things to do in the "Enchanted City of the South," and the years flew by. In 1903, a handsome twenty-eight-year-old bachelor moved into the apartment across the hall from the Boyers. Rosalie, who was twelve at the time, took great delight in teasing him when he came home from his job with the trolley system. Bascom Grooms had not the slightest inkling that the little girl who pestered him was to play a major role in the rest of his life.

In 1908, Grooms left Savannah intending to holiday in Cuba. En route to Havana the steamer made a scheduled stopover at Key West, and the vacationing conductor decided to ride the town's quaint trolley out to La Brisa, a dance pavilion located on the beach on the south side of the island near the trolley barn. By pure coincidence, he encountered an old friend, N. B. "Dusty" Rhoads. Rhoads had previously worked for the Savannah trolley system before he came to Key West and was now superintendent of the southernmost trolley system in the United States. After a brief conversation, Rhoads offered Grooms a job, and within an hour Bascom was the newest employee of the Key West Electric Company, the owner of the local trolley system.

For the Boyer family the departure of their neighbor for Key West was another reminder of the greatest disadvantage of living in Savannah: the remoteness of their friends and family. Harry and Beulah began thinking of going home. Several years later, Harry was promoted to official-in-charge of the Key West weather station, and the family moved back to the Island City.

Boyer's arrival in Key West in 1911 was considerably different from his first experience in 1885. The city was no longer the largest in the state, but its population had doubled to twenty thousand, and in less than a year it would be accessible by train, thanks to the vision of Henry Flagler. This time Boyer did not come ashore alone, but was accompanied by three attractive ladies, his wife and two grown daughters. But the most important difference for Harry Boyer as he became reacquainted with the sweet fragrance of tropical blossoms and walked among the noisy crowd on the dock was the absence of fear of contracting yellow fever.

The last epidemic in Key West occurred in 1899. Although 1,320 people had become infected, only sixty-eight died. In 1900, Dr. Walter Reed and a team of American and Cuban doctors working in Cuba had positively established that a mosquito spread the disease. They developed specific measures for preventing epidemics and for the handling of infected people. As the state health officer, Dr. Porter ensured that the State of Florida immediately began taking steps to control mosquito populations and to effectively manage yellow fever cases using the new information provided by the Reed Commission. In 1901, the last case of the disease was reported in Key West, and in 1905 the final case in Florida was recorded.

The official-in-charge of the Key West Weather Bureau was supposed to reside on the first floor of the Weather Bureau Building, but this was not possible when the Boyer family came to town because the building was undergoing major reconstruction. Built of concrete and stone in 1903 for the Department of Agriculture, the Weather Bureau Building was a very sturdy structure located at the corner of Front and Eaton streets near the docks and commercial district. Before the U.S. Navy added fill for its facilities, the site was on the island's western shore adjacent to the main ship channel, exposing the building directly to the wind and storm surge of hurricanes.

On October 11, 1909, a hurricane caused fifteen deaths and $1 million (1909 dollars) damage in the Keys. Nine miles southwest of Key West, the lighthouse and weather station on Sand Key were blown away. During a two-hour period, Key West endured 94-mph winds and torrential rains that dumped over six inches of water on the town. Four hundred buildings were destroyed, and the Weather Bureau Building interior was damaged. A year later, another hurricane inundated the Lower Keys with a storm surge that peaked at fifteen feet, sending seven feet of water into the Weather Bureau Building.

While the repair work was under way, the Boyer family lived in a rented house at the south end of Whitehead Street, and the weather station was temporarily located in the Island City Bank Building at 205 Duval Street. It must have seemed to Harry that the periodic relocation of his office was a routine part of being assigned to Key West.

The renovations of the Weather Bureau Building crept along and were finally completed in May 1913. There was a sense of urgency in the air as the Boyers moved into their official quarters for Rosalie was to be married in a few weeks and the wedding was to take place at their new home.

The gangly twelve-year-old who had pestered Bascom Grooms in Savannah was now a comely young lady in her early twenties. Bascom Grooms was still a bachelor and had formed a social club for unmarried men who worked for the Key West Electric Company. The name of the organization was the KWECO Club, and the bright, sharply dressed men regularly sponsored dances and other social events to which Key West's most eligible females were invited. By this time, Bascom was in his mid-thirties, still trim and handsome, and was now the superintendent of the trolley system. A new relationship developed between the attractive Rosalie and the debonair Bascom that eventually led to him asking for her hand even though he was sixteen years older than she.

The rooms of the living quarters of the Weather Bureau Building never looked so gay as they did on Monday evening, June 16, 1913, when Rosalie Sylindia Boyer and Bascom Lovic Grooms took their vows. A large number of people filled the rooms that had been lavishly decorated with many beautiful floral arrangements sent from well-wishers around the nation. The Rev. Wiltshire Winfield Williams, rector of St. Paul's Episcopal Church, performed the ceremony; refreshments were then served, and a band played for the listening and dancing pleasure of the couple and their guests. Among the many presents was a fine silver service from the bachelors of the KWECO Club.

Shortly before nine that evening, Rosalie and Bascom, accompanied by a large number of friends and the band, strolled down the street to the nearby dock, where the steamer *Olivette* was ready to cast off and take the newlyweds to Havana for their honeymoon. In the U.S. Department of Agriculture's weather station at Key West, a union had been forged that was to be celebrated for sixty years.

Rosalie and Bascom returned to Key West and made their home in a plain lapboard house on Washington Street near the trolley barn. On May 2, 1914, she gave birth to a daughter, Rosalind Boyer Grooms. Three years later, Rosalie's sister married Dr. George Tyler of Virginia and moved to Norfolk, where her husband had his practice. Harry and Beulah would now have the first-floor quarters of the Weather Bureau Building all to themselves for a while.

On December 11, 1921, the Grooms had another child, Bascom Lovic Grooms Jr. In a few years, Rosalind and her brother were frequent visitors at their grandfather's office, "helping" him take readings and watching in fascination as he squinted under a green eyeshade while meticulously plotting data on the large weather maps.

Harry was a weatherman through and through, and his easygoing manner and professionalism made him numerous friends throughout the meteorological community. The local newspaper described him as "the efficient official in charge of the local weather bureau."

One of the things that enabled Harry to be efficient was the "hurricane grapevine" he established. Growing out of the contacts he had developed from his initial tour of duty in Key West, the informal association of weathermen scattered throughout the Caribbean regularly exchanged weather data and theories by letter, telephone, and occasionally telegraph. Because of this network of mostly foreign and private-sector meteorologists, he was able to provide warnings of hurricanes well in advance of the official advisories issued by the central office in Washington.

People in Key West and throughout the Florida Keys—especially those in positions such as his son-in-law Bascom, who had become a manager in the Key West Electric Company—counted on Harry and his hurricane intelligence network for reliable, early information on storms. When Harry said a hurricane was coming, it was time to put up the storm shutters and batten down the hatches.

Harry Boyer had just completed his fiftieth year in the federal weather service when he died on July 15, 1931, with his wife and daughters by his bedside. The venerable weatherman had spent thirty-three of those years at the very place he had tried so hard to avoid.

Boyer's expertise and the weather data intelligence provided by the "hurricane grapevine" helped him become a recognized authority on hurricanes. His early, reliable warnings of approaching storms were said to have saved countless lives. According to the local newspaper, Harry Boyer was held in such high esteem that he was the only official-in-charge of a weather station that had blanket authorization from the central office in Washington to raise and lower hurricane warnings entirely at his own discretion. His successor did not enjoy the same professional status, and hurricane warnings issued subsequent to Harry's death came from the central office in Washington, D.C. The "hurricane grapevine" Harry had worked so hard to establish and maintain was allowed to wither and die and the early, locally issued warnings ceased.

On the day following his death, the U.S. Department of Agriculture Weather Bureau Building was once again crowded with family and friends. This time, though, the mood was somber as they paid their last respects to the weatherman and laid him to rest. Among the mourners at Harry's funeral was his granddaughter, an attractive seventeen-year-old who had just graduated from high school and would soon be off to college. The Reverend Bulkeley's words of human mortality and the inevitability of death rang true to her personal philosophy that life should be lived to the fullest every day for one never knew what tomorrow may bring.

Rosalind Boyer Grooms loved her grandfather and would miss him, as would the people of Key West and the Florida Keys. Four years later, Rosalind and many others would dearly wish Harry Boyer was still at his post.

Ready or Not

In the summer of 1935 at Jacksonville, Florida, an imposing new building with a limestone and granite exterior occupied the entire city block at 315 West Monroe Street. Housing the regional seat of the U.S. government and various federal agencies including the post office and federal courts, the Federal Building projected an aura of majestic strength and dignity just as its architect, Marsh and Saxelbye, intended. The building was also a monument to the New Deal and the promise of tomorrow, being adorned with almost forty symbols marking the nation's technological progress in the fields of aviation, communications, and motion pictures. Carvings of the open cockpit of an airplane and a steam locomotive graced the entrances. Huge stylized eagles gazed upon the spacious lobby, where voices and footsteps echoed off bronze fixtures and polished stone. Large murals and sculpted panels silently proclaimed that the "Land of the Free and the Home of the Brave" was entering the modern age, a theme that pervaded the public areas and was even carried into the elevator cabs. It took the Jacksonville sculptor Albert Bruner six months of intensive labor, but when he finished anyone visiting the building knew they were in a place where technological advancement was revered as the key to future prosperity.

Though Bruner's efforts were heroic, this message was most convincingly stated in an area of the building free of propagandizing ornamentation. Compared to the grandness of the main lobby, the fifth floor was drab, with an architecture driven entirely by function rather than form. Here ten people daily demonstrated the practical application of meteorological research and experimentation as they endeavored to predict the weather.

They were a new team recently assembled as part of a reorganization of the Weather Bureau's hurricane-warning service. Complaints of insufficient and untimely warnings had plagued the bureau for decades beginning in 1900, when a hurricane killed over six thousand people and devastated Galveston, Texas. In that instance, the chief of the Weather Bureau himself was accused of impeding the issuance of storm warnings because of his insistence that all storm warnings be issued by the central office in Washington. Dissatisfaction with the hurricane-warning service grew after a succession of natural disasters including hurricanes that struck Florida in 1926 and 1928 and killed almost 2,000 people.

When 1933 brought a barrage of twenty-one tropical systems, the most ever experienced in one season, public concern about the inadequacies of hurricane warnings became politically untenable, and a Presidential Science Advisory Board was appointed to analyze the service. The board published a report in 1934 listing various concerns including the practice of operating the warning system only twelve to fifteen hours a day during a hurricane event; the issuing of warnings during such events only twice a day; and the centralized preparation and issuance of hurricane warnings at Washington, D.C., far removed from the regions generally affected by hurricanes.

In late spring of 1935, Congress appropriated $80,000 to the Department of Agriculture for the purpose of improving the hurricane-warning service. Four centers (New Orleans, Jacksonville, Washington, D.C., and San Juan) were established and assigned the responsibility for monitoring the climatic situation in their designated regions and for the issuance of warnings related to any tropical systems existing therein.

In addition to establishing the hurricane-warning centers, the manner in which the Weather Bureau collected storm data and issued advisories underwent significant change, with new procedures effective July 1, 1935. These included increasing the frequency of reports ships were required to make during hurricane season and expanding the data to be reported. The Jacksonville and New Orleans centers were authorized to call ships and request reports as needed and to obtain weather information directly from the Coast Guard and other available sources within their districts while a hurricane was in progress. The Naval Radio Station at Key West was directed to transmit special bulletins issued by the hurricane-warning centers. More observations were to be obtained from West Indies stations.

The appropriation also provided for the establishment of a teletype circuit dedicated to the exclusive use of the Weather Bureau. The circuit connected twelve coastal stations: Jacksonville, Miami, Key West, Tampa, Pensacola, Mobile, New Orleans, Port Arthur, Houston, Galveston, Corpus Christi, and Brownsville.

Also addressed was a concern of the Weather Bureau that individual forecasters were being singled out for blame when weather-related disasters occurred. After July 1, 1935, the names of forecasters were to be omitted from all forecasts, warnings, and advisories relating to storms and hurricanes, and only the signature "Weather Bureau" was to be used on such messages for general distribution. Station officials were permitted to issue local bulletins providing they were preceded by a statement crediting them to the Weather Bureau.

Setting up the hurricane-warning centers in time for the 1935 hurricane season was no easy task, especially when the funding was not released until after the end of June. Staff had to be transferred, equipment installed, and training completed. This was an especially hectic time for the Jacksonville station, which in addition to becoming a hurricane center was upgraded to a forecast center to serve a new district comprised of North Carolina, South Carolina, Georgia, and the Florida Peninsula except for the extreme northwest part of Florida, which remained in the New Orleans district.

Fortunately hurricane activity was late in developing in 1935; the first tropical storm did not appear until after the middle of August. Even so, the season was to be one of the most demanding times in the lives of the forecasters manning the Jacksonville center. One of them would later say they worked so hard that first season "they were ready for the hospital!"

The official-in-charge of the new hurricane-warning center at Jacksonville and his forecasters epitomized the cadre of professional meteorologists General Hazen had set out to establish forty-five years earlier. Walter James Bennett had thirty-two years service with the Weather Bureau when he became head of the Jacksonville station in October 1932. He had joined the Weather Bureau as an observer in 1900. A year later, after brief assignments at stations in California and Kentucky, he was assigned to the

Forecast Division of the central office at Washington, D.C., where Edward Garriott, the chief forecaster, mentored him. With Garriott's encouragement, he attended George Washington University, earning a bachelor of science degree, and then did postgraduate work under Professor Cleveland Abbe, a highly respected bureau meteorologist who was considered the expert on forecasting at the time.

From 1905 to 1932, Bennett served four-year stints at Charlotte, North Carolina, and Canton, New York, and nineteen years at Tampa as an assistant meteorologist before replacing Alexander J. Mitchell, who had been in charge of the Jacksonville station since it was transferred from the Army Signal Corps to the Department of Agriculture in 1895.

Walter Bennett was a quiet man who enjoyed writing poetry and reading Sanskrit, German, Hebrew, and other languages as a hobby. He was active in Masonic affairs and in his church. According to one report, he stuttered; if true, he did not let this impediment prevent him from public speaking and teaching university courses. In his younger days, he was thin with a gaunt appearance. Now fifty-four, his hairline was receding and his face was fuller.

Bennett firmly established his reputation as a forecaster with the Jacksonville community when, in the third week of January 1935, he correctly predicted snow would fall in the city. On January 23 at 8:09 a.m., city residents were amazed to see snow flurries that persisted for an hour, a very rare occurrence for Jacksonville.

With that achievement as a start, 1935 held promise for being a great year for Walter Bennett. In June, he was promoted to senior meteorologist and received a 21 percent increase in pay. The weather station was allocated positions for three additional meteorologists and their assistants, and provided with the latest equipment. When the new teletype circuit was activated in July, the office came alive with the chatter of the machines and the air filled with the excitement of a new team coming together, ready to prove itself. The Jacksonville Weather Bureau was now a showcase of modern technology; a more appropriate location could not have been found for the office than in the crown of Albert Bruner's monument to progress.

With the increase in staff and his promotion, Bennett became primarily an administrator. Forecasting duties fell to Grady Norton and Gordon Dunn. Norton was born on a farm in Alabama and developed an interest in meteorology while in high school. He did not attend college, although he read extensively and occasionally took correspondence courses. He was a religious man with a deep faith in God, but was not active in church. Although his formal education was limited, Norton was said to be knowledgeable about history, Shakespeare, mythology, and the Bible.

In 1915 at the age of twenty-one, he joined the Weather Bureau only to be drafted near the end of the Great War. The Signal Corps still maintained a meteorology section, although it was exclusively for military use, so Norton was assigned to it and served ten months. During that time, he was selected to attend a special meteorology program set up for Signal Corps enlisted personnel at Texas A&M University. After his discharge from the army, he rejoined the Weather Bureau and worked in various stations in the southeastern United States, steadily advancing to more responsible positions.

In September 1928, while on vacation in West Palm Beach, Norton came upon a mass funeral being conducted for victims of a hurricane that had swept across Central Florida and Lake Okeechobee earlier in the month. Almost two thousand migrant workers and their families drowned. He was struck by the magnitude of the loss of life and by comments that the deaths could have been prevented by better warnings of the hurricane's approach. He resolved to do all he could to avert such losses in the future and dedicated the rest of his career to specializing in hurricane forecasts.

He worked hard, and when he was transferred from the New Orleans station to Jacksonville in June 1935, he was promoted to meteorologist and designated the senior hurricane forecaster. Wiry, bespectacled, with a hawklike face, Grady Norton at forty-one was described by colleagues as an outstanding forecaster and a salty, down-to-earth individual whose southern drawl and country manner enabled him to communicate very effectively with the general public even under the most dire of situations.

His colleague Gordon E. Dunn became interested in meteorology while a boy on his parents' dairy farm in Vermont. As a teenager he would hang out at the state's only weather station, which was located twenty-five miles from the family farm. The station was a one-man operation so the assistance of young Dunn was appreciated. It was not long before he was taking observations and learning how to read and plot weather charts.

Table 2.1. Jacksonville Weather Bureau Staff, September 1, 1935

Name	Working title[a]	Position class.[b]	Annual salary[c]	Pay raise	Previous station	Transfer date
Walter Bennett	MIC	SM	4,600	800	Tampa	Oct. 1932
Grady Norton	AF	M	3,800	600	New Orleans	June 1935
Gordon Dunn	AF	AM	3,600	600	Wash. D.C.	June 1935
Warren Johnson	A	JM	2,000	200	Wash. D.C.	July 1935
Harold Quattlebaum	A	O	1,800	180		
Ira Plummer	A	O	1,800			
John Hovde	A	AO	1,620	180	Evansville	June 1935
Philip Skillman	A	AO	1,620	180		
Milton Blanc	A	AO	1,620	180	Topeka	June 1935
Charles Walker	A	P	N/A			

Notes: All positions shown above were located in the Federal Building in Jacksonville. Four positions located at the airport are not shown.
[a] Working title abbreviations: A = assistant; AF = assistant forecaster; MIC = meteorologist in charge.
[b] Position classification abbreviations: AM = associate meteorologist; AO = assistant observer; JM = junior meteorologist; m = meteorologist; SM = senior meteorologist; O = observer; P = printer.
[c] Salaries in 1935 dollars. Includes promotional pay raise.
Sources: *Weather Topics and Personnel* (June 1935); Roger Plaster, former MIC Jacksonville.

After high school, he began studies at Brown University, but a bout of scarlet fever caused him to drop out. When he recovered, he became a messenger for the Providence, Rhode Island, Weather Bureau in May 1924 at the age of nineteen. Because of his substantial knowledge of meteorology and weather station operations, he was promoted to junior observer two months later and transferred to the weather station in Tampa, where he worked with Walter Bennett. Desiring to complete his college education, Dunn requested reassignment and was transferred in July 1926 to the Central Office in Washington, D.C.

Just as Bennett had done twenty years earlier, Dunn attended George Washington University part-time. While at work at the Central Office, he had the opportunity to associate with some leading authorities on weather theory. In 1931, he was promoted to junior meteorologist and assigned to the Forecast Division, where one of the Weather Bureau's top forecasters, Charles F. Mitchell, mentored him. Dunn was awarded a bachelor's degree in political science from George Washington University in 1932 and promoted to assistant meteorologist. He continued to work in the Forecast Division until June 1935, when he was promoted to associate meteorologist and transferred to Jacksonville. Of medium build and with a square face, Gordon Dunn enjoyed fishing and was described by a colleague as "a dedicated, polished forecaster." He celebrated his thirtieth birthday three weeks before Labor Day 1935.

As August 1935 began, Walter Bennett and his crew manned one of the best-equipped, best-staffed forecast centers in the hurricane-warning service. Now they needed a storm to hone their skills and test their equipment. Nature cooperated by providing a hurricane to exercise the newly reorganized hurricane-warning service.

On August 17, the San Juan hurricane-warning center detected a disturbance located about three hundred miles east-northeast of the station. The next morning, an American tanker encountered a northeast gale in the area and throughout the day radioed reports of increasing winds and decreasing barometric pressure. These reports were passed on to the Jacksonville station, where it was determined that the vessel had crossed the path of a tropical storm passing in front of its center.

On August 19, 1935, at 10 a.m. EST, the Jacksonville Weather Bureau issued the first advisory produced by the revamped hurricane-warning service. The advisory was described by a local newspaper as "laconic." It read as follows:

"Advisory 10 a.m.: Tropical disturbance apparently of slight to moderate intensity central about 400 miles northeast of Turks Island apparently moving northwestwardly. Caution advise vessels near path" (U.S. Congress, *Florida Hurricane Disaster Hearings*, 211–13).

For the weathermen, the hurricane was an interesting system. On August 24, three days before it left the Jacksonville center's zone heading north off the Atlantic coast, the storm became a Category 3 hurricane. It continued to travel northward, staying well offshore, and then began to curve toward the east. On August 25, the center of the storm became colder than the surrounding air, and the strongest winds were now found in the upper atmosphere, conditions opposite those found in tropical cyclones; therefore, the system was reclassified as an extra-tropical storm. It then curved back toward the northwest and came ashore in Newfoundland.

Walter Bennett was quoted as saying he was "greatly satisfied" with the performance of the equipment and staff and that the storm had given the Jacksonville station an opportunity to test itself.

With their first hurricane of the season out of the way, the weathermen at the Jacksonville Weather Bureau were kept busy receiving, plotting, and analyzing the hundreds of observation readings that came in daily from ships, land stations, lighthouse keepers, commercial airlines, and hundreds of volunteer observers like R. E. Chambers of Winter Haven, H. S. McKenzie of Tavernier, and James Duane at the Florida East Coast Railway Fish Camp on Long Key. In addition, the new teletype machines spewed forth typed data from the weather stations connected to the dedicated network.

As Labor Day neared, the Weather Bureau in general and the Jacksonville station in particular were as ready as they could be for the remainder of the 1935 hurricane season. Morale was high and there was even a degree of eagerness and professional curiosity to see how well the newly reorganized hurricane warning service would perform when a handling a full-fledged hurricane making a landfall in the United States. They did not have long to wait.

During the fourth week of August 1935, a complex of thunderstorms erupted 850 miles east of Key West and 420 miles north-northwest of San Juan, Puerto Rico. The event was not unusual in the North Atlantic at the end of summer. The waters of the northern tropics had been absorbing their annual dose of intense solar radiation for over five months. Like a pot about to boil over, the warm seas were beginning to release their pent-up energy, spawning moisture-laden clouds that became violent thunderstorms.

Such thunderstorms typically form and dissipate within an hour or so, but on some occasions they persist and begin to link with one another. When this happens the resulting unified updraft of steamy air can lower the atmospheric pressure over a broad area. If the updraft grows stronger, it interacts with the earth's rotation, causing the host thunderstorms to begin to rotate as an entity; in the Northern Hemisphere, this rotation is counterclockwise.

The weather system located north of San Juan and east of Key West evolved in the manner just described. Being close to the northern limits of the tropics, the thunderstorms continued to pass over very warm water, sustaining and strengthening the updraft and intensifying the flow of hot surface winds spiraling toward its center. Soon the thunderstorms lost their individual identity and blended into a single spinning mass, a heat-driven engine that was to live for almost two weeks and travel more than five thousand miles.

The rough seas and gusty winds associated with the system affected a small area far at sea that was not directly detectable at any shore stations. Only the barometers on a few ships sailing between the northeastern United States/Canada and the eastern Caribbean/South America registered the low pressure, yet the emerging pattern of disturbed weather was being monitored by the men at the Jacksonville Federal Building a thousand miles away.

By early morning of August 29, 1935, forecasters Norton and Dunn knew that a storm was brewing at 24.2 degrees north latitude, 68.3 degrees west longitude, and that it was moving toward the west with maximum sustained winds of 40 mph. Ready or not, Hurakan had made his first move in a deadly cat-and-mouse game with the Jacksonville weathermen, and the losers would be the people on the Florida Keys.

Rosalind and the Georges

At Key West on the same day the men at the Jacksonville weather station were taking note of what would become the second hurricane of the 1935 season, the granddaughter of Harry Boyer sat at the dining room table in her parents' home. Bascom and Rosalie Grooms's house was way out on the south side of town, just a block away from where the trolley barn and Bascom's office used to be. For their twenty-one-year-old daughter, the place where she had lived as a child had become a sanctuary, a refuge from the turbulence of her personal life.

She sat before a typewriter, and as her thoughts crystallized her fingers flew across the keys making sharp, sure strokes. The typewriter started clacking.

Thursday
Hi, kid!

Maybe someday I'll learn to treat the family to nice long letters like yours. Enjoyed it lots.

There's not much to write you about as I suppose that mother is taking care of that end of the business. Mike misses you. Can you imagine that! (Don't let me kid you!) He goes swimming occasionally with Manuel.

Her thirteen-year-old brother was up at Tavernier, staying with the Julius Collins family and making the most of his last days of summer vacation. He would be coming home on the train Monday because another year of school started the day after Labor Day. She continued to type.

Heard from George but he didn't say he had seen you so I suppose that he hasn't gotten down that way, and that you haven't made that bicycle trip as yet—where's your ambition?

Would like to be up that way enjoying the 'squitos and other varmint such as sand flies, but I'm through with trips for a little while.

Mrs. Collins gives a surprisingly good report of you thus far—here's to more and better surprises.

Anyway, since I can't write anything but nonsense had better knock off. Am inclosing fifty cents wherewith to buy Elizabeth a nut sundae.

Keep your nose clean and otherwise be a gentleman. My best to Jay and the rest of the Collins's.

Sister

The "George" she referred to was not her husband of one year and seven days; that George was somewhere on a navy ship cruising around in the Pacific Ocean. It is true she loved George, but the one she loved was not her husband. For many people this would be a problem; for Rosalind it was just one of the turns on life's road that made living exciting. Ever since she had graduated from Key West High School four years earlier, her life had become a series of events that began routinely enough and then took surprising turns. It was as if she had been swept into the whirlwind of fate and was still caught up in the vortex. This suited her, for Rosalind Grooms Palmer was a disciple of the spontaneous and a devotee to the concept of living for the moment.

Who could have guessed what would transpire? Not her, even though she had been the Senior Class Prophet and had predicted the destinies of her classmates. For herself, she had prophesied in the Key West High School annual:

Rosalind an artist fain would be;
Drawing pictures for all to see;
Wonder if she will make good in that line?
I hope so for she is a good friend of mine.

She had been far too busy to pursue art; the fulfillment of her prophecy would have to wait.

Rosalind was blessed with good looks. Even when she was a baby she was highly photogenic. Her eyes had an oriental quality, which was the inspiration for her nickname, "Chinkie." In high school she was an average student, doing her best work in English, Spanish, and music. A member of the Glee Club for three years, she acted in the senior play and was art editor of the yearbook. Norma Yates Dopp, a fellow member of the class of 1931, recalled: "Rosalind, Valerie Malone, Alce Curry, and Norma Yates buddied around together from the ninth thru twelfth grades. We had parties, went to movies, plays until we graduated—then we each went our separate ways." She described Rosalind as "Beautiful and lots of fun. Always out for a good time."

In September 1931, Rosalind made the long journey up to Tallahassee to attend the Florida State College for Women (FSCW) and enrolled in the School of Education. At first it was refreshing to be away from the static climate of Key West and experience a change of seasons among towering pine trees and mammoth oaks gracefully draped with Spanish moss. She was fortunate to be there, for in the midst of the Great Depression many families could not afford the luxury of a college education for their children. FSCW was well regarded scholastically and, with an enrollment of over 1,700, was the sixth-largest of the thirteen women's colleges in the United States.

The stately, ivy-covered, red brick dormitories rendered in collegiate Gothic architecture were the "home away from home" for students. The administration, in addition to its other duties, had the role of parent-in-residence and took this responsibility very seriously. The "girls" were expected to abide by a multitude of strictly enforced regulations. This was a difficult environment for the free-spirited Rosalind. She struggled with some of her classes, receiving failing grades in chemistry and history while barely passing Spanish. She did better the second semester, but while home on summer vacation Rosalind decided she had had enough of college and withdrew.

For the next two years, Rosalind worked for Judge Jefferson B. Browne, a highly respected jurist and historian in Key West. Judge Browne would later write of Rosalind:

She was beautiful, far beyond the lot of women; she possessed a brilliant intellect that scintillated like a diamond and reacted with the celerity of lightning; and her mind was stored with useful facts.

With her brilliance, she combined rare good judgment and common sense. She was a most interesting conversationalist, and a finished letter-writer. She took advantage of her educational opportunities and was a fine grammarian and rhetorician. Her knowledge of the classics and the best poets was unusual for one so young. Her wit was incisive, and although a bit of a cynic, her cynicism did not imbitter her—on the contrary, it made her charitable to the shortcomings of others.

On July 10, 1934, Governor Dave Sholtz appointed Rosalind Boyer Grooms the official court reporter for the Twentieth Judicial Circuit, a position she held until her marriage six weeks later to George Goldston Palmer.

Palmer was a handsome athletic naval officer stationed on a ship in Key West. He was from Cartersville, South Carolina, where his father had been one of the largest landowners in Florence County and a leading merchant. George Palmer Sr. had inherited a plantation and built and operated the largest, most successful hog farm east of the Mississippi. He was thirty-five years old and at the peak of his success in 1920 when he died, leaving his wife, Mary Keith Palmer, to raise twelve-year-old George and his four siblings. Mary Palmer continued to operate the plantation for a while and became active in local politics.

After completing high school and one year of college at Davidson, young George entered the Naval Academy at Annapolis, where his competitive nature and athletic ability earned him a place on the gymnastic team all four years. He was commissioned an ensign in June 1930 and received various assignments before being assigned to the USS *Perry* (DD-340) in May 1933. The *Perry*, a four-stacker destroyer of the Clemson class, operated out of Key West while conducting exercises in the Atlantic and Caribbean.

At twenty-six, Lt. j.g. Palmer had lost some of the baby-face look he had when he graduated from the Naval Academy, and he cut a dashing figure in his uniform. He was intelligent and came from a good lineage of successful businessmen, doctors, and military officers. His family in South Carolina was well-to-do and politically connected. For Rosalind, whose options were limited in Key West, George was apparently irresistible. The details of their courtship are not known, but it is a matter of record that George Goldston Palmer and Rosalind Boyer Grooms were married on August 21, 1934.

The circumstances of their union are intriguing. There was no formal period of engagement and no public announcement prior to the wedding. The marriage was performed in a Presbyterian church (Rosalind listed her religion on college records as "Episcopal") located in Miami instead of her hometown, Key West. According to a brief newspaper article that appeared in the *Miami Herald*, the bride was given away by her father and was attended by Carolyn Attanasio of West Palm Beach, a classmate of Rosalind's at the Florida State College for Women. The bridegroom was attended by his brother Joseph B. Palmer.

The Key West newspaper was not directly provided with information about the event and had to settle for reprinting the *Herald* story. Considering that Rosalind's parents were active in Key West society circles, the decision to have the wedding at a location over 150 miles away from the family's home and the apparent exclusion of the hometown media is baffling. Furthermore, none of Rosalind's high school buddies were invited. The wedding was a very private affair rather than the auspicious ceremony one would expect when the beautiful daughter of a prominent Key West family married a handsome naval officer of one of South Carolina's most influential families.

Whatever the circumstances, Rosalind and George were wed and the Palmers went to Timmonsville, South Carolina, to visit George's mother. After that the couple traveled to New York City for a brief honeymoon and then to Norfolk, Virginia, so that George could board his ship before its departure to San Diego.

Rosalind returned to Key West on September 17 by herself and stayed with her parents until the October 26, when she left by train to go to Columbus, Georgia, to join her sister-in-law, Mrs. Keith Palmer. The two then traveled by automobile to California, where George and Rosalind were to make their home at Coronado Beach.

Less than two months later for reasons not known, Rosalind flew back to Key West alone, arriving on the morning of December 23. She stayed with her parents for Christmas and left for Miami by seaplane on the afternoon of December 26. She went to Miami to buy a gown; the Casa Marina was having a grand reopening ball on New Year's Eve, and Rosalind planned to be there, as vivacious as ever.

When it was completed in 1921, the Casa Marina Hotel was Key West's most elegant hotel. Built as part of the Florida East Coast Railway's plan of creating destinations for its passengers, the reinforced concrete structure of Mediterranean architecture was placed on a thirteen-acre site on the south side of the island with two thousand feet of white sand beach on the Atlantic Ocean. Luxurious by Key West standards, the three-story hotel had two hundred guest rooms cooled by the ocean breeze, a large ballroom, a dining room, a kitchen worthy of its world-class chefs, a 20,000-gallon cistern, and immaculately groomed grounds landscaped with palms and other tropical plants. On its land-side face, the hotel featured an imposing drive leading up to sweeping verandas. As part of the Florida East Coast Railway System, the hotel's fortunes followed the railroad's.

The Great Depression had delivered the coup de grâce to the prosperity of the Florida Keys and of Key West in particular. In its heyday in the 1850s, Key West was the richest city per capita in the United States due to the lucrative business of salvaging of wrecks on nearby reefs. Thereafter the economy of Key West went on a roller-coaster ride.

The wrecking business declined dramatically after lighthouses were installed on the reefs along the Florida Straits. Hook sponging then came to the fore, and Key West became the sponge capital of the world. During the latter part of the nineteenth century, cigar makers left Cuba and moved to Key West to avoid the constant strife between insurgents and the Spanish rulers in that country, and the Island City became a center for the cigar industry. Then, in the late 1890s, fearing an invasion by Spain, the big cigar makers moved their factories and ten thousand jobs to Tampa. As the twentieth century began, Greek divers operating out of Tarpon Springs began to harvest sponges in the Keys, wiping out the deep-water beds that replenished the shallow-water beds harvested by hook spongers. Tarpon Springs displaced Key West as the sponge capital.

The construction of the Key West Extension of the Florida East Coast

Railway renewed hopes for an economic revival. Boxcars of pineapples were brought in from Cuba on ferries and a large pineapple cannery was set up next to the rail yards. It thrived until the U.S. Congress enacted tariffs to protect domestic growers and imported pineapples became unprofitable; it was not long before hundreds of people were out of work. As shipboard refrigeration came into widespread use, there was no longer a need to put into Key West to expedite the movement of perishable fruit from Central and South America to northern markets in the United States, and the economic promise of the Florida East Coast Railway extension faded away.

With the commencement of the Great War, the federal government took renewed interest in Key West. From 1915 to 1919, facilities were built for the dockage and repair of submarines and for torpedo research. The economic picture began to brighten as spending by military personnel and contractors flowed through the community; then, during the 1920s, postwar cost-cutting measures were implemented. The army's coastal defenses were reduced from a regimental post to a skeletal organization, and the naval base was deactivated. The district headquarters of the U.S. Coast Guard was removed from Key West.

The Great Depression began to exert its stranglehold on the Florida Keys during the early 1930s. As the nation's financial engine wound down, demand for fish declined, and the commercial fishing industry—the last remaining major underpin of the local economy—began to fail. In 1931, the Florida East Coast Railway declared bankruptcy and went into receivership. The Casa Marina Hotel was closed in the spring of 1932, putting more people out of work. By 1934, the $44 million military complex at Key West lay idle, and most of the civilian employees who had been crucial to its operation and had what they thought were secure jobs were unemployed.

The crisis was reached in the summer of 1934, when 80 percent of the thirteen thousand people in Key West were on relief and the city could no longer pay its employees and debts. On July 2, 1934, Monroe County and the City of Key West petitioned the governor to have the State of Florida take over their affairs, in effect declaring themselves insolvent.

Three months earlier Julius F. Stone, a federal relief administrator in Washington, had been sent to Florida to assist the state in reorganizing its emergency relief efforts. The Florida Emergency Relief Administration had become embroiled in controversy, and the embattled administrator had been reassigned. Stone took over the position and made sweeping changes that improved relations with authorities overseeing federal relief funding and caused the state's programs to operate more efficiently. When Monroe County and Key West petitioned for assistance, Governor Sholtz asked Stone to take control of the county and city to see what could be done to rescue the residents.

On July 5, Stone announced he would take on the task of looking after the welfare of the people of Monroe County and Key West. He focused his attention on Key West since most of the population was located there. He said he saw three options: do nothing and eventually put the whole island on the dole; evacuate the island, in which case the people would still be on relief and the problem would simply be relocated; or focus on the island's natural charm and transform it into the "Bermuda of Florida," using the residents to restore Key West's and Monroe County's economic vitality. He chose the latter.

Stone appointed B. M. Duncan, an engineer on loan from the State Road Department, to the post of administrator of a special district of the Florida ERA exclusively for Monroe County/Key West. Duncan went to Key West to perform an intensive study of the situation and reported his findings to Stone and Sholtz in Jacksonville on July 6. Among other things, he found that as of July 1, 1934, the City of Key West had $1,043 in cash and was faced with immediate demands for payments totaling $490,195. Taxes owed the city amounted to $1,060,651. Bonded indebtedness amounted to $1,314,400.

After meeting with Governor Sholtz, Stone announced that a program for the rehabilitation of Key West was taking shape. The first priority would be given to projects that improve public health such as sanitation and water supply. After that, projects for general painting and cleanup would be commenced using materials supplied by the Florida ERA and labor supplied by the city and county. People who owed taxes would be given the chance to work off their debt by working on rehabilitation projects.

The program was expanded thereafter to include a media campaign to promote Key West as a tourist destination, and initiatives were begun to improve access to the island. The latter included starting seaplane service to the city and planning the construction of a bridge system that would allow automobiles to travel from the mainland to Key West without having to use ferries.

The idea of building a continuous road from the mainland across the Florida Keys to Key West had been a dream since the island was settled in the 1820s. In 1923, with the Florida land boom picking up speed, the citizens of Monroe County approved a $300,000 bond issue to construct a segment of the roadway across the Lower Keys. In 1926, another bond issue for $2.5 million was approved for the completion of a link from the mainland to Lower Matecumbe Key. An additional bond issue of $500,000 provided for the construction of three ferryboats to provide passage across the forty-mile stretch of water from Lower Matecumbe to No Name Key, where the highway from Key West terminated. A final bond issue of $600,000 installed a beautiful boulevard around the eastern end of Key West and connected the island with the Lower Keys portion of the highway. When the work was finished in 1928, Monroe County owed $3.97 million for its highway system.

While the road provided vehicular access to the Keys, it was a challenge to negotiate, being in some places a "nightmarish jumble of crooked, oiled-marl trails and dangerous wooden bridges." The most frustrating element was the ferry service. The voyage was scheduled to take four hours, but often the ferry took longer and sometimes ran not at all due to bad weather or equipment breakdowns. The ferries only held twenty cars, so on holidays or other times when traffic was heavy, one traveling to Key West might have to wait for the next boat, which could mean an overnight stay in a rustic hotel on the Keys or returning to the mainland. The 150-mile trip by automobile from Miami to Key West was at best a day's journey.

The elimination of the ferry link was considered crucial to establishing convenient, reliable access to Key West. It could be done; most of the water was relatively shallow, but there were some channels to be crossed where powerful currents flowed with each change of the tide. It would require many men and millions of dollars. In 1932, civic leaders formed the Overseas Highway Bridge Corporation to make a loan application to a new federal agency that had been created to help communities with bridge projects. This same agency financed the Golden Gate Bridge in San Francisco.

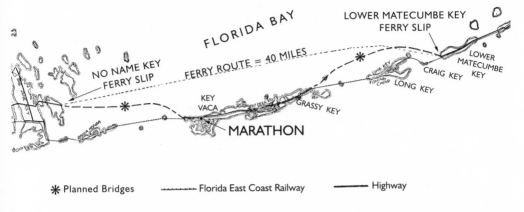

In 1928, funding was sought to construct two bridges to eliminate the ferries and make the highway continuous from the mainland to Key West. The onset of the Great Depression wiped out funding sources, and the plan lay dormant until 1935, when the federal government sent war veterans to work on the project. (author)

The Overseas Highway Bridge Corporation's engineers estimated it would cost $10.7 million to build 13.2 miles of bridges and 13.6 miles of causeway and fill, and to replace the Lower Keys highway, which after ten years of service was in a deteriorated condition. In the fall of 1932, the loan application was submitted and the following spring, after the Corporation was dissolved and replaced with the Monroe County Toll Bridge Commission, the loan was granted.

The next year, while the construction documents were being completed, the Depression struck the Florida Keys full force and Monroe County and the City of Key West sought assistance from the governor. With the arrival of Julius Stone and B. M. Duncan, the Keys had the leadership to see the project move forward. Stone, who had previously served as southern district administrator of the Federal ERA, had the contacts in Washington and access to relief funds to make things happen. Duncan, an experienced State Road Department engineer, had the technical expertise and practical experience to deal with a major transportation construction project.

On October 18, 1934, the Florida ERA office in Jacksonville announced that it would cooperate with the State Road Department to start construction of four miles of bridges and eight miles of road, which by tying into existing roads on some of the isolated islands would eliminate twenty-three miles of the existing forty-mile water gap. Additional funding for the project that had been sought in the form of a loan from the Public Works Administration had not materialized, so Julius Stone pledged to move the project forward as rapidly as federal funds could be made available. To keep the cost of materials as low as possible, limestone rock would be quarried on the Upper Keys. Because the work was labor-intensive and insufficient manpower was available on the Keys, Stone planned on using unemployed war veterans that the federal government was sending to Florida to work on public projects.

There was much to do before the main body of veterans arrived, and B. M. Duncan wasted no time in recruiting personnel for his staff. At the request of Claude Pepper, a Tallahassee lawyer and an up-and-coming politician, a young man was sent to Key West in the fall of 1934 to work with Duncan. Clean-cut, of polished appearance, and with a strong desire to succeed, George Truett Pepper would have been a good choice for Duncan's staff even if he had not been a first cousin of Claude Pepper.

George was born in Lineville, Alabama, on September 13, 1915, and had two older siblings; a brother, John, and a sister, Woodrow. His father moved the family to Florida during the mid-1920s at the high point of the economic boom. They settled in Titusville, where George played tackle on the high school football team. By the time he graduated in June 1933, the boom had evaporated, the Depression had settled in, and jobs were hard to find, especially for a high school graduate with no experience. After working odd jobs, George contacted his cousin Claude to see if he could help.

Claude Denson Pepper had already served in the Florida House of Representatives representing Taylor County. In 1934, he ran for the U.S. Senate against incumbent Park Trammell. He didn't have much money, but with the financial help of the Tallahassee Kiwanis Club, he toured the state, going all the way down to Key West. Traveling in a truck equipped with large loudspeakers, he won many votes with his direct, plain-talk speeches.

Speaking in Bayview Park in Key West, he told several hundred people he would support bonus payments to war veterans who could not support themselves. He also said that he believed "in the undying principle that every American citizen should be able to do an honest day's work and earn an honest penny for his labors." His speech was effective; the people of the Keys and Key West cast 1,204 votes for Pepper and only 423 votes for his opponent, Park Trammell. By the time George arrived in Key West, the Pepper name was well known and respected.

Claude Pepper's opponent was forced into a runoff and faced the prospect of his first defeat since entering politics in 1900. According to Claude, Trammell bought votes in Tampa's immigrant communities to ensure reelection. The runoff was decided by 4,050 votes. In Hillsborough County, the vote was 6,406 for Pepper to 16,789 for Trammell. It was the only county in the entire State of Florida to be so lopsided in favor of the incumbent. Even in defeat, Claude was gracious and maintained his popularity. To savvy people like Julius Stone and B. M. Duncan, this strong showing at the polls left no doubt that Claude Pepper was on his way to becoming a major political force in Florida.

During the summer of 1934, George Pepper went up to Tallahassee to see Claude and Claude's sister, Sara, and brother, Frank. The occasion was Sara's graduation from the Florida State College for Women. Frank Pepper recalled that he was seventeen at the time, and he and George, who was eighteen, spent the night at Claude's cottage on Lake Bradford. "We talked all night with our legs propped up on the porch railing, overlooking the moonlit lake," he said. Sometime during the visit, George let Claude know that he needed a job, and after a few words were spoken to the right people, the Florida ERA employed George.

When he arrived in Key West not long after his nineteenth birthday, George Pepper had a mature face and manner that combined with his receding hairline to make him look years older. He told his sister he had listed his age as twenty-five so he could vote for Claude in the next election. He was assigned to the publicity department of the Florida ERA District 9 headquarters in Key West to help with the media campaign to encourage tourism.

On November 1, 1934, an advance unit of fifty veterans arrived at Lower Matecumbe Key to begin construction of camps to house the main workforce that would build the highway bridges. An additional 250 veterans were to follow as soon as the housing was ready for them.

The same month, following a meeting of B. M. Duncan and the bankruptcy administrator of the Florida East Coast Railway, an annoucement was made that the Casa Marina Hotel would be reopened as soon as possible. Although the hotel began accepting guests on Christmas Eve, its official reopening would be celebrated at the grand ball on New Year's Eve. The New Year's Eve affair started with dinner at 8 p.m., followed by dancing from 9 p.m. to 2 a.m. The cover charge of $2.50 (about $30 in current dollars) per person was a bit stiff during hard economic times, but not out of line for a New Year's party at a major hotel. Of course, this ensured that attendance was limited to the influential and more prosperous citizens.

The ball was a grand affair held in the spacious ballroom and dining room of the hotel, with music provided by the Casa Marina orchestra under the direction of Richard Principal. The special dinner-dance program was "captivating and gratifying" according to the society column reporter for the *Key West Citizen*:

> Gaiety was spontaneous and wholehearted, and Key West society frolicked with grace and abandon. It was a picture worthy of a great artist's brush: the galaxy of attractive women in their lovely gowns, the men in their tuxedos, with a sprinkling of uniforms and mess-jackets, dancing and dining in an atmosphere of sophisticated charm and beauty.
>
> The colorful array of smart new gowns beggars description. Wherever one looked there was another delightful creation to catch the eye and hold it.

The list of attendees was impressive, anybody who was anybody or wanted to be somebody was there. Julius Stone, B. M. Duncan, the mayor, the commanding officers of the naval station and the army contingent, and the local civilian power brokers were there with their wives. As the president of the Key West Electric Company, Bascom Grooms was there accompanied by his wife, Rosalie; daughter, Rosalind; and mother-in-law, Beulah Boyer. Key members of the Florida ERA staff attended. Among the bachelors was George Pepper.

On December 31, 1934, the evening was pleasantly cool with a low of 68°F and clear skies. Above the courtyard adjacent to the ballroom, the stars twinkled brilliantly overhead, the water lapped softly against the beach, and the orchestra's music wafted through gently swaying palms; a more romantic place than the Casa Marina would have been hard to find that night. At midnight, the champagne corks popped and inhibitions were cast aside, strangers became good friends, and for at least one couple, a fateful relationship was begun. The Casa Marina on that New Year's Eve provided the perfect setting for the handsome young man from Titusville to meet a beautiful and venturesome girl from Key West.

Two weeks later, George was transferred from the public relations unit in Key West to Upper Matecumbe Key to augment the staff supporting the war veterans who would be building the new bridges for the highway. The separation must have had a reinforcing effect on their relationship, for George and Rosalind found ways to be together as often as possible over the coming months, and their love for each other blossomed.

At first George worked as an assistant to B. M. Duncan, who was overseeing the construction of the bridges. After a few weeks, he was assigned to work under John Good, the manager of stores for the veterans camps. In the summer, George was promoted and now had a job with significant responsibilities. He had never imagined that his first real job after graduating from high school would be in the Florida Keys, and involve the welfare of hundreds of war veterans. His pride in securing such a position was evident in the letter he wrote to his parents, postmarked at Islamorada at on August 14, 1935.

Dear Mother and Father,

Just a few lines to let you know that everything is coming along fine with me, and that I am now the chief steward here in charge of all food. Would you have ever thought that I would be a steward? And boy, is it a job? Just sit back and think how you would like to be responsible for ordering enough food for eight hundred men every day, and see that it was properly prepared.

They have not yet raised my pay but the man that has held the job before me got thirty five and I am going to put up howl for same pretty quick. The other steward that works for Duncan's men and feeds around a hundred men makes seventy-five per week. It's a big job and worth much more money.

At my assumed age of twenty-five, as they have it on record at the office, I am by eight years the youngest department head on the staff, and at that head of the largest department.

I've worked and worked hard. I have not gone up in my work because of any political connections. That makes me feel pretty good.

Will start sending the amount mentioned before next week, the 15th.

Much love.

Geo. Pepper

George's job was more important than he realized. Keeping the veterans well fed was an essential part of keeping them content, which is exactly what members of the Roosevelt administration had in mind when the plan to establish the camps was approved. It was all part of a strategy to avoid the disastrous political consequences that befell the previous administration when riots involving veterans of the Great War broke out in the nation's capital and had to be put down by the U.S. Army. The veterans had been and continued to be a very delicate problem for Washington, and people like George Pepper were critical to defusing this potentially explosive situation.

A few of the veterans in the camps on the Florida Keys had served in the Spanish-American War, but most of them had been young soldiers during the Great War. Sixteen years later, as they approached middle age, hundreds of the men who had served their country were unemployed and had been shuttled from the streets of Washington to Florida. For the Roosevelt administration, the camps bought time; for George Pepper and his colleagues, they brought jobs; for the veterans, they provided a new start; and for the people of the Keys, the camps were the means to fulfilling a long-standing dream. It seemed too good to last, and it was.

The Veterans

Construction of the veterans camps on the Upper Keys began in November 1934. Although the original master plan provided for four camps, only three were constructed. The first to be built was located at the northeast end of Windley Key near Snake Creek about 2½ miles northeast of the train station on Upper Matecumbe Key. Headquarters was set up at the Matecumbe Hotel, one mile southwest of the train station.

By the time the first contingent of 250 men arrived later in the month, a tent city had been constructed at the Windley Key site, which was designated Camp One. The tents were sixteen feet across and had wood-planked floors, canvas sides with screening in the window openings, and electric lights. Eight men were assigned to each tent. Other facilities in the camp included a tent that served as a canteen, a double-sized tent for the infirmary and dispensary, and several one-story frame buildings that served as field offices, tool storage, mess hall and kitchen, food locker, and powerhouse. The camp staff was housed in a two-story frame building that also served as their quarters. Potable water was brought down from the mainland in large cypress tanks carried on flatbed railroad cars and pumped into an elevated tank at the camp.

While the site for a second camp was being cleared at the west end of Lower Matecumbe Key next to the ferry landing, another contingent of 250 men arrived on December 19. For some unknown reason, the second camp to be constructed was designated Camp Three. It provided housing for the three hundred men assigned to work on the highway project.

The concept of using the unemployed to work on highways, schools, and other projects of benefit to the general public had been applied extensively during the peak years of the Great Depression as a means of distrib-

Top: Camp Three, located next to the ferry slip at Lower Matecumbe Key, housed veterans who were to build the four miles of bridges and eight miles of roads needed to complete the highway to Key West and eliminate the ferries. *Bottom*: Open-air kitchen at one of the camps. Food at the camps was said to be ample and of good variety and quality. (FPC)

uting aid to the general populace while allowing recipients to maintain their self-respect and learn new skills. The establishment of relief camps exclusively for war veterans in the Florida Keys and elsewhere in Florida was also a palatable response to a persistent and politically prickly problem that had plagued two presidents.

In May 1932, during Herbert Hoover's presidency, disgruntled veterans and their supporters began to travel to Washington. By the summer of 1932, about twenty-two thousand demonstrators, some with their families, had taken up residence in the city, living in makeshift camps. They became known as the Bonus Army.

The "Bonus" reference stemmed from a 1924 federal law that provided for veterans of the Great War (later known as World War I) to receive compensation for wages lost while they were in the service. Veterans who were to receive more than $50 were issued certificates that matured in twenty years (1945); those whose compensation was less than $50 received cash. By 1932, over 3.6 million certificates had been issued having a face (maturation) value averaging $999.34 per certificate. The government permitted up to half of the certificate's face value to be borrowed; by the spring of 1932, $1.25 billion had been loaned. The hard times brought on by the Depression caused veterans all over the nation to lobby Congress for the immediate redemption of the bonus certificates. This would place an additional $2.4 billion in the hands of the veterans.

The Bonus Army camped in Washington began as a grassroots movement to pressure legislators into passing the necessary statutes to release their money. Initially the cardboard villages were organized on a quasi-military basis and were fairly well managed. Their leadership visited members of Congress and the Hoover administration, urging that the bonus bill be passed. Bonus bills went before the Congress several times, and on each occasion the enabling legislation failed to pass, frustrating the veterans. When Congress adjourned in June 1932 without taking action on the issue, the movement's leadership and more conservative members left the camps and returned home.

According to a report prepared by the U.S. Bureau of Investigation, the predecessor of the Federal Bureau of Investigation, the remaining encamped demonstrators were mostly communists and people with criminal records; some were veterans, but many had no record of military service. Without leadership and deprived of the stability provided by the

War veterans, some with their families, camped at Washington, D.C., during the summer of 1932 as participants in a grassroots demonstration to urge Congress to expedite compensation for wages lost while they fought in World War I. (LOC)

more conservative members, the camps became unruly as well as unsanitary. By the third week of July, sewage and trash from the collection of shanties posed genuine health issues, and the inhabitants became more prone to violent encounters; community leaders as well as the federal bureaucracy became anxious to have the camps removed.

The breaking point came on July 28, 1932 when riots erupted in some of the camps. A young army officer named Douglas MacArthur was ordered to use U.S. Army troops to evict the demonstrators from the city and destroy the camps. The newspapers and tabloids made much of the incident, and the reputations of MacArthur and President Hoover were forever stained for the roles they played in using the U.S. Army to oppress American veterans.

In the spring of 1933, the bonus issue was still unresolved, and the veterans began to again assemble in Washington. Franklin Roosevelt was now in the White House, and he was not about to make the same mistakes his predecessor had made in handling the situation. The veterans were offered employment and other incentives to go to Civilian Conservation

Corps (CCC) camps in various states to work on forestry and other public works projects. Enough veterans accepted the offer that a repetition of the 1932 confrontation was avoided; however, by the fall of 1934, many of the CCC camps were being deactivated as the economy began to rebound. Out-of-work veterans once again began congregating in Washington.

The Roosevelt administration needed a quiet, voluntary way to move the unemployed veterans out of Washington. Julius Stone had what appeared to be the ideal way to resolve the dilemma: send them to Florida. In the Sunshine State, the veterans could work in a paradisiacal setting on projects that would ultimately help the state attract more tourists and thereby boost its faltering economy. It not only provided a nonconfrontational way to relocate the veterans from the capital, but it also provided the opportunity to demonstrate to the voting public that the Roosevelt administration was simultaneously working to improve both the economy and the welfare of unemployed war veterans.

Aubrey Williams, the deputy administrator of the Works Progress Administration (WPA) in Washington, whose office promoted the concept, said there were three reasons why Florida was chosen as the place to send transient veterans. First, the warmer climate made it less expensive to house the men. Second, the WPA was impressed with the work program that Julius Stone and the Florida communities had put together, which would allow the veterans to earn their pay and develop self-respect while working on projects of public benefit. The third and probably most significant reason was that other states did not want them; they had plenty of people out of work and preferred to take care of their own rather than provide employment for outsiders.

In the fall of 1934, an agreement was made between the Works Project Administration (WPA), the Veterans Administration, the Federal Emergency Relief Administration, and the Florida Emergency Relief Administration whereby the veterans would be recruited in Washington and sent to Jacksonville, Florida. There they would be screened for physical/psychological problems, and those who were determined to be sound enough in body and mind would be sent to camps in the state where the men would work on various projects for the public good.

The federal government reimbursed the state for a clothing allowance, housing, food, medical care, and a monthly salary for each veteran. The state paid for all materials and supervision related to the projects. The

American Legion members assist veterans arriving at the Islamorada train station in August 1935. On such occasions George Pepper manned an information booth set up at the station. He sent this photograph to his parents inscribed with "me" and an arrow pointing to his head. (Clark)

Veterans Work Program, as it came to be known, was vigorously pursued.

Not all the recruits stayed in the program; some decided to return home or elsewhere, some were rejected for medical reasons, and a few just never reported for duty at their assigned camp. By the end of August 1935, there were 1,458 war veterans in Florida stationed in seven camps around the state. Of these, 707 men were in three camps on the Upper Keys working on the highway bridges and other projects. At Clearwater on Florida's west coast, 234 veterans were employed beautifying and cleaning a city park, building an airport, and cleaning brick for road building. Another 227 ex-soldiers were at Leesburg in the center of the state, where they were engaged in the development of the Venetian Gardens, "a beautification and park project designed to rival in magnificence the famed Palatka Ravine Gardens." On the St. Johns River at Welaka, south of Palatka, 210 men worked on various civic projects.

Eighty-two veterans were racially segregated at a camp at Gainesville. According to a newsletter prepared by Conrad Van Hyning, administrator of the program, "The colored veterans at Gainesville were transferred to that point during June from their former camp at Mullet Key near St. Petersburg."

When word began to circulate about the Veterans Work Program, vets who had left Washington on their own began to return; the program intended to rid the nation's capital of unemployed veterans was actually attracting more of them to the city. Jane Wood, a social worker who interviewed some of the veterans at the Florida Keys camps in August 1935, described in her memoirs how the program worked: "You had to be a veteran and go to Washington and make trouble to get into one of these camps. They got thirty dollars a month, cots in tents, food, and plenty of time for fishing. The food was wonderful. Steaks and crawfish with drawn butter, and ice cream for lunch and dinner. The word was, 'Keep them happy and keep them out of Washington.'"

There were concerns about the problems that could arise by bringing in so many transient men into small communities and the impact such people may have on the morality of the residents. Aubrey Williams, the deputy WPA administrator, described the veterans in the program as "a very good group of men, greatly troubled and harassed by the lack of employment and by the frustrations that they had experienced since the war. They were, many of them, in need of the simplest forms of food and shelter as correctives to their condition. We found, while there was a small percentage, as there always is in any group of people, who had suffered so long and so greatly that it was very difficult to restore them without adequate hospitalization, on the whole they responded very excellently to the camp environment and to the food and to the work."

While investigating the feasibility of relocating the transient veterans to Florida, Julius Stone said they were described to him in the following manner:

They are persons who have never readjusted themselves after the war. They got through the war all right, but peace was too much for them.... [T]hey had come back and had found their jobs filled, and perhaps they were a little upset emotionally by their experience in the war, and if they had found employment, psychologically, they had been unable to adjust themselves to the regime of peace; ... they had been kicked from pillar to post for 20 years.... [T]he average

age was around 41 years. That was the average age: but it was, by no means, the top limit; and that the physical age, condition of the men was anything but good; that some of them were ill-clad, some of them had undernourished symptoms very definitely, and they were a peculiar problem.

Jane Wood thought that "They were good men who only got drunk once a month, because they only got paid once a month."

Ernest Hemingway, who was residing in Key West in 1935, was familiar with the veterans who frequented Sloppy Joe's Bar. He observed that they covered the gamut from good men who just enjoyed being in town to trouble-makers who went looking for a fight. Some had their heads on straight and others had mental problems, and there were always a few who saved their own money by conning their drunk comrades into paying for their drinks. He had seen men like them before in other countries after other wars; for Hemingway they were inevitable byproducts of war, a human residue left behind by combat.

Some journalists applied a broad-brush characterization to the veterans based on the comments of others without benefit of direct observation. It is not known on what experience Marjory Stoneman Douglas based her conclusion that the men were "broken-down army veterans, forlorn stragglers from the bonus army that had marched on Washington. Some were drunks. Some were shell-shocked and half-crazy. Some were hard, useless characters. All of them, one way or another, were misfits."

Wilbur Jones, a member of the camps' administrative staff, thought most of the veterans were decent men. He lived at the camp headquarters on Upper Matecumbe Key, and in the course of his duties had frequent contact with the veterans. He described the veterans at the camps as orderly, well behaved, and conscientious. "Sure," he said, "there were a few who were problems. But most of them were good men." One of Jones's duties was to go to the camps on the Fridays between paydays (they were paid once a month) and give the men who wanted it a one-dollar advance for spending money. He was always amazed how many of the veterans declined the advance and opted to save their money to send home.

Although some reports in the press gave the impression the veterans were duped or shanghaied in order to get them to Florida, this was not so. In some cases, people joined the program in the hope that going to a warmer climate would help their health. Such was the situation of Stephen Paschalls, a native of Greece who had fought in the Greek army during the Balkan Wars. When the United States entered the Great War, Paschalls joined the American army. He was injured, sent to Walter Reed Hospital for treatment, and discharged in 1920. He operated a restaurant on Seventh Street SW in Washington, D.C., for more than ten years until failing health forced him to retire in 1934. The talk about the good food, free medical care, and warm climate in the Florida Keys camps was irresistible. He joined the Veterans Work Program the next spring and was assigned to Camp Five, located at the northeast end of Lower Matecumbe Key.

"Frenchy" Fecteau was also assigned to Camp Five. Born in Canada, he moved with his family to Massachusetts when he was one year old. An ex-army aviator, Fecteau was one of the veterans who came to Washington in 1932. He stayed on after the Bonus Army was disbanded and worked for the Baltimore Transfer Company until 1934, when he was laid off. He then joined the Civilian Conservation Corps (CCC) and was sent to a camp in Georgia. He was subsequently transferred to a camp in Delaware and then to Foxboro, Massachusetts. In March 1935, Frenchy heard about the Florida Veterans Work Program and thought it was a good opportunity to learn a trade so he put in an application. He was accepted and sent to the camp at Clearwater, Florida, and then transferred on March 28 to Camp Five in the Keys.

Frenchy, whose given name was Joseph F. Fecteau, was assigned to the mosquito-control detail. His job was to spray a mixture of creosote and crankcase oil in swampy areas to kill mosquito larvae, a job that often involved wading through pools of the toxic substance. Creosote was developed as a preservative for wood pilings and telephone poles; it causes kidney and liver problems if ingested and is now believed to be a carcinogen. After several weeks on the job, Fecteau got the caustic chemical on his face and suffered severe eye burns. When he was released from the camp hospital at Snake Creek, he was reassigned to the position of assistant timekeeper at Camp Five. As a member of the administrative staff, he earned $36 a month and wore "whites" instead of the standard khaki pants and shirts issued to the workers.

Unlike most veterans in the camps, Frenchy owned a pickup truck and lived in a rented house located midway down Lower Matecumbe

Key. With him were his wife, Frieda; their daughters, Marie Madsden (18) and Dorothy Vester (16); and his grandchildren Ray Madsden (2½) and Dorothy Vester (1).

Benny Van Ness also had his family with him on the Keys. The thirty-six-year-old veteran had gone to Washington to join the Veterans Work Program and had arrived at Islamorada in February 1935. In May, he rented a bungalow near Islamorada and brought his wife, Laura, and their children, Doris (6), Catherine (5½), Benny Jr. (3), and Eugene (20 months) to Upper Matecumbe Key to live with him.

Like most of the men in the camps, Harold Langlois had no family in the area. A forty-four-year-old naturalized citizen who had been born on the Isle of Jersey in Europe, Harold had immigrated to America in 1908. He lived in Chelmsford, Massachusetts until the United States entered the Great War; he then served thirteen months overseas as a soldier in Battery F, 313th Field Artillery, 80th Division. After the war, he got married and then divorced. The last job he had held was as a foundry molder at the Toledo Machine Tool Company in Ohio. After that, he entered the CCC camps and worked in the Adirondacks. When his six months was up, he went to Philadelphia, where he learned that veterans were being sent to camps in Florida. Langlois said: "I heard they were sending men down to the Keys, and I wanted to go down there myself," adding, "I wasn't doing anything; I had come from the CCC camps, and thought I would go down to the Keys and stay there for the winter."

Langlois went to Washington to a place on Canal Street for transient veterans where "they had a committee of five, and they took our names and we showed them our discharges, and they picked out so many at a clip and sent them down to the keys." He and eighty others were put on the train in Washington on August 9, 1935, and arrived at Islamorada on August 13.

Harold was assigned to Camp One and worked at the limestone quarry on Plantation Key, cutting stone for a schoolhouse and pouring concrete. It was physically demanding work, but he was in good condition and the food was good. He recalled, "for breakfast we had fried eggs, fried potatoes, cereal, coffee, . . . at dinnertime we would have roast beef, roast pork, or roast lamb, and plenty of salads, and plenty of limeade, because there was plenty of limes to pick up."

At the end of each month, the men were paid, and some of them would go to either Miami or Key West. They paid their own way to get there. Special arrangements were in place to provide for the return of veterans who spent all their money and could not pay their way back. There were other opportunities to leave the camps for recreational purposes. For example, a baseball team composed of veterans went to the mainland and to Key West to compete with local teams.

The surroundings of the camps were not without temptations. Liquor was not allowed in the camps, but it was readily available on the Keys, as were hard drugs. Beer boats, floating bars, anchored close into shore. Frankie Newton and Bertie Wilson were reported to be partners in a beer stand across the highway from Camp One. Newton was formerly the owner/operator of the Homestead Country Club and previous to that had been caretaker of Al Capone's Palm Island home near Miami Beach. Mabel Gray, a Miami madam, brought her prostitutes down to the Keys for the convenience of men who did not want to travel to the mainland for such services.

The veterans did not lack for medical care. At Snake Creek a building that had formerly been a hotel was leased by the Florida ERA and used as a hospital. The director of medical services was Dr. Daniel C. Main, a fifty-nine-year-old veteran of both the Spanish American War and the Great War. Dr. Lassiter Alexander and his brother, Dr. A. Alexander, assisted him. Dr. Main reported to the director of the three camps on the Florida Keys.

In spite of the efforts of the medical staff, some of the veterans could find no relief from mental demons that persistently haunted them. This was thought to be the circumstance with Fred Griset, a veteran who had fought at Argonne. On August 4, 1935, Griset was walking beside the track on Lower Matecumbe Key when an unscheduled train sped down the straightaway from the mainland at 60 mph. The engineer saw him and blew the whistle several times to warn him of the approaching train. As the train drew very close, Griset raised his hand and stepped onto the track directly into the path of the hurtling locomotive. The train was delayed for an hour, the time it took to remove his remains from the engine and tracks. The incident reinforced the perception that the veterans were unstable relics of war.

At the beginning of August 1935, Ray Sheldon arrived on Upper Mate-cumbe Key and took over the management of the three veterans camps and hospital from Fred Ghent. Formerly director of Florida ERA opera-tions for Volusia, Flagler, and Lake counties, Sheldon was a forty-two-year-old construction engineer. Originally from Massachusetts, he had lived in Florida for twelve years, residing in West Palm Beach. He had been through the 1926 hurricane that struck north of Miami, two storms that hit West Palm Beach in 1928, and another hurricane that made land-fall just north of West Palm Beach in 1931. Ray Sheldon knew well the unpredictable behavior and danger of hurricanes.

Unlike Sheldon, his second-in-command had never experienced a hurricane and had no idea what one was like. Sam Cutler had been in Florida for only a year and a half. He came from New York, where he had worked for the Federal Emergency Relief Administration. When he ar-rived in Florida, Cutler worked for several months as a safety inspector at the Transient Bureau before being assigned as the works director for the Florida Keys camps early in March 1935. During the workweek, Sam stayed at the camp headquarters on Upper Matecumbe Key and spent weekends whenever he could with his wife in Miami. Cutler was fifty-nine years old and a graduate of the Lawrence Scientific School at Har-vard, where he had majored in mechanical engineering.

Each camp had a superintendent who reported to Sheldon, and each superintendent had several foremen who actually managed the veterans. By all reports, the superintendents and foremen were people who obeyed orders and were conscientious in looking after the men assigned to them. Will Hardaker was superintendent of Camp One, located on Windley Key, and supervised the quarry crew. Glenn Robertson was superinten-dent of Camp Five, located at the northeastern end of Lower Matecumbe, and Ben Davis was in charge of Camp Three, at the opposite end of Lower Matecumbe Key next to the ferry slip.

Also associated with the veterans camps were John Good, who headed up the Supply Department; Fred Poock, the trust officer; and D. A. Mal-com, who managed the auditing department. These men reported di-rectly to Fred Ghent. George Pepper reported to Good, and Wilbur Jones worked for Malcom.

Two residents of Upper Matecumbe Key were employed by the Veter-ans Work Program in responsible positions. O. D. King, who operated the

Rustic Inn on Upper Matecumbe Key, was hired to be the manager of the camps' central motor pool. Edney Parker, a native of the Keys, was signed on as the sanitation officer.

There was little fraternizing among the veterans and civilians. Even though there were no fences around the camps most of the veterans remained at their camps except when their work required otherwise. Veterans who brought their families with them to the Keys had more contact with civilian residents than the men living in the camps. Relations between the civilian residents and the veterans remained generally amicable.

With payday occurring on the weekend before Labor Day, many veterans made plans to go to Miami or Key West for the holiday. The week preceding Labor Day and especially the holiday weekend was traditionally a time for residents of the mainland and Key West to go visit family and friends who resided on the Keys. With summer coming to an end, tourists and fishermen flocked to the islands looking forward to enjoying the natural beauty of the Upper Keys before returning to the North. As they walked the beaches, swam, and fished, they had no idea that the clear, refreshing, bountiful waters would soon be threatening their very existence. Whether they were veteran or civilian, many would share a common fate.

The Civilians

The headquarters for the veterans camps in the Florida Keys occupied most of a two-story, frame hotel with a stucco exterior located on the ocean side of the highway near the middle of Upper Matecumbe Key. The Matecumbe Hotel was owned and operated by Ed Butters and his wife, Fern. They had originally settled around 1923 on Key Largo, where they built and operated a fishing camp and restaurant. The great inventor Thomas Edison would often visit the Butters' camp during the winter when he would go on expeditions searching for plants. In appreciation of Fern's wonderful cooking, Edison is said to have given her a vine, a plant that grew tall and healthy but that did not bloom until the day Edison died in 1931. Thereafter the vine became known as the Edison Miracle Vine. When the Butters family moved to Upper Matecumbe they brought the plant with them.

In addition to Ed, Fern, and their son and daughter, Ed's father and his sister's family lived at the hotel. The family was atypical for the Keys at that time in that all three adult males had attended college.

When he leased the hotel to the Florida ERA, Ed Butters retained the restaurant and continued to operate it. His sister, Loretta, managed the dining operation. A black couple, James and Hettie Burnett, handled the kitchen chores. All things considered, it was a good arrangement for the Butters family. The state's rent provided a steady income, and having the camps' headquarters located at the hotel assured a regular clientele for the dining room.

Personnel associated with the veterans' camps who resided at the hotel included Ray Sheldon, the director of the camps, and support staff including Sam Cutler, George Pepper, Wilbur Jones, and various draftsmen and clerical staff. Not all of the staff resided at the headquarters. John Good, who oversaw logistical support and was in charge of the supply warehouse, lived with his wife and two-year-old son in Tavernier. Fred Poock, a trust officer, rented a house at Islamorada and lived there with his wife, eighteen-year-old son, and two daughters, ages fifteen and nine.

The manager of the motor pool for the veterans camps was a newly arrived resident of the Keys named Orluff Dumond (O. D.) King. He and his wife, Betty, lived on Upper Matecumbe Key at the Rustic Inn, which they leased from Berlin Felton. The inn consisted of a restaurant with gas pumps out front and some cabins. Its name aptly described the patched-up complex of buildings.

O. D. King was a master chef who knew how to run a successful dining operation, and after the Kings arrived early in 1935, the restaurant began to attract locals and tourists. He was so good that he could have been a famous chef at a grand hotel or operated a gourmet restaurant if he had been able to stay sober. O. D. was an alcoholic, and he had squandered many opportunities to become financially well off.

It was a classic case of substance abuse. At the beginning of each cycle, O. D. refrained from drinking and, whether on his own or working for someone else, did very well. His cooking and marketing skills attracted a following, and the business would begin to grow. Then he started to drink again, and drink, and drink until absenteeism and poor performance brought about his downfall.

Before coming to the Keys, O. D. had run the counter operation at the Red Cross Drug Store in Miami. Hardly a prestigious position for a master chef, it was the best he could secure with his checkered past during the height of the Great Depression. It took several years, but his tenure followed the all-too-familiar pattern, beginning with him building up the trade and making the food service turn a handsome profit. Then the drinking and absenteeism started, and when he was at work he was drunk. Food quality suffered, and the trade began to decline along with the profits. He could not be relied upon to manage the inventory or cash. As had happened before, his irresponsible behavior reached a level where it could no longer be tolerated, and he was let go.

Six feet seven inches tall with brown neatly trimmed hair and blue eyes, O. D. was a kind, gentle man when he was sober who liked to help other people. He had the gift of gab and was a natural salesman; he could talk the shirt off just about anyone, but it was usually O. D. who ended up giving away his shirt to a fellow in need. That was the side of him that Elizabeth Murray Carter had seen before she married him. He towered over Betty, who was five feet three inches tall and eleven years younger than he. She was a slim, pretty girl with loads of energy and initiative. They both smoked and liked to have a good time. When O. D. was sober they had a good life together, but those periods became less frequent as the years went by.

O. D. was a different man when he was drunk, becoming moody, unpredictable, and obnoxious. He also became violent, something foreign to him when he was sober. Once during a drunken rage in Miami, O. D. hit his wife. Frightened, she called her brother John Robert Carter. John was not as big as O. D., but he was a plumber and was exceptionally strong, with muscles kept in shape from working with iron pipe and cast-iron fixtures. Normally very mild-mannered, John immediately responded to his sister's frantic call. When he arrived at the King's place, he found O. D. passed out on a cot. The plumber picked up the cot so that the canvas sling wrapped around King's body, lifted both the cot and O. D. up into the air, and flung them to the floor, breaking the cot into many pieces and rudely awakening King. John told O. D. that he would be in the same condition as the cot if he ever hit Betty again.

Not long after that incident, O. D. was let go by the drugstore in Miami. Unemployed during the Depression, the Kings faced an uncertain future. Then they heard about the veterans camps being established on the Keys. Betty, who had lived on the Keys as a youngster, learned from her childhood friend Eloise Felton that her husband had an inn available for lease right in the midst of the camps. By this time, O. D. had climbed back on the wagon and was making yet another attempt at rehabilitation. They scraped together enough money for the lease and sometime around the beginning of 1935 moved down to Upper Matecumbe Key. It must have been like a homecoming for Betty, awakening fond memories of the time when the Carter family had lived on the Keys.

Her mother, Karlie Murray, had auburn hair and blue eyes and had been voted the prettiest girl in St. Augustine when she was a teenager. Certainly Charles Lawrence Carter cast a confirming vote when he asked Karlie to marry him. The Carter family had strong ties to Key West. Karlie's father, an army surgeon, had been stationed there during the yellow fever epidemic in 1887, and her grandfather, the Reverend C. A. Fulwood, had been a beloved minister for many years at the Old Stone Church. She was well educated and strong-willed.

Karlie and Charles had ten children, including Betty and her brother John. Charles worked for the Florida East Coast Railway; in 1919, the family moved to Islamorada, where he was in charge of the pumping station. It was Charles's job to operate the pumps that refilled the two large elevated tanks with water brought down from Homestead in large, opened-topped, cypress-staved tanks carried on flatcars, and then to fill the locomotives when they stopped en route to Miami/Key West.

One of the benefits of the position was a large, sturdy house owned by the FEC Railway that had a pipe connecting it to the elevated tanks. The pumper's house was one of a few homes on the Keys at that time to have running water. Another perquisite was that the trains coming from Miami carried ice, and as they passed the pumper's house, they would slow and throw off a large block for the family while the engineer tooted the whistle, playing a tune in greeting. The Carters were the only family on Upper Matecumbe to have ice delivered to their front door by train twice a week.

Life on the Keys was generally an enjoyable experience for the children. Often when their friends came over to play, Karlie made ice cream and played the piano; she was an accomplished pianist. The children had to improvise their playground equipment, but that was part of the fun. On one occasion, Betty's brother Charles made a slide using planks of wood tied together with one end secured to the branches of a gumbo limbo tree. He rubbed the planks with Octagon soap and poured water down them to make the surface slick. The kids then took a piece of cardboard up into the tree, placed it on the top of the slide, and away they went.

On those frequent days when it was very hot or when the mosquitoes were bad, the children played in the attic of the two-story house. It was one large, open room that ran the length and width of the house. There were windows at the gable ends, and a cool breeze always wafted through. They went to church and attended school in a building located on the beach by the ocean.

During September 1919, a Category 4 hurricane passed over the Dry Tortugas and into the Florida Keys. Key West was hit hard, sustaining $2 million damage and three fatalities. On Upper Matecumbe Key, the Carter family safely rode out the storm in their home. As the wind-driven

Table 5.1. Veteran Camps Motor Pool Inventory, August 27, 1935

Vehicle type	Quantity	Cost ($)
Coaches	11[a]	4,475
Pickup trucks	10[b]	3,075
Dump trucks	7	5,250
Stake trucks	12	6,250
Tractor/trailer	1[c]	4,000
Fire truck	1	7,000
Ambulance	1	1,000
Bus	1	300
Totals	44	31,350

Source: U.S. Congress, *Florida Hurricane Disaster Hearings: Committee on World War Veterans' Legislation*, H.R. 9486, 74th Cong., 2nd sess., 1936, 324.
[a] One coach wrecked.
[b] One pickup truck burned.
[c] One tractor/two trailers.

rain pounded on the windows and doors, Karlie stuffed rags and towels in the cracks to keep the water out. It was a scary experience, but they were in a well-built structure and the worst of the hurricane bypassed them. After a nineteen-month stay on the Keys, Betty's father was transferred, and the family moved back to the mainland.

Sixteen years later, at the age of twenty-six, Betty returned to the Keys, and the Kings opened the Rustic Inn. Not long thereafter, O. D. talked his way into becoming the superintendent of transportation for the veterans camps. This was a job with substantial responsibilities. He had to see that the equipment was kept in good working order and that the vehicles were checked out only to authorized operators. An inventory taken on August 27, 1935, listed an impressive fleet of forty-four vehicles. Most of the vehicles were in satisfactory operating condition.

With O. D. managing the motor pool, the operation of the inn fell mainly on Betty's shoulders. She was normally up at six thirty in the morning and didn't get to bed until midnight. The restaurant had a gasoline-powered generator that started up automatically when a wall-mounted switch near the front door was turned on, so the diner had electric lights and was open evenings. Perishables were kept in a kerosene-powered cooler that was so efficient a gallon of fuel would last a month. Bread and other baked goods were delivered to the diner by truck from bakeries on the mainland.

The inn was not frequented by veterans, but several who worked with O. D. would stop by occasionally. Gilbert Thompson, a civilian, hung around the place all the time and helped out with chores. He was a good friend of O. D.'s, a relationship encouraged by O. D. giving him free beer.

In June 1935, Betty's younger sister Leone Barr and Leone's three-year-old son came to live with the Kings. Leone had separated from her husband and was very sick. By the end of August, she was still recovering, but was able to get up and take care of herself and her child. Leone was twenty-four years old and, like Betty, was five feet three inches tall, slim and pretty with her mother's auburn hair and blue eyes. Leone and her son lived in one of the inn's cabins.

In addition to the restaurants at the Matecumbe Hotel and the Rustic Inn on Upper Matecumbe Key, there was another diner on the adjacent island to the southwest. Lower Matecumbe Key is approximately four miles along on its longest axis, which lies southwest to northeast. The island is shaped like an elongated oval with a huge bite taken out of its mid-section on the bay side. The northeast end is about a half mile wide, and then it shrinks to one thousand feet across at its narrowest point before broadening out to the lower end, which is almost a mile wide. Although it had over eight hundred acres, most of it was not suitable for farming.

According to the census taken in the spring of 1935, there were no permanent residents living on Lower Matecumbe. Perhaps this was the reason two large camps for veterans were situated there, with Camp Five located on the northeast end on the ocean side of the railroad tracks, and Camp Three placed at the southwest end on the bay side of the tracks. The bulk of the veterans assigned to the Keys were housed in these two camps.

The railroad and highway traversed the length of the island, with the highway terminating at a ferry slip at the southwest end next to Camp Three. The ferry came in around noon most days if it didn't break down or encounter rough seas. After unloading the northbound cars and then loading the southbound vehicles, the boat returned to its other slip at No Name Key, forty miles to the west. There the vehicles disembarked and could take the highway all the way down to Key West.

The small harbor that served the ferry slip was one of the few places in the region where fishing boats could come alongside a dock conveniently located near the highway that went to the mainland. For this reason, the

Crosland Fish Company of Miami operated a fish house and refueling facility there for commercial fishermen. About seventy-five fishermen kept their boats there during the winter and early spring, when the great schools of fish ran along the reef.

Not far from the ferry landing were a diner, gas pumps, and marina operated by a young couple, Carson ("Cardy") Bradford Jr. (25) and his wife, Elizabeth (24). They had two children, Betty Ann (2) and Carson Bradford III (10 months). The family lived on a houseboat moored near the diner. Edna Arnold (36), the children's nanny, also lived aboard and did housekeeping chores.

They had a generator that provided lighting for the complex and its immediate area so they could operate when the daylight hours grew shorter in the winter months. At first the Bradfords' business catered mainly to people waiting for the ferry and to sportfishing and pleasure boats that relied on "Cardy" for provisions, fuel, and ice. When the veterans arrived business really boomed. The restaurant was expanded to include a country store, and Cardy had to hire a cook and waitress to keep up with the brisk trade. As Elizabeth observed, "It was a busy place."

The Bradfords' spacious houseboat was built on the hull of a barge and had two levels. On the top floor were four bedrooms and a large living room, while on the deck level there was a small bedroom, living room, kitchen, and bathroom. It was well appointed, having been built for Carl Fisher, who created Miami Beach and who, at his zenith in 1926, was worth more than $50 million.

Behind the diner were two garages made of corrugated tin built on top of a concrete cistern. Cardy used one for his car, while the other was reserved for his father, who often came down from Miami. Cistern water was used for washing; potable water was delivered by the railroad and stored in a water tank next to the diner. The Bradfords had all the necessities of life and many luxuries that few people on the Keys enjoyed.

When the State of Florida conducted a census in March 1935, the Bradfords lived in a rented house in Islamorada. They were among 13,335 people reported as residents of Monroe County at that time. Of the county's populace, 12,470 were living in Key West, and 865 resided on the other islands of the Keys and in the Everglades. Of the people living on the Keys, more than half (468 men, women, and children) resided on approximately 3,800 acres of land comprising Craig Key, Upper Matecumbe

Top: Vehicles line up waiting to board the ferry at the west end of Lower Matecumbe Key on July 4, 1933. The top of the ferry ramp's gantry at the landing can
be seen at the extreme left. The building in front of the gantry is the Crosland fish
house. The Terminal Lunch building is behind the bus. *Middle*: Carson Bradford's
Terminal Lunch diner in 1934. *Bottom*: Unloading Spanish mackerel at the Crosland
Fish Company dock. (Wilkinson)

Table 5.2. Resident Population Distribution: Craig to Tavernier, Spring 1935

Category	Craig	Islamorada[a]	Plantation	Tavernier[b]
WHITES				
Male adults[c]	13	85	13	46
Female adults	4	58	10	38
Male children	2	47	5	16
Female children	2	43	9	14
Total	21	233	37	114
NEGROES				
Male adults	0	4	4	19
Female adults	0	2	2	10
Male children	0	0	0	9
Female children	0	0	2	11
Total	0	6	8	49
Grand Totals	21	239	45	163

Source: State of Florida Census of 1935, State of Florida Archives, Gray Building, Tallahassee.

[a] Islamorada includes Upper Matecumbe and Windley Key.

[b] Tavernier includes the west end of Key Largo.

[c] Adults are defined as anyone eighteen or older.

Key, Windley Key, Plantation Key, and the western portion of Key Largo around Tavernier. Plantation Key was primarily farms and lime groves and was sparsely populated. No one was recorded as a resident of Lower Matecumbe Key. Veterans, camp administrators, and tourists were considered to be transients and were not counted as part of the census.

The census identified two racial categories, "Whites" and "Negroes." The population on these Keys was predominantly white, with only sixty-three people classified as Negroes. The latter category included all dark-skinned people, regardless of their ethnicity. Segregation was as deeply ingrained in the Keys as it was in the rest of the nation during the 1930s. Of the sixty-three people classified as Negroes, thirty-one were listed as having occupations. Of these, there were sixteen laborers, nine farmers, a carpenter, several cooks, and two laundresses.

The people on this section of the Keys ranged in age from six-month-old babies to a ninety-two-year-old laborer. Although most of the residents were born in Florida, twenty-three were natives of Georgia, and seventy-eight came from twenty-four other states. A total of thirty-nine

Table 5.3. Residents' Age/Gender Distribution: Craig to Tavernier, Spring 1935

Age	Male	Female	Total
0–6	38	30	68
7–17	41	52	93
18–29	48	46	94
30–39	53	31	84
40–49	33	25	58
50–59	26	11	37
60–69	16	4	20
70–92	5	4	9
Unknown	3	2	5
Total	263	205	468

Source: State of Florida Census of 1935, State of Florida Archives, Gray Building, Tallahassee.

Table 5.4. Students Enrolled in School, by Grade: Craig to Tavernier, Spring 1935

	1st	2nd	3rd	4th	5th	6th	7th	8th	9–12[a]	Total
White	4	10	10	11	10	9	9	9	8	80
Negro	3	4	1	0	0	0	0	0	0	8
Total	7	14	11	11	10	9	9	9	8	88

Source: State of Florida Census of 1935, State of Florida Archives, Gray Building, Tallahassee.
[a] Students in grades 9–12 attended school either in Key West or Homestead.

residents reported that they were born outside the United States; of this group, which identified nine countries of origin, 44 percent were from the Bahamas and 31 percent from the British West Indies. Eighteen of the foreign-born residents had become naturalized U.S. citizens.

There were 161 children, defined as anyone under the age of eighteen, reported to be living on the Keys from Craig to the west end of Key Largo during the spring of 1935. Of these, eighty-eight were listed as students. The schools on the Keys only went through the eighth grade, so students in the ninth through twelfth grades had to commute to Homestead or move to Key West to continue their education. Educational facilities were segregated.

There were 110 families, defined as a married couple whether or not they had children, living in the area from Craig to Tavernier in March 1935.

Table 5.5. Distribution of Families: Craig to Tavernier, Spring 1935

	White	Negro	Total
Craig	4	0	4
Islamorada	49	1	50
Plantation	8	3	11
Tavernier	35	10	45
Total	96	14	110

Source: State of Florida Census of 1935, State of Florida Archives, Gray Building, Tallahassee.
Note: The census defined a family as a married couple whether or not they had children.

Among the whites, the most common surname was Russell (50 people) followed by Albury (34), Pinder (31), and Parker (17). Two surnames accounted for over 40 percent of the Negroes; Williams with fourteen people and Albury with twelve. The above analysis counts only people with the same name whether or not they are related, and while it provides some indication of the size of a clan, it is by no means exact since a married daughter and her children would not be identified with her maiden surname. For example, although fifty people living in this area were registered in the census as having the Russell surname, the Russell clan is said to have numbered sixty-one members when the hurricane struck.

With regard to individual families, Edney and Edna Parker had one of the largest. The couple had a total of twelve children. The first died at birth, but the surviving siblings, five boys and six girls, and their parents formed the nucleus of Parkerville on Upper Matecumbe.

In June 1935, one of the Parker children, Etta, married Eddie Sweeting, and they moved into a rented cottage. There were still eight children living with Edney and Edna. With so many mouths to feed, it is no wonder that Edney held down three jobs; constable, bone fishing guide, and sanitation officer for the veterans camps.

It was not easy raising a family during the Great Depression, and it was even more difficult to do so in the Florida Keys. For many families, economic survival was a day-to-day struggle that took a heavy toll, especially on the breadwinners, homemakers, and older children. People such as Eddie and Mozelle Williams scraped a living from whatever the Keys would yield in order to keep their children fed and clothed. With remarkable resiliency, they overcame adversity to keep their family together. The Williams family could attest that life in Paradise was not easy.

Table 5.6. Census Data: Edney Parker Family, Spring 1935

Name	Age[a]	Sex	BP[b]	Education	Relation[c]
Edney Basil Parker	48	M	FL	Grammar Sch	————
Edna Pinder Parker	42	F	FL	Grammar Sch	wife
Janice Parker Reese	21	F	FL	Grade 8	daughter
Austin Lamar Reese	31	M	GA	Grade 8	s-i-l
Carl Nolan Parker	20	M	FL	Grammar Sch	son
Yvonne Parker Ryder	19	F	FL	Grade 6	daughter
R. W. "Jack" Ryder	53	M	NY	College	s-i-l
Etta Elizabeth Parker[d]	17	F	FL	Grade 8	daughter
Lois Lucy Parker	16	F	FL	Jr. High	daughter
Samuel Edney Parker	13	M	FL	Grade 7	son
Franklin Basil Parker	11	M	FL	Grade 5	son
Homer Earl Parker	8	M	FL	Grade 3	son
Fay Marie Parker	6	F	FL	Grade 1	daughter
Norman Frederick Parker	3	M	FL	n/a	son
Barbara June Parker	7mo	F	FL	n/a	daughter

Source: State of Florida Census of 1935, State of Florida Archives, Gray Building, Tallahassee.
[a] Age when census was taken in spring 1935.
[b] BP = birthplace (state).
[c] s-i-l = son-in-law.
[d] Etta Parker married Eddie Sweeting in June 1935.

Eddie and Mozelle lived with their son and two daughters on land created when the railroad placed a fill across Whale Harbor, the water opening between Upper Matecumbe and Windley Key. With some help from family and friends, Eddie built a wood-framed house that sat jacklegged over the sloping side of the embankment running from the tracks down to the highway. Almost level with the rails about twelve feet above sea level, the side of the home facing the tracks was only a few feet away from passing trains.

The fills were constructed by dredges and draglines scooping up coral rock from the shallow seabed adjacent to the railroad's route. In many instances, this created a channel paralleling a fill that could be used by fishing boats to access the natural channels leading out to the reef. Such was the situation along the fill where the Williams house was situated. It was probably one of the reasons Eddie chose this location. Directly across the highway from his home he built a nice-sized workshop/storeroom out over the water. From the back of the workshop extended a dock where he moored his thirty-foot fishing boat, the *Peggy*.

Six months before the hurricane struck, Eddie Williams completed this house on the Whale Harbor fill between Upper Matecumbe Key and Windley Key. The train tracks are at the top of the embankment. The highway lies between the house and Eddie's workshop, which sits out over water. His boat, the *Peggy*, is moored at the end of the dock on the right. (Chance)

The family had previously lived in a dilapidated rental house; their new home was a major step upward. The house that Eddie built had one large room that served as the living room, dining room, and sleeping quarters for his daughters. Mozelle and Eddie had a small bedroom that was partitioned off. Their eighteen-month-old son slept in there with them. There was also a separate kitchen.

It was far from perfect. The outhouse was a small shack built out over Florida Bay on the other side of the tracks. Mosquitoes, spiders, and other insects made it unusable at night, so chamber pots were a necessity. The house shook each time a train went by, and the passengers had a close-up view of the interior through the windows, which had to be kept open for ventilation.

There was no electricity and no running water; rainwater that fell on the roof was collected by gutters and stored in a barrel adjacent to the house. It was used for washing; potable water was purchased. Mozelle, according to her daughter Elizabeth, saw that every ounce of freshwater was put to good use: "After we swam in the daytime, mother would stand us on the porch and wash us off and let the water fall into a washtub and saved the water to do the laundry in. Of course, we weren't dirty because we had been swimming all day, but she wanted to get the salt off us so she would stand us in a washtub and rinse us off. Then she'd save the water to wash the clothes with it, and then sometimes she'd save the wash water to scrub the porch with! So it was recycled."

For lights, the family used kerosene lamps, although Eddie preferred the brighter light of his gasoline lantern, especially if he had to go outdoors at night. Cooking was done on a stove fueled by kerosene. The main fare was oatmeal for breakfast and fish and grits for supper. Occasionally they would have vegetables given to them by friends or brought down by family visiting from the mainland. They didn't have fresh milk so they used canned condensed milk on their oatmeal and got both the sugar and milk at the same time. Eddie kept the family supplied with different types of fish; Mozelle was a good cook and could fix seafood so many different ways that it did not seem like the same thing every night.

Eddie's and Mozelle's ancestors had come to Florida when it was still a territory. Eddie's father, Sam Williams, was for many years master of the *Island Home*, a schooner that plied the waters between Miami and Key West. For residents on the Florida Keys, the *Island Home* was their connection to the rest of the world, bringing in mail and supplies and taking their produce, fish, and other items to the markets in Miami and Key West. John (Johnny Brush) Pinder owned the vessel. From frequent trips with his father, Eddie learned the waters of the Keys and seamanship.

Some of his relatives thought Eddie looked like Humphrey Bogart. His skin was a dark mahogany color from all the hours he spent in the sun. He seldom wore shoes, and when he did he preferred tennis shoes. He wore khaki pants most of the time and smoked Lucky Strike cigarettes.

Mozelle's family settled in Hamilton County near Live Oak, Florida. She was born in May 1905 in Live Oak. Her family moved to Tampa after her father died in the 1918 flu epidemic. It is believed that Eddie Williams and Mozelle Law met in Miami when she went to visit some relatives. They were married in 1925 at Miami. Mozelle was a stout, strong woman who liked to have a good time. She enjoyed being with family and friends.

Eddie and Mozelle moved to Tampa, where their daughters were born—Elizabeth in 1926 and Evelyn in 1927. The family then moved to Tennessee, but life was hard, work was scarce, and it was not long before Mozelle and Eddie separated. Eddie moved back to the Keys and Mozelle took the children to Tampa. Eddie was a family man, and being separated from his wife and children must have been difficult for him to bear.

Smuggling was rampant in the Florida Keys, and heroin and rum were readily available; Eddie became addicted.

His father helped Eddie get treatment for his addictions, after which he returned to the Keys and as far as is known had nothing further to do with drugs. In 1929, Mozelle and the children went down to the Keys to visit him. The bond between them was still strong. "She dearly loved Daddy," recalled Elizabeth. The family was reunited, and they lived in a rented house on Upper Matecumbe Key. In 1934, Mozelle gave birth to a son, Robert Edward Williams, in a Miami hospital.

In the midst of the Great Depression, Eddie and Mozelle struggled economically. The couple had to make the best use of their talents. Mozelle's cooking skills landed her and Eddie jobs at the Caribbee Colony, a tourist resort at the south end of Upper Matecumbe. Eddie helped out in the kitchen, worked as a handyman, and took people charter-boat fishing.

The developer George Merrick built the Caribbee Colony in 1930. After the bankruptcy of his Coral Gables Corporation, he decided to begin again by developing a facility in the Florida Keys that would appeal to the middle-class traveler. The rich and famous had the Long Key Fish Camp for their exclusive use; Merrick wanted to provide a place for the common man. He built cabins, a marina, a long dock on the ocean side with a fenced-in swimming area at the end, a thatched pavilion similar to the large thatched lodges of the Seminole Indians, dining facilities, and a spacious outdoor dance floor. Leased and operated by Wade and Marie Dumas in 1935, the Caribbee Colony offered good food, private accommodations, and a variety of diversions including fishing, swimming, and nightly entertainment.

Occasionally the Williams children were allowed to spend the day at the Colony, helping out their parents and playing on the beach. Sometimes, as Evelyn recalled, they got into mischief: "Mother worked at Caribbee Colony during the wintertime. Mama was the cook and hostess. Daddy helped cook too. There were little cabins at the Caribbee Colony and just one bathhouse. The cabins didn't have bathrooms, they were just bedroom cabins. Everybody came to the dining room to eat. One day Liz and I went inside the bathhouse and locked all the doors to the stalls from the inside and crawled back out underneath. And people came up there (to the office) wanting to know why they couldn't get in." Evelyn and Elizabeth were typical young girls and had learned that enjoying life is what one makes of it.

It was such a carefree time. . . . We didn't think about that [being poor], after all what's to do except play on the beach and draw in the sand, and make orange juice out of bricks—we'd grate bricks and put the dust in water. We'd heard about orange juice, but didn't have any. We'd catch the jellyfish and put them up on the beach and watch them melt. We had lots of limeade made out of key limes.

The first movie we went to was at Tavernier [the only theater that existed on the Upper Keys at the time]. They would have amateur programs; people along the Keys if they had any talent would go in there and perform. . . . We went to see Shirley Temple movies, two different ones, and maybe cartoons.

They played with friends, going swimming at the beach and climbing trees to gather tamarinds. The girls were delighted when relatives visited from the mainland during the summer and they had their cousins for playmates. Sometimes they tested Eddie's patience, Evelyn recalled:

Daddy's language was pretty salty. He was a very gentle person. . . . He did [spank] me one time when we swiped that leaky skiff and we were going to hunt pirate gold on the island. We were looking for treasure. When we were living on the fill here, the four of us, our two cousins and Elizabeth and me decided we would go look for pirate's treasure on the islands over there [indicating the Gulf side], and we got out there and the boat started leaking, and we got caught in the current, and we started hollering, and the boys started fighting over the paddle, and telling us to bail the boat. It was just before the hurricane. And Daddy had to swim out and get us, and he gave each one of us a whop on the butt as we got out. It wasn't a beating. Mother was the one that disciplined us.

As with any children, the Williams girls suffered their share of bumps, bruises, and cuts. The nearest hospital was the one set up for the veterans at Snake Creek; the nearest hospital for civilians was at Homestead on the mainland, over an hour's drive away. Wounds that broke the skin had to be treated without delay because in the tropical climate gangrene was a likely consequence of ignoring such an injury. Kerosene was used as an antiseptic for cuts and punctures and also as an ingredient in homemade cough syrup and poultices.

Often the local drugstore was a plant or bush growing nearby. The aloe vera plant was a pharmaceutical cornucopia, and just about every home in the Keys had one or more growing in a handy place. When the stalk-like leaves are cut, a fluid emerges that soothes and promotes healing of scratches, burns, insect bites, and cuts. It was also used to make laxatives and an ulcer-relieving drink. The papaya tree not only produces an edible fruit, but juice from the green fruit was said to aid digestion. The leaves of the gumbo limbo tree were crushed to make a paste that relieved bee stings and insect bites.

As the end of summer approached in 1935, the Williams girls were looking forward to the day after Labor Day, when another school year would begin. A new school had just been completed in Islamorada across the highway from the post office. It had been built by the veterans out of limestone rock quarried on Plantation Key. The new school was much bigger than the one-room church in Matecumbe that Elizabeth and Evelyn had attended in prior years, and students from Tavernier to Lower Matecumbe would be there. Elizabeth said:

> We went to a little Methodist church on Matecumbe, and also it was the schoolhouse too. [It] was a little holiness church built by an elderly couple, and Evelyn and I would get ready and go to Sunday school in the afternoon. We always had church and Sunday school in the afternoons, never in the mornings. And it was right across the street; this was before we moved up to the fill. It was just the dearest old couple, Copeland Johnson and his wife.
>
> After moving to the new house on the fill, we'd get dressed in the mornings and walk up to the road and wait for the school bus. We'd take off our shoes and hide them under a palmetto bush so we could go barefoot. Most of the children went barefoot because their mommas and daddies didn't have enough money to buy them shoes. Mr. Charles was the principal, and Mr. Ferrin was the other teacher.
>
> They had built a new schoolhouse and we were to start at it the day after Labor Day. I worried that I wouldn't know where to go. The new school was at Islamorada.

The sad thing about it is that the schools only went to the eighth grade. The few that could afford it would have to go into Homestead or Key West to further their education, and mother had fears about this. I was in the fifth grade then and mother was worried.

Cash was a scarce commodity as far as Eddie and Mozelle were concerned. They worked hard when work could be had, but the Caribbee Colony only employed them during the winter and early spring when the tourists came down. The charter-boat business and commercial fishing were also seasonal. Sometimes Eddie worked on a barter basis, doing jobs such as fixing a farmer's truck in exchange for some farm produce.

On at least one occasion, Eddie worked for Edney Parker on a barter basis. Every now and again the rum smugglers would make a run, and Edney, as constable, needed help to locate and then dispose of their hidden contraband. Unfortunately, the constable did not have any funds to pay for deputies so Edney would ask Eddie and others he trusted to work for him on a noncash basis. Some weeks after Eddie had helped the constable with such work, Elizabeth made an amazing discovery: "Edney Parker worked for the government, and he would swear Daddy in as a deputy whenever the rumrunners would bring the rum over from Cuba and hide it in the Keys. Daddy and Mr. Parker would find it and see that it was taken care of properly. One afternoon I crawled under the house—it was built up off the ground—and I was so excited. I found some bottles wrapped in straw, and I crawled out from under the house and told mother, 'Look what I've got!' and she gave Daddy the devil!"

Mozelle's wrath stemmed from the very real fear that the liquor would once again bring Eddie down. He had freed himself from heroin, but alcohol still had a grip on him. Having a ready supply of rum right underneath the house was not conducive to controlling the situation. The rum did not remain in its hiding place for long; there were probably some drunk fish around the dock that day!

The *Peggy*, Eddie's boat, was kept tied up at the end of the dock across the highway from the house. About thirty feet in length, its spacious cabin could accommodate small groups on charters or the family on outings. The *Peggy* was important to the family in several respects. It provided opportunities to earn income from commercial fishing and charters, and

The Alligator Reef lighthouse was completed in 1873. With a focal plane 136 feet high, its light was visible from the bridge of a ship twenty miles away. Sixteen solid wrought-iron legs, each a foot in diameter and driven ten feet into the coral reef, supported the lighthouse. (Langley)

enabled Eddie to catch fish with which to feed his own family and use for barter. When he had a good catch, he shared freely with his friends and neighbors. His daughters were dispatched along the highway to spread the word. Evelyn remembers that soon people would begin to arrive at the dock with pots and pans. It was strictly a first-come, first-served basis:

> Every time Daddy had a big catch, he would send Liz one way and me the other way, up along and down along, and tell the neighbors if anybody wanted anything to come get what they wanted. There was no refrigeration. People had iceboxes. We had one, but it was very seldom that the iceman came.
>
> I can remember my father pulling the boat up on shore and scraping the hull and caulking the seams. It was just a boat that had bench type seats on the sides. He took fishing parties out from the Caribbee Colony. If he didn't take a big crowd he would sometimes take us out. I remember going out on the boat and getting bored.

A favorite place for family outings was the lighthouse on Alligator Reef. It was about five miles from the Williams house, a pleasant cruise across Hawk Channel. The lighthouse was manned in those days by rotating crews consisting of a keeper, a first assistant, and a second assistant. One of Eddie's sideline jobs was to take fuel and mail out to them.

The lighthouse was built on pilings driven into the submerged living reef and had no beach or land area. It was isolated duty, and the men were always glad to have friends drop by, especially if they brought something good to eat. Free of mosquitoes and flies with almost always a gentle breeze, the shady metal platform below the crew's quarters was a delightful place for picnics.

Usually a more peaceful place would be hard to find, yet there were times when it could become a scary place for a young girl, as Evelyn vividly remembered:

> The Fourth of July [1935] we went out there and we took the big boat and the skiff behind it. Daddy spotted a turtle, and he took the skiff and went out there and flipped the turtle into the skiff and then came back to the lighthouse where we were.
>
> They hauled the turtle up onto the lighthouse platform, and they butchered it there; they were going to make turtle stew. They didn't

think about the sharks. They threw the head and the entrails and everything in the water, and the sharks came up. And it was so scary—big sharks, I tell you! They got to fighting down there and banging around on those big metal pilings.

We had to catch the ingoing tide to go back home, and we had to go down those steel stairs with those sharks down there, and I wouldn't go, I began to cry, and Daddy had to take me down there in his arms. I was the crybaby of the family I guess.

About a week before Labor Day, Mozelle's brother Dan Law and his family arrived at the Williams home after driving down from Tampa. Dan (35); his wife, Carrie (31); their daughter, Markelle (6); and their son, Perry (9) planned to stay with the Williams family through Labor Day. Tall and thin, Dan was a salesman and was always telling jokes and being funny.

The adults got along well and enjoyed playing cards and talking. There were the usual diversions of swimming, fishing, and picnicking. As a special treat one night, Eddie made a spicy seafood gumbo. When there were slow periods. Mozelle pulled out an old Sears Roebuck catalog, and Markelle, Liz, and Evelyn would entertain themselves cutting out pictures of men, women, and clothes for paper dolls.

As the Labor Day Weekend approached, the tempo of life for the Williams and Law families and others on the Upper Keys shifted to a holiday mode. It was a time of good times that would soon come to a tragic end.

Friday and Saturday

Florida and South Carolina were the only two states that participated in the program to remove unemployed veterans from the nation's capital. By the end of March 1935, there were more than eight hundred veterans residing in eleven camps. The number declined to 749 in April, then rose slightly in May to 759 and remained at that level through June before almost doubling in July. The *New York Times* reported early in August that there were about 2,500 veterans residing in the South Carolina and Florida camps.

This surge in the population of the veterans camps was the result of the national economy beginning to improve. Believing the end of the Great Depression was in sight, many states began to cut back on their relief operations to save money. As state relief programs closed, veterans who had been served by those programs headed to Washington, where they were quickly processed and shuttled off to camps in South Carolina and Florida. The Florida camps—four located across the waist of the peninsula and three in the Florida Keys—saw a sharp increase in the number of veterans housed.

By August, the population of the Florida camps had stabilized at around 1,460 veterans. The white veterans were fairly evenly distributed among the camps located in the Florida Keys and at Clearwater, Leesburg, and Welaka, a small town about ten miles south of Palatka. All black veterans were assigned to the Gainesville camp.

In mid-August, the director of the Federal ERA, Harry Hopkins, announced that the veterans camps in South Carolina and Florida were to be closed by November 1. It was a matter of weighing the economics against the politics. The national economy was slowly, but steadily improving,

Table 6.1. Veterans Enrolled at Florida Camps, August 31, 1935

Location	Camps	Veterans
Florida Keys	3	707 (see note)
Clearwater	1	234
Leesburg	1	227
Welaka	1	210
Gainesville	1	80
Total	7	1,458

Source: *Review of Relief and Economic Statistics* (monthly newsletter prepared by the Research Department, Florida Emergency Relief Administration, Jacksonville, Conrad Van Hyning, administrator), August 1935, and September 1935, 8.
Note: This number appears to have been overstated. Frank T. Hines, administrator of the Veterans Affairs Department, stated in a letter to the chairman of the congressional committee holding hearings on World War Veterans' Legislation and the hurricane that there were 696 veterans on the Florida Keys camps's payroll for August 1935.

reducing the number of unemployed people, including veterans. This diminished the likelihood of a mass demonstration by bonus veterans.

Recurring incidents of drunkenness and rowdy behavior, a sit-down strike at the Florida Keys camps earlier in the year, and growing public awareness that the veterans were being shunted away from Washington for political convenience had turned the program into a liability for the Roosevelt administration. The camps were characterized in the media as "Playgrounds for Veterans," and the projects that the veterans were supposed to accomplish had become, in most cases, monuments of waste and inefficiency. The expenditures were not tolerable to the host states given the poor results and the demands of other needs. The Florida program cost a total of $862,326 from the beginning of 1935 to the end of August. Even with the federal government reimbursing $461,982, the hard-pressed citizens of Florida had to fund $400,344 for materials and other costs.

In this context, the decision to close the camps was not surprising. Although the closing was given some media exposure, most of the people in the veterans camps on the Keys, including the staff, were not aware that the camps were to be closed in November. Certainly some of them must have known that something was afoot when squads of social workers arrived at the camps in the latter part of July and began conducting interviews to evaluate the men to determine whether they would be sent home or relocated elsewhere.

The team dispatched to the Florida Keys camps consisted of a mix of experienced and novice social workers hastily assembled in Dade County. On August 30, 1935, they finished interviewing the last of the seven hundred veterans on the islands and boarded a bus for Miami. They were looking forward to a long weekend to unwind before returning to their regular duties tending to the poor and unemployed in southeast Florida.

The working conditions on the Keys had been physically arduous as the summer heat combined with suffocating humidity to make both people and paperwork go limp, and the mosquitoes relentlessly attacked any exposed flesh. It was emotionally draining work, listening to burned-out men talk about the experiences that had brought them to this situation. Some had forsaken their families while some had been abandoned, and others didn't care about anyone or anything anymore. Some had just arrived and did not understand why they were about to be sent home or elsewhere, while others were confused about everything.

For Jane Wallace Wood, an intelligent, perceptive, twenty-two-year-old who had recently joined the social work corps, it was especially trying to be suddenly immersed in a world that seemed littered with human debris. While she described herself as simply "a private in a task force of social workers," she was unlike many of her colleagues.

Born in Macon, Georgia, as a child her IQ was determined by reliable tests to be 167 (a score of over 140 is considered to be at the genius level). Her family moved to Miami when she was twelve. She finished high school at the age of sixteen. By the time she was twenty-one, Jane had spent two years in Greece soaking up the Aegean culture and had earned a bachelor's degree in physics from the University of Miami.

The Depression made work hard to find in 1934 so Jane took a job at the *Miami Daily News* writing obituaries and covering the food and fashion scenes. In the summer of 1935, a friend encouraged her to try social work. The salaries being offered were attractive, and she became a caseworker in Miami. Not long after that, she found herself drafted into the contingent of social workers organized to assist with the relocation of the veterans in the camps on the Keys.

They interviewed the veterans to find out who had a home to go to and who would require other arrangements. The information would be used to separate the ex-soldiers into groups and move them out like so many head of cattle. For many people, the veterans in the camps were a face-less group that was someone else's problem. Now the former newspaper reporter was in one-on-one sessions with them and could see the humanity and, in many cases, the tragedy. They were no longer just the statistics and prose of newspaper articles, but men with faces, names, voices, and burdens.

She returned to Miami with mixed feelings about her part in all this. She had done the best she could to make the processing as palatable as possible for the veterans; at the same time, she was part of the machinery that was manipulating the lives of these human beings, shifting them from here to there like abandoned cargo. For Jane Wood, the emotional aspects of this experience would soon be exacerbated by an act of nature of unbelievable ferocity, and by the foibles of mankind in trying to deal with the aftermath.

As Jane and her colleagues returned to Miami on the Friday before Labor Day, the teletype on the top floor of the Federal Building in Jacksonville clacked and busily printed out data from ships and observation stations. The weathermen had been monitoring the disturbed weather north of the Turk Islands since its discovery the previous day. As the latest data were plotted, there was no pattern of winds and pressures that suggested an organized system; it appeared to be a concentration of squalls and thunderstorms. There was no report of hurricane winds, but the composite plot of wind directions at the various observation locations suggested a weak circulation.

The men in the fledgling hurricane center were well aware that the Labor Day weekend was beginning and many people in South Florida were planning picnics and boating trips based on weather forecasts. The decision was made not to issue an advisory, but to promulgate a bulletin stating the facts as the weathermen had discerned them. The message was prepared and distributed at 9:30 p.m. EST to newspapers and civilian radio stations.

The bulletin was also sent to the U.S. Navy Radio Station at Key West, where three, 300-foot steel towers protruded into the night sky. Their bases were situated 500 feet apart at the points of a giant equilateral triangle. Thousands of feet of wire strung between the towers high above the ground provided an antenna system for the station's powerful transmitters that was capable of beaming strong signals across the Gulf of Mexico and over a large portion of the Atlantic Ocean. Another elaborate antenna system enabled the station's highly sensitive receivers to detect very weak signals from ships at sea.

The navy broadcast the Weather Bureau's message several times. The bulletin read: "Weather Bureau Jacksonville, Fla., August 30, 1935 9:30 p.m.,—Conditions remain unsettled and slightly squally east of the Bahamas and north of Turks Island with evidence of a weak circulation but no strong winds. Seems to be working north-northwest or northward."

One of the ships within receiving range of the Key West station was a freighter in the Gulf of Mexico. The MS *Leise Maersk* was far from her homeport of Svenborg, Denmark. Built in 1921 for A. P. Møller by the Odense Steel Shipyard Ltd. of Denmark, the *Leise Maersk* was the world's first single-screw freighter to be powered with an economical, long-stroke diesel engine. The ship sailed around the world on its maiden voyage to demonstrate the durability and economy of the diesel power plant and its suitability for the tramping trade, where a vessel sails from port to port depending on the demand of shippers rather than running a repetitive route on a set schedule.

The *Leise Maersk* had left New Orleans the previous day bound for New York City. From there the freighter was to sail across the Atlantic, through the Mediterranean and the Suez Canal to Massawa, Italian Eritrea. What the Italians saw in that barren land was something most people did not understand, but Mussolini apparently viewed it as a springboard to other resources. In any event, the Italian dictator was preparing to make a move against Ethiopia, Eritrea's neighbor to the north, in total disregard of the seven-year-old treaty of friendship he had with that country.

Mussolini, or "Il Duce," as he was called, was going to expand his African empire and take on the self-proclaimed leader of Ethiopia, Haile Selassie. Four years earlier, Selassie had bestowed upon himself the title "The Conquering Lion of the Tribe of Judah, Elect of God, and King of Kings of Ethiopia." The title itself was an outright challenge to any other egotist. It was Mussolini's plan to humble the "Conquering Lion," and for that he would need the cargo in the holds of the fourteen-year-old ship plodding across the Gulf of Mexico toward the southern end of Florida.

The *Leise Maersk* had loaded twelve thousand gallons of oil in drums at New Orleans earlier in the week, oil that was destined for El Duce's troops in Eritrea. It was Captain Richard Mortensen's job to see that the delivery was made. The voyage to Italy's first colony in Africa was expected to take a month of sailing. If everything went right, it would be a dull trip.

The *Leise Maersk* was built for durability, not speed. She just plodded along, pushing her 3,136 tons through the water at 10 knots or so. The weather at present was good, and the 321-foot ship sailed smoothly toward the Florida Straits. The Weather Bureau's bulletin was not alarming since "disturbed weather" was not unusual for this time of year in the reported location. The *Leise Maersk* kept to her course. In another two days, she would round the western end of the Florida Keys at the Dry Tortugas and begin to receive a welcome boost from the Gulf Stream.

Several hundred miles to the east on Lower Matecumbe Key, something unusual was occurring that Friday night at Cardy Bradford's restaurant and store by the ferry slip. The 350 men assigned to the adjacent veterans camp made up a good part of Bradford's regular customers. They were paid once a month, and in between paydays some of the men ran short of cash so Cardy would give them credit. Most times it was quite a while before they came in and paid on their accounts, but on this evening and during the next day just about all the veterans who owed him money came in and settled their debts. His wife would later recall that it was as if they knew it would be their last chance.

At 7:15 the next morning, the train to Key West pulled out of the Miami station with a larger than usual number of people on board. The heavy passenger load was in response to the Florida East Coast Railway offering a special Labor Day excursion fare of $2.50 round trip good for the weekend and holiday. Most of the travelers planned to stay the weekend and return on the Monday afternoon train. By midmorning Saturday, the train was making its way past the veterans camps in the Keys.

George Pepper must have felt a tinge of disappointment when he heard the whistle blow. He'd have been on that train and on his way to Key West to see his girl except that it was payday, and one of his collateral duties was to assist in paying the veterans. The train was the fastest way to get down to Key West from the Upper Keys except for a chartered seaplane, which few people could afford. He had a date with Rosalind that night and George did not want to be late. As soon as he finished his payday duties, he was going to board a speedboat that would whisk him through the Keys to the Island City in three hours.

He and Rosalind were going to attend a dance at the Key West Country Club. He looked forward to seeing some of the friends he'd made when he had worked down in Key West the previous fall, but best of all he'd have the weekend and holiday to spend with Rosalind.

Rosalind and George had grown closer together even though most of the time she was in Key West and he was at Upper Matecumbe. Being young, intelligent, and very much in love, they created opportunities to be together. She'd visit the Upper Keys, staying with friends, so she could be near him. Other times they would meet in Miami, where she was ostensibly visiting relatives and where he just happened to be visiting his brother.

On one occasion, they arranged for a session at a professional photographer's studio. Both were highly photogenic and the pictures of the handsome couple had a glow that only comes from being in love. One of the portraits was taken of George and Rosalind using props that made it appear they were on the rear platform of a train labeled the "Orange Blossom Honeymoon Special." She was his girl and he was her guy, and they were planning to spend the future together.

He was going to stay at the Grooms house on Washington Street; Rosalind's brother was still up at Tavernier, which made a room available for George. The invitation to stay at the home of Rosalind's parents was a signal that the couple's relationship was recognized and accepted by her father and mother. George planned to take Rosalind up to meet his parents in Titusville soon. Things were getting serious between him and the girl from Key West and that was just the way George and Rosalind wanted it. The fact that she was still married did not seem to bother anyone.

Wilbur Jones also had payday duties and had plans for the Labor Day holiday. Jones resided at the camps headquarters on Upper Matecumbe Key and usually stayed down in the Keys on weekends, but the Labor Day holiday was a traditional time to be with family and friends so he was going to spend the holiday at his mother's house in Miami. At noon he and two veterans, Rennie and Ayer, left the Matecumbe Hotel in a sedan and headed for the mainland.

Meanwhile, on the fifth floor of the Federal Building in Jacksonville, the weathermen were putting together the data from the latest observation reports. There were 150 reports in all, about a third from ships at sea and the remainder from land stations. The Atlantic Ocean, Gulf of Mexico, and Caribbean Sea were divided into zones for weather data–reporting purposes. Only two of the reporting ships were in the vicinity of the disturbed weather (Zone O). Another sixteen ships were traveling in adjacent zones. Of the land stations, four were in Zone O and twelve were in adjacent zones.

To overcome language barriers, the data coming from the ships were in an international numeric code. Two men worked the data, with one deciphering the message and calling out the data to another man who plotted them on a synoptic chart, a large map on which graphic symbols are placed to depict the existing weather at various reporting station and ship locations. Since the observations are made at approximately the same time, the chart provides a comprehensive snapshot of weather conditions. Because of the time it took to obtain and plot the data, the "snapshot" was typically several hours old by the time the weather summary or advisory was ready for release.

On Saturday morning, the synoptic chart showed the disturbance to be near the easternmost Bahamas island of San Salvador with winds above 60 mph. It was definitely a tropical storm, and even though geographically small, the approaching system was beginning to show some signs of organization. By midday on Saturday, the weathermen at the Hurricane Center felt they had enough information to justify issuing the following advisory:

> Jacksonville, Fla., August 31, 1935
> Advisory, 1 p.m.—Tropical disturbance of small diameter but considerable intensity central about 60 miles east of Long Island, Bahamas, apparently moving west northwestward, attended by strong shifting winds and probably gales near center. Caution advised southeastern Bahamas and ships in that vicinity. Further advises at 4 p.m. (U.S. Congress, *Florida Hurricane Disaster Hearings*, 211–13)

The director of the veterans camps on the Keys was not aware of the advisory when he drove down to Lower Matecumbe and left on the ferry. Ray Sheldon intended to spend Saturday night and Sunday in Key West. While he was gone, Sam Cutler was in charge at the camps' headquarters.

At the Matecumbe Hotel, Sam Cutler heard about the advisory around 1:30 p.m., but did not see a need for action because "the hurricane then was a long way off, and I had read up on hurricanes, more or less, and had charts of the previous hurricanes, and knew what a circuitous path they took at times, and there was no knowing as to what path this one would take. It was then assumed to be 200 or 250 miles away." Cutler would not become concerned about the storm until the next morning.

At midafternoon on Saturday, the Jacksonville Weather Bureau issued another advisory on the basis of only seven observation reports, two of which were from ships in the same zone as the storm.

Jacksonville, Fla., August 31, 1935

Advisory 3:30 p.m. Tropical disturbance of small diameter near Long Island, Bahamas, apparently moving west-northwestward, attended by fresh to strong shifting winds and squalls, possibly gale force near center. Caution advised Bahama Islands and ships in that vicinity. (U.S. Congress, *Florida Hurricane Disaster Hearings*, 211–13)

Apparently no one on board the ferry had a radio turned on—or at least not within earshot of Sheldon—and he remained unaware of the storm. In Key West, the printing of the local newspaper was held up so that an Associated Press story about the storm and the advisory issued at 1 p.m. could be placed on the front page. The story originated in Jacksonville and stated that the storm was about five hundred miles southeast of Miami.

At about 4:30 p.m., the speedboat with George Pepper aboard arrived in Key West, and Rosalind was at the dock to meet him. That evening they drove across the bridge to Stock Island to attend the dance at the Key West Country Club. The affair that night was exclusively for members and "out-of-town" guests. The weather was partly cloudy with showers expected during the night. They had no moon to look at because it had set early in the evening, but it is doubtful that they would have noticed. Rosalind's mother later wrote, "George and Rosalind attended a dance at the Country Club Saturday evening, & I have been told by many who were there that they have never seen such a divinely happy couple as they were that night."

Five hundred miles to the northwest of Key West on the north bank of the Mississippi River, the white superstructure of a large black-hulled ship was taking on a soft yellow hue as the sun hung low in the west Saturday evening. Wisps of golden steam swayed to and fro like small ghosts playing about the single smokestack mounted amidships of the 446-foot vessel. The ship was not supposed to be there, majestically moored alongside the dock at the foot of Bienville Street in New Orleans.

The SS *Dixie*, a passenger and freight steamer, had arrived on Tuesday and had been scheduled to depart at 11 a.m. local time on Saturday. The liner should have been well down the Mississippi Delta nearing the Head of Passes, but the ship had not been cleared for departure by the shipping line's agent. There were twenty-five people on the Southern Pacific's Sunset Limited who had booked passage on the *Dixie* and were not yet aboard. The train was supposed to have arrived in New Orleans early that morning but had been delayed eleven hours because of an unusual two-day torrential rainfall that had occurred a week earlier in Arizona. A half mile of track and a bridge approach on the Phoenix-Yuma mainline of the Southern Pacific had been washed out when the rampaging Hassaympa River flooded dry washes about thirty miles southwest of Phoenix.

The *Dixie* was part of the Morgan Line, a subsidiary of the Southern Pacific Steamship Lines, which was a subsidiary of the Southern Pacific Company, one of the largest corporations in the United States in 1935. The company owned the Southern Pacific Railroad and held part ownership in other electric and steam railways. Southern Pacific also owned bus, trucking, and transport companies, oil and timberlands, warehouses, ferries, steamship lines, terminals, express companies, and land development companies. The Southern Pacific Railroad was the mainstay of the company, with routes from Chicago and New Orleans to the West Coast and down to Mexico City. The Southern Pacific Steamship Lines had ships plying the Pacific to the Far East.

The Morgan Line's *Dixie* had been specifically built eight years earlier for the 1,800-mile run between New Orleans and New York City. The ship routinely made the trip to New Orleans in six days and the return to New York in five days, the difference in the duration being due to the effects of the Gulf Stream.

During its heyday in 1921, the Morgan fleet consisted of twenty-eight oceangoing steamers and sixty-five auxiliary vessels. Five of the steamers

The Morgan liner *Dixie* was advertised as "One of the staunchest ships ever built!" (author's collection)

were designed to carry both passengers and freight. Changes in maritime trade and the economic pressures of the Great Depression had forced the Morgan Line to sell some of its ships; now the *Dixie* was Morgan's only passenger and freight ship.

The Morgan Line had failed to generate net income since 1931 and was being closely monitored by its parent company. The commodore of the fleet was keenly aware of the precarious financial situation and the watchful eyes of the main office, and knew that in this competitive business maintaining on-time operating schedules was of the utmost importance. The delay of the *Dixie*'s departure was not helping matters.

In addition to being commodore of the fleet, Captain Einer William Sundstrom was master of the *Dixie*. Born in Brunswick, Georgia, in 1885, he was a descendent of a seafaring family of Swedish origin, and had always wanted to go to sea. At sixteen, he shipped as an ordinary seaman on the British barque *Madagascar* from Brooklyn on a ninety-two-day voyage. He spent three years in sailing ships, advancing through the grades until he joined the Morgan Line in 1904 as quartermaster aboard the freighter *El Siglo*. By 1917, he was appointed master of the *Topila*.

During the Great War, Sundstrom was commissioned a lieutenant commander in the U.S. Navy and served as commanding officer of the USS *Connelly*, a naval fuel and supply ship that made many dangerous trips to deliver supplies to the troops fighting in France. After the war, he returned to the Morgan Line and resumed command of the *Topila*. In 1921, Capt. Sundstrom became master of the *Tamaihua*, the largest tanker in the world at that time. He subsequently commanded other Morgan Line ships.

In 1934, in recognition of thirty years of stellar service with the company, Sundstrom was promoted to commodore of the Morgan Line fleet, the most senior seagoing official in the company. On July 10, 1935, the commodore became master of the SS *Dixie*. This was his third voyage aboard the *Dixie*. On Labor Day, Commodore Sundstrom would complete thirty-one years of service with the Morgan Line.

Sundstrom and his wife of twenty-five years, Marie, had two attractive daughters, Lillian (21) and Florence (17), who had sailed with their father many times and had weathered at least one hurricane on a ship under his command. They were not aboard on this trip, but remained at home with their mother in a neat, two-story brick house in Little Neck, New York.

Having been part of the transition from sail to steam, the veteran mariner had encountered many storms and other dangerous situations at sea. He knew the importance of being prepared and how critical the junior officers were in times of adversity. When he returned from his first voyage on the *Dixie*, he said of his junior officers: "They're just as good as we ever were, these youngsters who'll be commanding their own ships a decade from now. Men's brains have made life easier at sea for men's bodies— and why not? But the measure of a good shipmaster always will be: How does he meet the biggest emergencies that can possibly hit him? Today, the captain meets those emergencies infinitely better equipped than ever before in marine history."

The master of the *Dixie* was indeed well equipped for emergencies as well as for the more mundane aspects of sea travel. First and foremost, he had an experienced, well-trained crew of 120 men and women. Chief Officer Torges Nielsen and Second Officer Dennis Folds were former masters of ships. They were assisted by able seamen and experienced staff who had served continuously aboard the *Dixie* for many trips. Even the official hostess and pianist Doris Levings of New York had made nineteen voyages on the *Dixie*. The entire crew had recently completed special training in the handling of passengers during emergencies.

The ship itself was a masterpiece of marine architecture designed by A. S. Hobble, superintending engineer of the Southern Pacific Steamship Lines. Built in 1927 at the Federal Shipbuilding and Dry Dock Company's shipyard in Kearny, New Jersey, at a cost of $2.4 million, the *Dixie* made her first run to New Orleans in January 1928. Promoted as one of staunchest ships, her steel hull was constructed longitudinally according to the Isherwood system of design, with an elaborate system of watertight bulkheads and steel doors. Fire detectors and automatic extinguishing systems were installed throughout the ship. A special patented system had been installed that could speedily lower her twelve all-steel lifeboats that could hold 507 people.

The spacious bridge straddled the 60-foot-wide ship at the top, forwardmost point of the superstructure 55 feet above the waterline to provide a superb observation platform. The *Dixie* was equipped with a Sperry gyroscopic compass and a Sperry gyroscopic steering system, and had a highly sensitive radio direction finder that could detect government-maintained navigation beacons. Her steel superstructure was of the hurricane deck type. The promenade deck extended all around the passengers quarters and was protected at its forward end by a steel outer wall with sliding glass windows that continued 75 feet along both sides.

Chief Engineer George Gale and his men in the Engineering Department thought the best part of the ship was in the engine room. The *Dixie* was one of the first American ships to use a high-pressure, superheated steam turbine propulsion system. Oil-burning boilers fed the steam turbines that turned the armatures of large generators. The electricity the generators produced powered a 7,100-horsepower motor connected to a massive, single screw. The system was rated to push the *Dixie* through the water at a top speed of 16 knots; George and the engineering gang were rumored to have achieved 18–20 knots. Although the ship was built to endure the most severe seas, the *Dixie* could easily outrun most storms.

The commodore had told his wife in a letter that he thought they would be twenty hours late leaving New Orleans due to the train's delay, but by 6 p.m. the tardy passengers and their baggage had been placed aboard and the gangways were hauled up. Passengers lined the rails admiring the view of the Crescent City and waving good-bye to people on the dock, while others sipped cocktails and threw streamers. The sounds of the French Quarter cranking up for another frenetic Saturday night floated across the humid air. The music of Dixieland bands, the nonstop barking of the bar and restaurant hawkers, and the laughter, shouts, and other noises of people having a good time mixed with the whistles of the ship and its attendant tugs as they tooted directions and acknowledgments. The *Dixie*'s heavy hawsers were lifted off the massive iron bollards on the dock and hauled aboard. Her lines singled up, the command came to cast off, and the final bonds with the shore fell into the water; the *Dixie*'s voyage to New York City was finally begun.

Slowly, gently, the tugs pulled and nudged the 12,440 tons of steel, cargo, and people out into midstream. Once the ship was positioned to the river pilot's satisfaction, the engine room was given the command to engage the massive screw, and the ship began to move under its own power. When sufficient speed was attained for steerageway, the pilot dismissed the tugs and the *Dixie* was under way on her own power. The river pilot remained aboard to guide the ship down to the Head of Passes eighty miles below New Orleans.

About three hours after departure, the radio room of the *Dixie* received two advisories issued by the New Orleans Weather Bureau concerning two tropical disturbances, one in the Atlantic Ocean and one in the Gulf of Mexico. As the hurricane center for the western Gulf of Mexico and Caribbean region, the New Orleans office had been monitoring an area of disturbed weather in the Bay of Campeche north of the Yucatan Peninsula. The first advisory read as follows:

Advisory 8:30 p.m. CST (8/31/35)
The tropical disturbance apparently developing over Southwest Gulf of Mexico near latitude 20 longitude 92.30 attended by strong winds and gales near center, will probably move west-northwest-ward. Caution advised vessels in path. (*New Orleans Times-Pica-yune*, September 1, 1935)

This weather system would pose no threat to the *Dixie* unless the storm veered to the northeast, which was not expected.

The second advisory received from the New Orleans hurricane center was a rebroadcast of an advisory issued by the hurricane center at Jacksonville concerning disturbed weather in the Bahamas. By 8 p.m. EST, the storm's center had passed over Long Island in the Bahamas, and a barometer reading of 29.48 inches of mercury was reported. The maximum surface winds were approaching 70 mph. This information was derived from 139 observation reports including one ship and nine land stations in the same zone as the storm. The weathermen at the Jacksonville Weather Bureau felt they had a good fix on the storm's center, and an advisory was immediately issued at 9:30 p.m. EST:

Jacksonville, Fla., August 31, 1935
Advisory 9:30 p. m. The tropical disturbance is central tonight near or over the northern end of Long Island, Bahamas, moving rather slowly west-northwestward, attended by strong shifting winds and squalls over a considerable area and probably gale force near center. Indications center will reach vicinity of Andros Island early Sunday. Northeast storm warnings ordered 10 p.m., Fort Pierce to Miami, Fla. (U.S. Congress, *Florida Hurricane Disaster Hearings*, 211–13)

For the first time, the advisory carried a directive for signal stations to hoist northeast storm warnings along the South Florida coastline. This signal—composed of a red pennant above a square red flag with black center displayed by day, or two red lanterns, one above the other displayed by night—indicates the approach of a storm of marked violence with winds beginning from the northeast.

Regardless of the weather elsewhere, it was very pleasant as the *Dixie* moved down the Mississippi River. The wind was blowing gently from the northeast at 5 mph under clear skies. The moon, which had set just after sundown, was replaced by a brilliant display of stars. The watch on the darkened bridge could make out the cultivated fields of great plantations behind huge trees draped with Spanish moss. Occasionally lights from a farmhouse or village would twinkle in the distance. As the hours passed, most of the passengers retired to their berths to be rocked to sleep by the gentle motion of the ship as it moved ever closer to the Gulf of Mexico.

At 10 p.m. Saturday, Ray Sheldon arrived in Key West after driving down the Lower Keys from the ferry landing at No Name Key. He went to a restaurant and, while eating his supper, happened to notice a newspaper lying nearby. On the front page was the advisory about the tropical disturbance in the Bahamas. This was the first he knew of its existence.

He finished his supper, checked into his hotel, and called the Key West Weather Bureau.

At 11 p.m., the meteorologist-in-charge, George Kennedy, answered the phone and briefed Sheldon on the latest information about the storm. He told Sheldon that the storm would probably make landfall somewhere in the area between West Palm Beach and Fort Pierce, up on the mainland well north of the camps. Sheldon identified himself and his responsibilities for the camps and requested that he be called during the night if any further information came in. Too early the next morning, the jangling of the telephone in his room abruptly ended his sound sleep.

Sunday

One hundred miles below New Orleans, the Mississippi River splits into several branches known as passes that cut across the delta to the Gulf of Mexico. The SS *Dixie* had been steadily steaming down the river since departing New Orleans Saturday evening and reached the Southwest Pass early the next morning, the first day of September 1935. At about this time, a special bulletin issued by the Jacksonville Weather Bureau was received. (The time shown in the bulletin is Eastern Standard Time.)

> Bulletin, 2:56 a.m.—Tropical disturbance central about 50 miles west of Long Island, Bahamas, apparently moving westward about 8 miles per hour, accompanied by shifting gales and possibly winds of hurricane force near center. (U.S. Congress, *Florida Hurricane Disaster Hearings*, 211–13)

During the seventy-two hours that had passed since it was first detected, the storm system had moved 500 miles toward the west; it was now about 250 miles east of the Florida Keys. The message did not contain any information that required action by the crew. It was still too early to tell whether or not the "tropical disturbance" would affect the *Dixie*.

Under the guidance of a bar pilot, the ship completed the transit of the Southwest Pass without incident and moved out into open waters. Slowing briefly to allow the pilot boat to come alongside and remove the bar pilot, the *Dixie* cruised past the sea buoy and out into the deeper waters of the Gulf of Mexico. The weather was fair, and there was the seven-hour delay to make up if the liner was to arrive in New York on time. The throttles were opened, and the steam turbines and electric drive whined. The *Dixie* responded and quickly picked up speed as she headed southeast toward the Dry Tortugas and the west entrance to the Florida Straits.

At 4:45 that Sunday morning, the Key West Weather Bureau called Ray Sheldon at his hotel as requested to tell him the storm appeared to be moving toward the Florida Straits south of Key West. They advised that if Sheldon intended to return to the camps, he should do so on the ferry that would leave No Name Key in about three hours because the weather could worsen. As soon as the conversation was completed, Sheldon put through a call to his boss, Fred Ghent, at his home in Jacksonville. He briefed Ghent on the situation.

Ghent called the Jacksonville Weather Bureau and was told the storm had started to move northward but then reversed its movement. Ghent then called the Florida East Coast Railway dispatcher on duty in New Smyrna, the central dispatching office for the FEC Railway system. At 6:10 a.m., while Ghent was talking with the duty dispatcher, Chief Dispatcher J. L. Byrum came into the office. Byrum picked up an extension, and the three men discussed the possibility of putting extra cars on the Miami–Key West run. When that conversation was completed, Ghent called Sheldon and relayed the storm information and told him that he had talked with the FEC Railway about being ready to evacuate the veterans. They agreed that Sheldon should return to the camps on the 8 a.m. ferry. As a result of the phone call, Byrum had additional cars added to the Miami–Key West train so that it had a total of nine coaches.

Because of the special Labor Day excursion fare, the Miami station was again swarming with travelers headed for the Keys for the holiday. Even though it was Sunday morning, about 450 festive people were onboard No. 75 when it pulled away from the Miami station at 7:15 a.m. Doris Peacock and her fiancé, Roy Brady, were among the passengers going to Key West. They had a special invitation from Roy's brother, a contractor who was completing the renovation of the Gibson Inn. They could stay at the small hotel on Fleming Street free. The couple planned to return to Miami on the train Monday afternoon. They would not learn that a hurricane was headed that way until late Sunday afternoon after they had arrived in Key West.

Just before 8 a.m., Ray Sheldon guided his car across the ramp and onto the ferry at No Name Key. The ferry was part of the highway system built in 1924 with the proceeds of a $2.65 million bond issue. Ninety-five miles of paved road and six miles of bridges were constructed. The decks

The *Florida Keys* was one of three ferryboats built specifically to cover the water gap in the highway from the mainland to Key West. (FPC)

of the wooden bridges were only eight feet above the mean high-tide mark and were supported by creosoted piles. The highway was continuous from Key West to No Name Key and from Lower Matecumbe Key to the mainland.

Three shallow-draft ferries had been custom built with the highway bond proceeds to cover the water gap that separated the end of the highway from the mainland at Lower Matecumbe Key and the beginning of the highway to Key West at No Name Key. On September 1, 1935, one ferry was in Key West undergoing repairs and another was in Jacksonville being overhauled; only one of the ferries, the *Monroe County*, was operational. Each ferry had a steel hull with a reinforced main deck capable of carrying twenty automobiles. With two engines, each driving its own propeller, the boats had an average speed of 9 mph, meaning that on a good day, the forty-mile trip from No Name to Lower Matecumbe would take a little over four hours. Today will not be a good day for the ferry.

As the *Monroe County* dutifully makes its way across Florida Bay, the *Dixie* slips gracefully over the waves in the Gulf of Mexico toward the Dry Tortugas. After breakfast on Sunday morning, Commodore Sundstrom and his crew receive an advisory issued by the Jacksonville hurricane center.

Advisory, 9:30 a.m.—Tropical disturbance central short distance south of Andros Island moving westward about 8 miles per hour, attended by shifting gales and probably winds of hurricane force small area near center. Indications storm will pass through Florida Straits late tonight or Monday. Caution advised vessels in path. Northeast storm warnings displayed Fort Pierce to Fort Myers, Fla. (U.S. Congress, *Florida Hurricane Disaster Hearings:* 211–13)

The storm-warnings display directive covered the entire southern portion of the Florida peninsula from Ft. Pierce on the east coast to Ft. Myers on the west coast.

The *Dixie*'s route will take it around the Dry Tortugas and into the Florida Straits, right where the advisory said the hurricane was headed. The Commodore has two choices: he can slow down and wait for the storm to pass through the Straits and then maneuver around it, or he can use the speed of the *Dixie* to outrun the storm to the western throat of the Florida Straits and be well north of the area by the time the storm gets there. The first option would mean further delay and does not necessarily diminish the danger to the vessel as there is no way to tell where the storm will go after it passes through the Straits. Aware that the *Dixie* is a staunch, fast ship and will have an assist from the Gulf Stream after entering the Straits, Commodore Sundstrom decides to stay the course and rely on the 7,100 horsepower engine to propel the ship out of harm's way. The race is on, and the stakes are high. At risk is the survival of the premier ship of the Morgan Line fleet and the 356 souls aboard.

No announcement about the hurricane and the Commodore's decision is made to the passengers as the crew quietly goes about the business of preparing the ship for rough seas. It is Miss Doris Levings's job as hostess to see that the passengers think about fun things and enjoy the balmy weather while it lasts. There are ample diversions available. For exercise, one can walk a mile (eight laps) around the promenade deck. There are books and magazines available in the lounge/library. The more active passengers can play ping-pong, shuffleboard, or pitch horseshoes. Bingo games are popular. Radios in the sun parlor and dance room provide news, music, and a variety of shows if the static is not bad. Phonographs in the sun parlor and dance room also provide music. Pianos are available in the lounge-library, sun parlor, and the dance room. Cards games help

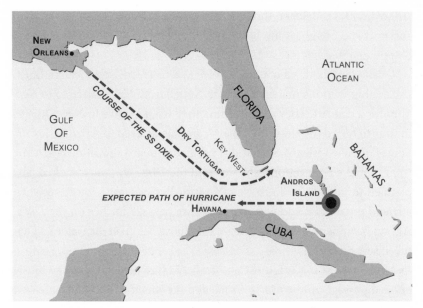

The *Dixie*'s course took the ship around the Dry Tortugas and then parallel to the Florida Keys through the Florida Straits. According to the advisory issued at 9:30 a.m. Sunday, the hurricane was situated just south of Andros Island and was forecast to move westward at 8 mph. (author)

pass the time away in the smoking room and at side tables in the sun parlor and dance room. For those who seek alcoholic refreshments while at sea, the bar is open in the smoking room from 8:00 a.m. until 11:00 p.m.

Florence Stieler noted, "it was a gay crowd that cavorted under the deck showers and played in the water and at other sports." Among the 233 passengers are three winners of a Pennsylvanian popularity contest, an actress, several musicians, a famous psychologist, teachers, civil servants, heiresses, a radio singer, several doctors, and several honeymooning couples.

Harry Burk of New Orleans, a music teacher, has an accordion he brought along. Herbert Shprentz, age eight, of Brooklyn has carefully stowed his prized stamp collection in the stateroom he shares with his mother. Sol H. Lupof, also of Brooklyn, is taking a brand-new car back to New York; the *Dixie* has a special port in the side of her hull through which automobiles can be driven on board and stowed in the hold. Carl Calman, a musician from Brooklyn, has his favorite $750 violin with him. Nan Belcher of New York, the wife of retired San Francisco grand opera singer Frank H. Belcher, thought it would be better to be prepared than sorry so she bought a life belt made for babies for her Boston terrier, Skippy, just in case.

Grisha Goluboff, who at age twelve is a renowned classical violinist, is traveling with his manager, Isidore Nobel, from San Francisco to New York for a concert. They did not think they would arrive in New Orleans in time to board the ship when their train was delayed in Arizona. Jeanne Soules of New Orleans almost did not get to board the ship. When she went to make reservations, she was told the *Dixie* was fully booked. She planned to take the train to New York for her two-week vacation when a friend intervened and was able to secure passage for her on the *Dixie*. Although vulnerable to seasickness, she enjoys being on the water and has taken several cruises.

Mrs. Beatrice L. Carter of Cambridge, Massachusetts, had previously booked passage on the *Morro Castle* and the *Mohawk* and had cancelled both trips because she had premonitions of disaster. Her visions proved accurate: a fire raged through the *Morro Castle* gutting the ship and killing 130 people, and the *Mohawk* collided with another ship and sank causing the loss of 45 lives. She had similar premonitions about the *Dixie* and almost cancelled her passage but decided at the last minute to sail anyway. William I. Bingham of East Orange, N.J. and his wife were not as clairvoyant as Mrs. Carter and had the misfortune to be on the *Morro Castle* the night the ship caught fire. Mrs. Bingham declined to accompany her husband on this cruise of the *Dixie*.

There are no diversions for the passengers aboard the ferry *Monroe County* as it plods across the calm waters of Florida Bay with Captain Charles P. Albury on the bridge. Albury, who is a native of Key West and resides there with his family, has been employed in the ferry service for nine years, working first for the private company that operated it and then for the Florida ERA when it took over the ferries in 1934. Also manning the vessel is the engineer Louis Cruze and deck hands Ansel Albury, T. L. Adams, Gordon Williams, R. Taylor, and Stanley Key. The boat is equipped with a broadcast-band radio receiver and a barometer.

Midway through the trip to Lower Matecumbe, one of the ferry's engines begins to rev up and the boat slows. The engine is shut down, and Engineer Cruze reports to Captain Albury that one of the propeller shafts has broken. Repairs cannot be made at sea so there is no choice but to continue the voyage on one engine. The ferry with Ray Sheldon aboard limps along at a pedestrian pace because not only has the power of one engine been lost, but the propeller of the shutdown engine now acts as a drag; the *Monroe County* will arrive at Lower Matecumbe four hours late.

At the veterans camps headquarters on Upper Matecumbe, Sam Cutler is becoming increasingly concerned about the storm and decides he needs more staff in the office to monitor the telephones and radio. Around 9:30 a.m., he calls Wilbur Jones in Miami. Jones is in bed enjoying the luxury of being able to sleep late on a Sunday morning when he is awakened to take the call. Realizing the seriousness of the situation, he responds quickly to Cutler's request and rounds up Rennie, Ayer, and two other headquarter staff members. The five men leave Miami and drive down to the Matecumbe Hotel, arriving by lunchtime.

At 10:30 a.m., Ray Sheldon is standing on the main deck of the ferry near a car with a radio. He hears an announcer reading the latest advisory issued by the Jacksonville Weather Bureau at 9:30 a.m. Sheldon knows that if the center of the disturbance is south of Andros Island and the storm continues due west, it will pass through the Straits between Key West and Havana and miss the Upper Keys. If that occurs, the brunt of the storm would be felt at Dry Tortugas, the Marquesas, Sand Key, and possibly Key West. Since the hurricane-force winds are confined to a small area near the center, the camps on the Keys should just experience some rain and perhaps gale-force winds. This is of little comfort to Sheldon, who has enough experience with hurricanes to know how unpredictable they can be.

Sam Cutler at the veterans camps' headquarters on Upper Matecumbe does not have any experience with hurricanes, so after hearing the 9:30 a.m. advisory, he seeks the counsel of Captain Ed Sheeran. Sheeran had been in charge of the ferry system, but on March 15, 1935, he was removed from that position when sweeping changes were made to the organization. Sheeran and several of his staff including his assistant, stenographer, and port steward were relieved of their duties. Norberg Thompson, an influential Key West businessman, became operations director, and Captain J. E. Demeritt, who was formerly master of the ferry *Monroe County*, was promoted to superintendent of the system.

The organizational shakeup was made with the blessing of the Florida

ERA. When F. E Albert announced the changes, he did not cite any cause for the action, but he did say the ferry service would be revamped to "make the trip across the water gaps from landing to landing pleasurable in every detail with nothing left undone to add to the comfort of the passenger." Ed Sheeran was reassigned to B. M. Duncan to assist with the bridge construction project at Upper Matecumbe.

Captain Sheeran is at Camp Three on the west end of Lower Matecumbe Key so Cutler drives down to see him; he does not want to talk with him on the telephone with other subscribers listening in. He finds Sheeran overseeing preparations for a big blow. Sheeran is convinced the Upper Keys will receive strong winds if not the full force of the storm. It does not take much talking with Sheeran to make Cutler apprehensive.

The camp administrator drives directly back to headquarters and places a call to Fred Ghent in Jacksonville. The call does not go through right away. Long-distance calls in 1935 were often delayed due the limited number of circuits available between cities. Unable to reach Sheldon on the ferry, Cutler begins making preparations for evacuating the camps. He alerts John Good so that he can coordinate arrangements for moving provisions and equipment with which to feed the men for several days.

Good telephones his assistant George Pepper, who is at the Grooms home in Key West and tells him that he might need to return to Upper Matecumbe to help with the evacuation. For George and Rosalind, it must have seemed that fate was being a terrible tease, first giving them a wonderful evening together and the next morning trying to separate them again. At 11 a.m., George calls Sam Cutler to get his assessment of the situation.

When Wilbur Jones and the men he rounded up in Miami arrive at the Matecumbe Hotel, various key personnel have begun to assemble at headquarters and are awaiting direction. In addition to his boss, D. A. Malcom, those present include Sam Cutler, Sheriff Woodham, Deputy Maloney, John Good, and a veteran named Patterson. As the situation is discussed, Cutler, Jones and Good are the only ones expressing concern about the hurricane and the need to prepare for the evacuation of the veterans on short notice. Jones later recalled that later when Ed Sheeran joined the group, "He [Sheeran] felt the situation was serious and that we might look for some very, very nasty weather."

After lunch, the telephone at the Grooms home rings; it is John Good calling again, this time to request that George Pepper return to headquarters on Upper Matecumbe as soon as he can. Traveling by car is not an option since the ferry left hours earlier on its northbound trip. He will have to take the northbound train that is scheduled to leave at 5:40 p.m. George decides to check with the Key West Weather Bureau to obtain the latest information on the storm. He and Rosalind go over to the building at the corner of Eaton and Front streets, where she and her brother had spent many hours with their grandfather Boyer. They are told that the latest advisory has the storm headed through the Florida Straits south of Key West.

Rosalie Grooms later recalled the conversation she and her daughter had when Rosalind returned home. Rosalind told her, "Well, George has to go back tonight, and I am going with him." When Rosalie started to object, her daughter said, "Mother, if Daddy was going, wouldn't you go?" Rosalie replied, "Yes dear, but Daddy is my husband." Rosalind then said, "Well George will be mine someday, and I want to be with him." There was no more discussion about the matter.

On Upper Matecumbe Key, Sam Cutler has proceeded with preparations for the storm. During the morning the boarding up of camp buildings was begun. The flimsy wood-framed structures with canvas roofs and side panels simply rest on concrete blocks and are not tied to bedrock. There is not much that can be done for them now. Cutler called the FEC Railway and told the dispatcher that in all probability the men in the camps will need to be moved from the Keys and suggested that they have two trains of passenger and baggage cars ready to send down to the Keys on a moment's notice.

At 2:42 p.m., the call that Cutler had placed several hours earlier to Fred Ghent finally goes through. Cutler tells Ghent what he has been doing and of the calls to the railroad. Ghent, who is on the golf course and had interrupted his game to take the call, is unimpressed. "When I talked with Mr. Ghent," Cutler recalled, "he said he had been in communication with Mr. Sheldon, and that Mr. Sheldon had the matter in hand and would take care of the situation on his arrival." By this time, Ray Sheldon has been on board the crippled ferry for 7½ hours.

An hour later, the *Monroe County* crawls into the ferry slip at Lower Matecumbe. John Cruze, the father of Louis Cruze, is employed as a dockhand at the slip and greets them. As soon as the boat is secured, Captain Albury goes to a telephone and calls his boss to report the damaged propeller shaft. Franklin Albert tells him there is a storm coming and he might as well tie up the boat and wait it out at Lower Matecumbe. The captain, Cruze, and the rest of the crew (Ansel Albury, T. L. Adams, Gordon Williams, R. Taylor, and Stanley Key) put out additional lines to secure the vessel for foul weather and make themselves comfortable; they plan to spend the night aboard the ferry. At least Louis will have time to visit with his father.

As soon as the cars are unloaded, Ray Sheldon drives directly to the Matecumbe Hotel. When he arrives, Cutler briefs him on what has been done and provides him with copies of all messages related to the weather. Not long afterward, the radio at headquarters crackles with another advisory:

> Advisory, 4 p.m.—Tropical disturbance central about 275 miles east of Havana, moving very slowly west or west-southwestward, probably accompanied by winds of hurricane force over small area near center. (U.S. Congress, *Florida Hurricane Disaster Hearings:* 211–13)

This advisory was based on a total of 102 observation reports. Five of the reports (including one from a ship) are from the same zone as the storm, while sixty-four reports were from adjacent zones. The weathermen at the Jacksonville hurricane center have concluded that the hurricane is moving toward Cuba. The center of the hurricane is actually located due west of the southern end of Andros Island and is beginning a turn toward the northwest, a course that will take it through the middle of the Florida Keys.

At 5:15 p.m., as a precautionary measure, Sheldon calls the district superintendent for the FEC Railway at Miami, P. L. Gaddis, and asks him how long after an order is placed will it take to get a train down to take the veterans out. Gaddis replies that it will take three to four hours to make up a train and get it to Matecumbe.

At this point, according to Wilbur Jones, Ray Sheldon was acting autonomously and did not consult with or seek the advice and opinions of the personnel who had gathered at headquarters. Ray Sheldon had always seemed to Jones to be somewhat arrogant and dictatorial: "I thought Mr. Sheldon was the type that wouldn't listen to anybody else, and would do what he wanted to, and what I could say would have no effect, and therefore, I would probably be better off if I just kept my opinion to myself."

It is quite possible that Ray Sheldon preferred to be remote and hard to approach. He had been sent down to oversee camps that were about to be deactivated and dismantled. The funds to build the highway bridge to replace the ferries had been exhausted. Layoffs of staff had already been announced in the Key West newspaper. Sheldon's job was to maintain order until the camps in the Keys could be closed. He was experienced enough as a manager to know that this task would require him to deal with all involved as objectively as possible and with a firm hand; his last concern would have been his popularity with the staff. He also was well aware that if anything were to occur that endangered the veterans assigned to the camps under his supervision, Ray Sheldon was most likely the one who would be singled out to take the blame. It was a thankless job that did not leave room for democratic decision-making.

Earlier that afternoon at about the same time the ferry arrived at Lower Matecumbe Key, Lt. j.g. W. L. Clemmer of the U.S. Coast Guard was flying near the northeast end of the island. During the morning the Coast Guard air station at Dinner Key near Miami had received the following message: "Delayed Weather Forecast: Jacksonville, Florida to Florida Straits, moderate N.E. winds over north and central portion, freshening off the coast, and increasing N.E. winds probably reaching gale force over extreme south portion, and possibly of hurricane force in the Florida Straits, tonight or Monday, with heavy Squalls in the Florida Straits."

True to the Coast Guard motto "Always Ready," the station soon had Clemmer in the air over the waters south of Miami dropping message blocks to boats. Message blocks were used to communicate with small vessels and isolated land parties who did not have access to a radio. This simple but effective device consisted of a block of wood to which was fastened a bright streamer of several feet. On this day the streamer bore the words "Hurricane Warning" stenciled in waterproof ink and large block letters. The block was inscribed with the location of the air station and a request that the block be returned to the Coast Guard station. Because of the number of boaters, Clemmer soon ran out of message blocks and had to return to base for more. These were expeditiously made up, and Clemmer took off in the afternoon, going as far south as No Name Key. He concentrated on small boats and picnic parties on offshore islands.

One such party was on Indian Key, a small island lying a quarter of a mile southeast of the northeast end of Lower Matecumbe Key. J. Early Horsley and twelve other people including the salesmen of his insurance agency, representatives of the American Fire and Casualty Company, and some of their wives had gone to Indian Key with the intention of spending the holiday picnicking and fishing. Although small in size (8.77 acres), its location provides convenient access to the reef and the Gulf Stream.

The Horsely party had set up camp on the island with the assistance of Leon Coulter (37) and Bill Hanlan (34), unemployed telegraph operators who were living on the Key where Coulter had built a summer home. They were friends of Horsely and were going to serve as fishing guides for the party. After arriving on the island, the group's attention was attracted by the sight of a solitary plane making low passes over fishing boats in the area. The familiar markings of the U.S. Coast Guard were plainly visible. The graceful lines of the seaplane were interrupted by twin engines mounted high above the wing on ungainly struts and by its wheels swung up so that they appeared to stick out the sides of the fuselage. The seaplane rose up in the sky, banked, and then seemed to hang in the air as it began a gradual descent directly toward the Horsely party. The racket characteristic of radial aircraft motors intensified as the powerful Wasp engines revved up for a low-altitude run.

The RD-4 Dolphin was one of ten purchased by the Coast Guard in 1933 from the Douglas Aircraft Company at a cost of $60,000 each. Equipped with two 450 horsepower Wasp engines manufactured by Pratt and Whitney, the amphibian could cruise at 110 mph and had a top speed of 147 mph. Topped off with 240 gallons of fuel, the Dolphin could fly out to a distance of 660 miles and return to base. The planes carried state-of-the-art electronic equipment including a powerful radio transmitter, an auxiliary receiver/transmitter, a highly sensitive radio direction finder, and a sophisticated frequency indicator. A crew of three flew the seaplane and operated the equipment.

As the Coast Guard plane flew over the Horsely party, the copilot thrust his arm out a side window just below the leading edge of the wing and dropped what appeared to be a small box. By this time, Clemmer and

A Coast Guard RD-4 Dolphin seaplane flies over a Greek sponger as a message block flutters (*left*) down to the water. The warning device (*inset*) consisted of a block of wood with an attached ribbon that was stenciled with the words "Hurricane Warning." (NOAA)

his crew had run out of message blocks again so they improvised using paraffin-coated containers with the storm information enclosed to which a tape tail of about two feet was attached. As the box spun, the streamer unwound, stabilizing the descent so that it landed within easy retrieval distance of the people on the island.

The ominous message "Hurricane Warning" were not words insurance men liked to see. They had planned to spend the night on Indian Key, but, perhaps as much for business reasons as well as for their personal safety, the Horsley group decided to depart immediately for the mainland. Coulter ferried them back in his small boat to the place they had parked their cars next to the highway. Hanlan and Coulter elected to stay on Indian Key, even though they had lived in Miami for ten years and knew firsthand the great destructive power a hurricane could unleash.

At 4 o'clock Sunday afternoon in Key West, the sky was overcast, and one-tenth of an inch of rain had fallen in the previous eight hours. The wind was fluctuating between 8 and 10 mph from the north and northeast, and the barometer was 29.34 inches and slowly falling. The Florida ERA had emergency crews out placing storm shutters on buildings so that they could be quickly closed and boarded up. Boats, rolling stock, and cabanas on beaches were being lashed down. Dredges that had been at work deepening the harbor were towed close to shore.

At the Grooms home on Washington Street, George Pepper and Rosalind Grooms Palmer packed their bags and drove with her parents to the station down by the harbor. FEC Railway Train No. 76 was alongside the loading platform ready to depart on schedule at 5:40 p.m.

The depot's configuration was somewhat unusual in that the station was part of a long line of one-story buildings sitting on a 135-foot-wide concrete-walled fill that extended almost a quarter mile into the water. The railroad tracks came out onto the fill and ran along one side of the buildings. A restaurant and the ticket office were about midway down. The pier arrangement allowed train passengers arriving on the Havana Special from New York to walk just a few feet to the gangway of the steamer that would take them to Cuba.

On the platform, George and Rosalind chatted away making plans for the rest of their holiday. It was obvious that they were happy just being together. Rosalind wanted to make contact with her brother before he left

Tavernier so that he could spend some time with her and George before returning to Key West. When the time came to board the train, they said their farewells. Rosalind wanted to kiss her mother. Rosalie recalled: "I started not to kiss her goodbye for I had a bad cold but something made me change my mind & I said 'Yes I will honey for it may be the last time.' And George called back, 'I'll take good care of her.'"

There were many seats available because of the extra cars that had been added to the train in case the decision was made to evacuate the camps that evening. In spite of repeated efforts to find out the intentions of the camp administration, the Islamorada agent could not get a definite answer. When the train pulled out of Key West shortly before 6 p.m. the three coaches ahead of the baggage car were entirely empty, the rear coach contained only seven passengers, and the coach next to the rear was not half full.

At 8 p.m. on Sunday night, No. 76 arrived at the Islamorada station. Rosalind and George left the train and went to the Matecumbe Hotel, where George would sleep in his room while Rosalind shared a room with Mrs. Butters's daughter. No veterans boarded at Islamorada, and the train continued on with 80 percent of its seats empty. With the capacity to transport eight hundred people, No. 76 had carried only 168 passengers and could have easily accommodated all the veterans on the Keys that night.

About an hour later the Jacksonville Weather Bureau issued the following advisory:

Advisory, 9:30 p.m.—Tropical disturbance central about 260 miles east of Havana, Cuba, moving slowly westward, attended by shifting gales and probably winds of hurricane force small area near center. Caution advised vessels Florida Straits next 36 hours. Northeast storm warnings displayed south of Miami to Fort Myers, Fla. (U.S. Congress, *Florida Hurricane Disaster Hearings:* 211–13)

The weathermen still thought the storm was off the north coast of Cuba and headed west toward the Florida Straits between Key West and Havana. It was actually about fifty miles north of where they thought it was, having just passed over the Hurricane Flats west of the south end of Andros Island, and was beginning a gradual turn toward the northwest.

The tropical cyclone had also continued to intensify and was now a Category 2 hurricane only 150 miles southeast of the Florida Keys.

Shortly after ten o'clock on Sunday night, Ray Sheldon called the home of P. L. Gaddis, the district superintendent for the FEC Railway at Miami. Gaddis remembered being in bed when his telephone rang:

> When I answered it, Mr. Sheldon stated he was at Islamorada and wanted to know how long it would take to get a train down there to move out about 400 men. Thinking I had misunderstood the number, I asked him to repeat it and mentioned that I thought he had a considerably larger number of men there. He replied he had but that they were scattered and not in that vicinity. I replied to the effect that our train had just come in from Key West and that this train was then at the Miami passenger station and that we could arrive there [Islamorada] with this train, with coaches enough to take care of 400 men, in about 4 hours. We then exchanged some remarks about the Weather Bureau advisory, both of us having the 9:30 p.m. advisory indicating that the disturbance was approximately 24 hours distant and moving westerly toward Havana. The last thing he said to me was that he would, when the necessity arose, order a train through his Jacksonville office.

W. L. Baker was the second work shift train dispatcher on duty at the FEC Railway office in New Smyrna on Sunday. About 11 p.m., someone called him from Islamorada and asked if a special train could be operated to move the veterans from Matecumbe, and if so, how soon could it get down there. Baker told the unidentified caller that No. 76 had just arrived at Miami; the engine was still hot; the operator, yardmaster, and switch engine were available at the passenger station; and the train could be on its way within an hour if the order were placed immediately. He added that if the order were placed later, after the engine had cooled, the operator was off-duty, and the switch engine had gone to the yard, it would require more time. Baker recalled, "For several minutes nothing was said as to whether the train was wanted or not and I again stated that unless the train was ordered at once it would take longer than an hour to get it out, to which a reply was made: They don't seem to know what they want so just forget the special train for the present."

The first sign that time was running out appeared in Miami at the northwest corner of the intersection of SE First Street and Second Avenue. There reposed a most impressive structure that had been built to house the offices of the Model Land Company, the real estate operation of the Florida East Coast Railway. The Ingraham Building had become a Miami landmark from its opening day in 1927. The monumental lobby featured a vaulted ceiling with gold-leaf inlays, Greek columns, arches, and friezes, highly polished marble floors, and gleaming brass doors. Even the six elevator doors in the lobby were distinctive, being embellished with heavy cast plaques depicting a beach scene of palm trees and waves upon which the initials "IB" were emblazoned in bold brass letters. On September 1, 1935, the most important aspect of the building was on the roof, where a device comprised of spinning cups and a weathervane sensed the speed and direction of the wind.

Like the building supporting it, the anemometer was the product of creative design and skilled craftsmanship. The Friez Selsyn recording anemometer had excellent exposure in all directions. The instrument was remarkable in that it made an ink and paper record for twenty-four, one-hour periods of various data related to the wind such as the average velocity, the direction from which the wind was blowing, the peak velocity of the maximum gust occurring during the period, and the number of gusts that occurred during the period in ranges of wind speed. The anemometer's recording showed that on this Sunday from 8 a.m. the wind had blown steadily from the northeast with the average velocity rising during the morning from 11 mph to 18 mph at noon. During the afternoon, the average speed varied between 18 mph and 21 mph. From noon through the 8 p.m. to 9 p.m. period, the maximum gusts measured between 34 mph and 39 mph. From 9 p.m. to 10 p.m., the maximum gust was 43 mph; during the 10 p.m. to 11 p.m. interval, there was one gust that measured over 65 mph.

The official-in-charge of the Miami Weather Bureau, Ernest Carson, associated this pattern with the "westward movement of the tropical disturbance." Carson would get only four and a half hours sleep over the next forty-eight hours; he would not be the only one deprived of sleep during the coming days.

Out in the Gulf of Mexico, it was the end of another boring day aboard the *Dixie* for twenty-seven-year-old Charlotte Evans, a supervisor of industrial research at the University of Pennsylvania. Having sailed on the *Dixie* from New York to New Orleans, she almost cancelled her return passage. In a letter to her mother, she wrote: "It's too monotonous, and I will be glad to get off. It's the quietest crowd I ever saw, and there's no excitement."

As Sunday drew to a close, the *Dixie* cruised smoothly across the Gulf of Mexico while Miss Evans and her fellow shipmates were for a second night rocked to sleep by the gentle roll of the ship. There was nothing to suggest that they were about to experience what was to become for many of them the most exciting time of their lives.

On the Whale Harbor fill after No. 76 rattled past Eddie Williams's house, the nine people comprising the Williams and Law families bedded down for a good night's rest exhausted from a full day of fun and fellowship. On Upper Matecumbe Key at the Matecumbe Hotel, the Butters family closed up the dining room; George Pepper and Rosalind Palmer retired to their separate rooms, as did Wilbur Jones and others of the headquarters staff. At the Rustic Inn, O. D. and Elizabeth King closed up the restaurant and switched off the generator; next door in her cabin, Elizabeth's sister Leone Barr put her son to bed and soon fell asleep. All were unaware of the danger that lurked about one hundred miles southeast of them.

The storm's intensity had increased all day. As midnight approached, the winds were topping 110 mph, and the cyclonic system that had been a Category 1 storm when the day began was transitioning into a Category 3 hurricane. More disturbing, had it been known, the hurricane stopped curving toward the north and was now squarely aimed at the heart of the Florida Keys.

In Jacksonville, the lights in the Weather Bureau's suite on the top floor of the Federal Building remained on; with a hurricane roaming their district, the hurricane center was being manned twenty-four hours a day. Their analysis of the available data led them to believe that the storm was skirting the north coast of Cuba and headed for Havana. The advisory issued at 9:30 p.m. EST, the last one issued that day, still referred to the hurricane as a "tropical disturbance attended by shifting gales and probably winds of hurricane force."

On the eve of Labor Day, the Weather Bureau's hurricane center was still vague and ambiguous in its description of the approaching weather system. Without the means to locate the small system precisely or to investigate its internal characteristics, all the weathermen could do was wait until better observational data became available and a true portrait of Hurakan's child could be rendered. By then it would be too late.

Labor Day

Prelude

The western entrance to the Florida Straits is defined on the south by the coastline of Cuba and on the north by seven small keys situated on coral reefs. In 1513, Ponce de León came upon the islands and named them Las Tortugas because of the numerous turtles in the area. The islands have no wells, springs, or sources of freshwater other than rainfall so early chart makers labeled them the Dry Tortugas.

The location of the islands is such that nineteenth-century military strategists considered the construction of a fort essential to the protection of U.S. maritime trade and ports located on the Gulf of Mexico. On one of the small islands named Garden Key, sixty-eight miles west of Key West, work began in 1846 on the largest coastal nineteenth-century masonry fort to be built in the United States. The hexagonal-shaped fort required 16 million handmade red bricks to form its massive 45-foot-high walls and internal buildings. The work continued for thirty years. Much of it was done initially with slave labor and with former slaves after the Emancipation Proclamation was issued. It was never totally completed.

In 1861, the fort was manned by the army and fitted out with various ordinance. By 1864, there were two thousand people living within its walls including military personnel, their families, and prisoners. The most notorious prisoner confined at Fort Jefferson was Dr. Samuel Mudd, who was incarcerated for aiding President Abraham Lincoln's assassin.

The facility was abandoned by the army in 1874 and fell into disrepair. The fort was again briefly manned for military purposes in 1898 during the Spanish-American War when coaling facilities were built there for deep-draft naval vessels. In 1908, the Dry Tortugas were proclaimed a wildlife refuge to protect sooty tern rookeries from egg collectors. On January 4, 1935, the area was designated the Fort Jefferson National Monument.

None of this is of interest to the men on the bridge of the SS *Dixie* as it speeds through the darkness early in the morning of Labor Day 1935. Their attention is being given to two navigational aids installed on Loggerhead Key, an island three miles to the west of Fort Jefferson. One them is a lighthouse of classical design, an upright brick cylinder with the focal plane of the light located 151 feet above the ground. On a clear night, the light can be seen from the bridge of a ship twenty to twenty-five miles away.

The other navigational aid is a radio beacon installed in 1926 that allows ships to take a bearing on the treacherous Tortugas reefs well before the light can be discerned. The *Dixie* is equipped with a radio direction finder that can detect the Dry Tortugas radio beacon.

At about 3 a.m., having been guided by the beacon and then the light, the *Dixie* changes from a southeasterly course to an easterly heading as the liner swings around the Dry Tortugas and enters the Straits of Florida. Soon thereafter an advisory is received from the Weather Bureau via the Naval Radio Station in Key West:

Jacksonville, Fla., September 2, 1935

Advisory, 3:30 a.m.—Tropical disturbance still of small diameter, but considerable intensity, is moving slowly westward off the coast of north-central Cuba, attended by shifting gales, and probably winds near hurricane force over small area. Will probably pass through Florida Straits Monday. Caution advised against high tides and gales Florida Keys and for ships in path. (U.S. Congress, *Florida Hurricane Disaster Hearings*, 211–13)

To the men navigating the ship, the advisory's report of the storm's slow westward movement and its location being near the north central coast of Cuba means Captain Sundstrom's plan to outrun the storm is still sound. The ship should be well to the north of the storm by the time it enters the Florida Straits.

The *Dixie* continues on course, racing past the Dry Tortugas, Rebecca Shoal, and the Marquesas as the eastern sky begins to glow with the dawn. The weather remains good, and at about 9 a.m. the lighthouse at Sand

Key, eight miles southeast of Key West, is visible on the horizon off the port bow. The Morgan Liner has been traveling almost due east since entering the Straits; as long as that course is maintained, the ship remains in the forecast path of the hurricane. Once past Sand Key, the *Dixie* begins a gradual turn toward the north, running parallel to the reefs that form the north edge of the Florida Straits.

At 9:30 a. m., the Jacksonville hurricane center issues another advisory:

Jacksonville, Fla., September 2, 1935
Advisory 9:30 a. m. Tropical disturbance central about 200 miles due east Habana, Cuba, moving slowly westward attended by shifting gales and probably winds hurricane force small area near center. Caution advised vessels Florida Straits next 24 to 36 hours. Northeast storm warnings remain displayed Miami to Fort Myers. (U.S. Congress, *Florida Hurricane Disaster Hearings*, 211–13)

While this advisory implies the weathermen knew the location of the storm with certainty, this was not the case. On the Daily Weather Map issued by the central office of the Weather Bureau in Washington, D.C., on Labor Day 1935, the tropical disturbance is represented by a single huge isobar (a line connecting observations where the pressure readings are the same). The oval is about four hundred miles across, reaching from north of Miami to well south of Cuba, a clear indication that the weathermen were not sure where the storm was located.

That uncertainty would exist is understandable. Of 172 observation reports processed by the Jacksonville Weather Bureau for the advisory issued at 9:30 a.m. on Labor Day, only one was from a ship in the same zone as the storm. The zone was approximately 350 miles wide, and it is likely that the reporting ship was well to the east of the hurricane. The closest reporting land station was Long Key, approximately 140 miles away from the hurricane's actual position; however, because of the compactness of the system, the barometer monitored by J. E. Duane, the volunteer observer, did not begin reacting to the storm until well into the afternoon. There were no reporting stations or ships positioned where accurate readings of the weather system could be obtained. While the weathermen could only estimate the probable position of the system with the data on hand, the wording of their advisories did not reflect the degree of uncertainty involved.

After the storm's passage, the Weather Bureau acknowledged in the *Monthly Weather Review* for September 1935 that tracking the Labor Day hurricane was problematic: "During the developing stage of the hurricane, as it was moving over remote islands and shoals of the southern Bahamas where there were no ships or island stations to report the passage of the small vortex, the problems of accurately locating the center and its line of advance and of forecasting its probable movement were extremely difficult. Nevertheless, timely and generally accurate advices were issued by the forecast center at Jacksonville, Fla., during this period." Without radar, weather satellites, or aerial reconnaissance, the small, intense storm eluded the meteorologists as it churned across the shallow waters of the Hurricane Flats off Andros Island. When it passed over the Santaren Channel, with its warm waters and depth of over a thousand feet, the updrafts increased and the winds intensified. With hurricane winds wrapped tightly around the compact eye, the storm continued to move toward the northwest, growing stronger and drawing ever nearer the Upper Keys.

On Upper Matecumbe Key, Betty King had been up at her usual rising time of 6 a.m. and was readying the Rustic Inn for the holiday's business. Betty's husband, O. D., went to the Matecumbe Hotel to get the latest information on the storm and then to the veterans camps motor pool. He had been given orders to take the keys from the drivers so they would not run away with the vehicles. At 8 a.m., he directed that all keys to motorpool vehicles be turned in immediately. Two truck drivers were told to hold onto their keys so that they could haul commissary and other supplies out if the men were evacuated. Both of them took their trucks and drove themselves to the safety of the mainland.

As the first rays of the sun fell on the maze of rails at the Buena Vista switchyard of the Florida East Coast Railway just north of Miami, railroad personnel went about the task of assembling the train for the scheduled run to Key West. Orders had come from the dispatching office in New Smyrna to add four extra coaches to No. 75 to accommodate holiday travelers and any veterans who wanted to come out of the Keys on the return trip that evening. The train pulled out for the station with a total of seven coaches.

At the lighthouse on Alligator Reef, Keeper Jones A. Purvis and his assistant, James O. Duncan, were on duty. On the flagstaff at the top of the lighthouse some 140 feet over the water flew a red pennant above a square red flag with a black square in the center; the international signal warning of the approach of a storm of marked violence with winds beginning from the northeast. At about 9 a.m., the pennant and flag were replaced as directed by the Weather Bureau with two red square flags with black squares in their centers, one above the other. This signal warned of the approach of a tropical hurricane. The ominous hurricane signal was visible to people on Upper Matecumbe Key. The lighthouse's barometer was read at 10 a.m. and logged; the reading of 29.80 inches was within the normal range.

Captain George W. Albury didn't get his newspaper on Monday morning, so the latest weather information he had came from the Sunday edition of the *Miami Herald*, which reported the storm to be 350 miles away. Born in Key West, Albury had lived on Plantation Key for forty-nine years. Described as a tall and gray-haired "grizzled veteran of the Florida Keys," the fifty-four-year-old fisherman had been through every storm that had hit the Upper Keys since 1894; he knew a thing or two about hurricanes. He had checked his barometer, and it did not indicate bad weather was on the way. He decided to drive over to Whale Harbor and see what another fisherman, Robert Ingraham, had heard. Ingraham told him that the radio had just broadcast a storm warning saying the hurricane was still two hundred miles east of Havana and was traveling at 8 mph. At that rate of travel, the storm was still a day away even if it came their way.

Nonetheless, Captain Albury, in an abundance of caution, went aboard his boat and moved it into a "hurricane creek," a narrow channel that winds its way among the mangroves that cloak many of the islands. The dense mangrove foliage looming up on either side and the twists and turns of the channel prevent a clear line of sight from the open water, making them a favorite hiding place for smugglers. In times of bad weather, the tough branches of the mangrove bushes moderate and deflect the wind and flying debris. A boat securely moored in one of these channels has a very good chance of coming through a storm unharmed. Albury used the boat's dinghy to get back to his car and return home. Both he and Robert Ingraham began to check their barometers regularly.

Ingraham was an industrious thirty-six-year-old fisherman who owned a house on the Whale Harbor fill east of Eddie Williams's place. Robert and his wife, Larimie (27), had made a comfortable home for their two sons, Everett (7) and Ervine (10), and their baby, Mary Ida (2½ months). On Labor Day morning, the house was especially cheerful as Ingraham's mother and sister had come to spend the holiday.

A naturalized citizen of the United States, Mrs. Edward E. (Mary) Ingraham was born in the Bahamas and had emigrated to the Keys, married, and settled in Key West. The sixty-six-year-old widow lived frugally with her daughter in a rented apartment and spent her time keeping house and doing church work. She was a devout member of St. Paul's Episcopal Church, where she participated in most of the church's activity groups and taught in the church school. Having only an eighth-grade education herself, she was especially proud of the scholastic achievement attained by her daughter Mary A. Louise Ingraham that summer.

Mary Louise graduated from the Monroe County High School at Key West in 1925 at age sixteen. Good at algebra, geometry, history, and Spanish, she wanted to become a certified teacher. With a widowed mother to help support, Mary Louise could not afford to go to college so she taught classes at the Harris Elementary School and began working on her teacher's certificate by taking correspondence courses from the University of Florida. By the summer of 1926, she had earned six semester hours and scrimped together enough funds so that she could attend the summer session at the University of Florida.

When she returned to teaching at the Harris School in the fall, she had a total of fifteen semester hours. Over the next five years, Mary Louise took eleven more correspondence courses from the university, bringing her total semester hours earned to forty. In June 1931, she was admitted to the Florida State College for Women at Tallahassee and attended summer school. She kept teaching at Harris School during the regular school year and attended summer school at FSCW in 1932, 1934, and 1935. After ten years of studying evenings, weekends, and summers, she had accumulated eighty-four semester hours; on August 2, 1935, Mary Louise Ingraham was awarded a two-year diploma and certified to teach primary-kindergarten. She was eager to return to Harris School after the holiday, looking forward to a higher salary and perhaps the social life she had been forced to postpone while she did her academic work. Whether or not she would get to enjoy the fruits of her labor would be decided in a matter of hours.

Ten miles down the railroad track from the Ingrahams' home on a small man-made island, Roland W. Craig began boarding up his buildings. When the railroad to Key West was constructed, many of the channels used by fishing and pleasure boats to go from the ocean side of the Keys to the bay side were closed off by solid fills. There were some channels crossed by viaducts, steel trestles, and concrete bridges with arched openings where the headroom was typically eleven feet and small boats could pass through.

For larger craft and sailboats with tall masts, it was a different story; there were only two places along the 130 miles from Key Largo to Key West where they could make the crossing. One was 45 miles east of Key West at the Moser Channel viaduct near Pigeon Key, where a swing bridge was installed. The other was 25 miles farther east between Long Key and Lower Matecumbe Key at Channel No. 5, where a drawbridge was installed. Because of this limited access, there were concentrations of boat traffic consisting mainly of commercial fishing vessels, yachts, and sailboats at Moser Channel and Channel No. 5.

On the east bank of Channel No. 5, a two-mile, L-shaped fill was constructed by the FEC Railway to accommodate a curve in the railroad track so that it crossed perpendicular to the waterway, thereby minimizing the width of the drawbridge and reducing its cost. The fill was wider than the straight fills found elsewhere along the Keys in order to provide the mass necessary to resist the reactive forces generated when a heavy locomotive and its cars made the turn. At the end nearest the drawbridge, the railroad constructed a sturdy two-story house for the bridge tender, which was occupied on Labor Day by R. G. Jackson, his wife, and their six children. A quarter mile to the east was a fish camp and marina owned by Roland W. Craig.

Craig was a shrewd entrepreneur who saw the drawbridge as a funnel bringing boats in need of provisions, mail service, and fuel by this tiny speck of land, so in 1930 or 1931 he moved onto the fill and set about establishing a facility for servicing the marine traffic. On the bay side of the island, he built a 200-foot dock next to the channel that had been dug by the dredgers when they created the fill. Between the dock and the track

Ivor "Ollie" Olson's boat was strapped down to his homemade marine railway with stout cables on the bay side of Craig Key. The ways was constructed from surplus railroad track and other salvaged materials. (Wilkinson)

he built a 20′ × 20′ combination store and post office. On the ocean side of the tracks, Craig built a 24′ × 30′ one-story house.

In 1932 he married, and he and his wife, Dorothy, lived on the island. The next year they established a U.S. Post Office at the fish camp, and Dorothy was appointed postmistress. They built some cottages to accommodate rich sportfishermen, and Craig, as the island had come to be known, was designated as a flag stop by the FEC Railway. There was no road to the fish camp, so Craig and others who drove cars from the mainland had to park them at the west end of Lower Matecumbe near the ferry slip and then walk along the railbed across the fill and the Channel No. 2 viaduct, a distance of about 1½ miles.

The 1935 census lists Roland, Dorothy, and twin daughters as residents of the island; however, after 1934, when Dorothy gave birth to the girls, she spent most of her time in Miami, preferring to raise the children on the mainland. On Labor Day there were fifteen people at Craig including the bridge tender's family and Ivor "Ollie" Olson, a fifty-two-year-old fisherman from Sweden. On the bay side of the island, Olson had pulled his boat up on a crude marine railway constructed from surplus railroad track and parts. The boat was not much to look at, but it was sturdy and was lashed securely to the ways with steel cables. On Labor Day, Olson was living aboard his boat.

On Saturday, Roland Craig was in Miami enjoying a visit with his wife and daughters when he heard about the storm. His friend Jack Crowe was taking care of the fish camp facilities while he was away. Craig became concerned about the storm and decided to return to the fish camp. He and another friend, Langdon Lockwood, drove Lockwood's new Graham-Paige roadster down to Lower Matecumbe and parked the car near the ferry slip then walked over the fill and Channel No. 2 viaduct. They arrived at the fish camp Saturday night.

On Sunday, Craig called the Miami Weather Bureau and was told that a storm with hurricane-force winds near its center was somewhere in the neighborhood of Andros Island and still in the Bahamas group. He monitored the party-line telephone and the radio during the day, trying to get more information. "Early Monday morning," Craig later recalled, "I called the telephone company in Miami to get the weather bureau advisory and was told the storm apparently had moved slightly and was located central over Cuba, 200 miles east of Havana and moving west." This didn't sound right to Craig. Using his charts and navigational skills, he calculated that the storm was about 150 miles southeast of his position. Aware of the unpredictable nature of hurricanes and somewhat amazed that the Weather Bureau thought the Keys would only receive gale-force winds, Craig began boarding up his buildings.

Offshore, the *Dixie* has made good progress on the initial leg of her passage through the Florida Straits. At around 10 a.m. on the morning of Labor Day, the lighthouse at Sombrero Reef was sighted. The *Dixie's* course runs parallel with the curvature of the reef protecting the Florida Keys. The ship is now on a northeasterly heading and every 3½ minutes is another mile away from the path of the hurricane as forecast in the Weather Bureau's advisories. There appears to be no reason to alarm the passengers so no announcement is made concerning the possibility of rough seas; however, the ship soon begins to encounter squalls. By 11 a.m., the rain is steady and most passengers have left the decks for their staterooms or the lounges. When lunch is served, none of the passengers are aware that this is their last opportunity for a hot meal on this voyage of the *Dixie*.

On Upper Matecumbe Key, Betty King and her sister Leone Barr are inside the Rustic Inn, sitting at one of the tables near an open window when James Edwin "Eddie" Carey comes by. Standing outside the window under the tilted Bahamas shutter, he tells them a storm is coming and advises them to secure the inn. He invites them to come out and stay with his family at his house on the beach. They thank him for the invitation, but say they would rather stay at the inn and keep an eye on the property. This decision probably saved their lives.

Eddie Carey and his wife, the former Clara Thompson, were born and raised in Key West, where they were married. In 1906, they moved to Key Largo and then relocated to Upper Matecumbe in 1913. The Careys' eight children were all born in Key West, some at her mother's house and some at a house rented specifically for the birthing. It was a common practice for women who were from Key West and lived on the Keys to return to their hometown for birthing. By 1935, the Carey clan had become a significant component of the Upper Keys community.

Although he had only an eighth-grade education, Eddie Carey was a hard worker, and by 1935 standards had done very well. At fifty-five, he was a successful farmer who grew limes, tomatoes, cantaloupes, and melons on land near the Rustic Inn. He was also a carpenter and for a while a grocer. In addition to his farmland, Eddie owned a two-story house, grocery store, and several cottages on the beach south of the Rustic Inn. He rented out the store and cottages.

After stopping by the Rustic Inn and talking with Betty King and Leone Barr, Eddie and other members of his family gather in one of the cottages to ride out the storm together. Eddie brings along his barometer; there is no doubt in his mind that they are in for a blow. Clara and their sixteen-year-old daughter, Rosalie, are in Key West, where they have spent two weeks visiting Clara's mother and attending to Rosalie's dental work. They plan to return to Islamorada on the northbound train that evening. Eddie's son Everett is with his wife at a hospital in Miami, where she was admitted on Saturday for an illness.

On the fill between Windley Key and Upper Matecumbe, the Williams family is enjoying the company of Mozelle's brother and his family. During the afternoon they make a trip to the grocery store and meet Ed Sheeran. A good friend of Eddie Williams, Sheeran tells him a storm is coming. Sheeran says, "Eddie, if I was you I'd get my family away from the fill." According to Mozelle Williams, this was the first they knew that a hurricane was headed their way. Without delay, they return to the house on the fill. While Mozelle and Carrie fix sandwiches and other goodies to eat, Eddie and Dan secure the house and boat. The four children gather up games and things to entertain themselves with.

As the wind freshens, they load up their cars and motor down to an old storm house that is sheltered by a grove of coconut trees. There is no concern among the adults and no discussion of taking their cars and going to the mainland. In fact, as they settle into their temporary quarters, they are all feeling the giddiness and excitement of embarking on a spontaneous adventure. "It was a lot of fun at first," recalled Eddie's daughter Elizabeth.

Over at the Matecumbe Hotel, the veterans camps staff has spent the morning doing mostly menial administrative chores while attempting to obtain the latest information on the storm via telephone and their radio receiver. Duties are light since it is a holiday, and half the veterans are on the mainland or in Key West. Down in the restaurant at lunchtime, Wilbur Jones sees George Pepper with a very pretty girl. While George and Rosalind Palmer are eating their lunch, they are unaware that the train to Key West is pulling out of the station at Islamorada after making a brief stop. One of the passengers is Rosalind's thirteen-year-old brother, Bascom Grooms Jr., who boarded the train at Tavernier and is heading home after a two-week stay with a friend. By now the balmy morning has given way to sporadic squalls and wind gusts. Even though the weather is inclement, there are drunk veterans all around the Islamorada station so Bascom stays on the train.

At the lighthouse on Alligator Reef, the barometer readings taken during the morning were in the normal range and had even risen to 29.85 inches at noon. Thereafter the pressure began to fall, gradually at first but steadily. At the Long Key Fish Camp, James Duane notes a decrease in barometric pressure and a rise in the tide. The reports of both stations are passed on to the Jacksonville Weather Bureau.

After lunch, O. D. King takes his pickup truck and begins transporting families of the veterans camps staff to the hospital at Snake Creek, where they can wait to be moved to the mainland if the decision to evacuate is made. On each trip he stops at the inn so that Betty and her sister Leone can fix them a bite to eat. Leone remembered one group of strikingly beautiful, blond-haired children O. D. brought by; she had no idea that was to be the last time she would see them alive.

On one of his trips, O. D. stopped at Frenchy Fecteau's place on Lower Matecumbe and told him he ought to get out while he can. Unlike most of the veterans, Frenchy owns a 1931 Chevrolet pickup truck. He later recalled: "Shortly after 1 o'clock I was notified by Mr. King to leave; that the storm would strike the keys. So I went on for the mainland. I had a truck down there, and I left with a party and got as far as Camp One at Snake Creek, that is, the old Snake Creek Hotel, which was turned into an emergency hospital down there for the camps. That is just about 12 miles from Camp Five." The party that Frenchy referred to was his wife, Frieda; his daughters, Marie Madsden (18) and Dorothy Vester (16); and his grandchildren, Ray Madsden (2½) and Dorothy Vester (1). They left Lower Matecumbe at 1:15 p.m. and drove up to Camp Five so that Frenchy could tell his supervisor, Glenn Robertson, that he was leaving.

Frenchy later recalled that the civilians offered assistance to the veteran and his family: "these natives did everything they could toward us, that is, before the hurricane did strike, they even told us if we were caught on the road to come into their storm houses. They have hurricane houses in different little buildings, but them things were built just to stand a breeze; they are not built to stand water."

Already there are six inches of water across the highway at low spots, but it is not the water or the wind that stops Frenchy and his family from reaching the mainland. When he arrives at the Snake Creek bridge, he is flagged down by law officers. They tell Fecteau the camp administrators have a train coming to evacuate the veterans and they want all the men to wait for the train so that the evacuation can be managed in an orderly fashion and the men can be properly cared for at their destination: "I was stopped down there by the sheriffs. They were flagging trucks across the road, of course, they were under orders they had received orders from the officials to stop all veterans, on account of the train, that the train would be there any time. . . . [T]he sheriff there was firing guns across the road. Of course, he had orders to stop us, even at a gunpoint, and hold us there until the train got in."

Thwarted by the roadblock, Frenchy and his family have no choice and go to the veterans hospital at Snake Creek. Once inside they receive some bad news: "The Snake Creek Hotel, that was hurricane proof, it had stood all the hurricanes they had in Florida. The lady who owned the building came there the day before, and she said to the doctors that she did not want them to keep the men—they were the sick men that were in the hospital—she said there were some cables broke on the building and it was not safe if the water did come up, to get the men out, the day before." With the weather deteriorating and the deputies blocking the only road to the mainland, the Fecteaus decide to stay at the hospital and wait for the train to come and evacuate them.

In Jacksonville, Grady Norton, Gordon Dunn, and Walter Bennett are trying to process observation reports and answer the telephone, which rings incessantly with calls from the media and public. It was a common problem for Weather Bureau stations in hurricane-prone areas because the public was allowed (and believed it was their right) to have direct telephone access to the forecaster on duty. As a result, when warnings were issued, the stations in the affected areas would be deluged with telephone calls from the press, business interests, and ordinary citizens. This meant that one or more station staff had to be assigned full time to handle telephone inquiries. In addition, as a storm approached, reporters from the Associated Press and United Press were often present at the stations. The incessant demand for information created pressure to expedite the labor-intensive work of collecting and plotting data, and sometimes pushed the weathermen to the extreme limits of their abilities and endurance.

During the morning, a check of barometric readings showed Miami was at 29.80 and the north coast of Cuba was 29.65, which the weathermen interpreted to mean the storm's low-pressure center was nearer to Cuba than Miami. In a letter written after the storm, Bennett states: "This disturbance passed through the Bahama Islands with little indications of any severity. The lowest barometer reported prior to noon of the 2nd was 29.46 (a very moderate depression) and the highest wind 34 miles per hour."

At 1 p.m., reports from the Alligator Reef lighthouse and the Long Key Fish Camp arrive at the Jacksonville hurricane center; the data show a decrease in barometric pressure, an increase in wind speed, and a rising tide. At 1:30 p.m., the weathermen issue another advisory derived from observations taken around noon based on a total of twenty-two reports, including three from ships and six from land stations in the same zone as the storm.

Jacksonville, Florida
Advisory, 1:30 p.m.—Hurricane Warnings ordered Key West. Tropical disturbance central noon about latitude 23 deg 20 min, longitude 80 deg 15 min moving slowly westward. It will be attended by winds hurricane force in Florida Straits and winds gale force Florida Keys south of Key Largo this afternoon and tonight. Caution advised vessels Florida Straits next 24 hours. Northeast storm warnings remain displayed elsewhere Miami to Fort Myers. (U.S. Congress, *Florida Hurricane Disaster Hearings*, 211–13)

This advisory differs from preceding advisories in two respects; it gives a specific position for the center of the tropical disturbance and states with certainty that the disturbance has hurricane winds. Earlier advisories gave the location in general terms and were indefinite as to whether it had reached hurricane strength. The location given in the advisory placed the center of the storm just a few miles off the north coast of Cuba about 150 miles east of Havana. Anyone who plotted the position and noted the phrase "slowly moving westward" would conclude that if the storm held to that track, the eye would pass just north of Havana and well south of Key West.

The weathermen were unaware that the hurricane was actually located where the Santaren Channel meets the Florida Straits, about eighty miles north-northeast of the position stated in the advisory. They were also unaware that winds near the center had increased to 150 mph, and that the "disturbance" was now a Category 4 hurricane moving dead-on for the Florida Keys.

Allegations were made after the storm's passage that the Weather Bureau did not give consideration to weather reports from Cuba, the Alligator Reef lighthouse, and the Morgan Liner *Dixie*, and ignored barometer readings throughout the Florida Keys from Miami to Key West. According to Weather Bureau records, this was not the case. Reports from three land stations in Cuba were used to prepare the 1:30 p.m. advisory, but the nearest reporting Cuban station was 275 miles away from the actual position of the hurricane. The reports of four ships were used, three of which were in the area of the western Florida Straits while the other ship was in the Gulf of Mexico.

When the readings were taken (believed to have been 11 a.m. EST), the barometers at the Alligator Reef lighthouse, Long Key, and Craig were within the normal range, leading the forecasters at the Jacksonville hurricane center to believe the storm was not nearing the Upper Florida Keys. Apparently the forecasters felt confident enough with the data to include a specific location in the advisory. Why this was the case is not known.

The 1:30 p.m. advisory was critical because it was the last advisory to be issued before the winds and rising tide made evacuation from the Keys to the mainland too hazardous. By the time the next advisory was issued, it was too late to leave the Keys by trucks and cars.

There is no question that the storm was difficult to track, given its compact construction and the absence of tools such as aircraft, radar, or satellites for making long-range observations. As Walter Bennett wrote after the storm's passage, "Regarding advices issued, we cannot tell more than we know and what we can logically figure from the reports received." In the advisory issued at 1:30 p.m. on Labor Day, it appears that the men at the Jacksonville hurricane center did exactly what Walter Bennett said they should not do; they told more than they knew or that they could logically figure from the reports received. By the time they became aware of the true position and heading of the hurricane, it would be too late.

Labor Day Afternoon

Four weeks earlier, when Ray Sheldon was sent to the Keys to manage the veterans camps, he astutely asked his boss, Fred Ghent, what provisions had been made in the event a hurricane threatened the Florida Keys: "I was informed by Mr. Ghent, in Jacksonville, that provisions had been made with the railroad, in case of a hurricane, to supply us with trains on very short notice." About two weeks after that, when Ghent and his boss, Conrad Van Hyning, went down to the Keys and toured the camps, Ray Sheldon asked for more detailed information regarding the evacuation arrangements: "At that time, we made an inspection of the camps and I requested a little more information as to just what I would do, how we would get these trains and I was informed that, in case of a storm, the railroad had already been in correspondence with the Jacksonville office, and that, if the request was made, it would only be a very short time—I mean in hours—before the train would be there."

The advisory issued by the Jacksonville Weather Bureau at 9:30 on Labor Day morning was received at the veterans camps headquarters in the Matecumbe Hotel at 10 a.m. Based on the advisory, Sheldon calculates that the storm is traveling at 5 mph. Since the advisory indicated the storm is holding to a heading that would carry it through the Florida Straits between Key West and Havana, he sees no need to implement an evacuation. He has the office staff monitor the radio and stand by the telephone.

At 11:23, Mr. Gilfong, of Key West, called me and said that Mr. Van Hyning had been endeavoring to get hold of me, but for some reason could not make connection; and he was very anxious to know in what shape we were there. I explained to him that my understanding was that we could get a train on short notice—and I meant by short notice 3 or 4 hours—that there was no reason for alarm from the reading of my barometer there at the hotel; that there had been no change at all; in fact, it was slightly rising; that there had been a slight rise the night before. The barometer reading then was approximately 29.81, or .09 less than normal. (U.S. Congress, *Florida Hurricane Disaster Hearings*)

The reading had been taken at around 11:30 a.m. and was not considered by Sheldon to be alarming.

That was a gradual drop. Now, there is also a rise or a drop of about 0.06, due to the tide, or due to other reasons. However, 29.81 is not low. . . . [T]here had been no change in the atmospheric conditions that would show that a storm was approaching any closer than we were led to believe by the reports that the Weather Bureau was giving. In other words, perhaps I should make it a little clearer this way: We knew there was a storm traveling west and was headed along the coast of Cuba, and that as it went along, it was parallel to the Keys, and it was not going to get any closer. This was as close as it would get if the Weather Bureau reports were correct. (U.S. Congress, *Florida Hurricane Disaster Hearings*)

Having received no further weather information either by radio or telephone, Ray Sheldon called the Miami Weather Bureau: "I asked them then if there was any danger to the people on the keys, at 12:52, and I was told that there was not, and I went down and had my dinner. When I left the dining room and went back up to the office, the barometer dropped .06. In other words, it showed a drop of .06 from 11:30, or approximately 11:30, until shortly after 1. That was alarming."

At 1:37 p.m., the call Sheldon had placed to Ghent at 11:45 a.m. finally came through. Sheldon told Ghent that his barometer is dropping and he thinks the hurricane is headed their way. Sheldon later recalled, "The Weather Bureau told me there was no danger, but I believed there was." While he is on the telephone with Ghent, a warning based on the 1:30 p.m. advisory is broadcast over the radio.

Hurricane warning 1:30 p.m. Key West district. Tropical disturbance central noon about latitude 23 deg 20 min, longitude 80 deg 15 min, moving slowly westward. It will be attended by winds hurricane force in Florida Straits and winds of gale force Florida keys south of Key Largo this afternoon and tonight. (U.S. Congress, *Florida Hurricane Disaster Hearings*, 211–13)

Sheldon relays this to Ghent and tells him he wants the evacuation train ordered: "I told Mr. Ghent what I wanted, that we should have the train ordered then, and I gave him my barometer reading and told him the condition of the weather. Some of the fellows were out in front, walking up and down the road. We had squalls of rain, gusts of wind, and the sun had come out."

After talking with Ray Sheldon, Fred Ghent calls the assistant to the general superintendent of the Florida East Coast Railway, F. L. Aitcheson. At 2 p.m., Aitcheson is at his home in St. Augustine taking a bath when Ghent's urgent call is received. Ghent requests a special train be sent to Matecumbe to evacuate the veterans and take them to Hollywood. Aitcheson says he will have a train assembled as soon as possible. He tells Ghent that if the train departs Miami by 4 p.m., it should reach the camps by 6:30 and that the veterans should arrive in Hollywood by 10:30 p.m. if there are no delays in loading the men. As soon as the call is over, Aitcheson puts on some clothes, "not taking time to dress fully," and hurries to his office.

Meanwhile, Sheldon calls the FEC Railway department that will assemble the train and alerts them that the order is being placed: "At 1:45, after completing the call to Mr. Ghent, I called the Florida East Coast operating department and told them that I had just talked to Mr. Ghent at Jacksonville and the order was going through from there to St. Augustine and then officially to him, saying that I was to have the train; that I wanted him to call me back and verify it, so that I would know the train was coming. He told me to hold the wire, that he thought it was coming in then. I held the wire for some 5 or 8 minutes, and whoever I was talking with—it was not Mr. Gaddis—told me that he had just got the order." Sheldon asks when the train will arrive at the camps. He is told, "We will have the train down there at 5 or 5:30."

Ben E. Davis, the supervisor of Camp Three, was in Miami on Labor Day when he received a call from headquarters to immediately return to the Keys. When he arrives at the Matecumbe Hotel in the early afternoon, he is handed written instructions from Sheldon stating that he is to make preparations to evacuate Camp Three at 5:30 p.m. He is told that a train will arrive at that time to take the veterans to Hollywood, a small town eighteen miles north of Miami. The orders instruct Davis to have all veterans and all kitchen utensils and surplus canned goods ready to load on the train. Davis proceeds directly to Camp Three, arriving there about 2 p.m. He immediately has the siren sounded to assemble the men in the mess hall. They are instructed to gather personal effects and blankets and make ready to leave on the train at 5:30.

As the afternoon progresses, the weather continues to deteriorate. At the veterans hospital at Snake Creek, the wind is blowing hard enough to cause loose materials to blow away. At Long Key, the cooperative weather observer James Duane makes an entry in his notebook: "Barometer falling, heavy sea swell and a high tide, heavy rain squalls continued. Wind from north or north-northeast, force 6."

East of the Keys in the Florida Straits, strong winds are buffeting the *Dixie*. The ship begins to pitch violently from bow to stern, moving up and down as the liner plows through the waves. The staterooms where most passengers are taking refuge soon become a scene of confusion and danger. Furniture and suitcases are thrown about and water finds its way into the rooms, sloshing from one side to the other.

Seventeen miles southeast of the Alligator Reef lighthouse, the American tanker *Pueblo* bound for Galveston is sailing close to the line of reefs trying to stay out of the opposing current of the Gulf Stream. The rough seas become a serious problem when the ship's propulsion system fails. The winds coming from the north-northeast push the helpless ship away from dangerous coral reefs and into the Gulf Stream. What Captain Walter Furst and his crew do not know until they see their barometer plummet is that the *Pueblo* is being swept into the path of a Category 5 hurricane.

The Florida East Coast Railway management moves into high gear to find the requisite equipment and personnel for the rescue train. By 2:17 p.m., Aitcheson is at his office and immediately calls A. I. Pooser, the superintendent of the Florida East Coast Railway. They determine that they can assemble six coaches, two baggage cars, and three boxcars, and confirm the estimate that it will be 6:30 before the train reaches the camps. They conclude their call at 2:30 p.m.

Pooser then calls the chief train dispatcher, J. L. Byrum, in New Smyrna to tell him they have an order for the special train and to start assembling the equipment. Byrum has no telephone operator on duty and has difficulty getting a call through to the Buena Vista train yard in Miami. He finally gets through to District Superintendent P. L. Gaddis, who has General Yardmaster G. R. Branch in his office. The yard clerk at Buena Vista joins the conversation and says he does not think he can get a crew together in time for the train to depart Miami by 4 p.m.

Branch tries to call the general foreman at his residence but cannot get hold of him, so he calls the assistant foreman at his home and tells him to get the coach on the repair track repaired. He then calls the locomotive department and requests that they have an engine hot and ready for service on short notice. As soon as that call is completed, he calls the Buena Vista yard office and instructs the chief yard clerk to have the foreman of the 3 o'clock yard engine gather the equipment needed.

At 2:45 p.m., Chief Dispatcher Byrum calls and instructs Branch to operate the train consisting of the five coaches and two baggage cars on hand in Miami and an extra coach to be taken from train No. 33, which is scheduled to arrive in forty-five minutes. Branch notifies the crew dispatcher and orders the crew to be called and told to depart at 4 p.m. Branch then phones the foreman of the 3 o'clock yard engine and instructs him to retrieve the coach on the repair track, the three coaches on track no. 6 in the north yard at Buena Vista located between Twenty-ninth and Thirty-sixth streets, move the engine from the engine house, make the train up, and move it to the Miami passenger station.

As the train is being assembled, the barometers in the Keys continue to fall. At Long Key, heavy rainsqualls persist and the wind remains from the north and northeast at 25–31 mph; however, the ocean swells have changed, and now large waves are rolling in from the southeast against the wind.

At the Alligator Reef lighthouse, the barometer has dropped to 29.6. It has been dropping steadily since noon at the rate of 0.125 in. per hour.

Southeast of the lighthouse on board the SS *Dixie*, the order is given for all hands to don life belts. The seas are so rough that the ship's radio antenna is carried away.

On the mainland at New Smyrna, Chief Dispatcher Byrum of the FEC Railway calls Miami again and instructs Branch to add three boxcars. This makes it necessary to switch the cars in the south yard at Buena Vista between Twentieth and Twenty-seventh streets, which requires the engine to come south of Twentieth Street to reach the cars, a process that adds more time to the assembly of the train.

At 3:30 p.m., train No. 33 arrives at the Miami station, and Branch rides the engine back to Buena Vista to pick up the crew. Will Walker (fireman), L. J. Carlisle (flagman), J. E. Gamble (conductor), and J. J. Haycraft (engineer) come aboard and ride back to the station on locomotive No. 447.

Engine No. 447 was built in 1926 and is one of ninety mountain locomotives operated by the Florida East Coast Railway. Called a mountain locomotive because its 4–8–2 wheel configuration is specially designed to provide the increased traction needed to climb inclines, it is a massive machine with each of its eight driver wheels standing as tall as a man. This particular series of locomotives can exert a pulling force of 44,100 pounds. The behemoth weighs 321,500 pounds, and with a tender carrying 10,000 gallons of freshwater and 4,000 gallons of fuel oil, the combined weight exceeds a half million pounds.

Hissing white clouds of condensation as steam is exhausted from the cylinders, the huge black locomotive moves down the track with the deep vibratory rumble associated with the passage of mass and power. No. 447 seems invincible, unstoppable—fully capable of carrying out the heroic mission assigned to it this day.

The special train stops at the Miami station to pick up a coach from train No. 33. Two empty baggage cars on the extreme south end of the spur serving the express track are repositioned and coupled to the special train. While this is being accomplished, Branch leaves the locomotive and goes into the station. At 4:05 p.m. he has a telephone conversation with Aitcheson and Pooser and tells them he has had trouble getting the equipment together but expects the train to be ready to leave Miami by 4:20 or 4:25. Pooser advises Branch to have the train back down to the camps so that once there the locomotive can be repositioned to the other end of the train and will have the use of its headlight while making the return trip in the dark. After completing the call, Branch climbs up into the cab of the locomotive; he will ride the train as the trainmaster.

At 4:25 p.m., the assembly process is complete and the train consisting of six coaches, two baggage cars, three boxcars, the tender, and the locomotive pulls out of the Miami station. At the controls is J. J. Haycraft, an engineer with sixteen years experience running trains on the Keys. He is familiar with hurricanes and especially with the effect of a crosswind upon a train on an exposed bridge or fill. He knows that a great concern of the FEC Railway is that a train may jump the track or be blown into the water, and for that reason special rules apply to the operation of trains on the Keys.

One rule requires trains to cross bridges at no more than 15 mph. Another rule forbids the operation of trains over bridges when the wind exceeds 50 mph. On the three longest viaducts, wind gauges are installed along the bridgework that sense when the wind is above the prescribed limit and automatically actuate switches to prevent an approaching train from proceeding onto the viaduct.

The special train is only going as far as the western end of Lower Matecumbe Key and will not have to cross any of the controlled-access viaducts. It will have to cross several bridges and a mile of exposed fill to reach Camp Three. Haycraft is aware that hundreds of people are counting on him to take them out of harm's way and that time is running short. The rules will not apply on this trip.

Nine and a half miles from the Miami station, the special train comes to a halt. The drawbridge at the Miami River has been raised to let a stream of holiday motorboats pass through. The train is delayed for ten precious minutes.

The hurricane in the Florida Straits has no such impediments. Increasing in intensity by the minute, the storm is toying with three ships, one southbound and two northbound. The southbound tanker *Pueblo*, her engines disabled, is being carried around the center of the hurricane like a chip of wood caught in a vortex. Without working engines, there is little the ship's crew can do except pray. Ever since 2:30 p.m., the northbound tramp steamer *Leise Maersk* has been in rough seas and is being blown toward the line of reefs. She is not taking on water, but the winds are so strong that the starboard mast has been blown into the sea, taking with it the ship's radio antenna. Another antenna was rigged, and that too was blown away.

The northbound liner *Dixie* is near the south side of the hurricane's eye wall, pitching violently. Like most of her fellow passengers, Florence Stieler has retreated to her stateroom. Taking refuge in her bunk, she is thrown out of it several times as massive waves crash into the port side of the ship. The wind drives rain and seawater through even the smallest openings. Three inches of water cover the floor of her stateroom, and large pieces of luggage careen back and forth across the small space.

In Leo Sumner's stateroom, the water level rises to three feet. He and his new bride struggle to keep from being knocked into the sloshing water that is littered with their personal effects.

Ivy Kitteredge, a New Orleans attorney, had looked forward to the rest and relaxation of a voyage, but now he is one of a score of passengers trapped in a tense situation in the salon. After being drenched by water leaking through the overhead deck, they are forced to play a dangerous version of dodge ball with large pieces of furniture that slide to and fro over the slick carpet and crash into anything in their way.

Father F. A. Winkenman, a Catholic priest from San Diego, gives several people absolution. At 4:30 p.m., an electrical short circuit plunges the ship into darkness. Then, as if the good Father Winkenman had worked a miracle, the seas and wind moderate, the clouds disappear, and the sun shines brilliantly against a blue sky. The ship steadies up and becomes eerily quiet. The *Dixie* has entered the eye of the hurricane.

Barometers at stations all along the Florida Keys are registering the storm's presence. At the Carysfort Reef lighthouse east of Key Largo, the barometer drops from 29.90 at 2 p.m. to 29.76 at 4 p.m. At Sombrero Reef near Marathon, the lighthouse readings drop from 29.75 to 29.64 during the same period. Halfway between the Carysfort and Sombrero lighthouses, the Alligator Reef lighthouse has readings that have dropped from 29.68 at 2 p.m. to 29.43 at 4 p.m.

The rapidly falling pressure readings come as a surprise to the weathermen in the Federal Building at Jacksonville. Instead of the hurricane heading west and passing through the Florida Straits between Key West and Cuba, it now appears to them that the hurricane has made a radical turn to the north and is headed across the Straits into the heart of the Florida Keys.

A total of forty-eight observation reports—thirty-two from ships and sixteen from land stations in the same or adjacent zones as the storm—erase any doubt. The only thing they can do is issue another advisory.

Jacksonville, September 2, 1935

Advisory, 4:30 p.m.—Tropical storm now apparently moving north-westward toward Florida Keys accompanied by hurricane winds over small area. Hurricane warnings displayed Key West and town of Everglades and northeast storm warnings elsewhere south Florida coast West Palm Beach to Sarasota. (U.S. Congress, *Florida Hurricane Disaster Hearings*, 211–13)

Although the forecasters believe the storm had been just off the north coast of Cuba and is now making a sharp turn toward the Keys, it had actually continued to move west northwest across the Hurricane Flats and the mouth of the Santaren Channel into the Florida Straits.

The three ships engaged with the hurricane have been no help to the weathermen. They cannot determine their positions because accurate sextant observations are not possible. Static electricity discharges associated with the storm interfere with radio direction finder reception and the violent pitching of the ships and poor visibility make it impossible to take bearings. If the vessels could have determined their positions, they could not communicate weather observations because the antennas on the *Leise Maersk* and the *Dixie* are down and the *Pueblo* is without power.

On Upper Matecumbe Key at the camps' headquarters in the Matecumbe Hotel, Ray Sheldon has tried unsuccessfully to call public officials in Hollywood to make arrangements for the veterans who will be taken there on the special train. At 4 p.m., he instructs Sam Cutler to take a government-owned vehicle and drive to the town north of Miami to see to the arrangements. Cutler leaves by himself in a two-door Chevrolet. It is raining and blowing hard at the time; he estimates the winds at 40–50 mph.

As Cutler departs, the agent/operator for the FEC Railway at Islamorada, Raymond S. Spitz, arrives at the Matecumbe Hotel. Spitz is thirty years old and lives with his twenty-two-year-old wife, Marjorie, and their five-year-old son in Islamorada. About a half hour earlier, he had called Pooser in New Smyrna and reported a reading of 29.36 from the barometer at the train station. Pooser told him to go get another reading. Spitz asks to check the camps' headquarter's barometer and obtains a reading of 29.10, then returns to the station to relay the information to Pooser.

Earlier in the afternoon, Wilbur Jones had told his boss that he would go around to the camps to collect the time books and take them on the train up to Hollywood. That way the camp superintendents would have the books available in Hollywood, and the timekeeping could be kept up to date. Since the records are used for pay purposes, they cannot be handled by just anyone. Jones is one of a few people allowed to have access to and custody of the records, so his boss accepts Jones's offer. As he walks through the hotel on his way to his car, Jones sees Rosalind Palmer and George Pepper: "The girlfriend of George, who was very attractive and who I had met, was waiting in the lobby area of our most modest living and headquarters hotel. As I was leaving in my vehicle to head south to Lower Matecumbe across the waterway on the railroad embankment, I waved to George and his friend who apparently were leaving the headquarters. This was the last time I saw George and Rosalind."

At 4 p.m., Ben Davis arrives at the Matecumbe Hotel. The superintendent of Camp Three wants to find out the status of the special train from Ray Sheldon. Sheldon tells him the train has been ordered and is on its way. Davis mentions that he intends to drive his personal car to Hollywood: "As I started out, I told Mr. Sheldon that I intended to drive my car out and that the boys on the train would be placed in charge of Top Sergeant Paul Pugh and that I would follow in my car alongside the train. Mr. Sheldon informed me that he would sooner have me with the men on the train and asked me to let George Pepper drive my car and take the women folks to Miami in it."

Davis agrees and drives back to Camp Three accompanied by George Pepper and Rosalind Palmer. Davis gives Pepper the keys to his Dodge sedan and bids the couple farewell. He later recalled: "On our arrival at the camp, I turned the car over to him, instructed him to make haste, and wished him good luck and good-bye. That is the last I saw of the car."

The highway from the mainland runs along the ocean side of the railroad tracks from Key Largo to the Caribbee Colony near the west end of Upper Matecumbe Key. There the road crosses the tracks and continues between the tracks and Florida Bay over solid fill for 2.16 miles to Lower Matecumbe Key. The tracks travel over an embankment that runs down the center of the fill. The embankment commences level with the road and increases in height to nine feet above the road at the midpoint, then descends down to road level at the Lower Matecumbe end. The road surface runs level along the bay side of the embankment approximately eight feet above mean sea level.

After retrieving the time books from Camp Three, Wilbur Jones has to drive back across the fill between Lower Matecumbe and Upper Matecumbe on his return trip to headquarters. The sky has darkened, and driving is becoming treacherous, especially across the fills where there are no structures or vegetation to deflect the wind. The darkness, wind, and rain make it difficult to see the road. Jones recalled: "When I drove down across that stretch of water and on my way back, waves were splashing across the top of the higher railroad embankment down onto the road pavement. It made me drive slowly and carefully."

As George and Rosalind leave Camp Three in Ben Davis's car, the wind is blowing from the northeast with hurricane force, and water covers the highway. The fill between Upper and Lower Matecumbe is pitch-black except for the probing headlights of the Dodge sedan. The tires kick up water, and the wind drives the rain almost horizontally, penetrating any crack or opening in the hood; the Dodge stalls out coming to a stop about midway across the fill.

Another car comes up from behind. The driver recognizes the stalled car as the one belonging to Ben Davis, but he dares not stop for fear of his own car stalling out. For George and Rosalind, there is no choice but to stay in the car. Attempting to walk the remaining mile across the exposed fill to reach Upper Matecumbe in the powerful wind would be suicide.

The train carrying Rosalind's brother arrived in Key West at midafternoon. There the weather was benign, with some rain and clouds but no strong winds. Bascom Grooms Jr. is just in time to make the matinee at the Monroe Theater on Duval Street. Having a fascination with aviation, he sits engrossed watching Wallace Berry and Maureen O'Sullivan in *West Point of the Air*. Bascom and his parents are totally unaware that a real life-and-death drama is taking place on the Upper Keys and of the desperate situation Rosalind and George are facing.

Across town from the theater, train No. 76 has been made up for the evening run to Miami and begins loading. Clara Carey and her sixteen-year-old daughter, Rosalie, are among the passengers boarding the north-bound train. Their two-week visit and Rosalie's dental work completed, they are headed for their home on Upper Matecumbe Key. Before boarding the train, Clara sent her husband, Eddie, a telegram saying they would arrive at Islamorada that night. While they are sitting in their seats waiting for the train to depart, a Western Union boy comes up and gives her a telegram. It is a four-word reply from Eddie that reads: "Don't leave. Weather bad." Clara and Rosalie get off the train and return to Clara's mother's home. Meanwhile, the conductor of the train announces to the passengers remaining on board that a hurricane is crossing the Keys and the train cannot depart until the winds subside. Packed with excursionists who had taken advantage of the low holiday rates, the fully loaded train remains at the station.

South of Miami, the special train requested for the evacuation of the veterans arrives at Homestead at 5:15 p.m. A railway motorcar and line-man are taken aboard. Various other people also board the train including six veterans returning to the camps to collect their personal effects, a reporter named William Johns, and Fred Long, who is going down to look after his boat moored by the ferry slip at Lower Matecumbe.

Homestead was the southern terminus of the FEC Railway before the Key West extension was built and has a "Y" table, an arrangement of track and switches that enable a train to be turned around without using a turn-table. As earlier suggested by Superintendent Pooser, the tender is uncoupled from the cars and the locomotive and tender are turned around on the "Y" table and then run back to the cars, which are coupled to the front of the locomotive.

From Homestead the locomotive will back down onto the Keys, pulling the cars with the tender in the lead. This arrangement will allow the train to pull onto a siding on the Keys where the locomotive and tender can be uncoupled, run around on the mainline, then backed down the siding and coupled to the other end of the cars, thereby placing the locomotive at the front of the train and allowing the headlight to be effective on the return trip.

Loading the motorcar and reversing the locomotive and tender take fifteen minutes. An hour has passed since the train left Miami, and it has only gone twenty-eight miles. Camp Three at the western end of Lower

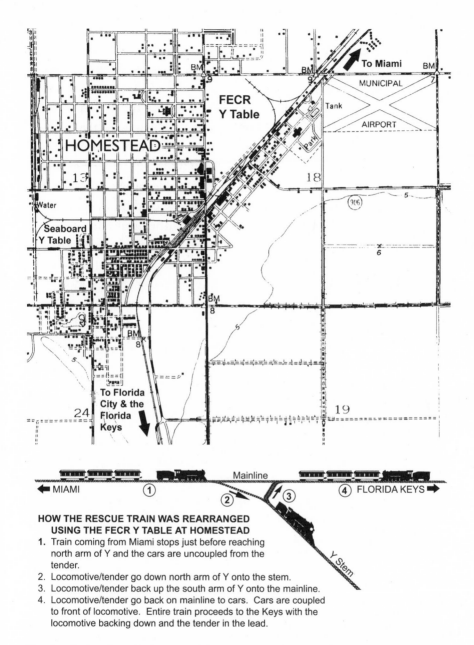

**HOW THE RESCUE TRAIN WAS REARRANGED
USING THE FECR Y TABLE AT HOMESTEAD**

1. Train coming from Miami stops just before reaching
   north arm of Y and the cars are uncoupled from the
   tender.
2. Locomotive/tender go down north arm of Y onto the stem.
3. Locomotive/tender back up the south arm of Y onto the mainline.
4. Locomotive/tender go back on mainline to cars. Cars are coupled
   to front of locomotive. Entire train proceeds to the Keys with the
   locomotive backing down and the tender in the lead.

The Florida East Coast Railway "Y" table at Homestead was used to turn around part or
all of a train without the use of a turntable. A competing railroad (Seaboard) also had
a "Y" table (*middle left on map*) at Homestead. (author)

Matecumbe is twice that distance away. Because the engine is backing down, the fastest speed the train can safely make is 30 mph.

At 5:30 p.m., Ray Sheldon and all other staff at the Matecumbe Hotel headquarters move to the train station at Islamorada in order to expedite the boarding process. Ray Spitz is on duty monitoring the railroad's private telephone circuit. He tells Sheldon the train has just left Homestead.

Southeast of the Matecumbe Hotel between the highway and the beach, the Williams and Law families have hunkered down in an old storm house. The four adults and four children have been in the low structure sheltered by a grove of palm trees for over four hours. Outside the wind howls and palm fronds thrash, coconuts and other objects sporadically bounce off the walls and roof, and the rain pounds down. The picnic atmosphere that initially prevailed had turned to boredom and now has been replaced by a growing fear. At 4:30 p.m. Carrie Law and Mozelle Williams set out an early supper, anticipating that conditions will become worse. Mozelle later described the storm house as "a little house braced in every way that a brace could fit." The building was old, and at 5 p.m. the roof and shuttered windows begin to fail. Eddie Williams musters the group near the back door.

His daughters recalled the events clearly. Elizabeth said: "Daddy went out and drove the 1930 Model A Ford up into a nest of palm trees. It was his car. He came back and took Evelyn out first. By then the wind had blown the windows out, the roof off, and the front door in. We went out the back door." Evelyn recalled: "We couldn't stand in the wind. He sort of crouched and tucked me in and carried me out to the car. He had a time closing the car door. It was just wind at that time. I was screaming the whole time. And then he went back and got the others one by one. By then we had to crawl out to the car."

Elizabeth, Evelyn, their cousin Markelle, and her mother, Carrie, cram themselves onto the back seat. Eddie Williams takes the driver's seat, and Mozelle, holding her seventeen-month-old Bob, sits next to him. There is no room in the car for Mozelle's brother Dan Law or his son, nine-year-old Perry. They take refuge behind a large palm tree and make a handhold by passing their belts around the trunk of the tree and hooking them together. This arrangement allows them to hold on while moving around the tree as necessary to stay on the lee side.

In Key West, the U. S. Navy Radio Station receives a call at 5 p.m. from the Key West Weather Bureau relaying the advisory issued by Jacksonville at 4:30 p.m. Lt. William Kraus immediately has the advisory broadcast to all ships in the Florida Straits. The broadcast is repeated ten minutes later.

At 5:30 p.m., the *Dixie* has spent the last hour transiting the relatively calm waters of the eye when heavy, dark, fast-moving clouds quickly obscure the sun. The wind springs up with a fury greater than that experienced just before the ship entered the eye. The waves that had been hammering the ship on the port side before the calm now pound the starboard side. Captain Sundstrom and his crew on the bridge strain to pickup landmarks or navigational aids. Sundstrom later reported: "I had not seen a light since we picked up and passed the Sombrero Lighthouse. . . . At times I could not see a foot ahead. I have been in hurricanes before—in 1915, 1919, 1926, and 1932—but never in one as bad as this."

The *Dixie* is southeast of the reefs that line the western edge of the Florida Straits. The strong winds have caused the ship to drift west, and her northerly heading is now taking her toward the jagged coral rocks. Captain Sundstrom thinks he is well offshore and farther north than his actual position. No one aboard is aware the *Dixie* is running out of sea room.

Labor Day Evening

By 6 p.m. on Labor Day the center of the hurricane is fewer than fifty miles from the western end of Lower Matecumbe Key. Strong gusts are blowing from the north-northeast across Camp Three. At the ferry slip where the *Monroe County* is moored, Captain Charles Albury and the crew listen to the radio and watch the barometer. It had started falling at 4 p.m. and now is plummeting. From their vantage point in the lounge above the car deck, they can see the hook sponger *Gilbert* at anchor in the wave-tossed channel. She had arrived earlier in the afternoon seeking a safe haven.

After advising the five men in his crew to go ashore and find shelter, the master of the *Gilbert*, George "Muggins" Albury, along with Frank Harris and Walter Russell, go aboard the ferry. Also taking refuge on the ferry are a veteran assigned to Camp Five, Karl Cordell; a veteran from Camp Three, "Jersey" Corlin; a Matecumbe fisherman, Bruno Ellison; and others.

The *Monroe County* is moored with heavy hawsers securely attached to strong steel pilings. As the winds pick up, the people on the ferry leave the relative comfort of the elevated lounge for the cramped but much safer spaces below the main deck. It would be hard to find a more secure place to ride out the storm than inside the reinforced steel hull.

The space below the car deck is normally inhabited only by the engineer Louis Cruze and his assistant. With Louis is his father, John Cruze, who works as a dockhand at the Lower Matecumbe ferry slip and had come aboard to visit with his son when the ferry tied up. In all there are twenty-one people crowded among the engines, fuel tanks, pumps, and other equipment.

As driving rain and windblown waves wash over the boat, water trickles inside, prompting Louis to secure the hatches. At first the air is just thick with the smell of oil, fuel, bilge water, and other odors typical of an engine room in a working vessel. With so many people in a closed-up space, the air rapidly becomes foul.

Nearby, George Kelly has loyally stayed at his post at the office by the ferry slip. As the winds increase and debris begins to pound the small shack, the former ferryboat captain, along with a forty-six-year-old veteran from Camp Three named Elmer Krietsburg and two other veterans, flee to Cardy Bradford's diner.

At Camp Three, most of the men are in the mess hall with the camp superintendent, Ben Davis. The train is already an hour late. The mess hall is one of a few all-wood buildings at the camp that has been holding its own; but it is beginning to creak and groan as the intensifying wind continues to blow unimpeded off Florida Bay. When the roof of the mess hall begins to come off, most of the men follow Davis over to Cardy Bradford's store.

At the Alligator Reef lighthouse, Keeper Jones Pervis and first assistant James Duncan are inside their metal-walled living quarters. The barometer that had started falling at 2 p.m. now takes a dramatic plunge from 29.00 inches at 6 p.m. to 27.84 inches at 6:30 p.m. The wind is howling through the structure, and waves crash against the pilings supporting the lighthouse as the men climb the enclosed spiral staircase to the watch room. The small room is just below the glass-enclosed space housing the lamp and Fresnel lens. As they climb the ladder to light the lamp, the red sector panes on the northeast side of the lighthouse explode inward from the wind pressure, and a fusillade of shards of ⅜-inch-thick laminated glass destroys the lamp and lens. The men quickly close the hatch and scurry down to the living quarters. There they watch in horror as the steel outer doors begin to bulge inward.

To the west at Long Key, James Duane, caretaker of the fish camp and cooperative weather observer, dutifully takes his 6 p.m. readings with great difficulty. He notes the barometer is reading 28.04 inches and falling. Heavy rain is coming down and the wind is out of the north at hurricane velocity. The seas are now very, very rough. Although the hurricane is approaching from the ocean side, he observes the water rising on the

bay side. All he can do is write the information down because the telephone lines are down.

Forty-five minutes later, the needle on Duane's barometer has dropped
to 27.84 inches. An 8-inch square beam eighteen feet long that had been
in a storage area is picked up by the wind and hurled three hundred yards
into Duane's house, nearly killing him and two others. The house is completely wrecked. The air becomes filled with flying timbers of all sizes,
propelled like spears and heavy rams flung by giants. The wind begins to
swing to the northwest, which Duane correctly interprets to mean that
the center of the hurricane will pass to the north of the fish camp. The
water on the bay side is within three feet of the top of the railroad embankment, which is now functioning as a dam. It has risen sixteen feet!

The special train from Miami with its locomotive backing down
crossed over the drawbridge at Jewfish Creek and moved onto Key Largo
at 6 p.m. The wind is blowing at gale force by the time the train passes
through Tavernier at the south end of the island. Rain beats into the open
cab of the locomotive as J. J. Haycraft and G. R. Branch peer over the back
of tender, trying to see the road ahead. It is dark as a moonless night.
The headlight is of little help since the locomotive was turned around in
Homestead and its lamp now faces the cars connected to the front of the
engine. At about 6:30 p.m., the train crosses over the Snake Creek trestle
and onto Windley Key.

Windley Key is basically a solid coral rock formation, making it unfit
for farming. The ease with which the rock can be accessed and the fact
that it can be dug some depth before salt water intrudes interested the
railroad builders, who established a quarry on the island to supply the
large quantities of crushed rock that were needed to stabilize the railroad
fills.

Once the railroad's needs were satisfied, the quarry continued in operation, mining large blocks of coral that were sent to the mainland, where
they were cut into slabs and polished to produce an attractive stone facing
for buildings. A hoisting gin was erected near the FEC Railway track to
facilitate loading the blocks onto flatcars for the trip to the finishing plant.
The gin has a mast stabilized by long heavy cables.

As the special train comes abreast of the quarry, one of the hoisting
gin's 1½-inch-thick cables suddenly appears out of the mist and rakes

At Windley Key, blocks of coral rock were lifted from the quarry onto railroad flatcars by means of a hoisting gin. The derrick was made from heavy timbers spliced together and held in place by thick cables anchored in the coral rock. The dark mass at the top of the gin is an osprey's nest. (FPC)

across the top of the tender. Haycraft later recalled the harrowing moment: "A gravel pit boom line, which usually hangs high above the track, was sagging, and we backed into it at about 10 miles an hour. The line was high enough to slip over the tender but struck the back of the cab and almost cut Trainmaster G. R. Branch in two. I put the air brakes on. Since it was dark, I didn't know whether we had had a wreck, a washout, or what. We might have been at a bottomless pit, it was so dark."

Before the powerful locomotive can be stopped, the strong cable wedges into the cab's steel frame with such force that the wire is welded to the frame. The locomotive is caught tight and cannot break free. The lineman and crew struggle in the 65-mph wind and stinging rain to remove the snagged cable; it is not an easy task, and precious minutes tick away. While the train is stopped, six veterans who had taken refuge in the rock quarry and the Cale family board the train.

Charles Cale (36) and his wife, Alice (23), had seen the glimmer of the train's headlight. Charles operates the rock quarry with Lewis Moore, Alice's brother. When he realized the storm was approaching, Charles drove his car between two palm trees on the high ground next to the quarry and lashed it down. Alice and he have a six-month-old son, and they were not about to take any unnecessary chances with his safety. The family was in the car prepared to ride out the storm when they saw the train's headlight and decided it would be prudent to evacuate on the train.

At 7 p.m., the Jacksonville Weather Bureau issues another advisory. By this time, advisories are of no value to anyone on the Upper Keys. Earlier the men at the hurricane center believed the storm had been skirting the northern coast of Cuba when it made a sharp turn to the north, taking it toward the middle of the Florida Keys. The wording of this advisory indicates they now expect the hurricane to continue turning and proceed north along the east coast of Florida.

Jacksonville, Fla.
Advisory, 7 p.m.—Hurricane warnings ordered 7 p.m. north of Key Largo to West Palm Beach and northeast storm warnings north of West Palm Beach to Titusville and storm warnings continued elsewhere south Florida coast Titusville to Sarasota. Tropical disturbance, hurricane intensity, approaching Matecumbe Key, appar-

ently moving north northwestward with recurving tendency will cause winds of about hurricane force over extreme southern Florida and strong winds over central Florida late tonight or early Tuesday morning. (U.S. Congress, *Florida Hurricane Disaster Hearings*, 211–13)

At the Long Key Fish Camp, all of the people have gathered in the main lodge. Duane and his companions watch as the barometer continues to fall. Flying timbers are beginning to wreck the two-story lodge; it shakes with every blast of the wind. Water has now reached the level of the railway tracks on the north side of the railroad embankment and threatens to inundate the camp. Wind gusts are timed and found to hold their strength for a full ten to eleven minutes.

Back on Windley Key, heroic efforts by the train crew finally free the train from the hoisting gin's cable. After a delay of one hour and twenty minutes, Haycraft releases the air brakes and eases the throttle forward; the train begins to move again. As it crosses the Whale Harbor fill, the train is fully exposed to the wind. Fortunately the wind is blowing almost parallel with the engine and cars. Haycraft can see little of the track up ahead with the engine turned around and the headlamp facing the first car. In the darkness and heavy rain, they roll onto Upper Matecumbe, the massive locomotive pushing its tender ahead and pulling the trailing cars, the whole affair looking like some strange creature crawling over a water-drenched landscape.

By 7 p.m., the tanker *Pueblo* has been without her engines for five hours and is eight miles southeast of her 2 p.m. position. The storm nourished by the warm waters of the Florida Straits has intensified and is now a Category 5 hurricane moving directly toward the helpless ship. The seas have become exceedingly rough as the storm's center moves to within sixteen miles of *Pueblo*. The crew continues to watch the plunging needle on the barometer. The *Pueblo*'s aneroid barometer has a scale with the lowest reading on the dial being 27.80 inches of mercury. The needle moves lower and lower until it is finally off the bottom of the scale. When it stops falling, the lowest excursion is marked on the glass cover with a grease pencil. Two weeks later, the Weather Bureau at Galveston, Texas, determines that the mark indicates a reading of 27.18 inches. Lying helpless in the path of a very powerful hurricane, the *Pueblo* seems doomed to certain destruction.

On this day the *Pueblo* is a lucky ship. The hurricane's winds push her aside into the southern, less dangerous region of the tropical cyclone. For the next three hours the *Pueblo* rides around the center as if on a carousel, staying just outside the eye wall, where the devastating winds are concentrated. As the ship is swung around the backside of the storm and enters the northern region of the hurricane, the *Pueblo* gradually spins out of her dangerous dance.

By 10 p.m. the *Pueblo* is out of the grasp of the storm, but she is not out of danger. The ship is now only seventeen miles off the reefs east of Key Largo. With the passage of the storm, the wind is coming from the southeast, and the *Pueblo* is being carried toward Molasses Reef. The rough seas have made work on the engines extremely dangerous and arduous, but the crew manages to get the engines running, and the *Pueblo* pulls away from the reef and the hurricane just in time. After ten hours of being at the whim of a powerful hurricane, the tanker is only twenty-nine miles northeast of its original position and has miraculously suffered no major damage. The *Leise Maersk* and *Dixie* are not as fortunate.

The *Leise Maersk* is a tramp steamer and is smaller than the sleek liner *Dixie*. Today the ships have one thing in common; they both sailed into the worst hurricane their masters and crews had ever experienced. Captain Richard Mortensen remembers that for him and his crew aboard the *Leise Maersk*, tangling with the hurricane in the Florida Straits quickly became a dangerous situation:

> We left New Orleans on the 30th of August and headed for the Florida Straits, never expecting to run into a hurricane. Everything was going along smoothly until Monday afternoon at 2:30.
>
> The Florida Straits are always dangerous, even in the best of weather, but it is even more dangerous in times of hurricanes. We knew that the hurricane season was on, so we were worried when the storm first hit us. There was nothing to do but attempt to ride it out. If we had been out in the ocean it would have been easy, but in the Straits there is no place where we could turn without hitting a reef or a sandbar. The steadily increasing gale drove us slowly towards the shore.

Unlike the *Pueblo*, which was directly in the path of the storm and, being without power, was swept around the south side of the hurricane, the *Leise Maersk* is north of the hurricane's center and is caught in its most dangerous quadrant. The ship is assailed by the strongest winds of the hurricane. It is a nightmare become reality for Captain Mortensen: "The wind velocity was so great that my clothing and that of a member of the crew was stripped from us. We were left almost naked. The waves smashed our equipment and the ship was in darkness. Our bridge was smashed, boats torn away, and the whole ship was littered with wreckage. We lost both top masts. The crew was helpless. Men were thrown about until every soul aboard was groggy."

On board the *Dixie*, Captain Sundstrom thinks his ship is near Carysfort Reef, but the coastal steamer is actually about thirty-eight miles to the south. The *Dixie* entered the eye of the hurricane at 4 p.m. When the ship emerges on the north side of the storm at 5 p.m., the winds resume blowing with ferocious intensity. The passengers and crew are flung about by the blasts of wind and crashing waves. Marie Shields (25) of Highland Park, Pennsylvania, found it impossible to stand up. She later said: "We were tossed against walls and we were told to stay in the music room. People just clung to objects. The officers and crew tried to reassure us, but by night we knew we were in deadly peril."

Newlyweds Lorraine and George Weatherby are in the music room, which is now a cluttered shambles of wrecked furniture. They have their life preservers on and struggle to avoid injury from the violent motions of the ship. "It was lurching so badly that the jerks snapped table legs in the dining saloon," wrote Lorraine.

Most of the passengers abandon their staterooms and stay in the spaces in the superstructure. The situation below decks is very unpleasant at best and treacherous at worst. Devona Doxie, a radio singer, thinks the ship has sunk. "We had a cabin on C Deck on the *Dixie* and the portholes stayed underwater so long that we thought we were trapped. Water poured into the stateroom. It backed up from the bathroom and rose level with our beds."

Edward Rommel is in his berth when water pours in through the porthole. He struggles to get it closed and then is thrown across the cabin by a sudden lurch of the ship. A steward is able to work his way into the disheveled room and shouts to him to put on his life belt and get out. "As

I did so, I heard a woman scream, 'Save my baby!' I had been panicky, but that scream steeled me and after that I tried to help others and forget my own fears."

The lights have been turned off in order to prevent short circuits. The companionways and passageways are no longer innocuous stairs and hallways, but are now dangerous trails in a dark maze of caverns. Slimy water backed up from toilets and drains sloshes about. The interior of the luxury ship has been transformed into a dank, black labyrinth filled with terrible odors and vile liquids that heave with unpredictable and violent motion like the disturbed bowels of some monstrous sea serpent.

When the stateroom that Herbert Shprentz shares with his mother begins to flood, the lad grabs his stamp collection. Sensing the gravity of the situation, the eight-year-old asks his mother if he will be able to collect stamps in heaven.

Carl Calman, the musician who was worried from the beginning of the voyage about protecting his $750 violin no longer has anything to worry about; the instrument is smashed beyond repair. Dr. Sandor Lorand, a prominent New York psychologist, said he was so engrossed observing the other passengers that he did not have time to become frightened. "When they strapped on their lifebelts they showed hysteria. Life and death were written on all their faces," he later reported.

Martha Mayo, a Broadway actress who appeared with Will Rogers in his most recent stage production, *Ah, Wilderness!* is returning from visiting her mother in California. She fights her way to the music salon and is immediately thrown against some heavy furniture. "Someone grabbed my hand to support me. I heard a priest praying for us."

Captain Sundstrom tries to make his way across an exposed area going from the bridge to the after deck. As he crosses the sun deck, the part on which he is standing is blown away. Frantically groping for something firm to hold onto, he grabs an awning brace and saves himself from going over the side. He manages to get back to the bridge, but the fifty-year-old man has suffered injuries to his back and both ankles. Ignoring his injuries, he stays on the bridge.

James W. Hodges, the *Dixie's* senior chief wireless operator, knows the ship is in danger and knows that he cannot call for help should it become necessary because the long wire antenna that was strung between the stack and aftermast was lost at 3 p.m. Since then the wind and violent seas have made it impossible for Hodges and the junior wireless operator Richard O. Schroeder to rig an emergency aerial. Henry Treger, a passenger from Plainfield, New Jersey, stops by the radio room to offer his services to Hodges. Treger works for the National Broadcasting System as a transmitter engineer at radio station WJZ. His offer is promptly accepted.

At 8 p.m., the *Dixie* is about twenty-eight miles northeast of the center of the hurricane and is experiencing sustained winds of 109 mph, with gusts of 135 mph. Treger and able seaman Heinze Lahmeyer volunteer to rig an emergency antenna. Because of the wavelength of the transmitter (565 kilocycles), the antenna has to be a long wire stretched horizontally as high up as possible. This requires one man to climb up the smokestack and another to climb up the aftermast to secure the ends of the wire to their respective mounts.

Treger had booked passage on the *Dixie* "just to be doing something different this summer." The voyage was to become one of his most memorable experiences. "I climbed the chimney stack to help get the antenna rigged and never expected to get down again safely. The wind fairly burned me, and I had to grope blindly about the work."

It took three attempts, but finally in the darkness, with heavy seas tossing them about and high winds threatening to blow them off their perches into the water at any moment, the men rig the wire and come down without suffering significant injury. With the antenna rigged, Hodges can concentrate on getting the transmitter and receiver working. It is a good thing. Time is running out, and Hodges will soon need to send the dreaded SOS.

Harry Boyer at seventeen years old was the youngest man undergoing military and meteorological training at Fort Myer in 1881.
(Grooms)

Top left: The Boyer family in Savannah; Rosalie, Harry, Beulah, and Viola, ca. 1905; *top right*: Bascom, Beulah, and Rosalie in Key West, ca. 1912; *bottom left*: Bascom Lovic Grooms in his conductor's uniform, ca. 1905; *bottom right*: Rosalie Boyer Grooms with her children, Rosalind and Bascom Jr., 1924. (Grooms)

Top: The Dept. of Agriculture Weather Bureau building located at the corner of Front and Eaton streets in Key West, 1920. *Bottom left:* Harry Boyer shows his granddaughter Rosalind Grooms the instrument cabinet, ca. 1915. *Bottom right:* Harry and Beulah Boyer on the grounds of the Weather Bureau building, ca. 1930. (Grooms)

Rosalind Grooms and her brother, Bascom Jr., on August 21, 1934, the day she married George Palmer. (Grooms)

Rosalind Grooms Palmer is believed to have been wearing this ensemble on Labor Day 1935. (Clark)

On one of their trips to Miami during the spring of 1935, Rosalind Palmer and George Pepper went to a studio and had these pictures made. The bottom photo suggests where their relationship was headed. (Grooms)

Above: George Pepper in Key West, 1935. He told Bascom Grooms Jr. that he received the scars on his right cheek during a swordfight. George's sister said the scars resulted from a dog that attacked him when he was a youngster (Clark). *Right*, Bascom Grooms Jr., 1934. (Grooms)

George Pepper (*left*) was nineteen when this picture was taken in Key West. His demeanor and a receding hairline allowed him to easily pass as being twenty-five. (Clark)

The men seated on the orange crates in this 1948 photo were Florida's political power brokers. *Left to right*: U.S. Senator and former governor Spessard Holland, U.S. Senator Claude Pepper, Governor-elect Fuller Warren, and Governor Millard Caldwell. Claude Pepper's political career began in 1928 when he was elected to the Florida legislature and ended when he died while serving in the U.S. Senate at the age of eighty-nine. (FPC)

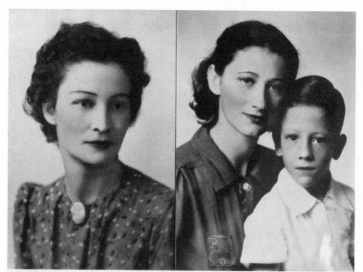

Left, Elizabeth "Betty" Carter King; *right*, Leone Carter Carey and son, Bob, ca. 1937. (Carey)

Left: O. D. King and his brother (dark trousers). O. D. was a master chef and an effective restaurant manager when he was sober. *Right*: John Carter poses with his sister Karlie. John was a plumber in Coral Gables and was very strong. (Carey)

Karlie and Charles Carter had ten children. He operated the pumping station at Islamorada in 1919. (Carey)

Five of the Carter children stand beside the railroad track on Upper Matecumbe Key in 1919. Left to right: Lillie Belle, Karlie, Leone, Charles Jr., and Betty. The Florida East Coast Railway provided a house (upper left) for the pumper and his family. This photograph was taken from the back of a train that stopped to take on water. It is one of a few family photographs that survived the hurricane in a leather album. (Carey)

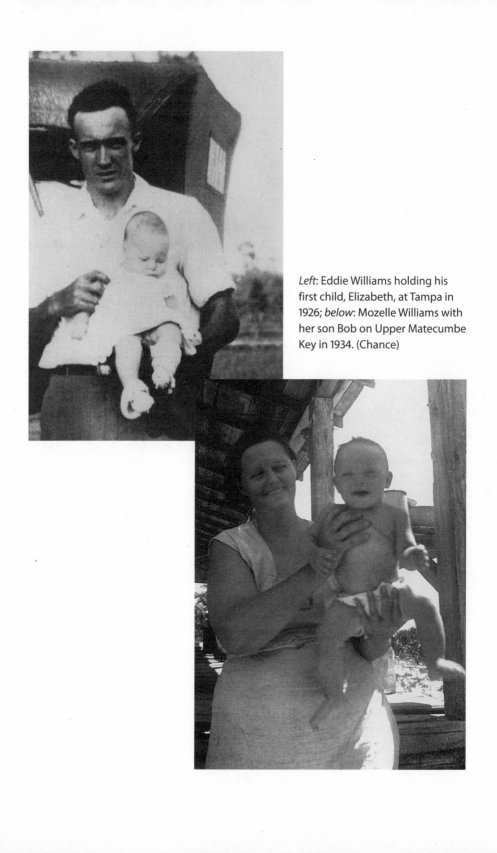

Left: Eddie Williams holding his first child, Elizabeth, at Tampa in 1926; *below*: Mozelle Williams with her son Bob on Upper Matecumbe Key in 1934. (Chance)

Right: Dressed in their best, Elizabeth, Evelyn, and Bob Williams are almost ready for Sunday School. This photograph was taken during the spring of 1935. *Below, top*: Many adventures were had using the old skiff. Elizabeth walks toward the shore as Evelyn prepares to climb over the side and cousin Paul Saunders helps his brother Cecil. *Below, bottom*: Mozelle Williams, Grandma Bea Williams, Aunt Virginia Saunders, Jack Saunders, Elizabeth Williams, Paul Saunders, and Evelyn Williams standing outside the house on Upper Matecumbe Key rented by Eddie Williams until he finished building the house on the fill, 1934. (Chance)

Top left: Henry Reno was a crime reporter for the *Miami Herald* who was trusted both by the mobsters and the police. *Top right*: Jane Wood was a highly intelligent young woman with a degree in physics who, as a social worker, interviewed many of the veterans at the camps on the Keys. *Above*: Henry often fished the waters off the Upper Keys in his boat, the *Vagabond*. *Right*: Henry and Jane met when she went to work for the *Miami Herald*. They were married in 1937. (Reno)

Top: Walter Bennett joined the Weather Bureau in 1890 at the age of twenty-one and had a career spanning forty-nine years (NWS-Jacksonville). *Bottom*: The Federal Building in Jacksonville, Florida was built in 1931. The Weather Bureau was on the top floor. (FPC)

Top: Grady Norton at the Miami Weather Bureau in 1948. He managed the hurricane center at Jacksonville. *Bottom*: Gordon Dunn was Norton's assistant at Jacksonville. Later in his career he became the meteorologist in charge of the Miami Weather Bureau succeeding his friend and colleague Grady Norton. (NOAA)

Left, Helen Muir (Muir); *below*: The Miami Daily News Tower. (FPC)

The Surge

Part 1

At 8 o'clock on Labor Day night the lighthouse on Alligator Reef is being savaged by the right-hand front quadrant of the hurricane, where the most intense winds of the Category 5 hurricane are concentrated. The wind shrieks as it goes through the iron framework, and the entire structure shudders as massive waves pound the reef. The three people manning the lighthouse were barely able to secure the doors to the first assistant's room, where they took refuge after an unsuccessful attempt to light the lamp at the top of the lighthouse. The sound of the wind is deafening until 8:10 p.m.; then the noise dies down as the wind and seas subside.

Keeper Jones Pervis, first assistant C. Turner, and second assistant James Duncan cautiously open the metal door and emerge onto the platform that surrounds the living quarters. Damage to the lighthouse is extensive. At the top, the thick laminated glass panes that normally provide a protective shield around the lens and lamp have been blown away. The Fresnel lens, a masterpiece of glass craftsmanship, has been completely destroyed. The watch room below the lens is littered with glass and pieces of metal, and everything is thoroughly soaked. The metal doors to the keeper's and second assistant's rooms are bent inward.

The rowboat has been washed away, but the motor launch is still in its hoist. No one says anything about leaving the lighthouse at this time; they know this is not the peaceful end of a violent storm and that more is yet to come. The barometer indicates 27.30 in. and then begins to pump violently between 27.30 and 27.40 in. The atmospheric pressure gradient is so deep that only thirteen miles to the northeast at Tavernier the barometric readings are an astonishing 1½ inches higher.

Duncan goes down onto the lower platform of the lighthouse to check for damage. Things are relatively calm for the moment so he decides to have a smoke. The sky has lightened since they are in the eye near its northern perimeter. He leans against the rail and feels wafts of air as the wind begins to pick up. He later tells Edney Parker: "Edney, I looked up and there was a wave coming at me that I fully believe was ninety feet high. I barely made it to grab hold of the ladder when it broke over the light, and how I held on and why I wasn't drowned I can't say. Then the wave went on. The three of us in the light spent the rest of the night sitting on the stairs halfway up to the top of the light."

When the storm surge went over Alligator Reef, the water welled up and around the 135-foot structure. Although the *Leise Maersk* is fewer than two miles away on this stormy night, neither the men in the darkened lighthouse nor the men on the *Leise Maersk* see each other, which is just as well because there is nothing they can do to help each other.

Captain Mortensen knows the wind and surging water is driving the *Leise Maersk* toward the reef. In a desperate attempt to stop the careening vessel from being smashed on the rocks, he orders the anchors let loose. The anchors have no effect. As long as a football field and weighing over 6.2 million pounds, the ship rides the crest of the huge swell over the jagged coral shoals and into Hawk Channel. As the anchors rake across the bottom of the channel, they snag a Western Union submarine telegraph cable. The cable is ripped from its bed and pulled apart, sustaining damage so extensive that over a mile of it will have to be replaced. The destruction of the cable absorbs the ship's momentum and it comes to rest on the mud flats of the channel's bank a mile southeast of the Islamorada train station. Remarkably, the hull has no punctures and the crew, though dazed, will ride out the hurricane safely aboard the stranded ship.

Off Key Largo, the *Dixie* continues to slug its way through the rough seas. For twelve-year-old Eleanor Shields, the massive waves and awesome display of power being put on by Mother Nature is a show not to be missed. She is traveling with her adult sister Marie. Eleanor, who has a streak of stubbornness, wants to be out on deck and is going to be out there no matter what! She later recalled: "We knew early Monday that we were going to run into some rough weather that night, and when I insisted on staying on deck to watch the waves, one of the stewards tied me to a deck chair. I was in the chair when the *Dixie* struck the reef."

At 8:12 p.m., Mrs. C. H. Colgin of Brownsville, Texas, is on B Deck and sees an elderly lady who appears to need assistance. As Mrs. Colgin walks toward the woman, she hears a loud thud and the ship stops for an instant; the kindly Mrs. Colgin is thrown across the deck into an open hatch, fracturing her ankle.

To Anna Chambers of New Orleans, the ship reacted like a wounded animal. "The sound was horrible, even above the roar of the wind and the thunder of waves. A crunching, grinding sound, and the *Dixie* shivered like a live thing that had received a death wound."

Two minutes later, there is another shudder as the *Dixie* runs hard aground on French Shoal, about 15 miles south southwest of Carysfort Reef.

"A bouncing thud and scraping of the plates as if the ship was jouncing along a huge washboard awakened me to the fact that we had struck something," said Leo Sumner of New Jersey.

"It was the most thrilling experience I've ever had," said Miss Clara M. Shaffer, the winner of a recent popularity contest in her hometown of Tarentum, Pennsylvania. "When we hit the reef, they told us to grab something solid and lie down. We stayed that way for several hours and then everyone was sent to their staterooms for life preservers."

At 8:16 p.m., the *Dixie* starts sending the distress signal SOS. The radio receiver is not working so there is no way to tell if anyone is receiving the message. James Hodges works the key with a professional's rhythm, hoping someone will pick up the call for help and home in on the transmitter with a radio direction finder. Three dots, three dashes, three dots—the radio frequency pulses race up the saturated wiring and onto the makeshift antenna that emanates a feeble signal. It will go undetected for over an hour.

The *Dixie* is lodged on the reef with heavy waves pounding her hull and an unrelenting wind beating upon the superstructure. Captain Sundstrom leaves the bridge and circulates among the passengers, reassuring them that they are safe on the sand bar. Joseph Lombardo recalled, "When we hit the reef and the captain told us we were in the sand, we were all greatly relieved." What Captain Sundstrom does not tell them is that the layer of sand is of unknown thickness and beneath it is hard coral rock, rock that can easily pierce the metal hull of the ship. After a while, water begins to seep into the *Dixie's* double bottom.

The great swell that put the *Dixie* on French Shoal and the *Leise Maersk* on the muddy bank of Hawk Channel was part of the storm surge, a massive dome of water that is typically pushed ahead of the front right-hand quadrant relative to the path of a hurricane. In deep water away from land, the dome is not constrained and the elevated water is indiscernible among the waves. As the water surges ashore, its height can increase many times its open sea height.

The formation of the mound of water and its position are the result of many factors at work within and around the hurricane. One is the atmospheric pressure. If the atmospheric pressure is constant over a body of water, the surface of the water is level; however, if the pressure is lower in one area than it is on the rest of the body of water, the areas of higher atmospheric pressure will push water up into the area of low pressure until the weight of the raised water equals the force caused by the difference in pressure.

During good weather, the normal atmospheric pressure at sea level is around 30 inches of mercury. If a low-pressure area exists such as at the center of a hurricane, for every one-inch difference in atmospheric pressure, the water will rise thirteen inches. The central pressure of this hurricane was measured at 26.38 inches at Craig: a pressure that would generate a dome of water almost four feet high in the open sea. It is likely the pressure was even lower just before the storm made landfall.

If a hurricane did not move, the dome of water would stay in the center of the storm where the lowest pressure occurs. The forward motion of a hurricane causes the dome to lag into the eye wall, the area where the surface winds have greatest velocity.

The surface winds interact with the mound of water and create currents that cause the dome to move and remain intact. The effect of the water's viscosity, the earth's rotation, and spiraling high-speed wind streams moving across the surface push the dome out into the right-hand quadrant of the storm. Given enough open deep water and other favorable conditions, the surge can pick up momentum and move well ahead of the center of the storm. The storm surge in this storm had just formed as the hurricane came across the Florida Straits and had not had time to move very far forward of the storm's center.

When the storm surge approaches land, various factors can affect the severity of its impact and the height of the water as it sweeps over the

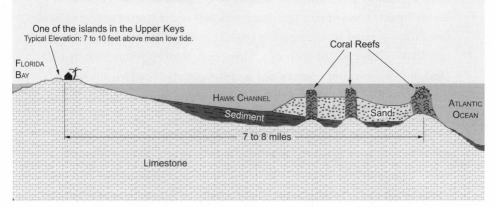

This cross-sectional view shows the gentle slope of the sea bottom from the islands of the Upper Keys to the reefs. Vertical dimensions have been exaggerated in order to show the features of the reefs. (Modified version of graphic obtained from the U.S. Geological Service)

shore. One of these is the angle at which the storm surge approaches the shoreline. An angle less than 90 degrees causes the storm surge to be confined between the land and the storm's leading outer edge, which can result in a funneling effect producing higher water and more severe damage. This hurricane approached the Keys at an angle of approximately 60 degrees. The path of the storm in relation to the arch of the Keys was such that the mound of water rode over the islands north of Craig at approximately the same time, about 8:23 p.m.

Another factor is the sea bottom leading up to the shore. A sea bottom that gradually slopes up to the shore forces the water upward as it moves toward the shore. The rapid change in depth at the face of the reef would have caused water to well up along the reef, resulting in the large wave observed at the Alligator Point lighthouse. Once over the reef, the mass of water moved into Hawk Channel then followed the gentle slope of the bottom for four to seven miles up to the shore.

One of the worst conditions for storm surge occurs when tidal flows caused by the gravitational pull of the moon act upon the dome of water and literally pull it toward the shoreline. Such was the case when this hurricane arrived at the Florida Keys. When the storm surge passed over the

Keys, the moon was exerting its maximum tidal pull, moving water from the Florida Straits into Florida Bay, the same direction the storm surge was traveling.

There was also another factor that initially directed the rising water onto the islands. The railroad fills between the Keys were solidly constructed, with a center core of sand, rock, and marl covered by an outer layer of marl. Marl was dredged from the shallow sea bottom along the railroad's route. A mixture of mud and coral rock that is plastic when dredged, it becomes a hard, solidified mass somewhat like cement. In its hardened form, marl has the ability to resist the erosive forces of waves and tide. The fills were constructed so that the elevation increased from the ends to the midpoint, with the midpoint being as much as ten feet higher. The fills not only blocked the natural water passages between the Atlantic Ocean and Florida Bay, but their design directed surging water around the fill and onto the lower, adjoining islands.

The mound of water slowed and grew in height as it crossed the sloping bottom of Hawk Channel. The storm surge stretched a distance of twenty miles from the western end of Lower Matecumbe Key to north of the train station at Tavernier on Key Largo, and maintained a peak height of seventeen to eighteen feet above mean sea level over most of this span. In a period of fifteen to twenty minutes, huge amounts of seawater poured into shallow Florida Bay, spreading west toward Cape Sable and north into the Everglades. Some of this excess water was swept south toward Long Key.

The storm surge did not come ashore as a towering wall of water collapsing tons of water onto objects in its path, but was characterized by a rapid rising up of water upon which a succession of smaller waves were superimposed. Alonzo Cothron experienced the event on Upper Matecumbe Key and provided one of the most detailed accounts of the behavior of the storm surge.

The water started coming up over Upper Matecumbe about 7:30 p.m. that evening. And by 8:30 p.m. there was about 15 feet of water above the normal high water level. I had my watch and flashlight and noted the rise.

By 8:30 p.m. the water covered the whole key. It was about five feet over the railway track at that time. And then the fill across Whale Harbor must have been washed away about that time because from then on the water fell so rapidly you could actually see it going down. The wind was still blowing at its full intensity but by 9:30 p.m. we were standing on solid ground again. I don't believe it was more than 10 minutes before the water had dropped from where it was neck deep to where it was ankle deep. When it went, it went fast. I never saw the water drop so rapidly in my life.

There were powerful forces at work as the mound of water moved across the land and into Florida Bay. As the water level rose and immersed objects, anything that could float, including houses and railroad cars, was subjected to hydraulic lifting. Homes that had withstood the fury of the wind were wrenched off their foundations, boats were pulled out of their moorings, and metal tanks and drums popped loose from brackets, shooting upward like rockets to the surface. There was also the kinetic force exerted by the mass of the water as it moved from the ocean to the bay; it was the same force that carved the Grand Canyon. The momentum of the moving mass of water stripped the land clean, bulldozing structures and anything else in its path.

The solid fills between Upper and Lower Matecumbe and between Upper Matecumbe and Windley Key could not withstand the tremendous pressure of the water and burst apart; natural channels that had been blocked for almost thirty years were blasted open by the torrent in a matter of minutes. That any living thing could survive such an onslaught is incredible, and yet a surprising number of people in harm's way lived to tell about their experience that terrifying night.

Shortly after 8 p.m. on Labor Day, the Upper Keys are feeling the full fury of the hurricane's most powerful winds. At Snake Creek, the sustained winds blow from the northeast, ranging from 126 to 132 mph, with gusts much higher. Harold Langlois (44) and six other veterans are standing in one of the shacks at Camp One when the water begins to rise up through the floorboards. The water gradually rises until it is up to their armpits. As the shack begins to float off, Langlois goes out into the storm and wades through the salt water toward the highway. It is dark and the wind and rain blind him. He finally crawls up onto the railroad embankment. As he lies down, a piece of wood smashes into his leg, destroying his kneecap. Another windblown object breaks his arm in two places. Somehow he holds onto the track.

Further west at Islamorada, a small crowd has gathered at the train station. Among the group are the station manager, Ray Spitz, and the men who had come up from the Matecumbe Hotel headquarters to meet the special train, including Ray Sheldon, John Good, Wilbur Jones, deputy sheriff Louis Malone, and three veterans.

Judge C. Marvin Thompson and his two brothers run to the station after Judge Thompson's home starts to come apart. Marvin's title derives from his service as justice of the peace from 1927 until 1934. Born in Key West in 1900, he moved to the Upper Keys in 1919 after a failed romance soured his taste for the Island City. He worked hard and bought property on the Upper Keys. He was positioned to make a fortune in the real estate boom and was in the process of subdividing his land to place it on the market when the boom collapsed in 1926. His brothers Robert and Anthony are both deputy sheriffs.

The train stations built on the Keys were designed and constructed to withstand the onslaught of hurricanes. The station at Islamorada had successfully withstood many previous storms, but this hurricane was different. The sustained blasts of wind begin to take their toll, and by 7 p.m., the structure shows signs that it is weakening. An hour later, the southwest wall of the station starts to shake. Fearing the building will collapse at any moment, the men decide to abandon the station and make a dash for two boxcars parked on a nearby siding. One is loaded full with sacks of concrete; the other is partially loaded with forty 55-gallon drums of oil. The wheels of the boxcars are immobilized with wood blocks. The boxcar with the oil is brand-new, and its door on the bay side is unlocked. As the station starts to come apart, the fourteen men run for their lives and scramble into the unlocked boxcar.

They enter the boxcar on the lee side. Wilbur Jones recalls that little could be seen through the open door except rain and the debris being blown over the car. The wind howls and objects bounce off the car, but its stout walls protect the men. At 8:15 p.m., someone shouts that he sees a flashing light through the heavy rain. Ray Sheldon looks out and deduces that the flickering glow is from the special train's headlight. Sheldon and Sam Perdue, one of the veterans, exit the boxcar, as does John Good and another man.

Sheldon and Perdue make their way around the boxcar and run to the train that has stopped only fifty feet away. At first there is no standing water on the ground, but by the time they reach the locomotive, water is up to their waists. They climb up into the cab of the engine. In the cab are Haycraft and Branch, along with the fireman Will Walker and the conductor J. E. Gamble. Sheldon checks his watch using the lamp over the engine's gauges; it reads 8:20.

Branch later recalled they had not encountered any water over the track until they reached Upper Matecumbe:

> First water we could tell we were in was when we stopped at Islamorada. I instructed the engineer to stop at the depot to see what conditions were and let Miami know where we were. It was storming so badly that he didn't see the passenger station and I called to him that he was passing the depot and he stopped two or three cars south of the station building. I told him to back up, which he did, and just as he stopped Mr. Sheldon and another gentleman came to the engine. Mr. Sheldon asked me what I thought our chances were of going to Lower Matecumbe. I told him I could not say, but thought we could get through if we could get water in the locomotive [makeup water for the steam engine]. I doubted if any man could stay on top of the tank long enough to get water in the locomotive, but suggested we might form a chain of about 10 men and try it. I wanted first to communicate with Miami. Sheldon told me I couldn't, that the wires had been out since about 6:30.

Sheldon tells Branch about the men in the boxcar on the siding. Branch suggests that they go back and check on them, but the weather is so bad that Sheldon rejects the idea. They wait for five minutes to give the men a chance to board the train. Then Sheldon tells the engineer to head for Camp Three: "I told the engineer to head south. There was something said about taking on water, but the tank for the water was south of Islamorada, was in the direction that we were going. The engineer manipulated the levers. As I looked out the door I thought we were traveling too fast.

I told him to slow up or we would go off the track. As a matter of fact, it was simply the water going by the locomotive and we were not moving."

Haycraft had moved the lever that releases the air brakes, but the brakes did not release. Nothing happened. The train would not budge. Realizing that this problem can be caused by one of the air hoses between the cars becoming disconnected, Branch and Perdue decide to investigate and climb out of the cab onto the catwalk attached to the side of the locomotive's boiler then enter the car coupled to the front of the engine. Branch later recalled his determination to get the train down to the veterans camp:

> I suggested that the boxcars must have blown over and went back to see about them, and did so over the protest of the train crew, and was accompanied by the man who got on the train—the engine with Sheldon. We succeeded in getting through the first coach and went on through the train to the rear and found the boxcars turned over behind the baggage cars; and by that time the water had risen to the level of the coupling between the cars, preventing our separating the cars. We started back, thinking we would endeavor to cut the baggage cars off behind the rear coach by opening a vestibule door on the other side, but we found the baggage car in front of us turned over, which trapped us in the baggage car until the storm subsided.

The surge of water that turned the baggage car on its side also put out the fire in engine's boiler, disabling the locomotive. There was nothing Ray Sheldon or the people in the cab could do but to look after their own safety. Sheldon recalled:

> The next instant there was another wave which went over the cab floor and shut off the draft to the oil burner, and there we were. Now, we all grabbed what we could to hold on. The windows in the locomotive had been broken. It really was no protection except that you had your head up against the roof of the cab. There was no other protection. I stood on the seat, holding onto a channel bar and a valve over my head. The water was sufficiently high at times to hit me in the knees, back of the knees, and there were times that

we were unable to breathe due to the water breaking over the loco-motive.

According to Haycraft, chaos raged around the men crowded in the lo-comotive's cab: "The safest place we could find was the west corner of the cab, the only one that had [unbroken] windows. Gamble [the conductor] got in the corner, the Negro fireman, Will Walker, and I crowding around him. Bits of debris blew through the cab, but nothing hit us. The water rose to the top of the 'drivers,' the biggest engine wheels, that is about seven feet from the ground, and big waves came over us time after time, almost drowning us."

William Johns, a reporter who had boarded the special train in Home-stead, later wrote: "I was in the smoker in the last passenger car when the wave hit. The car crashed over on its right side and water poured in the broken windows on the ocean side. I grabbed a seat and hung on while the water poured in. Somehow I got outside the smoking compartment and lay against the side, a few inches from a broken window through which water, coconuts and debris poured in."

Wilbur Jones and nine other men remain in the boxcar where they had taken refuge after fleeing the train station. Through the open door they see water suddenly covering the ground and quickly rising. The car begins to lean over on the side with the open door. As it does so, water wells up through the opening. Jones, who is a good swimmer, thinks that if things really get bad inside he will dive down and swim out from under the boxcar. The water continues to rise, and the boxcar leans farther over. The water rises to the men's waists and then to a level where they must tread water to keep breathing. Some of them cannot swim and thrash about in desperation. The others pull the nonswimmers over to where the oil drums are secured, pushing some drums out to make room for them. The boxcar begins to move, floating, bumping along, then settles on its side; Jones's escape route is now blocked. They do not know if they have drifted to sea and sunk to the bottom or if they are still on land.

Three deputy sheriffs are in the group. One of them pulls his pistol out and says he is going to try to shoot the lock off the other door, which is now above their heads. A clear shot is not possible because the lock is out of sight on the outside of the car and is shielded by the door's metal latch and a layer of thick wood. If the bullet strikes metal there is a high probability that it will ricochet or shatter, either of which would likely injure or kill the men struggling to keep their heads above the water. For these reasons his comrades strenuously object to the deputy's plan, and he finally abandons it.

Water continues to fill the interior of the boxcar, and now there is only a bubble of trapped air just big enough for their heads. Had the boxcar not been new and tightly sealed, the air would have escaped and they would have surely drowned. They are in total darkness except when one or another of the men turns on his flashlight, and then in the dim yellow light Jones can see the faces of the men around him stricken with panic and terror as they gasp for air in the small void.

The water level rises and falls, almost as if death is toying with them. After fifteen minutes that seem like an eternity, the water recedes and does not come back. A flashlight shined at the open door reveals they are still on land and not at the bottom of the bay, but the boxcar is laying flat on the door opening, and there is not enough clearance for a man to crawl out. They remain trapped and have no idea if there is anyone left alive outside who knows of their situation.

At Islamorada in the vicinity of the train station, the top of the rails was 8.9 feet above mean sea level. The U.S. Army Corps of Engineers later determined that the water sweeping over the island reached a maximum height at Islamorada of 18 feet above mean sea level. According to Haycraft, the engineer of the special train, the water rose up to the top of the locomotive's driver wheels, which on No. 447 were seventy-three inches in diameter. On top of that, successive waves were superimposed that inundated the men in the engine's cab. One or more of those waves carried the water four feet above the top of the driver wheels. The whole island was inundated with waves cresting almost ten feet above the ground at the point of the highest elevation.

On Windley Key next to Snake Creek, forty people are inside the two-story wood frame building that serves as a hospital for the veterans. About half are veterans who fled the adjacent camp when the hurricane began to blow away the flimsy canvas and wood tents that made up most of the structures. There are also seven women, some accompanied by children. The group includes Frenchy Fecteau, a veteran assigned to Camp Five, and his family, who were stopped by armed deputies before they could cross the Snake Creek Bridge.

At 7:20 p.m., the people in the hospital see the headlight of the train as it crosses Snake Creek. T. F. Russell, a deputy sheriff, decides to move the refugees over near the tracks so that they can board the train as it makes the return trip. He does not realize that the train has become snagged on the quarry's hoisting gin cable. Russell later described how, as the wind howled and debris pelted the walls of the former hotel, he tried to organize a human chain over to the nearby tracks:

> The storm was getting worse all the time and the winds kept increasing in intensity. We talked among ourselves, and I suggested that the others at the hospital should join in forming a whip by linking hands. I told them I would lead the whip in an attempt to make the railroad crossing so we could get on the train when it passed again going north. It was about 150 to 200 feet from the hospital entrance to the railroad track.
>
> I opened the door and the water outside was waist deep. When the women saw the water they went into a sort of panic and were afraid to leave the hospital.

Another deputy sheriff, Dan Loper, and his wife agree to go with Russell. Russell is in the lead, holding one of Mrs. Loper's hands while her husband holds her other hand. More people join in, and a human chain begins to form.

As Frenchy Fecteau emerges from the building to join the chain, he is swept away. "I swam back as quickly as I could and reached shore just as the hospital collapsed. I heard my wife calling my name, but I was unable to get to her in time." Fecteau's wife, Frieda; his teenage daughters, Marie Madsden and Dorothy Vester; and young grandchildren, Ray Madsden and Dorothy Vester, die when the building falls down on them.

Mrs. Loper glances back and sees the building collapse. "As we were leaving I looked back, and it seemed to me the hospital jumped about a foot off the ground." The cables that tied the building down, one set of which was defective, apparently snapped, and the two-story building shot upward due to the hydraulic pressure of the surging water.

Dr. Lasser Alexander is inside the building with Dr. Daniel Main when it collapses. Alexander is the medical officer at Camp One, and Main is the medical director of the veterans camps in the Keys. As the building comes apart, Alexander sees Main killed by falling timbers.

Dr. Alexander said later: "When the building toppled over, I was able to walk out through a hole in the wall into about three or four feet of water filled with floating timbers and debris. The wind was about 50 or 60 miles an hour and carried flying timbers that caused most of the casualties." Alexander leaves the wrecked hospital and heads for the railroad embankment. Wading through the water, he walks about 150 yards and is knocked down many times by flying timbers. For a while, he and some other men take cover behind a four-foot-high block wall, but the rising water forces them to move: "When we found the water still rising, we made our way to the railroad track. Placing ourselves behind the grade, we dug holes into the earth under the cross ties so we could protect our heads from flying debris. This was the only way we could find to keep our brains from being crushed out."

Eight miles southwest of Snake Creek, Melton Jarrell is at Camp Five on the northeast end of Lower Matecumbe when the entire camp is demolished. Sixty veterans jump into trucks and head across the exposed fill toward Upper Matecumbe; they are never heard from again. As the water starts to rise, the remaining men try to make their way to Camp Three at the other end of the island 3½ miles away. When the water surges, some climb into trees or grab onto anything they can reach; others are washed out to sea. Jarrell recalled making it to the railroad embankment and hanging onto the track: "A heavy sea came along and washed it [the track] up and as it settled back down it pinioned my left leg under it. After lying there for what seemed countless ages, suffering horrible agony I decided to try to cut my foot off but I couldn't get to my penknife. After that I passed out." When he regains consciousness, Jarrell is in a mangrove bush and rides out the rest of the storm frantically holding onto its branches. He is one of only twelve survivors of Camp Five.

Near Camp Three adjacent to the ferry slip, Cardy Bradford's store and restaurant starts to come apart; those inside make a dash for shelter elsewhere. As Elmer Kreitsberger goes out the door, a broken piece of a two-by-four is driven into his chest and protrudes out his back. Captain George Kelley and two veterans help Kreitsberger, with the board still in him, into a nearby car. As the storm surge passes over the car it partially fills with water and bounces around. The men stay in the car, and the water recedes. Krietsberger, who survives the night and is awake most of the time, dies at six o'clock the next morning when the board is pulled out of him so that his wound can be bandaged.

On a siding near Camp Three, about seventy men cling to a tank car full of freshwater. The storm surge wrenches the tracks and ties of the mainline up from their bed and twists them like a ribbon. A segment is pushed against the heavy tank car, causing it to lean a little. The men grope for anything to grab; it is hard to hang on. Gusts of wind pick up grains of sand and blast the skin off fingers or other exposed parts of the body. Splinters and rock ballast shoot through the air as lethal as bullets. Many of the men are only partially shielded by the metal tank; the weaker ones gradually let go and are swept into the mangrove bushes down by the shore. Some of these manage to grab onto the tops of the tough plants and are able to save themselves, while others are carried into Florida Bay and never seen again.

"Matecumbe," some sources say, is a corruption of the Spanish phrase "matar hombre," which translates to "kill a man." According to Spanish lore, the islands were so named because they were notorious places where Indians killed or enslaved crews of shipwrecked sailing vessels. On the night of September 2, 1935, they became a killing ground once more.

The Surge

Part 2

Upper Matecumbe Key is an island about four miles long and less than a half mile across except at the ends. The island stretches southwest to northeast with a relatively straight shoreline on the ocean side and an irregular shoreline along Florida Bay. At each end the land swells out so that the island taken as a whole looks something like an elongated dog bone.

In the 1880s when the early settlers filed homestead claims, their charters divided the habitable land of the island into four sections, each having approximately 165 acres and extending from the bay side to the ocean side. The easternmost section was known as "Islamorada" and extended from Whale Harbor southwestward including the area where the train station and post office were located in 1935. Mary Ann Russell, who migrated with her husband from the Bahamas and settled in the Upper Keys in 1854, filed this claim. In the spring of 1935, there were over fifty people comprising this clan of Russells who resided in the area. One of the most prominent members was the postmaster, John Augustus Russell.

The next two sections southwest of Islamorada were claimed by two brothers, Cephus and Adolphus Pinder, descendants of Richard and Sarah Pinder. Their claims included the area around the Matecumbe Hotel that locals often referred to as Pinderville. The 1935 census listed twenty-three Pinders as residing on Upper Matecumbe Key; Jerome Bramwell "Brammie" Pinder is a respected elder of the clan.

From Pinderville to the southwest end of the island is Parkerville, where the family of William Henry Parker homesteaded. Parker was originally from Eleuthera in the Bahamas and migrated to Key West. Sometime after 1887, he moved his family to Plantation Key and then relocated them again to the southwestern end of Upper Matecumbe where they grew soursop, watermelons, tomatoes, sweet peppers, and pineapple. In the 1935 census, there were fifteen people recorded as having the Parker surname living on Upper Matecumbe. The father of most of these was Edney Parker, a man known for his pragmatism.

Most of the homesteading families built their homes on the ocean side either directly on the beach or close to it. They were strong wood-framed structures built on piles standing four to five feet above grade that had survived many hurricanes. The houses often began as modest one-story buildings with additional space being appended as a family's size and economic resources increased. As a result, most of the houses had multiple peaked roofs joined together. Sometimes, instead of expanding horizontally, the roof was raised to create a 1½- or 2-story building.

The families tended to be large in order to provide the labor needed to farm and fish, the primary sources of income. As the parents died off and their estates were distributed to their children, the concentration of holdings by clans became somewhat diffused. For example, Edna Pinder married Edney Parker and brought her inherited Pinderville land into the Parker clan. In some cases, significant tracts were sold to mainland investors. Such was the case with the land where the Caribbee Colony was built on the southwestern, or Parker, end of the island.

While the Russells, Pinders, and Parkers continued to be major landowners in 1935, other families had acquired substantial holdings on Upper Matecumbe Key. James Edwin "Eddie" Carey was one of these hardworking people.

During the afternoon on Labor Day, Eddie takes his barometer and goes to one of his wood-frame cottages located near the beach southeast of the Rustic Inn. There he is joined by his son Franklin (28); his daughter Ellen Moore (19); her husband, Lewis (20); another son, Charles (24); Charles's wife, Maude (27); and their children Rose (8) and Beverly (2). Eddie's other son Everett is in Miami, where his ailing wife has been in the hospital since Saturday.

In the late afternoon, Eddie receives a telegram from his wife saying she and their daughter Rosalie are boarding the train in Key West to come home. By now the squalls are becoming more frequent and the wind is blowing with some strength. After sending a short message telling Clara not to leave Key West, Eddie returns to the cottage and begins checking his aneroid barometer frequently.

The barometer reads something just over 26 inches a few moments before the walls of the cottage begin to collapse. As the walls sway, the family tries to get out, but the doorframe is twisted and the door will not open. Lewis Moore smashes it down, and the group flees toward one of the other cottages. Eddie carries his barometer with him. On the way, he is hit in the head by flying debris that stuns him, but he does not loosen his grip on the barometer. Lewis Moore, who is leading the way to the cottage, sees Eddie stumbling and goes back for him. Moore later described the scene: "All of us managed to keep together so far, and had reached the other cottage and entered it when it blew over on its side. Almost trapped, we fought our way out, with the water lashing over our heads at times. We went into another cottage 10 feet from that one and no sooner had gotten into it and see that we were all together, when it went to pieces." The moving water disintegrates the cottage and pushes the family out into the maelstrom.

Lewis Moore and Ellen become separated. He and Franklin Carey survive without serious injury. Ellen is found after the storm floating on a board with lacerations and bruises, naked except for one shoe. Charles Carey, his wife, and their two children are not as fortunate; their bodies are found later in the debris. Eddie Carey is swept over to the highway near his grocery store. He still clings to his barometer, even in death. When Clara Carey returns from Key West, she will find nothing where her home had stood except an eroded sand ridge next to the beach.

During the hurricane, Clara's niece Carolyn Lowe is in a house near the Carey's home. Carolyn Royce Curry was born in 1915 in Key West. The daughter of Frank and Myrtle Curry, her father was a butcher and her mother is Clara Carey's sister. When she was a child, Carolyn lived with her grandparents Ellen and Johnnie Thompson on Lower Matecumbe and attended school at Islamorada. After finishing the eighth grade, the highest grade taught at the school, she went back to live with her mother in Key West to continue her education and to enjoy more social opportunities. Carolyn said coyly, "I went back to Key West when I started to take an interest in boys."

Cyril Harvey Lowe lived nearby and used to take a shortcut across her family's yard. Cyril was 3½ years older than Carolyn. He was known by the nickname "Baby," as was his father, Harvey Lowe. Cyril did not take a fancy to Carolyn at first. In fact, she said he hated her until he was sixteen, and then he fell in love with her. After a courtship of five years, they married in 1932. A year and a half later, they had their first child, a son they named Frank Harvey Lowe.

In August 1935, Cyril, Carolyn, and their son moved to Upper Matecumbe Key because work was scarce in Key West and Cyril, who loved to fish, had found employment as a fisherman in Matecumbe. Cyril was a handsome twenty-three-year-old, well built and trim with dark brown hair and blue eyes. Carolyn, with her blond hair, brown eyes, and slim build, was an attractive twenty-year-old. Described by his mother as a "nice, big, fat, baby," Frank was almost two.

Until they can get settled, the Lowe family is staying at the home of Cyril's stepfather, Brammie Pinder (61), and Cyril's mother, Mary "Mamie" Pinder (45). She married Brammie after Cyril's father died.

The Pinder home is located on the ocean side of Upper Matecumbe Key at the end of the road that runs by the Matecumbe Hotel to the beach. The house is a one-story wood-frame structure with white lapboard siding; it faces the ocean. Spacious for those days, it has three bedrooms, inside plumbing, a wood-burning stove, and an icebox. Ice is delivered from the ice plant in Florida City. They have no telephone or radio; the nearest ones are at the Matecumbe Hotel. Carolyn said that people who had a radio then were considered to be very fortunate. Brammie does have a barometer.

On Labor Day, the Pinder home is full of family looking forward to a pleasant time together. Two of Mamie's sisters and a nephew are visiting for the holiday. Ruby Baker (Mrs. Robert F. Baker) drove down from Miami with her son, Billy, on Friday. Ruby is in her early forties. She and Billy plan to stay for a week. Billy (William F. Baker) is eighteen and works as a bookkeeper at the First National Bank in Miami. He is unmarried and very well liked by everyone. Mamie's other sister, Winnie Curry, is forty-eight and unmarried. She works as a saleslady at a shop in Key West and arrived by train on Saturday.

They had read about the hurricane in the Sunday edition of the *Miami Herald*, but took that "with a grain of salt" for over the years there had been many hurricane warnings issued, and few turned out to be relevant to the Upper Keys. Although the article said the Weather Bureau thought the hurricane would pass south of Key West, when the barometer started dropping they shuttered the house and made preparations just as they had always done in the past. Carolyn said they had no idea the storm would be as bad as it was and did not think of going to the mainland. Sometime between 8 and 8:30 Labor Day evening, they had finished eating supper and were all in the kitchen doing dishes and talking when the wind really started to blow.

Carolyn is wearing navy blue slacks and a pullover, a knit pale blue blouse, and tennis shoes. Cyril is wearing a blue chambray shirt with dungarees and tennis shoes. Without warning, water bursts through the front door and gushes through the house. Carolyn and Cyril are standing next to the kitchen table; he is holding the baby. Everyone is pushed out the back of the house by the force of the water. Carolyn loses consciousness. When she wakes up she is lying on the ground in a lime grove on the bay side of the train tracks.

Through a haze of pain and the drumming rain, she can hear Cyril searching for her in the darkness, calling her name. When she tries to move, the pain is so great she almost passes out again. Even trying call back to Cyril hurts; she has broken her ribs. Soon he locates her. As Cyril draws near she can see his clothes have been shredded like hers. He has some cuts and bruises, but it is what he does not have that sends a spear into her heart. Her husband is not holding their baby, Frank.

Cyril has a strong spirit and is not given to being emotional, but when he sees her, his relief in finding her alive is quickly replaced by grief as he tells her in a breaking voice that he had been knocked unconscious and when he woke up Frank was gone. All they can do is gingerly cling to each other, their sobs obliterated by the wind, their tears washed away by the rain. They stay in the lime grove through the long night.

On Labor Day afternoon, Edney Parker was given a warning that this storm would be different. In addition to being constable, he had signed on as the sanitation officer for the veterans camps. It was in this role that he had driven up to Camp One at Snake Creek to help tie down loose materials and equipment. When preparations for the storm were completed, he climbed into his motor pool pickup truck and started for home. Along the way, he picked up his son-in-law Jack Ryder. Jack and Edney's daughter Yvonne have a home in Islamorada.

At this point, the truck is carrying a good load. Jack weighs 240 pounds, and in the bed of the truck is a heavy 55-gallon drum filled with insecticide. As the truck negotiates the highway running along the ocean side of the fill between Windley Key and Upper Matecumbe, a strong gust of wind hits the vehicle. Edney later recalled: "When I crossed Whale Harbor fill, a puff of wind blew that truck, Jack, drum and me off the road, almost in the water, before I could get it back on the road. That was the first I realized what a wing-ding jackass of a hurricane this one was going to be."

After dropping Jack off in Islamorada, Edney goes home and tells his wife, Edna, this storm is going to be different from the others. Their house is right on the beach on the ocean side close to the shore, so close that his daughter Fay said she could "practically jump off the front porch into the water." They decide to move the family over to a recently constructed cottage behind her brother Brammie Pinder's house about a half mile away. Edney and his sons batten down the windows and doors of their house.

The Parkers gather up their things along with some food and move over to the small wood-frame bungalow that is the home of newlyweds Eddie and Etta Sweeting. Etta is the Parkers' third eldest daughter. She and her husband are over at Eddie's grocery store getting it ready for the storm when her family arrives at the cottage. There are seven men in the group, including Edney (48), his sons Nolan (22), Sam (13), Franklin (11), Earl (6), and Norman (3), and another son-in-law, Austin Reese (22). Austin is married to Edney's daughter Janice (21). She is one of five women in the entourage, the others being her mother, Edna Parker (52), and her sisters Lois (16), Fay (6), and Barbara (11 months). The Parkers' other daughter, Yvonne Ryder (19) is with her husband at their home in Islamorada.

Janice and Lois start preparing stewed fish for supper. Around 6 p.m., the wind is blowing and squalls are coming across the island with increasing severity. Etta (17) and her husband, Eddie Sweeting (22), arrive with Eddie's brother Alton (18). They had decided it would be safer to stay at the cottage than in the two-story grocery store. As Fay and Earl watch in awe, the elevated water tank that serves Brammie Pinder's house comes crashing down. Edney and the other men secure the shutters over the windows and batten down the doors of the cottage.

Supper is served, and all sixteen people eat what will be their last warm meal for the next two days. Outside, the wind begins to scream. After the meal, Janice makes a large pot of Cuban coffee and, as is customary, hangs the bag with the grounds on a nail placed in the wall for that purpose.

The room where the meal is served is crowded so Janice, Austin, and Nolan go into another small room. Edna sits in a rocking chair, overwhelmed by the shrieking of the wind that grows louder with each passing minute. Around 8 p.m., Edney tells Eddie they should take the battens off a window and move Edna over to Brammie's house. Edney checks his barometer, tapping the glass cover with his finger; the needle does not budge, remaining on 26.55 inches. Fay said, "they took the battens off a window and turned around to get my mother sitting in the rocking chair and the roof went off and the water came in busting out the windows."

The kerosene lamps go out, and they are in total darkness as water pours in over the roofless walls and through the broken windows. The water level inside the house rises, reaching the windowsills and beyond. Janice begins to panic as the water quickly immerses her up to the neck. Nolan sees the fear in the eyes of Janice and her husband, Austin. He later recalled picking them up: "I had my sister in this arm and my brother-in-law in my other arm; they were short people and they couldn't swim so I was holding them up out of the water." Then the house lurches and breaks free of its foundations. The water drains from the cottage as it begins to float.

When Austin turns on his flashlight, they are amazed to see that the house has become a strange-looking raft. The wood floor is awash, and the exterior walls are gone as is all the furniture except for a heavy cast-iron bed frame that has a leg caught in a hole where one of the studs pulled out.

Edney grabs his diminutive wife and places her on the bare metal bedspring, and the other women crowd around her. The men grab hold of the side rails and ends of the bedstead and hang on, hunching over the women to protect them. Edney feels a bump and finds two mattresses that have floated up. He grabs one and yells to the other men to grab the other mattress and pull it up over themselves for protection against flying debris.

The house bobs up and down; there is no question they are afloat. Edney figures that with the wind coming out of the northeast they are being blown into Hawk Channel south of the island. The rain and wind-blown seawater is so intense that they cannot see where they are.

After about an hour the wind suddenly moderates. It never quite stops blowing, but there is a definite lull. Then, as Edney later related, something strange happens: "There were two minutes in that lull that I think if they had been drawn out to three minutes, none of us would be alive now. We breathed and got no air. We gasped and our lungs got no good of it. Before the storm broke, there had been some thunder and lightning, but there was none during the hurricane. But there were balls of fire in the air during the lull. Suddenly here and there, all around, they would appear and be gone in the instant." Another man not with Parker family also observed balls of fire, describing them "as big as a five-gallon tin."

As the storm surge moves inland on Upper Matecumbe Key, O. D. King; his wife, Betty; her sister Leone; and Leone's son are in the kitchen of the Rustic Inn. Gilbert Thompson, O. D.'s friend and beer-drinking buddy, is with them.

The Rustic Inn is an all-wood structure located on the highway southwest of the Matecumbe Hotel and several hundred feet from the beach. It is shielded on three sides by lime groves and a stand of mature gumbo limbo trees. The building has wood shutters that normally tilt out and act as awnings, but are now closed and secured by battens. Like most buildings in the Keys, the inn is not tightly sealed, and the wind whistles through cracks around the windows and doors. They have purposely left the windows on the lee side open to equalize the internal pressure and let the air flow through; otherwise, the air pressure would steadily build and a sudden gust could cause the building to explode.

Leone is still recovering from her illness and is frail. When water starts to come into the building, O. D. and Gilbert clear off the top shelf of the pantry and push Leone and her three-year-old son onto it. Leone is petite, so she and her son almost fit into the cramped space. To keep them from rolling off, Gilbert, O. D., and Betty stand beside the pantry with their arms raised so they can brace Leone and her son. As the surge of water builds, it floods the restaurant until it floats off its foundations. The building rocks to and fro, and every time it sways Leone thinks she and her son will be thrown off the shelf into the water.

For Betty King, standing in the water beside the pantry in total darkness with her arms raised to keep her sister on the shelf is an especially trying time. The water feels warm and gradually rises until it is up to her armpits. At one point, she feels something in the water nudging her and screams: "There's something touching me! Something's trying to move me! Something's bumping me!" The wind is so loud Leone can just barely hear her. O. D. said after the storm that it was a body that had floated into the building. He said he just pushed it back outside.

Unknown to the group in the kitchen, a veteran from Camp Three, Joseph Crusse, has taken refuge in the seating area at the front of the inn. This was an addition to the original building, and when the structure comes free of its foundation, the seating area breaks off. Weighing less than the main building that contains the kitchen, the addition is more buoyant. As the portion he is in floats, it appears to Crusse that the water level remains constant. He later recalled: "It seemed to me the water just came up there and stayed level all the way through. It got about knee deep in the store. Then it went back down."

The mangled main building floats around the gas pumps and would have been swept away except that a corner of the structure catches on the sturdy limbs of a gumbo limbo tree. The snagged inn is spun completely around by the torrent and gently deposited on the other side of the gas pumps, severely damaged but with the floor, walls, and some of the roof somewhat intact. When the water subsides, Leone and her son are finally taken down from the shelf. She is bruised from holding him so tight for so long but is otherwise all right. Sections of the roof decking have blown away so they all huddle in a corner to try and stay out of the wind and rain as much as possible.

Several hundred yards east of the inn between the highway and the beach, Eddie Williams's 1930 Model A Ford is wedged between two coconut trees. Eddie; his wife, Mozelle; and their young son Bob occupy the front seat, while their daughters Elizabeth and Evelyn, and Mozelle's sister-in-law Carrie and her daughter Markelle are crammed into the back seat. Evelyn said her father anticipated the rising up of the water and prepared them for it: "He told us what was happening and what to expect; he had been through these things before. He told us that the water would be coming up, and he tore the [cloth roof] lining and tore it out and there was wire up there, and he told us to hook our fingers around the wire, and when the water came up to pull our heads up as close to the roof as possible. The water was warm, real warm, each time that it surged in." Elizabeth recalled how terrifying it was for them:

> It was raining and blowing still, and the car was rocking. We were out of the wind, but the water was extremely warm. Timbers and debris were washing up under the car and would lift the car some. Each surge of water filled the car, and we had to hold our heads up to the roof to keep from drowning. My little brother was seventeen months old at the time. A time or two Mother thought that he had drowned. She had to hold his head up.
>
> The water in the car surged. Came up and went down, came up and went down, and each time it surged, more debris was piling underneath and around the car. By then, the debris was the houses that were being blown down.
>
> Daddy said, "Stay in the car and do not get out!" And when the water started coming in the car, I was so desperate I opened the door and I was floating away. It was like a nice comfortable dream—I was just floating away. Somebody grabbed me by the hair and pulled me back—Daddy put me back in the car.

Eddie Williams had been through many hurricanes and knew very well the dangers posed by windblown objects and rising water. He knew better than to go out into the storm, but sitting in the car with his family worrying that at any moment something may break through the windshield or rip open the roof was not easy. As the bands of rain and wind came across the island, there were moments when the wind was less ferocious. Elizabeth recalled that her father tried to go for help: "Daddy said he saw a light. He got out of the car. We were just packed in there. He said he saw a light and thought it might be a boat or house or something that would bring some help. He got out of the car and went to go get help, but never did find who it was as far as we know. He had to get back in the car because the weather was so bad. While he was out, he got hit in the head by a heavy timber of some sort. He was kind of unconscious, but made his way back to the car."

Eddie was not outside the car very long, but when he returned he was not the same. Even nine-year-old Elizabeth sitting in the back seat could tell something was wrong:

Daddy came back and was in the car, but kept saying that he couldn't find the light and that he had been hit. He kept telling mother to help him open the door. Mother kept reassuring him that he was in the car and that he was all right. He said his head hurt. Then he was real quiet for a long time; then he started praying. And that was the last we heard him say anything.

Daddy's head was bleeding real bad and Momma told me to slip off my panties so she could use that as a compress/bandage. Aunt Carrie was in the back seat with us. During the night, Aunt Carrie asked mother did she realize what was happening, and mother said yes.

And all during the night, I kept asking, "Why is my Daddy so cold?"

There was nothing anyone could do to help Eddie Williams. The storm continued to roar around them, piling up debris until they were entombed in the car.

At Islamorada earlier in the day, the Russell clan went through their usual preparations for a hurricane. They battened down their homes on the beach, stowed loose gear, collected valuables, and packed up food and other supplies. John Augustus Russell and his brother James Clifton Russell then loaded up their vehicles and took their families across the tracks to the packinghouse located in their lime grove next to a railroad siding.

The packinghouse easily accommodates the two families and is reinforced with heavy timbers to strengthen its wind resistance. Sheltered somewhat by the lime trees, the building had proved to be a safe refuge during two previous hurricanes.

In addition to being lime growers, the Russell brothers run the Islamorada Post Office, which is located in John's store. John is the postmaster and Clifton is the assistant postmaster. The store is built of coral rock and located on the highway a half block south of the train station. An attached cafeteria caters to train passengers and crews.

With the forty-seven-year-old postmaster are his wife, Emma (46), their son, Bernard (16), and daughters Marjorie Spitz (22), Irene (14), and Rose Mary (7). Marjorie has her four-year-old son with her; her husband, Raymond, is the Florida East Coast Railway agent-operator at Islamorada, and as such he has to be at the station to meet the special train. Clifton

Russell is thirty-eight and his wife, Charlotte, is thirty-nine; their family consists of their sons, Floyd (9) and Glenwood (7), daughters Phyllis (5) and Florine (3), and the latest addition to the family, James (16 months).

As the weather continues to deteriorate, the men secure the packinghouse while the women tend to the children and unpack the food and supplies. It is not long before the wind is blowing hard and debris begins to hit the building. The glass windows are closed and although boarded up, the roaring wind forces air through vents and small openings until the internal pressure is so great that the panes shatter outward and the occupants are menaced by shards of glass striking the boards nailed over the windows and bouncing back into the room.

The Russells now know this is a much more intense storm than any they have previously experienced. The rugged building continues to hold together, but when muddy water seeps under the door, there is great concern. The packinghouse is situated on some of the highest ground on the island, and water has never come into the building. The infiltrating liquid is full of sediment. John reaches down to get his hand wet and then takes a lick; the salty taste confirms that it is seawater, which can only mean that the whole island is being flooded.

The relentless assault by wind and water is too much for the packinghouse, and it begins to show signs of coming apart. John knows that if they remain, the heavy rafters and posts will crush them. He tells the group to line up and form a chain by holding each other's hands. A door on the lee side is opened, and they make ready to leave.

Marjorie Spitz cannot join hands with the others because she insists on holding her son. Bernard tells his older sister to let him hold the boy and for her to hold onto the two of them. Marjorie is adamant and holds tight to the boy as the human chain begins to move out the door.

Outside the packinghouse, it is pitch-black, the noise of the wind is deafening, and the driven rain hits so hard it feels like a sandblaster. A flashlight reveals there is moving water everywhere. On the water's surface, pieces of houses and coconut trees float by. Debris flies through the air. It is an act of desperation to go out into such a wild melee, but there is no choice; the building is beginning to collapse.

Bernard grabs his sister Marjorie, who has her arms locked around her son. He recalled: "I wanted to hold onto him and then she could hang onto me. But she wouldn't do it so I held onto her. And we went out of the building together and once we were outside the wind spun us around and she went one way, he went another way, and I went a different way. I never saw them again."

Struggling to stay afloat, the teenager is swept into a grove of thorny lime trees. Something lodges against his back and pushes him down submerging his head. Just as he thinks he cannot hold his breath any longer, the object pulls away, and as it does, he shoots up to the surface. Somehow Bernard Russell stays alive.

Floyd Russell recalls going out into the storm, but after he is whacked on the head by debris, it is all a blur. Seriously injured, the boy and his father, Clifton, miraculously find each other in the dark tempest and take refuge in an overturned railroad car.

Before the surge came ashore, almost a mile down the track from the Russells' packinghouse, Andrew Booth and his wife, Ruth, are in the sturdy house built by the Florida East Coast Railway for the pumper and his family. It is the same house that holds many happy memories for Leone Barr and Betty King from when they lived there sixteen years before as members of the Carter family; it is the place where their mother, Karlie, played her piano and the trains tooted greetings as they passed.

The pumper's house no longer resonates with the frenetic comings and goings of ten children and two adults as it did when the Carters lived there. Andrew (27) and Ruth (20) are just starting their family. Now it is only the cry of a two-month-old baby that occasionally breaks the tranquility of the home.

Andrew Booth had lived in St. Augustine for many years and then moved to South Florida in 1933. Employed as a pumper by the FEC Railway, he was assigned to Upper Matecumbe Key. There he met Ruth, the daughter of Clarence and Rosie Knowles. Rosie's brothers are the postmaster and assistant postmaster, John A. Russell and Clifton Russell.

The most important thing in Ruth's life now is her baby, Andrew J. Booth Jr.; with a name like that good things were surely in store for him. The only other achievement in her life that came close to her fine baby was the completion of her education at the Monroe Graded School in Islamorada. When she finished the eighth grade in 1932, her mother was so proud of her that she scrimped together the money to buy her daughter a genuine gold ring emblazoned with the letters *MGS* and the school's seal on it. The ring, which even had her initials engraved on the inside of the band, was always on Ruth's finger.

On Labor Day afternoon, the Islamorada station manager Spitz notified Andrew that a special train was coming down to pick up the veterans and he should have his equipment ready to provide freshwater since it would be going right back to Miami. As the day progressed and the weather deteriorated, Andrew began to ponder just how he would manage to get the cumbersome folding spout out over the tender and keep it there in a heavy wind.

That evening, Andrew keeps a lookout for the headlight of the locomotive. The train is late, and the rain and wind are becoming worse by the minute. The sturdy house holds up well in the wind, shrugging off repeated hits by debris, but when confronted with the force of tons of moving water, it is no contest. The water pushes open the door, bringing the darkness inside as it knocks aside the hurricane lamps and sweeps anything in its path out the back toward the bay. The horrific sounds of rending walls and screeching wind are the wicked accompaniment of the powerful, unseen forces set loose that night.

Ruth holds her fragile son with all her might as they are flung outside into the cruel wind and waves. In the dark wetness she feels her legs scrape over things and then nothing but water. She struggles to keep her head and the baby's out of the water. There is no sign of her husband. Her world has become full of blackness and the shrill noise of rushing air punctuated by stinging rain, the splashing of waves and the bumping of unknown objects. She is determined to protect her baby, to fight to the death if need be.

West of the pumper's house, members of the Woods family will also try to protect a young child from being claimed by the rushing waters. James Woods was born in Tennessee around 1881 and as a young man served in the coastal defense artillery. Assigned to Key West, around 1910 he met and married Effie Roberts. After the Great War he retired from military service and the family, which now included several children, moved to Greenville, Tennessee. In 1922 they moved back to Key West, where James worked at the navy yard. Seven years later, when the naval base was deactivated, the Woods family moved to Upper Matecumbe Key. Effie's sister

Camille was already living on the island with her husband, Russell Pinder, and Effie and Camille's father, Robert I. Roberts.

On Labor Day, the Woods family is in a house they rent next to Sweeting's grocery store. James (54), with only a fourth-grade education, is employed as a caretaker. Effie (41) has her hands full in her roles as homemaker and mother of an eighteen-month-old baby girl. Their daughter Dorothy (16) is away getting ready to attend high school the next day. Since there is no local high school, Dorothy is not at home during the school year to help out, but the other daughters, Ruth Lee (11) and Mary Camille (9), do what they can to help with chores and taking care of the baby.

James and Effie's sons, Robert Lee Woods (22) and Charles James (Jimmy) Woods (19), live with them and are commercial fishermen. Jimmy in particular loves to fish and is happiest when he is out on the water. His aunt Camille (34), uncle Russell (37), and grandfather Roberts (74) live in another house down the road.

James, Effie, their two sons, and three of their daughters are in their wood-frame house when the water surges and the house begins to come apart. The roof blows off, and the house starts to tilt over. Jimmy sees a large icebox fall over, smashing his mother against the floor. Thinking his mother has been killed, he picks up his baby sister, Beverly, and makes a dash for the door.

Jimmy holds the baby tight as he runs out of the disintegrating house. The girl's head is pressed against the left side of his face when something hits the other side of her head with such impact that it crushes the skull of the little girl against his head and she goes limp. He is stunned by the force of the blow, and her little body slips from his grip into the turbulent water.

Although dazed, Jimmy can see his other two sisters struggling. He tries to go to their aid but is struck in the back of the head by a metal water tank flung by the wind and falls to the ground becoming entangled in the wreckage of the house. The injury is severe; the back of his head has been laid open. Jimmy later recalled, "That thing hit me and before I passed out, my 11-year-old sister said 'Lord Save Me' and she came through the storm without a scratch!"

On Upper Matecumbe, Windley Key, Plantation Key, and the south end of Key Largo, tragic episodes are taking place that terrible night. Entire families are being wiped out, and in other instances, fathers and mothers are being forced to confront the classic nightmare of parents, "Which child do I save?"

For those within a five- to six-mile radius of Craig, there is a respite coming. The eye of the hurricane contains a circle of calm ten to twelve miles in diameter. Craig, Long Key, and Lower Matecumbe experience the deceptive serenity. There is no way for anyone to know that the massive amount of water dumped into Florida Bay is now being redirected. Constrained by the mainland on the north the excess water is pushed by the wind and hydraulic pressure back toward the islands. Hurakan has yet another card to play: the resurgence.

The Resurgence

The combination of Category 5 winds and massive storm surge took a heavy toll among the people on the islands that night. Hundreds of people of all sexes, ages, callings, and physical conditions were either killed outright by objects propelled by the wind and surging water or were drowned when they became trapped in collapsing buildings or entangled in lime trees or mangrove branches. Others were condemned to a lingering death as a result of being injured or were swept away to sea or remote islands, where they became victims of exposure and starvation. The storm savaged both man and one of his most physically imposing accomplishments, the overseas railroad, and yet its destructive work was still unfinished.

The eye of the hurricane reached Craig at approximately 8:49 p.m. EST. Estimated to have had a diameter of about ten to twelve miles, the center passed directly over Craig with the calm extending to Long Key and Lower Matecumbe Key. It probably was not perfectly circular and may have encompassed the lower end of Upper Matecumbe for a time.

At the west end of Lower Matecumbe Key near the ferry slip, when the calm commences the veterans of Camp Three begin to come out and congregate. Some think the storm has come to an abrupt end. Ben Davis, the camp superintendent, circulates among them and tells them the storm is not over yet, and they must seek shelter quickly before the wind returns. Davis and some of the men proceed to a nearby tank car that is full of freshwater and is very heavy.

The twenty-one men who had sealed themselves in the steel hull of the ferry *Monroe County* had ridden out the first part of the hurricane enveloped in fumes of fuel oil, sweat, and bilge slop. They are desperate for a breath of fresh air. T. L. Adams leaves the vessel and finds the ferry's engineer, Louis Cruze, on the railroad embankment with a badly injured

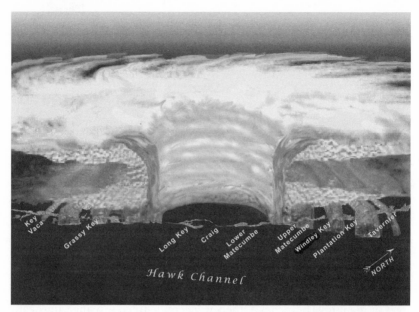

Cross-sectional view of the hurricane as it moves over the Florida Keys into Florida Bay. The storm is moving away from the viewer, toward the northwest. The calm of the eye was experienced at Long Key, Craig, Lower Matecumbe Key, Alligator Reef lighthouse, and the west end of Upper Matecumbe Key. (Based on National Hurricane Center models of hurricane structure and chart prepared by Corps of Engineers, dated October 1935)

arm. Before the calm arrived, Cruze along with Captain Richard "Dick" Albury and Gordon Williams left the vessel to seek shelter elsewhere. Cruze tells Adams he was placed on the embankment by Williams, who has a serious injury to the back of his head and went back to the ferry. With the assistance of Louis's father, Adams moves the injured man to a hut, where Albury bandages his arm.

Captain George "Muggins" Albury and Clarence Jones of the sponger *Gilbert* leave the ferry to go look for their shipmates. They learn that the vessel was thrown onto the beach and the four crewmembers aboard ran to the railroad tracks, where they clung to the rails as the raging water engulfed them. Two of the men, Felipe Perdomo and Joe Lowe, could not hold on and were swept to their deaths. Frank Harris and Walter Russell survived the storm surge.

A few miles from the ferry landing, R. W. Craig, Jack Crowe, and Langdon Lockwood come out of Craig's bungalow and see the stars shining bright and clear above their heads. Craig later said: "The wind fell virtually to nothing. We went out to look at what was left of my buildings on the other side of the tracks. We found—nothing! Not even a scrap of lumber. Everything as clean as if you had swept the floor of this office with a stiff broom. My 200-foot dock had been reduced to three fragments of piling."

Down at the west end of the small island R. G. Jackson and his family leave the bridge tender's house, which had been designed to withstand hurricanes. The steel-reinforced structure located adjacent to the eastern end of the Channel No. Five viaduct is now without its roof, the windows are shattered, and the doors hang listlessly from their frames. Jackson, his wife, and their four children walk a quarter mile up the tracks to Craig's place.

Craig asks Jackson if he thinks it will be safe to stay in the bungalow during the second part of the storm. Jackson says he has been through sixteen hurricanes and this is the worst one he has ever experienced. He warns Craig to seek good shelter for when the storm resumes, it will be as bad or worse than the first part; then Jackson and his family go over to the north side of the small island to take refuge aboard Ivor "Ollie" Olson's boat.

The boat is up on a makeshift ways and tied securely down with steel cables. Ollie Olson and several others successfully rode out the first part of the hurricane in the boat. During the lull, Olson reads his aneroid barometer; the indicator is far below the lowest value engraved on the dial. He notes that it is aligned with the +10 degree Centigrade mark on the temperature scale. When the barometer is subsequently tested by the Weather Bureau, it is found to be accurate and that the +10 degree Centigrade mark on the temperature scale corresponds with a reading of 26.40 inches, the lowest atmospheric pressure ever recorded in the United States and the second-lowest in the world.

Craig, Lockwood, and Crowe decide to try and get to Lower Matecumbe, which is almost two miles away and requires crossing the Channel No. 2 viaduct. By the time they start, the wind has begun to rise again. About halfway to the viaduct, it becomes clear that they will never make it, so they get down on their knees on the north side of the track and dig small foxholes in the ballast under the crossties with their bare hands. As the wind begins to blow with a vengeance, each man burrows in his own hole and waits for the next onslaught.

At 9:20 p.m. on Long Key, cooperative weather observer James Duane notes: "Wind has abated. We now heard other noises than the wind and knew the center of the storm was over us. . . . During this lull the sky is clear to the northward—stars shining brightly and a very light breeze continued throughout the lull—no flat calm."

The lull lasts fifty-five minutes at the Long Key Fish Camp. During that peaceful period, James Duane and his companions move from the lodge to the only cottage he thinks may be strong enough to withstand the remainder of the hurricane. The cottage is known as the "Wahoo" and belongs to an English woman, Lady Ashley, the countess of Suffolk. It cost $25,000 to build and is elegantly furnished with objects d'art. Lady Ashley stays at the cottage only a few weeks each year and was last there during the winter; she is not at Long Key during the storm.

Duane enters in his log, "A section hand reports that a white man, his wife and four children are in an unsafe place a half mile down the track." The man is a section foreman named Rousch. He and his family had just arrived on Long Key that morning after being transferred from farther up the line. Duane notes, "Aid is given them and now all hands, 20 in number, are in this cottage waiting patiently for what is to come."

Midway through the lull, Duane goes out to record weather observations and makes a frightening discovery:

About middle of lull (which lasted a timed 55 minutes) the sea began to lift up it seemed and rise very fast, this from ocean side of camp. I put my flashlight out on the sea and could see walls of water, which seemed many feet high. I had to race fast to regain entrance of cottage, but water caught me waist deep. An idea as to the rapidity with which we were inundated may be gained when it is known that the writer was about 60 feet from the doorway of cottage. By the time I had gained the entrance the water was waist deep as just described. All people inside house now; water is lifting cottage from foundation. Cottage is now floating.

In a letter to Ernest Carson at the Miami Weather Bureau, Duane wrote: " Never will I forget the water raising—no not a wave but looked like the Vacuum drew it right up—Then let it go—raising very, very, very fast—Then it started to Pound."

During the first part of the storm, massive amounts of seawater were dumped into Florida Bay. The bay is a shallow, saucerlike depression bounded by the Everglades to the north and by the long arc of the Keys on the east and south. Because of the hurricane's path and the wind patterns, the excess water becomes trapped between the Everglades and the Keys until the wind and hydraulic pressure cause it to move south. As the storm continues on its northwesterly path and the center passes beyond Craig, the winds swinging around the eye redirect the water back toward the islands.

R. W. Craig holds onto the cross ties under which he and his friends have dug small holes. As the first wave sweeps over the embankment, he feels the cross ties lift, move, and then settle back into place. Submerged, he holds his breath as the impact of debris and water being swept over the rails is transmitted through the cross ties. To his relief, the water quickly subsides, and he can breathe again. The wind screams and then the ground shakes as another wave generated by the shrieking wind comes ashore. This is followed by two more inundations. Sand, splintery debris, and small crabs work their way into his clothing. In total darkness, deafened by the roar of the wind, there is nothing he can do but stay in his hand-dug foxhole, clinging to the cross ties and praying.

At the ferry landing on Lower Matecumbe, when the water begins to come over the railroad embankment again, people scramble for cover. Ferry captain Dick Albury, Louis Cruze, and Cruze's father seek shelter behind an ambulance parked at the veterans camp. Louis has a badly damaged arm and can only use one arm to hold on. Water rushes over them as they hang onto the vehicle. After being inundated several times, a large wave overturns the ambulance and the three men are washed away. Albury does not see his companions again. Adrift, he hangs onto floating timbers for about forty-five minutes and then comes upon and climbs onto an embankment about five feet above the water running out about three hundred feet from the shore. He remains there until the storm begins to abate.

Stanley Key, T. L. Adams, and another man who works at Camp Three take refuge in a car only to find the water rising over the car seats. On two occasions they see waves breaking over the railroad tracks and washing down upon the car in which they are sitting. Most disturbing are the bodies that drift by the car windows. One particularly gruesome corpse has a large stick protruding from its side.

During the first part of the storm, when the roof blew off his diner and store, Cardy Bradford ran out and jumped into the car his father had left parked in the garage built on top of the concrete cistern. Other people sought refuge in the car until there were seven people and one stray dog inside. The garage blew down and covered the car. After the lull, the wind blows the wreckage of the garage back the other way, and in so doing creates a shield that deflects flying objects. The car becomes completely covered by sand and debris, further protecting those inside.

Many of the people who had been in Bradford's place when the roof came off ran from the disintegrating building and took shelter by clinging to the lee side of a tank car full of freshwater. Others grab hold of the railroad track. Ben Davis, one of those holding on to the tank car, recalled the scene: "I watched the water coming in on us from the top of the tank car. It was at least 25 feet high and completely submerged us [the men on the top of the tank car] with approximately 5 feet of water. . . . Men were washed from the track as the track was completely torn up by the water, and the men on the tank car were saved by the track falling against the side of the car."

Off the south shore of Upper Matecumbe, the situation of the Parker family seems hopeless; they are still adrift on the wreckage of the wood-frame cottage that was wrenched free of its foundations by the storm surge and swept along the south shore. For a while Edney Parker thinks they may end up in Hawk Channel or possibly out in the ocean. They are on the north edge of the eye, and the wind never completely dies down. The winds intensify soon after they observe balls of fire in the air. With the wind howling and waves breaking over them, the sixteen people, including Edney, his wife, and ten of their twelve children, continue to hang onto an old iron bed frame.

Blowing from the opposite direction, the wind pushes the floating wreckage of the house back toward the shore. Edney hears something brushing along the side and reaches out; it is the limb of a lime tree. They are back on land after a voyage of about three hours. The water subsides, and they are gently deposited back on Upper Matecumbe about a mile southwest of where the cottage had originally stood. As soon as the water recedes, Edney, accompanied by his son Nolan and son-in-law Austin Reese, goes to look for his brother-in-law Brammie Pinder.

At the southwest end of Long Key, James Duane and nineteen other men, women, and children are afloat in the cottage belonging to the Countess of Suffolk when they enter the trailing part of the eye wall. Duane dutifully notes the times and conditions in his report:

> 10:10 PM—Barometer now 27.02 inches, wind is now beginning to blow from South-southwest.
>
> 10:15 PM—This was our first blast from S. S.W. which came full force. Seemed blast took one section of house away. House now breaking up, wind seemed stronger now than at any time during storm. I glanced at barometer which read 26.98 inches—dropped it in water and was blown outside into sea—got hung up in broken fronds of coconut tree and hung on for dear life. Could see cottage now going to sea as parties inside were flashing a light. I was then struck by some object and knocked unconscious.

The wind continued to blow at hurricane strength for seven more hours.

On Upper Matecumbe Key, Wilbur Jones and nine other men have been trapped for several hours in a boxcar. The storm surge pushed the car onto its side, blocking the unlocked door through which they entered. Nearly drowning when water from the surge almost filled the car before subsiding, they are anxious to get out. The door opposite the one they entered is above their heads and locked on the outside. A small ventilator grill at one end of the well-constructed boxcar does not yield to efforts to smash a hole through it. Without tools, the situation looks hopeless.

One of the men has been shining a flashlight through the ventilator grill in hopes of attracting help. Finally someone on the outside sees the light and comes to their aid. An ax and sledgehammer are retrieved from a nearby passenger car. Using the sledgehammer, the men on the outside are able to break out the ventilator's grid. The resulting hole is small and not big enough to accommodate a man, but the ax can be passed through. Jones and the others inside the boxcar take turns with the ax trying to enlarge the opening in the ventilator.

After the better part of an hour, a sufficiently large hole is made, and the men squeeze through. Outside, the wind is still blowing very hard. The

Only the foundations (*just above top right corner of inset*) of the train station remained at Islamorada after the storm surge came through. The cars of the rescue train were pushed by the storm surge off the main line, with some coming to rest on two boxcars that had been parked on a siding. The arrow points to the boxcar in which Wilbur Jones and others became trapped. The Islamorada train station (*inset*) was a sturdy structure that had withstood many previous hurricanes. (Photo, Langley; inset, FPC)

passenger cars of the special train lie nearby on their sides, their broken-out windows glowing eerily from battery-powered interior lights. Jones and his companions run to one of the cars and huddle together away from the smashed windows, trying to stay out of the reach of windblown debris and stinging rain.

On Labor Day night in Miami, Helen Lennehan sits alone in the city room of the Miami Daily News Tower. The huge space filled with desks is normally one of the busiest places in the imposing building known simply as the "Tower," but on this night all the reporters are out covering the storm, and she has been left to anchor the city room and handle rewrite. As the reporters call in, she cradles the phone on her shoulder and types the story as they dictate, rewriting it on the fly. It is not a job just anyone can do.

When there is a slack period, she calls the duty man at the Western Union office and takes down the latest wire service stories as he reads them to her. The wire service lines to the Tower are not working this evening, and this is the only way the paper can get the national and international stories. The problem is the Western Union man cannot pronounce Addis Ababa and other names of landmarks and people associated with the situation in Ethiopia, which is a hot topic.

The city room is on the second floor of the building and has one wall that is almost entirely large windows. Every now and again, a gust of wind shakes the large sheets of glass, and the thought flashes across her mind that at any moment she could be showered with sharp pieces of glass and meet a grisly end. Then the phone rings, and she is back at her typewriter taking broken sentences and making them whole.

She has no idea what a hurricane is, much less know what to do when one happens along, but the man who is courting her was in Miami during the 1926 hurricane and told her of the damage the strong winds can inflict. After hurricane warnings were issued from Key Largo north to West Palm Beach indicating that the weathermen now believed the storm could strike near Miami, Helen's suitor called her at work and insisted on taking her to her apartment to make sure everything was secure. At the apartment, located on Thirty-third Street right on the waterfront, Helen put the photograph of her mother under her bed for safekeeping and changed into her heavy London wool suit and Knox hat because they were her treasures and that is the type of clothing one wore up north during a storm. Feeling suitably dressed, she returned to the Miami Daily News Tower.

Elegantly slim, vivacious, and sophisticated beyond her twenty-four years, Helen's considerable talent for writing, and her energetic personality had already taken her far both professionally and geographically. Just last December she had been well ensconced in New York City, writing a column for the *New York Journal* and working for Carl Byoir Associates, a public relations firm.

As the nation dragged itself out of the Great Depression, shrewd businesspeople knew that advertising was key to priming the economic engine, and bright young people like Helen were the spark plugs that advertising and public relations firms provided for firing up effective marketing campaigns. In late December 1934, she was sent down to Miami to direct public relations for the Roney Plaza, a hotel located on Miami Beach. She was considering a job offer in Persia at the time, and the Roney Plaza assignment would end in February at the close of the winter season. She would have been in New York now or maybe London or Persia but for two people; Jane Wood and Bill Muir.

Helen had been packing for her return to New York City in late February when Frank Malone of the *Miami Daily News* called and pleaded with her to come work for the newspaper. Jane Wood, who had been working at the *News* writing obituaries and covering food and fashions, had left to become a social worker.

Malone sounded desperate and really in a bind to find someone to cover Jane's duties and to do rewrite as well. Not eager to return to the snow and slush of New York City, Helen accepted the offer. Soon she was writing feature articles, film reviews, and even became church editor, all under the byline of Helen Hansl. Then she met Bill Muir.

Muir had been an attorney for Carl Fisher when Fisher made his millions developing Miami Beach. Athletic, cultured, and handsome, he seemed to be the perfect match for Helen. At the same time, her communications skills were not going unnoticed, and by August 1935, career opportunities were beginning to overwhelm her. Job offers were coming in, and the glamour of New York City beckoned once more. Her romance with Muir was complicating her life so she boarded a steamer and returned to New York to visit her parents and sort it all out. Bill Muir was not about to be outdone by the bright lights of New York City; he hopped on an express train and was waiting on the pier when her ship docked. Eloquent and charming, he convinced her to return to Miami. She did— just in time for the hurricane!

By 10 p.m., the weathermen are saying that the storm is in the Upper Keys and headed northwest across Florida Bay toward the Gulf of Mexico instead of Miami. Even so, the automatic anemometer atop the thirteen-story Ingraham Building records an average wind speed of 52 mph, with gusts as high as 128 mph. Each blast of wind seems to shake the large glass windows in the city room of the Tower more violently, as if to remind Helen of the storm's presence.

The heavy wool suit she had put on is becoming more uncomfortable by the minute. The temperature is in the low eighties and the air is saturated with moisture, an environment that, combined with a wool suit, makes for a portable steam bath. Nonetheless, Helen continues to diligently crank out the reporters' stories and to gather the international news from the duty man at the Western Union. She has to—the Miami Daily News is fighting to maintain its readership.

In November 1934 a new newspaper began publishing in the Miami area. Less than a year later, using a tabloid format and a heavy dose of exposé reporting, the *Miami Tribune* boasts the largest readership in Florida and is pulling readers away from both the *Miami Daily News* and the *Miami Herald*. South Florida in 1935 is ripe for such a publication. Gambling and prostitution are rampant in Miami and Miami Beach. Of course, the only way such a condition can persist is with government corruption, and there is no shortage of that. Bribed judges, gangland executions, and policemen paid to look the other way provide the *Tribune* with ample material of sufficient juiciness for bold headlines and spicy stories. The *Miami Herald* is seen as lethargic and conservative, and while the *Miami Daily News* is viewed as more energetic, it does not have the boldness or flashiness of the *Tribune*. The *Tribune* staff is young and hungry, and has made it their mission to regularly scoop their rivals.

The *Tribune*'s upstart editor, Paul Jeans, who has been described as "aggressive, suspicious, and cynical," seems to have an unusually good knack for sniffing out a story and getting it into print before his competitors. In order to do this, Jeans works his staff hard and has no qualms about putting them in harm's way.

On Labor Day evening, while Helen Lennehan and her colleagues of the *Daily News* cover the storm in the Miami area, Jeans is focusing on the Keys. During the day, he had been skeptical of the Weather Bureau's advisories, so he sent a man to the Miami Weather Bureau to obtain a copy of the latest weather map. While the Weather Bureau was saying the storm would pass south of Key West, Jeans used the weather map and an elementary knowledge of meteorology to determine that the hurricane would make landfall somewhere on the Keys; hence, that is where the big story would be.

At 7 p.m., as the paper's workforce readies the presses to print the Tuesday edition, the *Tribune*'s plant loses electrical power. A call for assistance to the *Miami Herald* is politely stalled with a response that no one of sufficient authority is present to authorize the *Tribune* to use their press. The

Miami Daily News agrees to help, but the power outage spreads to their plant and thwarts that plan. Arrangements are finally made with the *Fort Lauderdale Daily News* to use their plant, and the necessary *Tribune* staff and materials are loaded up and moved twenty-eight miles north of Miami. It will prove to be a fortuitous inconvenience.

Seventy-one miles south of Fort Lauderdale, the situation is looking bleak aboard the *Dixie*. At 9:34 p.m., Captain Sundstrom orders his officers to make preparations to abandon ship. With the hull hard aground on a sand-covered portion of the reef, the vessel has assumed a noticeable list. The alarm gong is not sounded, and the order is quietly passed from the bridge to the stewards, who inform the passengers. The storm continues to rage as the passengers make their way to their lifeboat stations. Many find that their boats have either been washed away or have been damaged to the point of being unusable. The stewards herd them out of the weather and into small corridors amidships, where they are instructed to wait for further orders.

Some of the passengers are without outer clothing, shoes, coats, glasses, and other personal items, so the stewards are kept busy running back to cabins. Later, coffee, sandwiches, and fruit are distributed. Most of the interior of the ship is now saturated with moisture from one source or another. Water continues to pour through smashed or unclosed portholes, and ugly liquids and solids well up from toilets and drainpipes. Foul odors permeate much of the ship.

Up in the radio room, James Hodges and R. Schroeder have been working the sending key in relays, while passenger Henry Treger, an engineer and operator of a New Jersey broadcasting station, fine-tunes the emergency transmitter. The *Dixie* has been sending SOS for over an hour. Even with the antenna rigged earlier at great peril by Treger and crewman Heinze Laymeyer, they do not know if their message for help is being heard because the ship's receiver is not working.

At 9:40 p.m. their persistence pays off, and the Naval Reserve Communications Station in the Federal Building in Miami hears a weak SOS call on a frequency of 565 kilocycles. The signals are too weak to enable a fix on the originating position. At 9:50 p.m., the Naval Radio Station at Key West is notified of the distress call. A watch on 565 kilocycles is immediately established, and the Tropical Radio Telegraph station WAX in Hialeah, Florida, just north of Miami, and the Radiomarine Corporation Station WOE at West Palm Beach are notified. The Tropical Radio Telegraph station is a subsidiary of the United Fruit Line, which has many ships plying the Caribbean and Florida Straits.

Aboard the *Dixie*, the men in the radio room realize they do have another receiver available. The radio direction finder on the bridge is basically a radio frequency receiver with a highly directional antenna. They make some minor modifications and adjust the set for maximum sensitivity. Finally, confirmation is received that the ship's plight is known to the outside world.

Tuesday

Part 1

At fourteen minutes after midnight the Tropical Radio Telegraph station receives the first coherent distress message that enables the sender to be identified as the *Dixie*. The message gives the ship's location as Carysfort Reef. It is also heard by the *Platano*, a United Fruit Company passenger-carrying freighter plowing through the waves in the Florida Straits on its way to New York from Cortez, Honduras. Capt. C. D. McCrea immediately steers his ship for Carysfort Reef, which is only thirty miles to the northeast of *Platano*'s position.

The Tropical Radio Telegraph station immediately contacts the divisional headquarters of the Coast Guard at Jacksonville and forwards the *Dixie*'s message, "aground Carysfort Reef; 275 passengers. Pounding. Antenna and receiver out, using direction finder. Please get bearings on him and send assistance." The Hialeah station widely broadcasts a report of the *Dixie*'s distress. Naval radio stations in Key West, New York, Norfolk, Balboa, and the Panama Canal receive the message. The Naval Radio Direction Finding Station at Jupiter, Florida, tries to get a fix on the position of the *Dixie*'s transmitter, but the incoming signals are too weak.

At 12:20 a.m. an urgent message is received in the communications room of the Coast Guard National Headquarters in Washington, D.C. A Coast Guard station in Miami teletypes: "Call letters WCIX . . . SS Dixie . . . aground Carysfort Reef with 372 passengers . . . pounding . . . antenna and receiver out . . . try get bearings and send assistance." The chief of operations and acting Coast Guard commandant, Capt. L. C. Covell, is called at home. He orders the oceangoing tug and rescue ship *Carrabasset* based at Port Everglades north of Miami, and the patrol boat *Saukee* stationed in Key West, to proceed to the aid of the *Dixie* as soon as possible. At 12:30 a.m. the *Dixie*'s radio direction finder yields a welcome message as Tropical Radio Telegraph sends: "Coast Guard assistance coming now from Key West and Port Everglades."

The *Miami Tribune*'s staff has set up shop temporarily at the offices of the *Fort Lauderdale Daily News* and is preparing to print the Tuesday edition when city editor, Howard Hartley, is notified that the naval reserve station at the Federal Building has picked up a call from a ship in distress. The SOS was faint and did not give the name of the troubled vessel. A half hour later Hartley learns that the Coast Guard station in Fort Lauderdale thinks the ship involved is a passenger liner.

A ship in distress always makes an interesting story, and a ship stranded on a treacherous reef with hundreds of people aboard during a raging hurricane provides the makings of a great story. Editor Paul Jeans quickly reassigns his reporters and photographers, leaving a skeleton crew to cover the Miami situation, dispatching a reporter and photographer down to the Keys, and assigning a team to cover the vessel in distress. When he learns that the Coast Guard is planning to dispatch the oceangoing tug *Carrabasset* to the aid the *Dixie*, Jeans calls the commanding officer of the vessel. Lt. Cmdr. John McCann says a newsman can come aboard if he gets there by 4 a.m., when they are scheduled to get under way. With all his other reporters already assigned, Jeans orders Virgil Pierson, a reporter who normally covers sports, to get aboard the ship.

At 2 a.m. the incessant ringing of his telephone rudely awakens Cecil Warren. The *Miami Daily News* reporter picks up the earpiece and hears his boss, Hal Leyshon, the city editor for the *News*, telling him to get up; the Coast Guard is sending a ship from Port Everglades to a stranded liner in the Keys, and he wants Warren on it! Leyshon tells Warren he has to be aboard the *Carrabasset* by 4 a.m. Warren hangs up and starts collecting his thoughts about the assignment. He has a lot to do, including picking up his photographic gear and supplies. He is unaware that Virgil Pierson of the *Miami Tribune* has a similar assignment.

For the people on board the *Dixie*, it has been a sleepless night. Because the possibility exists that the stranded ship could lurch free and sink, the passengers and nonessential crew have been herded into groups in spaces along the main deck of the ship. They are not comforted by the continuing howl of the wind and the disturbing shudder underfoot

The USS *Carrabasset* was an oceangoing tug used by the Coast Guard as a rescue vessel. (USCG)

caused by the huge waves pounding the hull. Everything is wet. Even the coffee tastes of salt water, and the sandwiches are soggy.

At 3 a.m. an officer makes his way among the passenger-filled compartments and spreads the word that two Coast Guard cutters are standing by, ready to take them off as soon as the sea subsides enough to make the transfer safe. Immediately spirits lift and singing breaks out in various parts of the ship. In reality, the extremely rough seas have kept the *Carrabasset* at Port Everglades and the *Saukee* at Key West.

Three hours earlier in Key West, in a house on Whitehead Street across from the lighthouse, a thirty-eight-year-old man alternated catnaps with checking the barometer placed on a chair by the side of his bed. On Tuesday morning just after midnight, his eyes flicker open, and he reads 29.50 on the dial. This is lower than the previous reading, which means the storm is closer. It is time to go. He pulls on some clothes, grabs a flashlight, and leaves his two-story home to check on his boat. His car drowns out so he abandons it and sloshes through the stormy weather. The wind comes in gusts of sufficient strength to occasionally knock down a tree branch, but not strong enough to fill the air with flying debris. He makes his way to Southard Street and turns left to the Naval Station and the piers where the submarines used to be moored during the Great War.

The Naval Station was deactivated during the 1920s. In an attempt to stimulate tourism, the Florida ERA made an arrangement with the navy to allow the idle docks with a basin protected by a massive concrete breakwater to be used for berthing yachts. On this windy night, there are a number of private vessels moored there, including several yachts with families living aboard.

The man hurrying toward the piers does not own a yacht. His boat is not for pleasure cruising; it was custom-built to his specifications to be a forty-foot sportfishing machine. He had gone deeply in debt to acquire the boat. When it was delivered from the shipyard fifteen months ago, he gave it the nickname of his wife.

The *Pilar* glistened in the dim dock lights, showing lines more akin to a commercial fishing boat than a graceful yacht. Her owner checks the bollards and mooring lines, then goes aboard to check the cleats. He is prepared to stay as long as necessary; he isn't about to take any chances of another boat breaking loose from its moorings and ramming her. He periodically shines his flashlight around the basin and on adjacent craft, keeping a watchful eye out for anything that might pose a threat.

The storm is not too bad, and at 1:30 a.m. the barometer stops falling. An hour and a half later, the Key West Weather Bureau records the maximum wind velocity of the storm as 46 mph; it comes from the west, indicating the center of the hurricane has passed to the north. When the winds ease a bit and there is no longer a threat to his boat, the man returns home to catch up on his sleep. He will need his rest, for when word spreads to the Island City about the destruction on the Upper Keys, Ernest Hemingway will be among the first to join a rescue mission.

Out in the turbulent Florida Straits several large merchant ships are making their way through mountainous waves toward Carysfort Reef, the position reported by the *Dixie*'s crew. The *Reaper*, a tanker of the Texas Company, reports that she is about fifty miles away and making slow progress through the heavy seas. The *Watertown*, a tanker of the Cities Service Transport Company, is ninety miles distant. The *Platano* and *Limon*, both United Fruit Company ships, are fewer than fifty miles away.

With the 4 a.m. deadline for boarding the *Carrabasset* fast approaching, Cecil Warren fights a strong crosswind as he makes his way up the highway to Port Everglades. The *Miami Daily News* reporter is worried he will not get there before the ship sails. When he arrives, the vessel is still moored to the pier. The decks are brilliantly lit, and everything appears ready to go. The wind remains high, and large waves are coming down the throat of the channel that leads out of the harbor. Warren finds Lt. Cmdr. John McCann, who tells him the ship will get under way at dawn, roughly an hour and a half away. When Warren says his editor has sent him to sail with the ship, McCann informs him that only one newsman is allowed on the voyage, and there is one already aboard. Virgil Pierson of the *Tribune* had come aboard earlier.

Frustrated, Warren pleads with the commanding officer, but McCann remains unyielding. The reporter goes ashore, finds a telephone, and calls his editor and anyone else he thinks can get him aboard the rescue ship; the calls do not change the situation. In desperation, he calls Paul Jeans at the *Tribune* and asks him to pull his man off the boat. Jeans has his staff spread thin and would rather have Pierson doing sports than bouncing around on the ocean. Warren is a seasoned reporter and agrees to share his reports with the *Tribune*. Jeans says he will send a *Tribune* man down to go with Warren and tell Pierson to come back to the office.

By the time Warren completes these arrangements dawn has arrived and the *Carrabasset* is singling up her mooring lines, indicating departure is imminent. Warren jumps aboard the ship and frantically looks for Pierson to tell him to get off the ship. By the time he finds Pierson and informs him of the arrangement, the *Carrabasset* has pulled away from the pier. Fortunately for them the commanding officer is devoting all his attention to getting his ship through the channel that runs between two breakwaters; a wrong move could sink the ship. The waves are so large that the deep-draft tug is in danger of hitting her hull on the floor of the channel when she bottoms out in a trough. It will be a voyage the two reporters will not soon forget.

At 5 a.m. the *Platano* arrives off Carysfort Reef and determines that the *Dixie* is not there. Captain McCrea starts to search for her with his radio direction finder. It is difficult to get an accurate fix, but the weak signal indicates the *Dixie* is south of Carysfort Reef. McCrea is determined to find the liner and orders the helmsman to put the *Platano* on a southerly heading.

The center of the hurricane is now about fifty miles west of Craig and beginning to swing around Cape Sable on a track that will take it northward, just off the west coast of Florida. This change in direction causes the feeder bands to remain over the Florida Keys for an extended time. Although the sustained winds have dropped below hurricane force, powerful gusts still rake the islands and seas, and rain continues to fall. To people ashore and those at sea there seems to be no end to the hellish weather.

Aboard the *Carrabasset* reporters Virgil Pierson and Cecil Warren are holding onto anything they can for dear life. Lt. Cmdr. McCann maneuvers the ship out to the open sea, where fifty-foot waves greet the craft. The vessel spends more time traveling up and down the face and back of waves than it does going forward. A wave catches the ship at an awkward angle and tons of water crash down on the bridge, smashing one of the windows and sending shards of glass across the confined space. A deep cut is inflicted on Quartermaster Claude Simmons's leg, and another man has to take the helm.

Seawater and rain come through a broken ventilator and drench the crews' quarters. Stale air and soaring temperatures make the spaces below decks an oven. With waves washing over the ship, it is not safe to go topside. The *Carrabasset* is only able to make about two miles each hour.

At 11 a.m. Tuesday the Coast Guard cutter *Saukee* gets under way from Key West and moves northeast, staying outside the line of reefs. She encounters violent seas and has to heave to near the lighthouse at Sombrero Key, forty-five miles southwest of the *Dixie*.

Captain McRea aboard the *Platano* continues to search for the passenger liner with his radio direction finder after it becomes obvious that the *Dixie* is not at Carysfort Reef as stated in the distress message. Six hours after beginning his search, McRea fixes the liner's position as French Reef, about seven miles east of the middle of Key Largo. At 11 a.m., he broadcasts the new location. Another United Fruit Company freighter, the *Limon*, reaches French Reef at 11:45 a.m., followed by the *Platano* fifteen minutes later. The tanker *Reaper* appears soon thereafter. At 1:30 p.m. the Morgan Lines freighter *El Occidente*, commanded by Captain E. S. Campbell, arrives. The four ships commence a vigil, waiting for the weather and seas to moderate so they can begin the task of transferring passengers.

By 2 p.m. Tuesday the rain and wind have decreased somewhat and the rescue fleet can periodically see the *Dixie* on the reef a quarter mile away. From the decks of the stranded ship the sight of an array of large ships ready to lend assistance provides a needed boost to the morale of the passengers and crew. High wind and rough seas continue throughout the day, thwarting plans to remove personnel from the *Dixie*. The hours pass slowly for the passengers who remain in the shelter of the upper decks.

As darkness falls, the men aboard the *Carrabasset* can see two landmarks, the Miami Daily News Tower and the lighthouse at Fowery Rocks, meaning they are off Biscayne Bay northeast of Key Largo. Lt. Cmdr. McCann now knows the *Dixie* is on French Reef, thanks to the *Platano's* midday message to that effect. They are halfway to French Reef, and his crew is exhausted from fighting the storm all day so he orders the ship to heave to for the night. All hands except those on watch try to find a place where they can sleep without being washed overboard or being roasted or suffocated in a closed-up space. Cecil Warren sits down on the couch in the wardroom and falls over on his side sound asleep. It will be daylight when he opens his eyes again.

At 11 p.m. Tuesday night the *Dixie's* chief engineer, George Gale, reports the results of his latest inspection of the ship to Captain Sundstrom. The captain has the following message transmitted: "Chief engineer reports floor plates in fireroom up two inches. Making no water except in double bottom. Ship pounding slightly. Morale of passengers high."

As midnight approaches the 135-foot Coast Guard cutter *Pandora* is about three miles inland on the St. Johns River assisting a yacht into Mayport, a town near Jacksonville. The radio operator hands the captain an urgent message directing him to disengage from his present operation and proceed at full speed to assist the *Dixie*. The stranded liner is 310 miles away.

Late Monday night James Duane was knocked unconscious. When he wakes up he is sitting on the top of a palm tree twenty feet above the ground at the Long Key Fish Camp. The last thing he remembers is being swept out of the Wahoo cottage, grabbing onto some palm fronds, and watching the flashlights held by his companions grow smaller as the cottage drifted out to sea. Although soaked with rain and seawater, his watch is still working; it is 2:25 Tuesday morning. Not far away he can make out the seagoing cottage sitting on the beach. All the seawater has receded from the island, but the wind is still blowing so strong that sand carried aloft by the gusts is making his skin raw. He climbs down from the tree and with great difficulty begins to make his way through wreckage to the cottage. Along the way he finds a barometer that shows the pressure is beginning to rise, indicating that the storm is moving away from the island.

It is 2:30 a.m. when Duane gets back to the cottage and discovers the others safe except for the two men who were swept into the sea with him. The men are found later in the morning under debris along the railroad embankment where they were trapped but otherwise all right. Some Scotch wool blankets are retrieved from a cedar closet and are used to rig a bed for the children, who sleep peacefully through the rest of the night even though the wind continues to rip pieces off the cottage. Duane notes: "Hurricane winds continued until 5 a.m. and during this period terrific lightning flashes were seen. After 5 a.m. strong gales continued throughout day with heavy rain. No lives were lost but whole camp was demolished, damages will amount to hundreds of thousands of dollars. The FEC Railroad crossing Long Key was considerably damaged."

In Key West at 4:30 a.m. Tuesday, the northbound train that had been scheduled to leave the previous afternoon finally departs. On board are over one hundred passengers, most of whom are anxious to get back to their homes and jobs on the mainland. The train proceeds to a point a few miles east of Marathon then comes to a halt when substantial amounts of debris block the track. Some of the crew go forward on foot to survey the situation. Eventually word gets back that the track is destroyed up the line, and the decision is made to return to Key West.

Sunrise in the Florida Keys can be a colorful, even spectacular event, but on the morning after Labor Day feeder bands from the hurricane cover the sky with clouds heavy with moisture. This morning there is no appearance of the sun, just a lessening of the night.

After brushing the western face of Cape Sable, the hurricane is now off the Ten Thousand Islands and headed northwest along the west coast of Florida. Having been over shallow water since it passed Alligator Reef, the storm's intensity has diminished, although it is still a dangerous Category 3 hurricane with maximum sustained winds near 130 mph.

At Islamorada near where the train station used to be, the man responsible for the safety of the hundreds of veterans assigned to the camps on

The only parts of the rescue train that remained on the track following the storm surge were the locomotive and tender (*bottom center*). The arrow indicates where the Islamorada station used to be. (FPC)

the Keys peers out of the battered cab of the rescue train's locomotive. The 50-mph wind propels drops of rain with sufficient force to sting his eyes so he squints and through the grayish half-light and sees a disturbing sight. It was then that Ray Sheldon realized just how devastating the storm had been: "The locomotive was the only thing which stood upright. It just looked as if a giant broom had swept across there. The cars, some were on this side, some were half way over. This car with the 720 sacks of cement was washed a considerable distance and toward the east there was a Danish freighter [the *Leise Maersk*] blown in, possibly within a mile of shore."

Sheldon and several other men hike northeastward to see if they can get to Tavernier. At Whale Harbor, they find that the fill that had connected Upper Matecumbe Key to Windley Key has disappeared for the most part. Sheldon was impressed with the scene: "The pile which had been driven for the railroad tracks stood up, but the fill itself and the track had gone. We attempted to swim. We waded as far as we could. . . . The wind was blowing water in from the east and it had found this new passage or channel through here and was just sweeping over into the Gulf toward the west. It was impossible, after going out some, I do not know, 200 or 300 feet, to get across, so we headed back down to the hotel here, or where the remains of the hotel were."

Sheldon finds twenty-nine people, including Ed Butters and his family, at the Matecumbe Hotel. Ed had been in Miami on Labor Day but raced down the highway when he heard the storm was headed for the Keys. He

Devastation at Islamorada was extensive. This view looks north from the ocean side toward Florida Bay (*top left*). The train station site (*extreme right middle*) is nothing but a bare patch of ground. The locomotive and tender are located out of view at the lower left. The positions of the train cars relative to the track indicate the direction of the storm surge. (FPC)

Although badly damaged, the Matecumbe Hotel was one of a few structures where survivors could find some shelter from the rain while waiting for help to come. (FPC)

arrived at the hotel at 5:30 p.m., just before the worst of the hurricane struck.

Most of the survivors at the hotel are bruised and scratched; some of them are seriously injured. The physically able begin scavenging for food. "There was no drinking water," Sheldon recalled. "There were a few bottles of soft drinks floating around—not floating, but around there, laying around. There were a great many cases of canned goods, which had the labels washed off, and we would have to open them to find out what was in them, and that was the only food that we had." Fortunately, Ray Sheldon's cigarette lighter worked long enough to get a fire started. "We did manage to make one pot of coffee, and I believe it was made out of salt water."

As other survivors join the group, Sheldon learns that the fill that ran between Upper Matecumbe Key and Lower Matecumbe Key where Camp Three and Camp Five are located is completely washed away. Upper Matecumbe Key is cut off from the rest of the Keys, and they wonder if anyone on the mainland even knows of their plight.

There are at least two people doing their best to find out what the situation is on the Keys. *Miami Tribune* reporter Bill Freeze and his photographer, H. S. Willoughby, had been trying to get onto the islands ever since Monday night when their editor, Paul Jeans, assigned them to cover the hurricane. High winds and large waves in Card Sound made it impossible to negotiate the 2,800-foot wooden bridge between the mainland and Key Largo until dawn. As they approached Tavernier, the light filtering through the clouds began to reveal the storm-ravaged landscape. About two miles northeast of Tavernier the destructive force of the hurricane became pronounced. Driving carefully to avoid debris, especially boards that may have protruding nails, they made their way through the small town. Pieces of roofs were missing, and some shacks and small houses had been moved off their foundations. The farther they went, the more severe and extensive was the damage.

The highway bridge and railroad trestle at Tavernier Creek were intact so they went on to Plantation Key. Now they began to see small groups of people, some injured, standing in the rain with dazed looks upon their faces. They encountered crushed houses, uprooted trees, and groves washed away; it was evident that substantial amounts of water had come across the Key. Most disturbing were the bodies they saw in increasing numbers.

At Snake Creek, the banks on both sides were severely eroded where enormous amounts of water had passed through, ripping up railroad track, demolishing the trestle, and lifting the planked deck off the piles of the highway bridge. The approaches to the trestle had been washed away, and water poured through the newly enlarged gap at an extraordinary rate. Freeze and Willoughby get out of the car and stand on the western end of Plantation Key, a spot that had previously afforded a pretty view of the northeast end of Windley Key with the Snake Creek Hotel/veteran's hospital in the foreground and Camp One in the background. Now there is nothing there, just land stripped bare.

Across the way where the approach to the west end of the trestle began, there are people trying to attract attention by waving their arms. They shout something but cannot be heard because of the noise of the rain, wind, and rushing water. Separated by the torrent of water flowing through Snake Creek, Freeze hollers to the frantic figures on the other side as loud as he can, asking how many are dead. After several attempts they make out a response. "Five hundred! For God's sake send help. There's

Hell over here!" Freeze shouts some words of encouragement then hops in his car and drives back to Homestead where the nearest working telephone is located. He calls in a preliminary story and tells the person on the other end to send medical and other help. Willoughby stays on the scene to take photographs. The media race has begun.

Tuesday

Part 2

On his way to the mainland, Bill Freeze probably passed a taxi headed for Snake Creek carrying a crime reporter for the *Miami Herald*. Henry Reno was in the unique position of being trusted by both the Miami police and the city's criminal underworld. He was very good at his craft, and some years later the *Miami Herald* would be awarded a Pulitzer Prize for crime reporting due in large part to his work.

At this moment Reno's focus is on the Upper Keys. For most of Labor Day night, Henry had been at the Miami Police Station hoping to pick up a good story, but the criminals had sense enough to stay out of the stormy weather, and the stories had been mostly weather-related incidents. As he headed home in the early morning, Henry heard rumors that the hurricane had caused extensive devastation around Tavernier and Snake Creek. He had spent some happy days fishing the waters off Plantation Key and Key Largo, and had friends in the area. Without hesitating, Reno called the city room at the *Herald* to alert the staff about the situation and to tell them to send a photographer to meet him at Snake Creek. Then Henry picked up a bottle of booze, jumped in a cab, and began to compose the lead-in for a story sharing swigs with the driver as they raced over the wet roads to the Keys.

Reno was not his name when he was born in Denmark in 1901. Before Henry's family immigrated to the United States in 1910, his father, Robert Marius Rasmussen, thought that it would be wise to change the family name to one more easily pronounced by and less foreign-sounding to Americans. He placed an opened map of the United States on their dining room table, closed his eyes, and made a stab with his index finger; it landed on Reno, Nevada. So the Rasmussens became the Renos, and off they went to America, first to Wisconsin, then to Florida (Bartow), and eventually to Tennessee. Henry attended the University of Tennessee for two years, majoring in agriculture before the family moved to Miami in 1923. His father, who had been a photographer in Denmark, was hired by the *Miami Herald* and was able to get his sons Henry and Paul jobs there as well.

The bottle of booze was nearly empty when the cab arrived at Snake Creek and Henry began surveying the situation. Before noon, additional *Miami Herald* reporters and the photographer Henry had requested arrived. He told the reporters to go back to Tavernier and interview the people there while he looked for a way to cross the water gap and get the story as to what happened to the rescue train.

He watched as a veteran made an unsuccessful attempt to swim across the fast-flowing waters. A man from Homestead attempted to swim across while carrying a rope, but he was forced to turn back. Someone retrieved a small rowboat that had been purposely sunk to protect it in a nearby mangrove creek. After some rough going, the first successful crossing was made in it.

The first survivor from Windley Key to be brought back to the Plantation Key side of Snake Creek was six-year-old Dorothy Van Ness. She, her mother and father, two brothers, and a sister had been waiting at the veteran's hospital for the rescue train. Her father, brothers, and sister were killed when the hospital collapsed; her mother was missing. As the little boat headed back to Windley Key, Doris sat on the shore asking if she would ever see her mother again. When the rowboat returned after completing its third trip, Laura Van Ness stepped ashore, and the little girl ran to her mother's arms.

The trip across Snake Creek was extremely dangerous due to the strong current flowing from Florida Bay and the hazards posed by floating debris and submerged wreckage. Initially only a few small boats without motors were available, which severely limited the number of people brought across.

It was just as well for at that time there was little in the way of aid for survivors after they were brought to the western end of Plantation Key. For a few lucky ones there were friends and family who had come down and had a car to take them to the mainland. Others had to hitch a ride 6½ miles to Tavernier, where the residents were themselves trying to recover from the storm. Fortunately for the refugees coming out of the hurricane-ravaged area, the people of Homestead were quick to appreciate the magnitude of the devastation on the Keys. They prepared facilities for receiving the survivors with remarkable rapidity and generosity.

During the day on Tuesday, the survivors reaching the mainland consisted of people who had been on the south end of Key Largo, on Plantation Key, and the few who could be brought across Snake Creek from Windley Key. The fills between Windley Key, Upper Matecumbe Key, and Lower Matecumbe were washed out and the islands were isolated by expanses of fast-flowing water. Wind and rain still lashed out with a severity that made rescue operations impossible even for the Coast Guard.

On Matecumbe Key Carolyn Lowe sits on the wet ground in what had been a lime grove but is now a lonely grotesque landscape of twisted stalks and leafless branches. It seems as if she and her husband are the only two people left alive. Her back rests on the stub of an old lime tree. She moves slightly from time to time, trying to ease the constant pain of her broken ribs, but it is impossible to find a comfortable position. Cyril tries to keep the wind and rain off her as much as he can by shielding her with his body. The vacant look that comes with the sudden loss of a loved one is etched on both their faces.

When the rain and wind ease somewhat, they discuss the need to get help. Cyril doesn't want to leave her alone, but they have seen no one, and Carolyn needs medical attention. She tells him to go see what he can find and passes out from the pain as soon as he leaves. When she wakes up, Cyril is back with some men and a litter fashioned out of boards. Carefully, as gently as they can, they place the small woman on the litter and carry her to the Rustic Inn.

Other survivors have found their way to the inn. The wind is slowly diminishing, but the rain continues, sometimes hard and sometimes just an annoying drizzle. O. D. King, his wife, Betty, and her sister Leone have cleared up the kitchen enough to get the kerosene stove going and make hot cocoa for the children. There is not enough powdered milk and chocolate to make some for the adults. As more survivors gravitate to the inn, it takes on the appearance of a military field hospital set up in a bombed-out building in a combat zone.

Betty King has a cedar chest with linens, and when some of the children come in naked, she makes gowns for them by cutting arm and neck holes in pillowcases. As the hours pass, more survivors congregate at the inn. A little girl comes down the road without any clothes on, so Gilbert Thompson takes one of Betty's sheets and wraps it around the child. She is a young girl about eleven years old looking for her family.

It becomes so crowded in the wrecked building that people are standing shoulder to shoulder, and some of the Pinder boys sit up on the exposed rafters. The injured are placed on makeshift beds. There is precious little space protected from both wind and rain, but a niche is found for Carolyn Lowe. She is made as comfortable as possible on a soggy mattress, her broken ribs bound tightly by ripped sheets.

Back toward the beach in his 1930 Model A Ford that is wedged between two palm trees and covered with debris, Eddie Williams sits in the driver's seat, slumped over the steering wheel with his daughter's panties tied around his head. He has been dead for almost eight hours. Mozelle sits next to Eddie with her son Bob in dirty diapers still on her lap. Her daughters Elizabeth and Evelyn are scrunched on the backseat with their Aunt Carrie and her daughter Markelle. They are all soaked from being inundated in salt water and from perspiring the cold sweat that comes with being afraid. They are very thirsty, hungry, and tired after having been confined to the car for over twelve hours without food or drinkable water.

The wind no longer has a ferocious roar, and it is clear to Mozelle that the hurricane has moved away from them. All that can be seen through the windows are slivers of grayish light that slip through the pile of timber and rocks heaped over the car. Mozelle tries to open the door, but the debris is tightly wedged against it. She passes Bob over to her sister-in-law in the back seat, then winds down the window and works at loosening the top pieces of obstructing wreckage. A strong woman, she succeeds in clearing a hole big enough for a child to get through. She tells Elizabeth to go get help.

Elizabeth is scared and not eager to go but musters up her courage and wiggles through the splintery wood and scratchy branches: "I got out and it was total desolation. It was like being on another planet. There was no life; there was nothing alive, everything was white, just the white sand. And I just started walking; the little side roads were all tore up."

Upper Matecumbe Key after the hurricane. The land was covered with white sand, and the tops of coconut trees snapped off. Only a concrete cistern remains where a house once stood. (FPC)

The brave nine-year-old walks slowly, picking her way over the ground strewn with rocks, glass, and boards with sharp nails as the sputtering rain and gusting wind buffet her body. She thinks she is on the side road leading to the highway, but can't be sure since sand is spread over everything. The houses and other landmarks are gone, and even the trees have been stripped of their identity. Elizabeth finally reaches the highway and finds some survivors at what remains of Eddie Sweeting's grocery store. It was made of stone and had gas pumps in front of the store. The roof, part of the walls on one side, and the back are gone.

Elizabeth guides some men back to the car, and they remove enough debris to extract her aunt Carrie and the children through a window. Because of her size, Mozelle cannot get out through the window, and the timbers that keep the front passenger door from being opened are too heavy for the men to move without special equipment. They have to leave Mozelle in the car while they hunt for some tools to cut open the heavy canvas roof. Carrie Law takes the children to find something to eat and drink.

Mozelle is left alone beside the corpse of her husband. She later wrote: "and two men come and got all out but my self and they left and went for an ax to cut the top of the car out. and only (god) knows what I went thro and to haft to leave my dear one there. so cold." Eddie's body is left in car since there is no better place to store it.

Elizabeth recalled: "They got mother, Evelyn, and Bob and my Aunt Carrie and Markelle out of the car and took us up to the service station that was partly left. All during the day the rescuers brought in the few survivors, some of them unconscious. I mean, the water was so strong they brought in some of these people with all their clothes washed off of them. The snakes were real bad down there. They had to be very, very careful."

South of the Williams's car near the beach, Edney Parker's son-in-law Eddie Sweeting makes his way through the surreal landscape looking for better shelter for his wife, Etta, and the Parker family. Near a pile of wreckage that had been Brammie Pinder's fine house he hears a voice calling for help. He finds Billy Baker, the eighteen-year-old bookkeeper from Miami, pinned underneath some wreckage next to his mother, who had been killed when the house collapsed. Eddie tries to free Billy, but the weight of the timbers is too great so he leaves to find help. As he approaches the Rustic Inn he can see that some of the cottages and the inn are still standing. A crowd of survivors has gathered there. He rounds up six men, and they go back to free Billy. Baker has suffered cuts and apparently has internal injuries so they carry him back to the inn.

Meanwhile, Edney and the other members of the Parker clan have made their way to the inn. There are now forty people at the disheveled building, including Carolyn and Cyril Lowe, O. D. and Betty King, and Leone Barr and her son. O. D. salvages a first-aid kit with which only rudimentary treatment can be rendered to those with cuts and puncture wounds. Carolyn Lowe and Billy Baker need professional medical treatment, but until some way to evacuate them can be found all O. D. King and the others can do is make them as comfortable as possible.

Exposure and stress place enormous demands on the physical reserves of the body, and many of the survivors have had nothing to eat since the previous afternoon. Elizabeth Williams recalled: "There was very little food. A few cans of corned beef and some waterlogged bread and a few soft drinks, and they divided it among everybody." The cisterns where drinking water was stored had become contaminated with salt water and debris. Eddie Sweeting and others who were still physically able went scavenging for food. He recalled, "We fared fairly well. . . . We gathered some canned goods which had been scattered from my store about the ground, and found bottles of Coca-Cola and beer, though we had no water."

Even in the midst of disaster, the resilient children made a game of finding food. "It was fun because the labels had been washed off the cans so you didn't know what was in it until it was opened," said Edney Parker's daughter Fay. Physically and emotionally drained, many of the adults sit listless, waiting for help to come.

After helping rescue Billy Baker, Eddie Sweeting makes his way over to the bay side of the island, where he had secured his small sailboat in a narrow channel between clumps of mangroves. To his amazement, the boat is intact and has come through the storm in usable condition. He casts off and makes his way through the riled waters of Florida Bay to Lignumvitae Key about four miles to the west. To his relief, he finds his father, Willard Sweeting, has survived the storm. Willard is employed by the owners of the island as caretaker and rode out the storm in the main house, a stout two-story building constructed of coral rock.

As Eddie and Willard sail along the shoreline of the island on their way back to Upper Matecumbe Key, they see two boats trapped in a mangrove channel by wreckage swept in by the storm surge. One of the boats is overturned; it belongs to Horace "Coley" Albury (60) of Miami. The other boat is from Key West and belongs to Charley Pinder, who is with his brother-in-law, George W. Johnson. The men had been crawfishing, and when the weather turned bad they had sought refuge among the mangroves that grow thick along the southeastern shore of Lignumvitae Key.

Pinder and Johnson are uninjured; Albury was thrown from his boat into the mangroves when it was capsized by the surge and received minor scratches. Since the three men say they do not require assistance, Eddie and his father sail on to Upper Matecumbe Key. The three men free themselves and make their way to Snake Creek in Pinder's boat the next day. Albury almost drowns when the driver taking him back to Miami swerves to avoid a parked gasoline truck and the car lands in a canal adjacent to the highway. Coley Albury believes he has been jinxed!

At Miami Beach early Tuesday morning, Cardy Bradford's wife is worried. All telephone and telegraph lines to Lower Matecumbe are down. There is no way to find out if her husband is alive, hurt, or dead. Twenty-four hours have passed since she, her two young children, and their nanny left the houseboat at the ferry landing and went with Cardy's father to his home on Miami Beach. The wind was already picking up when Cardy waved good-bye. Last night while they were talking with him on the telephone, the roof was coming off the diner and Cardy said he could see the sky, then the phone went dead.

When the power went out on Miami Beach, Elizabeth Bradford and her father-in-law went out and sat in the car, listening to the radio for news about the storm and the Keys. They stayed up until the station went off the air. They were up early the next mornng trying to find some way to communicate with Cardy or someone down on the Keys to see if he was all right, but had no success. Feeling that all other options have been explored, Elizabeth decides to fly down to the Keys.

She checks with Pan American and with regular charter services only to learn that none of them are flying because of the weather. Even the Coast Guard at Dinner Key with their rugged seaplanes is not flying any rescue missions because of the strong winds. She keeps asking, determined to get to her husband; eventually someone says the only person they know who is crazy enough to fly in this kind of weather is Charles Collar. She goes out to the airport on a hunch and finds Collar checking the tie-downs on his amphibian. At first he refuses, but her persistence overcomes his resistance, and he agrees to take her down to the Keys.

It is midafternoon by the time the plane rolls down the runway on wheels protruding from the bottom of the two large pontoons attached to the underside of the fuselage. The single-engine seaplane struggles into the air against the strong wind. The drag created by the pontoons is enormous, and at one point the plane appears to be standing still. Just when it appears the wind will win the battle, the aircraft begins a slow climb, barely clearing a stand of trees at the end of the runway. They fly along the coast and then over the Keys. The lateness of the day and low visibility due to the clouds and occasional rain make it impossible to locate Lower Matecumbe Key so they fly north and land at Snake Creek.

By this time the Plantation Key side of Snake Creek is a beehive of activity with a mix of volunteers, relatives and friends, and a few government people trying to get rescue efforts organized. As darkness falls, several cars are maneuvered close to the water gap and their headlights turned on to provide illumination for the small boats that continue non-stop to ferry survivors across. A long rope had been rigged so that the boat crew can pull the vessel across instead of rowing. Flashlights flicker here and there, and occasionally a photographer's flashbulb goes off.

The Miami Red Cross has been busy assessing the situation and mobilizing resources during the day. The fruits of this labor are seen at dusk when three ambulances, doctors and nurses, first-aid supplies, food kits, and a canteen wagon arrive.

At about the same time, members of the American Legion's Harvey W. Seeds Post 29 of Miami bring four boats with outboard motors. They set up operations on a slab of decking that was lifted off the highway bridge by the storm surge and carried over to bay side of the island, where it now lies half submerged and half on shore. Situated near the mouth of Snake Creek but far enough away to be out of the swirling current, the improvised dock/launching ramp becomes the center of rescue activity. Soon the Legionnaires have their outboard-powered boats running regular trips between Plantation Key and Windley Key and across Whale Harbor between Windley Key and Upper Matecumbe.

A steady stream of dazed men, women, and children are brought across and moved up to Tavernier to await transportation to the mainland. Elizabeth Bradford talks with many of them, but no one has any information about Cardy or the situation at Lower Matecumbe. Worn out from a hectic day, she finds an abandoned car and bunks down in its backseat; there is nothing more that she and Charles Collar can do until daylight.

At 8:40 p.m., amateur radio operator Fred Bassett (W4AKI) arrives at Tavernier with his portable short-wave transmitter and receiver. With batteries provided by the Red Cross, Bassett and Frank Duckett (W4EB) set up a temporary station at Tavernier and establish a radio link with Alonzo Bliss (W4COT). Transmissions on the 80-meter band commence at 9:20 p.m. and continue around the clock with E. G. Little, George Hill, and H. G. Higgs assisting Bassett and Duckett.

Bliss, age thirty, owns Tropical Camera Stores and a real estate company. He never attended school, but received his education at home. He has been a ham for sixteen years. The radio equipment in the garage of his home on Twenty-eighth Street in Miami is said to be worth $12,000 and powerful enough to be heard around the world. Little, Hill, Higgs, Bassett, Duckett, Bliss, and twenty-nine other hams form the membership of the Miami Amateur Radio Club.

Throughout the night, the Legionnaires from the Harvey Seeds Post continue to operate their ferry system, transporting survivors to the Plantation Key side of Snake Creek. It is difficult navigating through the darkness, the strong currents, and the wind. The crossing from Upper Matecumbe Key to Windley Key is about a half mile, but because of the current the boats have to swing out in a wide arc; a round trip with loading and unloading takes almost an hour. Once they are brought over to Windley Key from Upper Matecumbe, the evacuees have to walk or be carried 1¼ miles across the island to Snake Creek and then ferried across to Plantation Key.

As rescue operations became more organized, responsibilities are formally divided between the American Legion and the Red Cross. The Legionnaires provide transportation from the cut-off islands to Snake Creek, where the evacuees are handed over to the Red Cross. The Red Cross provides logistical and medical support and manages landside transportation for the evacuees. Later that night a National Guard unit from Miami arrives to maintain order and assist with rescue efforts.

During Tuesday sketchy bits of information about conditions on the Upper Keys begin to filter into Key West. Although communication lines from Key West to the mainland are out, the submarine cables between Key West and Havana are operational, as are the circuits from Havana to the mainland of the United States. A news story sent by the Associated Press via telephone from New York reports among other things that at least thirty miles of FEC Railway track on the Upper Keys have been washed out and that it is not known when train service might be resumed. This information is most disquieting to a group of men in Key West who reside in a unique train car parked at the FEC Railway yard on Trumbo Point.

From the outside, the 83-foot-long railroad car looks much like a mail car except for a group of windows at one end. Inside, one-third of the car provides living quarters, including a bathroom and kitchen, for six people who collect and tend the fish and other aquatic specimens carried in the remainder of the car. In addition to sixteen, 5-foot-long, 200-gallon cypress transport boxes, there are twenty smaller tubs and equipment

Top: The custom-built car *Nautilus* hauled aquatic specimens to Chicago for display at the John G. Shedd Aquarium (*background*). *Bottom*: Men at the Trumbo Point rail yard in Key West tend submerged cages containing specimens. The *Nautilus* (*left*) was parked beside the slip for the duration of its stay. (Shedd)

for aerating and heating/cooling the water that sustains the specimens. Named the "Nautilus," the special car was custom built in 1929 by the Pullman Car Works in Chicago and outfitted with tanks, pumps, air compressors, electric generators, refrigeration and heating equipment, and crew accommodations at a cost of $40,000. It is one of the most technically complex cars to ride the rails in 1935. The sole purpose of the Nautilus is to transport aquatic specimens to the John G. Shedd Aquarium in Chicago.

The aquarium's elegant 300-foot, octagonal building covered with white Georgian marble was built on land created by filling the shoreline of Lake Michigan at the foot of Roosevelt Avenue, and was substantially complete at the end of 1929. Over the next several months, 1 million gallons of seawater from the Florida Keys were hauled in 160 railroad tank cars for its salt-water exhibits. The final aquatic exhibit was opened for display in 1931; 4.69 million people visited the Shedd Aquarium that year. Many of the specimens on view had been brought to the aquarium by the Nautilus, which made regular trips to Key West from 1930 to 1935.

The 1935 collection team, led by Dr. Max Mayer, arrived in Key West on August 22. They were greeted with inclement weather: rain that poured steadily for twenty-four hours. The trip was not off to a good start, with the weather costing the team a day of precious time. The bad weather was an omen of things to come.

Four days later, Mayer wrote to the director of the Shedd Aquarium, Dr. Walter H. Chute, to give him a progress report of the expedition and advise him of the arrangements for their return to Chicago. The plan was to have a small switch engine pull the Nautilus to Miami, where it would be attached to a regularly scheduled train for the long haul to Chicago. Mayer wrote, "They only have a switch engine here four days a week so my best bet will be to leave here Labor Day."

By Labor Day, the collection team had brought aboard the Nautilus 1,300 tropical fish belonging to approximately eighty-five species, including yellow tangs, bluehead wrasses, black-and-white pennant butterflyfish, as well as brilliant coral and colorful anemones. Dr. Mayer had dearly wanted to catch some small tarpon, but time was running out and what they had in their tanks was, in his opinion, one of the best collections obtained since he began coming to the Island City.

Over the Labor Day weekend it was learned that a hurricane was approaching and the departure was postponed. While the storm did little damage in Key West, the railroad's telegraph system between Marathon and Homestead stopped working and the telephone circuits failed, a sure sign that substantial damage had occurred along the mainline. Rumors began to circulate that some of the track had been destroyed, causing Mayer to become concerned that further delay might endanger his collection.

Other people in the town were also becoming concerned, but not about Dr. Mayer's fish. Rosalie and Bascom Grooms have not heard from their daughter, Rosalind, or her boyfriend, George Pepper. Clara Carey and her daughter wonder if Eddie and the other members of their family are all right and how their house fared with the storm. At the Harris School, the principal has had to find a substitute for Mary Ingraham, who failed to report for the first day of school and has sent no word as to when she will be back.

Claude Brown from Cincinnati and twelve other veterans are concerned about getting back to their camps on the Keys. The men had come to Key West with about fifty other veterans for the weekend. Brown and his buddies elected to remain another day even though they knew their pay would be docked for overstaying their leave, which expired Tuesday morning. Other people whose friends, relatives, and employees had gone to the Upper Keys for the long weekend are beginning to ponder the possibilities, and irritation about not receiving information is transforming into frightful worry.

The situation is not helped by the return at 8:45 Tuesday night of the Miami-bound train that had left Key West very early that morning. The train had been stopped all day at Marathon while the extent of damage up the line was probed. When it was determined that the train could not safely proceed, the decision was made to return to Key West. The entire train had to be backed down the Lower Keys since there was no facility for turning it around. After spending over sixteen hours on board with little to eat and drink, the weary passengers and crew are exhausted and hungry.

One of the items unloaded from the baggage car is the body of Henry Lilija, a shark fisherman employed as a watchman at the Thompson Fish

House on Key Vacas. He is the first victim of the hurricane to be brought to Key West. A sense of foreboding begins to creep over the city.

Doc Mayer realizes the situation of the Shedd collection team is not good at all. He sends the aquarium's director a Western Union night letter:

MAROONED AT KEY WEST LENGTH OF TIME UNKNOWN RAILS OUT
EVERYONE SAFE WILL TRY TO HOLD FISHES PLEASE NOTIFY CREWS
WIVES OF SAFETY WILL KEEP IN TOUCH NO DIRECT COMMUNICA-
TION MAY NEED MORE MONEY INVESTIGATE RETURN TRANSPORTA-
TION= M V MAYER.

As soon as the main line is clear of the retreating northbound train, the switch engine pulls out of the Trumbo yard and heads toward Marathon. It is not towing the Nautilus; the small engine is being dispatched to test the track and see how far it can go. It will get no farther than Grassy Key where two miles of track are washed away.

More than twenty-four hours after the storm's center passed over the Keys, the hurricane is in the Gulf of Mexico about fifty miles due west of St. Petersburg, Florida. With winds near 100 mph, it picks up speed and heads north.

As the day after Labor Day comes to an end, the *Dixie* lies hard aground on the reef east of Key Largo, while the *Leise Maersk* is stuck on the mud flats off Upper Matecumbe Key. The survivors ashore have congregated in the ruins of the Rustic Inn and the Matecumbe Hotel, the only remaining structures on Upper Matecumbe that offer some shelter. On Lower Matecumbe Key, most of those left alive are at the west end near Camp Three, where they find shelter as best they can. On Craig, the men, women, and children seek refuge in Ollie Olson's boat and the wreckage of the store and cabins. On Long Key, J. D. Duane assures his group that the storm is now far away from them, and they bed down in the remains of the countess's cottage. The common despair of the people stranded on the ships and islands is the knowledge that they are marooned; the common hope is that rescue will come soon. For them, the only relief from the nightmare of reality is sleep.

Saving the Survivors

For many of the survivors coming off the Keys Tuesday night and Wednesday morning, the place where recovery begins is located forty-eight miles away from Snake Creek in the Redland District of southeast Florida. The Redland District covers an area of approximately fifteen square miles in the southern half of Dade County and stretches from the shores of Biscayne Bay to the eastern edge of the Everglades. The district's highly productive farmlands yield a variety of vegetables and fruit; its name derives from the red soil found in its Pine Lands section. The Redland District is nationally known for its avocados. In 1935 there are several towns within its borders, the largest of which is Homestead, occupying an area of five square miles with a population of more than three thousand.

A thriving community, Homestead has doctors (including some equipped with X-ray machines), a very nice movie theater, a Rexall drugstore, six churches, and an impressive array of clothiers, furniture stores, grocers, and other businesses, including several feed and seed stores. The Redland District Chamber of Commerce described its citizens as "a culling of the best folk from almost every State of the Union with staunch native stock, noted for its hospitality and honesty of life and purpose." The small country town ambience is evident in a notice that appeared in the *Leader-Enterprise*, the local weekly newspaper.

If Anybody Has
Married,
Left town,
Had a fire,
Sold a farm,
Been arrested,

Been your guest,
Left you a fortune,
Elected new officers,
Met with an accident,
Organized a new club,
Swiped your chickens,
That's News
Phone us

Homestead has social, religious, educational and business ties with the residents of the Upper Florida Keys. The Methodist church's Matecumbe Mission holds services on Upper Matecumbe Key on the first and third Sundays and on Plantation Key on the second and fourth Sundays. Many dwellers on the Upper Keys go to Homestead to do their shopping, and some have children attending the Homestead high school. Ben Archer, the owner of the local newspaper, also publishes the newspaper produced by the veterans for the camps in the Keys. An edition of the *Key Veteran News* was being run on Archer's press when the hurricane struck; it was never distributed.

When groups of rain-soaked survivors began to straggle into Homestead on Tuesday, the citizens of the town rallied to their aid. Whether the dazed and bedraggled people were friends, relatives, customers, or strangers, it did not matter. They were people who needed help; all were hungry, dehydrated, and in need of baths and clean clothing. Many had bruises, scratches, and cuts while a few could not walk and were carried on litters. The refugees were civilians and veterans, men, women, and children. Some of the veterans brought along dogs they had saved during the storm and talked to them as if they were war buddies, which in a way they were.

As awareness of the number of possible survivors grows, the Sunday schoolrooms of the First Baptist Church are hastily converted to an improvised infirmary and assistance center. There the survivors are doctored, clothed, and fed. Telephones are made available so friends and relatives can be contacted. It is a welcome refuge where they can rest until arrangements are made to send them to a hospital, or someone comes to get them, or a place can be found for them to stay. Their names are taken, and a list is maintained of whether or not they are injured and where they are being sent from there. Jane Wood was impressed with the way the town responded:

> Now that is a town—Homestead—that met all proper commitments to human decency. Nothing they had there wasn't used. Mayor Preston Bird slopped about in the rain getting everything ready for the survivors. The druggist opened the drugstore and gave all his medicines. The furniture stores opened up and they had all the hurt people on the mattresses. Nobody told them they had to do what they did. They did everything they could. Not so Miami.

All through the night, people arrive at the makeshift aid center. The flow of survivors increases during the day on Wednesday as the wind abates and rescue operations begin in earnest. At 3 a.m. Wednesday morning, there are nearly one hundred men, women, and children being cared for at the Baptist Sunday school building.

Not all the survivors are processed at the Homestead church. The badly injured are taken directly to hospitals in ambulances. Some survivors are removed from the Keys to Miami by seaplanes and taken to a place eighteen miles north of Homestead.

During the Great War, the U.S. Navy established a base for its fledgling seaplane service southwest of Miami on a small island attached to the mainland by a strip of fill. Situated on Biscayne Bay, it had been a popular place for picnicking, a recreation that gave the island its name, Dinner Key. Sheltered by the outlying islands that make up Miami Beach and the northernmost part of the Florida Keys, Biscayne Bay is an ideal environment for seaplane operations. Of special appeal to the navy was the proximity of Dinner Key to the narrowest part of the Florida Straits between Bimini and Miami. Navy seaplanes could easily monitor ships passing through the fifty-mile-wide throat of the Straits.

Prior to the United States entering the Great War, a runway was dredged for seaplanes, and the spoils were used to expand the size of the small island by filling in the shallows between it and the mainland. Dinner Key was transformed from an island to a bulge on the waterfront of Coconut Grove. Nonetheless, the area continued to be referred to as Dinner Key.

In 1918, the first naval air station in the United States was commissioned at Dinner Key. After the Great War, the navy deactivated the base, and private companies operated seaplanes from the facility. Ten years later, the New York, Rio, and Buenos Aires Line (NYRBA) acquired much of the property. No sooner had operations commenced than the stock market crashed. Pan American Airways acquired the NYRBA and took over the Dinner Key facility.

Over the next four years, Pan Am bought adjacent bay bottom and conducted extensive dredging that created a basin and channels deep enough for its large, intercontinental seaplanes. The dredged fill was used to expand the land area many times beyond its original size. Two large hangars and a modern terminal were constructed to serve as a base for Pan Am's international flights to Central and South America and the Caribbean. The spacious art deco terminal also served as the airline's corporate headquarters. From here one could board a seaplane, which Pan Am called "clippers," and fly direct to Havana or even Rio de Janeiro.

In the early 1930s, the Coast Guard began to use seaplanes for rescue missions in addition to conducting aerial patrols. Advancements in aviation had produced aircraft with sufficient range and sturdiness to make such missions a reality. The former naval air station site located at the northeast corner of the Dinner Key was a logical choice for its South Florida base. In June 1932, the U.S. Coast Guard Air Station-Miami was commissioned.

At dawn on the Wednesday after Labor Day 1935, the wind was blowing off Biscayne Bay at a brisk 30 mph. That was a light breeze compared to the 80-mph gusts experienced when the hurricane made its closest approach thirty hours earlier. For most of the day on Tuesday, 50-mph winds had blown directly against the large doors of the Coast Guard's hangar, causing them to jam so hard that they could not be opened. At 3:30 a.m. Wednesday, the wind abated to the point that the hangar doors could be pushed back and one of the new Douglas Dolphin RD-4 amphibians, CG-133 was rolled out. As the crew warmed up its two radial engines, a survey boat sounded the taxiways and runways to ensure there were no wrecked boats or other submerged debris that could pose a danger to the aircraft. Several private boats had broken their moorings during the heavy weather and lay wrecked along the Dinner Key bulkhead.

Lt. C. B. Olsen, the commander of the air station and pilot for this first poststorm flight, made a final check of the aircraft and then climbed into the cockpit. Slowly the plane rolled down the ramp and into the choppy water. As it taxied out into the bay, a crewman turned cranks that caused the wheels on either side of the cabin to swing up out of the water. When they were at a 45-degree angle from the fuselage, the struts were locked into their takeoff position. Picking up speed, the seaplane rose up onto the hull's step—a protrusion on the bottom designed to break the surface tension of the water—and lifted into the air.

Aboard the aircraft in addition to the three-man crew was an employee of the State Health Department—who was representing the Red Cross and the Florida ERA—and a Universal News cameraman. For 3½ hours they conduct an aerial survey of the Keys and Florida Bay; for the first time since the storm had struck, the full extent of the destruction of the Upper Keys became known.

At 6:25 a.m. CG-133 flies over Snake Creek where Elizabeth Bradford and her pilot, Charles Collar, are preparing to resume their flight down to Lower Matecumbe to find Elizabeth's husband. Before they leave, her brother-in-law and a friend arrive by car, and the foursome boards Collar's amphibian. As the plane taxies toward the open water, a gust of wind blows it into some mangrove bushes, where it becomes snagged. The new arrivals earn their passage by jumping overboard and freeing the aircraft from the tangle of branches. There is a small tear in the varnished fabric that covers one wing and another in the tail. Collar does not think them serious enough to abort the flight, and the plane takes off.

In a few minutes, they are over Lower Matecumbe. Now it becomes clear why they had not been able to find Lower Matecumbe the afternoon before. Parts of the island are still covered with water so high that only the tops of trees are exposed. From the air, the four-mile-long key appears to be a series of small islands. As the seaplane descends, the scene that unfolds beneath them is one of utter destruction. They can see bodies in the treetops. Much of the exposed land is swept clean of vegetation and structures. And then the ferry landing comes into view.

The large black hull of the ferry *Monroe County* is aground on the bay side of the approach to the Channel No. 2 viaduct. With its superstructure pushed into the water alongside the hull, the ferry looks like a big barge. The main-line railroad track has been lifted off its bed still affixed to its ties and lies fifty to one hundred feet to the northwest twisted like a ribbon. Up on the beach near the ferry's hull, Elizabeth can see the houseboat that had been her floating home. It looks intact except that the second floor is gone. A large patch of white sand now marks the area

The west end of Lower Matecumbe Key was a scene of utter destruction. In the foreground, the hull of the ferry *Monroe County* lies hard aground and stripped of its superstructure. Just above it, the Bradfords' houseboat is beached with its top deck ripped off. Veterans Camp 3 (*top left*) has been swept bare. The railroad track has been lifted from its bed, twisted like a ribbon, and moved toward Florida Bay. (FPC)

where the numerous tents and buildings of Veterans Camp Three had been. Cars and trucks are scattered about—some with their roofs ripped off, others overturned. Out on the loading dock at the ferry slip stands a lone car apparently unscathed.

The water in the vicinity of the ferry slip is a jumble of wreckage. Most of the Terminal Inn restaurant and store is gone, and the two adjacent garages are a pile of twisted sheet metal and broken timbers. Charlie Collar flies low over the water looking for safe place to land. He has to be careful because there appear to be logs or thick timbers about six feet long floating on the water. When the plane is low enough, they realize that the logs are bodies. Is it possible that Cardy Bradford survived such carnage?

On the ground, the superintendent of Camp Three, Ben Davis, and a group of veterans stop their grisly work of retrieving bodies to look at the airplane as it drones overhead. Davis and some of the veterans survived the storm by holding onto a tank car filled with freshwater that was parked on a siding. They spent Tuesday searching for survivors and looking after the injured as best they could. There was not much they could do because the camp's ambulances where the medical supplies were stored had been destroyed. They had been picking up bodies since 6 a.m., stacking them on the pier for removal to the mainland.

Charlie Collar lands his seaplane and taxies in as close as he dares among the debris and floating bodies. The men on the beach have a row boat and ferry Elizabeth and her companions to the shore. Then comes the moment that makes all her trials and tribulations since Monday night worth tolerating; she finds Cardy alive and well. In contrast to most of the other survivors, who are still dazed and say little or nothing, Cardy bubbles over with excitement telling them about the storm until he realizes they have come to take him back; then he is ready to leave.

Collar's plane can hold seven, so Cardy and two seriously wounded men are taken aboard. The heavily loaded seaplane with tears in the wing and tail becomes airborne after a few breathless minutes, and they are on their way home. It is not known how much Charlie Collar was paid for the charter, but whatever the amount, he certainly earned it.

At 10:30 a.m., a Coast Guard amphibian lands, and some doctors come ashore at the ferry slip. There is little they can do for the injured because they did not bring any medical supplies with them. In the early afternoon, a Coast Guard cutter arrives, followed at 2 p.m. by the arrival of a private yacht on loan to the Red Cross.

The *Byronic* is a high-speed boat owned by Byron S. Miller, executive vice president of the Woolworth Company. The *Miami Daily News* arranged to have the boat made available to the Red Cross for the evacuation of injured people from the Keys. Captain Percy Branning, master of the *Byronic*, has a volunteer crew that includes James Moore, whose brother Lewis is a son-in-law of Eddie Carey. After departing Miami early in the morning, the *Byronic* went directly to Snake Creek and took aboard doctors, nurses, and medical supplies. The sleek-hulled vessel then headed for the ferry slip on Lower Matecumbe Key.

Of course, the *Miami Daily News* had a reporter and a photographer aboard to document the good deeds the mercy mission accomplished. In addition to medical personnel, the *Byronic* carried two Catholic priests, a representative of the American Legion, and J. Marvin Dowde, who in 1933 received some attention in the media for surviving in the "wilds of the Keys" for six weeks equipped with only a knife.

Fifty veterans and three civilians are loaded onto the seventy-two-foot yacht while it is at Lower Matecumbe. Ben Davis and twelve volunteer veterans elect to remain at the camp to continue to search for survivors and retrieve the dead. The *Byronic* casts off and heads for Craig.

At 4 p.m., a vessel from No Name Key arrives at the ferry slip with a detachment of the Florida National Guard unit in Key West. The detachment is composed of three officers and fifty-one men under the command of Major William V. Albury. Albury informs Davis he is taking over the island. His troops begin to comb the area for dead and injured. According to Albury, they find that bodies in accessible places have nothing in their pockets while bodies that remained in the mangrove swamps almost invariably carried papers, army discharges, and frequently money. Since the survivor veterans had been the only ones collecting and stacking the accessible bodies, it appears to Albury that looting has been occurring. He asks Davis to move his men to the dredge *Panama* and to keep them there until they can be evacuated.

The *Byronic* arrives at Craig at 5 p.m. Because of space limitations, only women, children and injured men are being taken aboard. W. R. Craig and Langdon Lockwood do not board the vessel. They have come through the hurricane with only minor cuts, scratches, and bruises, and are otherwise in good shape. Their comrade Jack Crowe has not been as fortunate. When the trio had tried to run across the railroad tracks to Lower Matecumbe Key, they were caught in the open as the winds resumed and had to burrow under the tracks for shelter. Jack Crowe became claustrophobic, panicked, and rose up, sitting fully exposed on top of the railroad tracks with his back to the wind. In no time, his clothes were ripped from his body. From his ears downward his back looked like raw meat where the flesh was blasted away by wind-driven sand. Crowe and the bridge tender's wife and children are taken aboard the yacht, and the vessel heads out into Hawk Channel. Four and a half hours later, the *Byronic* pulls up to the Royal Palms Hotel docks in Miami.

At Snake Creek, congestion along the only road to the mainland is hampering relief operations. Early Wednesday morning, ten trucks arrived with medical supplies, food, and clothing collected by the Red Cross. More convoys follow, bringing drinking water, gasoline, and other supplies for the rescue teams. Eighteen ambulances carrying fifteen doctors struggle through the traffic to get to the west end of Plantation Key.

Scores of private vehicles are parked along the road near Snake Creek as people arrive to check on their homes, boats, and businesses or to assist friends and relatives. The two-lane highway becomes jammed with cars and trucks.

The backed-up traffic on the highway is not a problem for Lt. j.g. W. L. Clemmer as he flies over Snake Creek in a Coast Guard seaplane to begin cruising the coastline of the Everglades and the small islands in Florida Bay. During the patrol, the aircraft, CG-255, makes several landings to pick up survivors. One of these is east of the small village of Flamingo at the southern edge of the Everglades, where the debris-strewn water makes landing very dangerous. With luck and skill, Clemmer brings the plane onto the water without puncturing the hull, much to the relief of his crew and the three people who are clinging to a partially submerged houseboat. The rescued boaters are taken to Snake Creek, where they are turned over to the Red Cross for treatment and transportation to the mainland. Upon learning that there are injured people who need to be evacuated from Upper Matecumbe Key, Clemmer and his crew rev up the engines of the seaplane and get under way.

CG-255 is a Fokker Flying Life Boat and is somewhat similar in appearance to the Douglas RD-4 (CG-133) that Lt. Olson is flying. Both are monoplanes with the fuselage hung under the wing and twin engines mounted on struts above the wing. On the Fokker, the engines face aft and the propellers push the plane forward, whereas on the RD-4, the engines are pointed toward the nose and the propellers pull the aircraft. With a wingspan of almost seventy-five feet and a length of fifty-five feet, the Fokker is larger than the RD-4 by fourteen feet on the wings and ten feet nose to tail. The plane cruises at a stately 95 mph, but what it lacks in speed is made up with a range of 1,100 miles, almost twice that of the RD-4.

As CG-255 flies over Upper Matecumbe, the *Leise Maersk* can easily be seen. The large freighter is very close to the island, so close that one newspaper reports the freighter has come in to aid the stricken island. Much of the land has been scoured clean, with the debris being swept into Florida Bay. A stretch of railroad track has been ripped up and lies twisted beside its former bed. A string of railroad cars lie on their sides before a locomotive and tender that stand upright facing the northbound direction. A group of people can be seen walking along the highway. Everything is either white, where the coral rock has been laid bare, or grayish black or blackish brown, where groves once stood. All the greens and yellows of the vegetation are gone as are the bright colors of painted structures.

Mud flats surround Upper Matecumbe Key except at the ends, where the fills have been washed out and the natural channels are flowing once again. The deep water near the island is too turbulent so Clemmer decides to land on the flats, where the water is only eighteen inches deep. After making an inspection pass, the Fokker gently settles onto the water and anchors in Florida Bay off Islamorada. The pilot and the mechanic wade ashore to see if they can render any assistance. A team of doctors and a Coast Guard shore party that had come ashore earlier are tending to survivors. Chief Boatswain Mate Karcher reports difficulty in getting the women, children, and injured men to Snake Creek.

Clemmer decides to try to evacuate as many as he can. In addition to its three-man crew, the Fokker is designed to accommodate eight passengers if the stretcher carrier is stowed. Small children and some of the injured cannot wade out to the seaplane and have to be ferried over in the aircraft's inflatable rubber dinghy.

The dingy is small so the loading process is dreadfully slow. The wind is still blowing, but the air is warm and humid. As people are transferred to the seaplane, the metal cabin becomes hot and stuffy, a situation that worsens as more and more people come aboard. After sixteen passengers are in the cabin, eight more than the aircraft is supposed to carry, Clemmer has the hatch secured and starts the engines.

For most of the evacuees, this is their first time in an airplane. Packed into the cabin like sardines in a can, the experience will not be very enjoyable. Radio equipment occupies one side and blocks half the windows; the other windows are blocked by passengers, so for most there is no view. The noise from the eighteen cylinders firing in the engines a few feet above their heads is terrific, and the heat is becoming unbearable.

The Fokker is now considerably heavier than it was when it landed and squats deeper in the water. Instead of brushing over the mud as it did when they arrived, the hull is sledding across the bottom, the aluminum plates of its hull making worrisome grinding noises as if to protest the abuse. The engines are revved up to push the plane through the sea grass and mud.

It would only take one large rock or piece of debris or even a tenacious clump of seaweed to halt the aircraft's forward progress and trap it for hours in the mud, but Clemmer's luck holds, and the Fokker picks up speed. Air rushing through the cabin brings sighs of relief from the human cargo. The aircraft vibrates so violently it seems a wonder that the plane stays together; then the hull breaks free of the water and they are airborne.

In little more than a half hour, the overloaded Flying Life Boat is coaxed onto the waters of Biscayne Bay. A brisk breeze is blowing as the seaplane approaches the ramp at the Coast Guard air station. Considering the wind and the heavy load, Clemmer decides not to risk running the seaplane up the ramp and anchors off the base. The passengers are ferried ashore by the station's crash boat. For one seriously injured passenger, the evacuation does not come soon enough, and he dies on the apron. Not long thereafter, Clemmer and his crew are back in the air headed south.

The Coast Guard seaplanes can be heard and sometimes seen by Mozelle Williams and the other people at the Rustic Inn as they wait for rescue workers to reach them. After Mozelle was extracted from the car that now serves as a tomb for husband, she was taken to the Rustic Inn, where she was reunited with her children and her brother Dan and his family. Dan suffered a head injury during the storm, and his head was bandaged. His son Perry was uninjured. Considering that he and his son had endured the brunt of a Category 5 hurricane outside with only the trunk of a coconut tree for a shield, they were very fortunate.

During the morning, aid workers from the mainland come by and tell them that the fills at both ends of the island have been washed away. Mozelle now knows that her home is gone and that all she and her children have left are the clothes they are wearing. The aid workers also say that if they can get up to Whale Harbor, a boat will take them over to Windley Key. From there they can walk across the island to Snake Creek, and another boat will take them over to the aid station on Plantation Key where transportation will be provided to the mainland.

Whale Harbor is about 1¾ miles from the Rustic Inn. The hike across Windley Key is another 1¼ miles. The journey to the aid station will require walking three miles over the debris-strewn highway; it will not be easy for men, women, and children suffering from shock and exposure.

Dan Law with his head injury is not up to making the trip, so he and his wife decide to remain at the inn to await medical attention and assistance in being evacuated. They urge Mozelle to take the five children and get them off the Keys. With Mozelle carrying her son Bob and the children in tow, they set out for Whale Harbor, slowly making their way along the littered road. It was a walk nine-year-old Elizabeth Williams never forgot:

> They said they were going to try and get some boats and get transportation up to Miami, but we would have to walk. Mother took Evelyn and Bob and me and Markelle and Buck [Markelle's brother Perry], and we walked up here, and Momma kept saying, "Don't look, don't look" because they had already started stacking up bodies. And I can remember seeing the bodies, they were stacking them up, stacking them up like cordwood, and all of them were bare. And so mother kept telling us, "Just keep your eyes on the road." And I can remember seeing the seaweed hanging on the telephone wires and wondering how it got there.

It was slow going, but they made it to where the fill used to go across Whale Harbor. There was no trace of the Williams home; nothing was there except pilings and flowing water. A man with a small boat powered by an outboard motor helped them aboard, and a black man pushed the boat out from the shore and climbed in. The outboard strained as it fought the strong current. The man running the motor was drunk and was unable to control the boat.

Just when it seemed to Mozelle the boat was going to capsize, the black man yelled to the man to cut the motor off and grabbed the oars. The inebriated man was coherent enough to know they were in serious trouble and shut off the outboard motor. The black man used the oars to row the boat out of the current into some mangroves, where they waited until another boat came along and towed them to Windley Key. Mozelle and the children finally reached Snake Creek, where they were evacuated by a Coast Guard seaplane.

By Wednesday night, Mozelle and the children were in Miami at the home of Sam and Beatrice Williams, Eddie Williams's parents. For Elizabeth and Evelyn the familiar surroundings of their grandparents' home was the best tonic in the world, but the joy of being rescued was dampened by the realization that they would never see their father again. Later

By the second day after the hurricane's passage, the bodies of the dead were discolored, swollen, and stiffened into grotesque positions. It was a horrible sight, especially for children. (FPC)

during the day, Dan and Carrie Law were evacuated and taken to Riverside Hospital in Miami, where Dan was admitted for treatment of a scalp wound and an infection on his right arm. Carrie remained with him while their daughter and son stayed with Mozelle and her children.

The exodus of survivors continued throughout Wednesday. O. D. and Betty King with Leone Barr and her son joined the line of people trekking up to Whale Harbor. They had done all the good they could do at the makeshift aid station that used to be the Rustic Inn. Now that the rescue workers had arrived and taken charge, the Kings, Barrs, and other survivors needed to get off the Keys and see to themselves.

Those who cannot walk are put on an old pickup truck that remained upright during the storm. The truck won't start, so it has to be pushed—a difficult task on a road littered with boards and rocks. Leone helps push the truck as do other people they encounter along the way to Whale Harbor.

A small boat takes them across to the west end of Windley Key. When they cross a low spot on the island, they have to wade through rivulets of salt water that still flow across the land from Florida Bay. As they near the site where the hospital and Camp Five had stood, Leone puts her hand over her son's eyes and guides him around body parts and entrails scattered on the ground. The first bodies they come across that are recognizable are those beautiful blond children that O. D. had brought by the inn just before the storm. She turns away and holds her three-year-old boy closer to her breast.

When they reach the west bank of Snake Creek, Leone is surprised how fast the water is flowing even though this is the second day after the storm. The small boat they have to board does not look up to the task of transporting them over the rushing water, and she is concerned. She later recalled: "I can't remember the name of the man who took us across Snake Creek, but he was a tall man. I was so scared because I'm scared of the water anyway. I was so scared and he knew I was scared, and I'm hanging onto my child, and he put his hand on my shoulder to calm me and he was shaking. I could just feel him shaking! It was a little old skiff going across that water and when the current hit it you could feel it, the current was still gushing."

The boats ferrying people across Snake Creek to the improvised landing on the Plantation Key side are met by people looking for friends and relatives. Among them are Leone and Betty's brothers, John and Charles Carter. They had driven down on Tuesday morning and had been camping out in their car, hoping that Betty and Leone and her son would be among the survivors finding their way to Snake Creek. When they finally see Leone and Betty, they run to greet them. Leone is holding her son when both brothers envelop her in a big hug.

As Leone makes her way through the throng at Snake Creek, she sees a familiar face. Her doctor from Coral Gables is at the aid station giving people tetanus shots. As she approaches, Dr. Cleveland looks up and says, "My God, Leone! What are you doing down here with your heart!" and that was how she learned she had a heart murmur!

O. D., Betty, Leone and her son, and the Carter brothers all pile into John's car and drive up to Homestead, where they stop at the Baptist Church Sunday School Center so that Leone can replace her water-soaked shoes that are falling apart. They then drive up to John's house in Coral Gables, and the horrific experience of the last three days becomes a bad dream.

It is after midday on Wednesday when Wilbur Jones and some of the other survivors who had taken shelter in the overturned cars of the rescue train leave Upper Matecumbe Key. As they walk toward the eastern end of the island, they encounter a group of survivors pushing an old car that has a bare bedspring across the trunk on which a black boy in great pain has been placed on his stomach. The boy had climbed up one of the FEC Railway water tank towers to escape the storm surge and had held onto one of the tower's legs during the peak winds. His clothing and the portion of his skin on his back, arms, and legs that had been exposed to the wind were blasted off by sand and debris.

Various ones come up and take turns pushing the car; many of them are suffering from exposure and shock themselves. Wilbur and other members of his party lend a hand. At one point, they meet some men walking in the opposite direction. From the condition of their clothes and the state of their health, Jones knows they have just come from the mainland. One of them says he is with the American Legion and is looking for veterans. When asked if he will help push the car carrying the injured boy, the man hesitates, then says he has a heart condition and declines. Sixty-seven years later when he recalled the incident, Jones was still infuriated, "After all we'd gone through and doing our best to help the injured, they send down a bunch of sightseers who won't give us a hand to get this boy to the mainland!"

On Windley Key as Jones approached Snake Creek on the high ground of the railroad track embankment, he looked down and recognized a friend. Jack Bell was getting out of a skiff that had just arrived from the Plantation Key side. A veteran of the Great War where he lost an arm, Jack Bell is sports editor at the *Miami Daily News*. Because of the scope of the hurricane disaster, he has been assigned to help cover the situation on the Keys. Looking across the water, Wilbur sees his brother standing on the other side. Bell tries to convince Jones to stay and go back to Upper Matecumbe with him, but Jones tells Bell he has "been through Hell and was not about to stay!" Once across Snake Creek, Jones joins his brother and the two drive to their mother's home in Miami.

Jack Bell goes on, and what he sees compels him to do some of his finest writing in an article that appeared the next day in the *Miami Daily News*. Among the grisly scenes he eloquently describes are a young woman clinging in death to her piano and the body of a black man hung up in the top of a telephone pole by the storm surge and left high above the ground as if to warn of the death and destruction that lay ahead.

Edney and Edna Parker and their family made the long walk past the gruesome sights and the harrowing trips across the two turbulent water gaps. Their six-year-old daughter, Fay, saw the bodies, some of them still oozing blood. She later recalled, "We walked by all the bodies and some of the group we were with became very upset by what they saw. I don't know why, but all the bodies didn't bother me."

When they reach Homestead, Edney contacts a friend and arranges for a place where the family can stay. He returns to the Keys as soon as they are settled. Being the constable and a longtime resident of the area, he feels it is his duty to help his surviving friends and neighbors find and bury their loved ones.

On Wednesday morning, the survivors at Long Key become concerned that rescuers have not investigated the situation at the fish camp. The limited amount of canned goods and bottled drinks that have been salvaged will not last long for twenty people. Duane decides to hike to Marathon and get help. The Long Key viaduct appears to be intact. What lies beyond that he does not know, but as a weather observer he is aware that the hurricane's center passed above Long Key so it is likely the area farther down suffered less damage.

He walks along the railroad right-of-way, finding that eleven of the seventeen miles of track from Long Key to Marathon are damaged. Duane arrives at Marathon late in the morning and gets his first good meal since Monday evening. After briefing aid workers about the situation at the fish camp and FEC Railway personnel about the condition of the line, Duane boards a work train and goes to Key West.

At the Trumbo railroad yard in Key West, Doc Mayer is still trying to learn the extent of damage to the railroad and how long it will be before the Shedd Aquarium collection car can be moved to the mainland. Wednesday evening he sends another update to his boss at the Shedd Aquarium.

BACK AT SLIP FISHES DOING WELL OUR GAS PUMP GONE I HAVE
ANOTHER MAY BE HERE WEEK OR MORE YET TWENTY MILES RAIL
OUT NO DEFINITE INFORMATION WILL NEED TWO HUNDRED WATER
HERE FAIR EXPECT TO HOLD WHAT I HAVE MUCH WEED BUT NO
RESULTS WILL GET WHAT I CAN= MAYER

Members of the Parker family arriving at Snake Creek on September 4, 1935. Edney Parker is standing in the stern. The curly-haired woman in front of him is Etta Parker Sweeting. The little girl to her right facing aft is Fay Marie Parker. Lois Parker is at the left sitting on the gunwales. The little boy to her right is Earl Parker. Edna Parker is holding her daughter Barbara. The two boys in the foreground are unidentified. (Carey)

During Wednesday morning, the hurricane raced up the west coast of Florida and made its second landfall in Florida near Deadman's Bay north of the Cedar Keys. The winds rapidly fell below hurricane intensity as it moved across north Florida. Although a tropical storm, the system still topples trees and unleashes torrential rains. As the second day after Labor Day comes to a close, the storm is west northwest of Savannah, Georgia, moving on a course that parallels the eastern shoreline. For the time being, Hurakan is through with Florida.

In a report prepared for President Roosevelt, the assistant administrator of the Federal Emergency Relief Administration stated, "by Wednesday night it was reported that all injured and able bodied who wished to leave the Keys had been evacuated." Although this was true for the situation ashore, there were people still aboard the Morgan Liner *Dixie* who definitely wished to leave.

Saving the Ships

At dawn on Wednesday, the Coast Guard's oceangoing tug *Carrabasset* arrives at French Reef and takes up a position about a half mile east of the *Dixie*. Lt. Cmdr. John McCann reports to his base that the ship "bucked mountainous waves and a fifty-five mile wind." The crew is worn out from fighting the sea. The two newspapermen aboard, Cecil Warren from the *Miami Daily News* and Virgil Pierson from the *Miami Tribune*, are sound asleep as the anchor plunges toward the bottom thirty-six hours after departing Port Everglades.

The wind is still blowing briskly, but the weather system associated with the hurricane is finally letting go of the Keys. At 6 a.m. Captain Sundstrom sends a message saying the *Dixie* is "resting easily" and all is well. Fifteen minutes later Captain E. S. Campbell of the Morgan liner *El Occidente* sends: "Strong southerly winds rough seas continue. Moderating slightly. DIXIE advises no immediate danger. Standing by, awaiting instructions from DIXIE."

The passengers and crew aboard the liner have adapted as well as can be expected in a waterlogged environment. Everything is wet or soggy. Broken glass litters many areas, and the passengers are still confined to the salon and other spaces on the upper decks. The panic and fear that prevailed during the storm and much of Tuesday have been replaced by boredom and a reluctant tolerance. At 6:30 a.m. L. D. Ransom, assistant manager of the Morgan Line, who is aboard with his wife and son, radios to the company's New York office: "All well. Every member crew has rendered perfect service. Passengers calm and in good spirits throughout entire event due their confidence ability master and officers."

Thirty minutes later the *Warbler* arrives and takes up station near the *Carrabasset*. The ship left Key West Tuesday morning, but the rough seas delayed her arrival. A wooden-hulled minesweeper built toward the end of the Great War, the *Warbler* saw six months of convoy duty with the Atlantic Fleet before being decommissioned in 1920. At that time the 188-foot vessel was loaned to the United States Shipping Board and converted to a salvage ship. Manned by a civilian crew under an arrangement with Merritt, Chapman, and Scott, a New York-based salvage firm, the *Warbler* brings the resources necessary to manage almost any damage-control situation.

At 9:30 a.m. the *Dixie's* captain orders his crew to make preparations for transferring the passengers. Many of the lifeboats have been damaged; those that are serviceable are swung out on their davits, and rope ladders are put over the sides. An hour later the *Dixie's* radio transmits the disturbing message: "No. 2 hold making water. Ten feet at 10 A.M. Have pumps on it. Still too rough to transfer." The *Dixie* has four holds and seven watertight compartments. The situation is considered manageable. Captain Sundstrom and the Morgan Line are reassured by the knowledge that the *Warbler* is standing by with a crew of experienced damage-control specialists.

Captain McRae of the *Platano* is concerned that his cargo of highly perishable bananas will spoil if he has to remain at French Reef, and he radios the United Fruit Company for direction. The company arranges for another fruiter, the *Atenas*, to be diverted to French Reef as a replacement for the *Platano*, which resumes her voyage to New York City.

By midday an armada of fifteen rescue ships has gathered off French Reef, including the *El Mundo* and *El Occidente* of the Morgan Line; the tankers *Watertown* and *Reaper*; Coast Guard vessels *Carrabasset*, *Pandora*, and *Saukee*; the salvage tug *Warbler*; and the fruiters *Limon*, *Atenas*, and *San Benito*. The larger ships are arranged in a semicircle 1½ miles southeast of the *Dixie*. The Coast Guard ships and salvage tug are able to take positions a half mile off the *Dixie* because of their lesser draft. As the morning wears on the seas continue to abate. Two of the *Dixie's* holds are taking water, but after pumps are activated the water level drops from ten feet to eight feet in about two hours.

At 1:30 p.m. the *Dixie* sends: "All ships with motor launches put them over and transfer passengers." Only the *Warbler* has a motor launch, which is put into the water and dispatched to the *Dixie*. The other rescue ships launch their boats and a convoy of small craft slowly begins to form.

All except *Warbler*'s launch must be rowed across 1½ miles of rough water.

The prospect of boarding a small boat bobbing on the seas and tossed about by the waves is very intimidating to many of the *Dixie*'s passengers. A request is put out for male volunteers to go in the first lifeboat to demonstrate that a safe transit is possible. At 2 p.m. they board one of the *Dixie*'s lifeboats and head for the *Carrabasset*, the closest vessel. Rowing against the wind and waves, it takes one hour for the small boat to cover the half-mile distance to the Coast Guard ship.

Captain Arne Pederson, master of the *Reaper*, had put his boats in the water as soon as the message came from the *Dixie* to commence the transfer operation: "We sent over two boats immediately, in charge of the chief officer and third officer. Other ships standing by sent over lifeboats at about the same time. The sea was still a little disturbed and rather rough alongside the *Dixie*, which made it difficult to take passengers aboard the lifeboats, and consequently few passengers were taken off compared to the number of lifeboats that were ready to take them to their respective ships." Crewmen of the rescue vessels and the *Dixie* struggle for five hours against the wind and sea; after moderating at midday, the wind begins to freshen toward evening.

An Associated Press reporter flew over French Reef in a chartered airplane in the late afternoon and observed: "Choppy seas and winds made the task difficult. As we flew over, there were three lifeboats in the water carrying passengers. A powerboat was towing them, but all boats had their oars in the water. The boats were bobbing up and down like corks in the rough water—sometimes you could see them, sometimes waves hid them. But the passengers, apparently unworried by the danger, seemed cheerful. They waved eagerly at us."

By 7 p.m. a gale is blowing out of the southwest and the sea has become too rough for the small boats. Captain Sundstrom wisely suspends the transfer operation. Of the 384 people aboard when the *Dixie* went aground, 164 passengers and crew have been safely taken over to rescue ships.

Six of the rescue ships with *Dixie* personnel aboard begin to get under way as darkness descends. The *Carrabasset*, *El Mundo*, *El Occidente*, and *San Benito* weigh anchor and head for Miami. The *Reaper* heads for Southport, North Carolina, while the *Atenas* proceeds to Charleston,

South Carolina. The Texaco tanker *Watertown*, the cutter *Saukee*, the salvage tug *Warbler*, the fruiter *Limon*, and two other vessels continue to stand by at French Reef.

Time passes slowly for the 131 passengers remaining aboard the *Dixie* on Wednesday night. Some become so bored they try to clean the decks, getting down on their knees and scrubbing. Jane Bryant of New York realized it was a hopeless cause, for just as the scrubbing showed promise, the slightest movement of the ship sent brown water over the cleaned area, leaving a deposit of filth and scum. "We were up to our knees in swill and contaminated water," she said.

During the early hours of Thursday morning four ships carrying a total of eighty passengers and fifty-five crewmembers from the *Dixie* arrive at the Clyde-Mallory docks in Miami. As they come down the gangways to the pier, hundreds of people and a blinding barrage of flashbulbs and camera lights greet them. Some family and friends are there, but most of the people are associated with wire services, newspapers, and newsreel production companies. Police and representatives of the Morgan Line herd the refugees through the throng, but the reporters and cameramen swarm about like the sharks on the reef, looking for tidbits of news and personal stories.

Some of the evacuees are talkative; others just want to get a bath, a decent meal, and some rest. "We lived on crackers and apples for 24 hours before the rescue," said one. Mrs. J. G. Fisher of New Orleans gave a concise summary of her experience: "First we were ordered to don lifebelts, which seemed to me a warning of approaching danger. Then the lights failed. Later the nightmarish experience of having a rope tied about you and lowered apparently into nothingness; the comparative relief of feeling even a bobbing lifeboat under your feet, and then the sound deck of the larger ship. It was a harrowing experience to feel a ship under you bound on a reef, buffeted by mountainous seas, but too much cannot be said for the officers and crew of the *Dixie*." Most of the passengers praised the calmness and professionalism of the officers and crew.

"More exciting than a movie thriller!" was the way a movie actress from Los Angeles described the rescue. A doctor and his wife from Rhode Island said they were frightened by the hurricane winds, but twenty-four-year-old Miss Myra Barnard of New York City said: "I was not frightened for a moment. The crew was wonderful." August Wade of New Orleans said, "I feel fine, although I haven't slept for three days and nights." Florence Stieler of San Francisco, who was on vacation from her job as an insurance underwriter for the New York Life Insurance Company, said she considered herself lucky to be alive. Eleanor Shields, the plucky twelve-year-old who had insisted on staying on deck to watch the waves and was tied to a deck chair when the *Dixie* struck the reef, proudly displayed her life preserver with the autographs of sixty of her shipmates on it. "Gee!" she said, "being stranded was the biggest thrill of my life!" Many others carried their life preservers with them as souvenirs.

By dawn Thursday the seas and wind on French Reef have greatly moderated. The cutter *Saukee* radios Coast Guard headquarters in Jacksonville at 6:30 a.m. that the transfer of personnel from the *Dixie* has resumed. Better weather and the previous day's experience help the shuttle operation proceed more efficiently. Two powered launches from the liner and one from the cutter *Pandora* are used to tow the lifeboats in convoys. The tug *Warbler* is able to come alongside and directly board evacuees. By 8:50 a.m. all personnel to be evacuated from the stranded ship have been taken off. The last group of *Dixie* evacuees is brought to Miami that afternoon by the cutters *Saukee* and *Pandora*, the tug *Carrabasset*, and the Morgan liner *El Occidente*.

Among the last of the passengers to arrive at Miami are newlyweds George and Lorraine Weatherby. Lorraine, a beautiful socialite to whom proper grooming and dressing are priorities, said: "We started this honeymoon a week ago looking our best. We've finished the *Dixie* part of it looking our worst. . . . But we're here now—and so glad that we don't even care how we look!"

The *Dixie* refugees are escorted from the Clyde-Mallory docks by representatives of the Morgan Line and taken to the Alcazar and Everglades hotels, where they are put up until transportation to New York can be arranged. The Morgan Line spends $50,000 in Miami for clothing, housing, and other needs of the rescued passengers and crew.

That night at 10:47, a special Seaboard Airline Railway train consisting of two engines, ten Pullmans, two dining cars, and a combination coach/baggage car pulls out of Miami and heads north. Aboard are 166 passengers and 65 crew members from the *Dixie* accompanied by several doctors and nurses. Early Friday morning the train stops at Baldwin, Florida, to discharge people who want to return to New Orleans. They are taken to Jacksonville, where they board the Seaboard's New Orleans Limited. After brief stops in Philadelphia and Trenton to discharge other evacuees, the special train rolls into New York City, arriving at Pennsylvania Station at 8:38 Saturday morning. Less than a half hour later the Havana Special pulls into the station carrying twenty passengers who had been taken to Charleston by the *Atenas*.

Over a thousand people meet the trains in New York. Reporters scribble frantically to get down the story of one evacuee before moving on to another. Newsreel cameras whir and microphones are thrust into the faces of the passengers and crew, many of whom stare through the blinding light of flashbulbs trying to find friends and family in the mass of people beyond the area roped off for the media.

At a bank of microphones surrounded by motion-picture and still cameras, some of the passengers describe their experience. Herbert Shorentz holds up his prized stamp collection album in triumph, unabashedly proud as only an eight-year-old can be at having brought it safely through the wet ordeal. Jean Marshall, age nine, announces she had not been afraid at all, but she had had to sing to her dolly and her mother for two days to keep them calm. Many praise the officers and crew of the *Dixie*, recounting noteworthy deeds.

At 5:15 p.m. the last of the evacuees arrive on a regularly scheduled train. All the passengers are escorted to the Hotel Pennsylvania, where they order clothes and meals and enjoy the comfort of a full-size bed. Members of the crew are put up at the Seamen's Institute. The Morgan Line announces that it is paying the evacuated crewmembers a month's pay "to take care of them at least temporarily." In addition, $3,000 is loaned to passengers who left their money on the *Dixie*.

With all of the passengers and over half of the crew removed from the *Dixie*, Captain Sundstrom and 52 crewmembers remain aboard to look after the stranded ship. Likewise, Captain Richard Mortensen and his crew remained aboard the *Leise Maersk* off Upper Matecumbe. The men on both ships turned their attention to refloating their vessels.

By Thursday afternoon when A. S. Hebbie boards the *Dixie*, the fleet of rescue ships has departed and the only vessels standing by to provide assistance are the *Relief* and the *Warbler*. Both vessels are operated by the

Merrick, Chapman, Scott Company, which has been placed under contract by the Morgan Line to eliminate any basis for a salvage claim being made against the *Dixie* and her cargo.

Hebbie is responsible for managing the removal of the *Dixie* from French Reef. He is a marine architect and, as the supervising engineer of the Morgan Line, oversaw the design and construction of the *Dixie*. He immediately begins a stem-to-stern inspection of the hull to determine if the vessel is seaworthy enough to be refloated. Engineers from Knight and Chapman, New York salvage specialists engaged by the Morgan Line, had boarded the *Dixie* Wednesday night and were already making their own evaluation of the ship's condition.

Hebbie and the salvage engineers come to the conclusion that the ship is seaworthy and can safely be refloated. Over the next two weeks, barges and laborers brought from Miami to French Reef offload cargo to lighten the *Dixie*. On September 19, the *Relief* and the *Warbler* pull the liner into deep water a safe distance away from French Reef. After divers visually inspect the hull, the ship is towed to Turtle Harbor, an anchorage east of the north end of Key Largo. While temporary repairs are made to strengthen the hull, cargo is reloaded and provisions are brought aboard. On September 22 at 6 a.m. the tug *Relief* takes up slack on the towline and the *Dixie* begins the final leg of her ill-fated voyage to New York.

The reason the *Dixie* was not towed to Miami or some other port prior to going to New York lies with a maritime disaster that occurred the year before. Early in the morning of September 8, 1934, the 11,530-ton *Morro Castle* of the Ward Line was heading for its home port of New York after a one-week Labor Day excursion cruise to Havana. While the ship sailed through a storm with gale-force winds off the coast of New Jersey, a fire broke out. Fanned by the high winds and feeding on flammable materials used in the finishes and furnishings of the luxurious liner, the blaze quickly spread throughout the ship. Eighty-six passengers and forty-nine crew members perished either from the fire or by drowning. The incident was intensely investigated. An official inquiry produced an extensive list of findings of negligence that included failure to construct the ship in accordance with applicable fire codes for passenger vessels; lifeboats that were stored improperly, causing access to them to be blocked; fire hydrants that had been capped because they were leaking; and failure to train the crew in the use of fire-protection equipment.

At the time of the *Morro Castle* disaster the federal law that determined liability for maritime accidents had been passed in 1851 and had never been amended. It limited the extent of the ship owner's liability to the value of his remaining interest in the vessel and freight aboard after the accident. In the *Morro Castle* case, the cargo was a total loss, and the proceeds from selling the burned-out hulk for scrap were grossly inadequate for compensating losses sustained by claimants. Furthermore, many passengers' claims were denied on the basis they were filed too late and did not comply with the terms of the contract established when tickets were issued. In the fine print on the back of the passenger tickets was a statement that required any claims against the Ward Line to be made within thirty days of the loss or the claim would be null and void.

The media extensively covered the numerous hearings, inquiries, and disputes related to the disaster. J. Edgar Hoover even had the FBI look into the incident. The public became outraged that such flagrant code violations and negligent actions resulted in no significant punishment or compensation. Politicians were quick to jump into the fray, and in the following session of Congress, Representative William Sirovich of New York sponsored a bill that substantially increased the liability of the ship owners and mandated that claimants have six months to file for compensation after suffering such losses. President Roosevelt signed the amendment into law two days before the *Dixie* went aground.

The *Dixie*'s grounding was the first maritime accident subject to the amended maritime liability law. Claimants would have the potential to recover substantial damages if negligence could be proved on the part of the ship owners or its employees. Although there were several hundred passengers and crew aboard the *Dixie* when the ship went aground, there were no deaths and very few significant injuries. The most serious injury was to an elderly female passenger who suffered a fractured hip. The other injuries were of the ordinary variety, including sprained ankles, bruises, and cuts.

The Morgan Line moved quickly to attend to the passengers' medical and other needs, and to minimize the passengers' out-of-pocket losses due to stranding incident. The company and its corporate parent, Southern Pacific, would make tempting targets for liability lawyers if negligence of any of the ship's licensed officers or the Morgan Line could be proved. The official inquiry would be crucial to determining liability exposure.

In 1935, the primary governmental entity in the United States responsible for investigating steamship incidents that involved liability was the Bureau of Navigation and Steamboat Inspection of the Department of Commerce. The bureau had offices in major ports throughout the country. Each office was assigned a jurisdictional district comprised of the ports in geographical proximity to the office. In the event of an incident at sea involving liability, the responsibility for conducting an official inquiry fell to the bureau's office having jurisdiction over the first port the involved vessel put into following the incident.

Given this situation it is not surprising that the *Dixie* was moved to Turtle Harbor and effected temporary repairs and provisioning at that anchorage instead of at Miami. The Morgan Line much preferred that the inquiry be conducted in New York, where its corporate legal staff was located and presumably where it wielded some degree of influence. By towing the ship directly to New York City, that office of the Bureau of Navigation and Steamboat Inspection became responsible for conducting the official inquiry.

The *Dixie* arrives in New York on the afternoon of September 29, 1935, and ties up at Pier 51 North River, located at the foot of West Twelfth Street. The once-black hull has turned a dark gray from salt spray and shows scrapes here and there; stains of rust can be seen on the white superstructure where it was battered by cables and parts of masts torn loose by the wind. Even so, there is still an aura of majesty about the ship as it docks. Standing on the pier are family and friends of the crew, including Mrs. Sundstrom and daughters Lillian and Florence. Captain Sundstrom is still sore from his back injury and strained muscles, but he walks down the gangway on his own and feels the firm footing of land for the first time in almost a month.

On October 1, 1935, the second day after his reunion with his family, Captain Sundstrom and other members of the crew appear before a special board convened by the New York, N.Y., supervising inspector of the Bureau of Navigation and Steamboat Inspection of the Department of Commerce to consider a supplementary report of casualties and violations of steamboat laws—File No. 26950. Two days after the grounding, the Department of Commerce had sent two steamboat inspectors from the Jacksonville office to the *Dixie* to begin investigating the grounding.

On October 14, 1935, the final report of the board is released, which states, "After carefully considering the testimony, the Board finds the accident was due to extreme and unusual weather conditions and there is no negligence on the part of any licensed officer and the case is hereby dismissed." The Morgan Line quickly and quietly settles any claims made for damaged belongings and injuries.

The freighter *Leise Maresk* has been almost totally ignored in the media coverage of the storm. Located on the shoreward bank of Hawk Channel about a thousand yards east of where the rescue train's locomotive stands on Upper Matecumbe Key, the 321-foot ship looms over the muddy flats that hold her hull in a tight grip. Once the storm surge carried the ship over Alligator Reef and deposited it onto the bank, there was nothing more that Captain Richard Mortensen and his crew could do but keep the hatches closed and the pumps running. The hull remains intact, and her diesel engine and single screw are undamaged.

Initial efforts to back the ship into deeper water failed. As the weather returns to a more normal pattern, the crew is able to begin offloading onto barges more than two hundred drums of the oil the *Leise Maersk* was carrying as cargo. Two weeks after going aground, the lightened ship comes free of its mud bed on the high tide. Under its own power, the *Leise Maersk* moves out to sea and heads for Miami, tying up at the Meteor Dock the next day. Two days later, with the cargo reloaded and minor repairs completed, the freighter departs for New York City.

Both the *Leise Maersk* and the *Dixie* had incredibly good fortune in that they were lifted over the hull-ripping rocks of the reefs and came to rest on sand and mud that cushioned their hulls. The successful removal of the *Dixie* and the *Leise Maersk* from the sensitive environment of the living reefs eliminated the dangers posed by oil (both fuel oil and the twelve thousand gallons of oil bound for Il Duce's army) and other contaminants related to the ships.

While the environmental threat to the fish at French Reef and in Hawk Channel had been removed, in Key West the almost two thousand specimens contained in the tanks and tubs aboard the Shedd Aquarium's collection car Nautilus are becoming more imperiled each day. The damage to the FEC Railway's Key West Extension is now known to be great and will take months to repair; the word on the street is that the line will probably be abandoned by the bankrupt railroad. On September 5, Doc Mayer has a great idea, so good that he sends a full-cost telegram to Director Walter Chute:

RAIL IMPOSSIBLE ARRANGE MOVEMENT BY FERRY VIA HAVANA–
NEW ORLEANS GOING GOOD= MAYER.

The next day, Chute responds with a night letter:

FERRY MOVEMENT IMPOSSIBLE. HAVANA–NEW ORLEANS SIZE LIMIT
FIFTY SIX FEET COST OVER TWO THOUSAND MUST BE PATIENT WAIT
UNTIL TRACKS REPAIRED SECURE MORE FISH IF NECESSARY WILL
WIRE MORE FUNDS IF NEEDED WILL BE IN FLORIDA SEVENTEENTH
SEE YOU THEN IF STILL THERE NOTIFY OFFICE IMMEDIATELY YOU
START BACK= CHUTE

Obviously, the people in Chicago did not understand the enormity of the damage done to the railroad. They would soon know; Spearman Lewis of the *Chicago Tribune* has arrived in the Upper Keys, and his first-hand accounts are being wired direct to the Windy City. In the meantime, Doc Mayer and his team continue to tend the fish already collected. At least now they have time to search for the tarpon and other fish that have eluded them.

On the Upper Keys amid the wreckage of homes and buildings, and in the remnants of groves and tangled clumps of mangroves, a menace is quietly growing. The cloudy skies and rain that had continued throughout Tuesday had slowed the process of decomposition of the hundreds of bodies that are scattered from Plantation Key to Grassy Key and across Florida Bay. Now the bodies floating in the water, stuck in mangrove bushes, or just lying on the ground are rotting with unbelievable rapidity in the tropical heat. Add to this the amazingly fast recovery of the fly population and the situation is ripe for a plague. The corpses are time bombs of putrefaction, and time is running out. The dead are about to threaten the living; the Grim Reaper's crop must be quickly harvested.

The Harvest

Even before the survivors left the demolished islands of the Upper Keys, undertakers in Miami were rushing hearses down to Snake Creek. For $100 (equivalent to $1,581 in 2008 dollars) per body they would place a corpse in a plain box made of pine planks that cost all of $2 to make and haul it up to Woodlawn Cemetery. It was reported that an order had been issued for three hundred of the pine boxes.

When Ernest Hemingway arrived at Lower Matecumbe Key on the Wednesday after Labor Day he was shocked at the extent and savagery of the carnage. In a letter to his editor written three days later, he said it was the first time he had seen so many bodies since June 1918, when he stood on the banks of the Lower Piave River in northern Italy and observed one hundred thousand corpses littering the battlefield after the Italians had routed the Austrians. It was not just the number of dead that impressed the former war correspondent, but who they were and how wantonly their bodies had been treated by the storm surge and high winds. In particular, the sight of two naked women wedged high up in the trees, their bodies so bloated that it took him awhile to realize they were two nice girls who had operated a sandwich shop, brought home to him the ruthlessness of the destruction that occurred on Labor Day night.

People outside the Keys were just beginning to hear about the disaster and had not come to grips with the realities involved. The same day that Hemingway was walking through the destruction on Lower Matecumbe Key, President Roosevelt was at his Hyde Park home in New York telling his aides to see that the dead were treated with respect, and that the veterans should be buried in Arlington National Cemetery unless their next of kin preferred otherwise.

The need for rapid action was made clear on Thursday morning to Conrad Van Hyning, Florida Emergency Relief administrator and the state welfare commissioner. He and other officials went to survey the damage on the Keys, flying from Dinner Key down to Lower Matecumbe in a Coast Guard seaplane. Even at several hundred feet above the islands, a strong, sickening odor filled the cabin of the plane. When they landed at Lower Matecumbe, the peculiarly sweet-obnoxious scent of decomposing bodies was overwhelming. Lt. J. E. Fairbanks, the commander of Coast Guard forces assisting relief workers, was reported to have recommended that "the entire Keys from Snake Creek to and including Lower Matecumbe be burned."

Unlike the situation at the Piave River, the collection of the dead was not a matter of bringing carts up to the bodies and hauling them away. There were some bodies in accessible locations on land, but many had been swept into Florida Bay and others into Hawk Channel on the ocean side. As Dr. J. T. Googe of the Florida State Board of Health later testified, these bodies had to become "floaters" before they could be recovered.

Many of the bodies had to be recovered from the sea, I guess perhaps a third or maybe one-half of the bodies, and before they would be recovered from the sea, they had to be floaters they would not come to the surface until they were floaters. That meant that the gas bacilli had been working on the bodies, and they were bloated, as the Governor suggested in the letter. As I say, the bodies were in a high state of decomposition, and it was dangerous, in our judgment, to transport the bodies over the road between Snake Creek and Miami.

On the day after the storm's passage, the winds were too high and the waters too roiled to do anything even if recovery forces had been available. On Wednesday, while the emphasis was on finding and removing survivors, some collection of the more accessible bodies was done. Not until Thursday did the harvesting of the dead begin in earnest. The National Guard coordinated recovery operations ashore, while the Coast Guard oversaw the collection of floaters and bodies brought in from the small islands in Florida Bay.

Hemingway came with a group of volunteer rescue workers from Key West aboard one of their fishing boats. Other people came down in boats from the mainland. Even the Border Patrol was engaged. As described in a report submitted by Border Patrol inspector Murphy Steen to his superior officer, the typical procedure was for small boats to work with a Coast Guard cutter.

Following instructions received from you on the night of September 5th, 1935, Patrol Inspector Todd and the writer left their official station at 4:00 a.m. on the morning of September 6th with Government owned Chevrolet No. 26, and trailer with boat and outboard motor. We arrived at Snake Creek on the Florida Keys about 6:45 a. m. where we reported to Lieutenant Fairbanks, Commander of Coast Guard, for duty in the storm area and were assigned to Coast Guard Cutter No. 212 for duty. We got a crew of Negroes and put the boat with outboard motor into the water and fastened it to the Coast Guard Cutter and boarded the Cutter and proceeded to patrol to Matecumbe Key. Reaching the Keys we went ashore to look for bodies. After recovering several bodies, we returned to the boat and took the outboard motor and towed in several bodies that were afloat in the water of Almarado [Islamorada]. About four o'clock in the afternoon we were ordered back to Snake Creek and remained there until about 8:00 p.m. when we started out to anchor off shore for the night.

Anchoring offshore on the windward side of the island whenever possible gave the crews some relief from the stench and flies/mosquitoes—if there was a breeze.

On board the Coast Guard cutters bodies were stowed on the afterdeck or other topside location. At the end of the day, the vessels put into Snake Creek and offloaded the corpses. Everything did not always go according to plan. One cutter was bringing in seventy-five bodies stacked on the afterdeck when it ran aground. With a falling tide, the crew could not free the vessel so they had to wait until the tide came in. To pass the time, the crew went below decks to play some cards. Just as they were beginning to relax and enjoy the game, a pounding on the sides of the hull began. The incessant thumping was caused by sharks drawn to the boat by blood and urine from the bodies running off the deck and into the water. The game was called off when a steady stream of blood began to drip onto the table from the bodies lying on the deck above. For obvious reasons, the cutters were periodically sent to the Coast Guard base in Miami for fumigation.

Ashore, the National Guard was being assisted by relief workers from the Florida ERA, Civilian Conservation Corps men from a nearby camp, and volunteers. Some of the latter were kin of people who resided on the affected keys and were looking for loved ones.

At first bodies were taken to Snake Creek and then on to Miami. In a few cases bodies were sent to their next of kin, but many ended up at the Woodlawn Cemetery in Miami. By Thursday night 110 coffins were sitting on the ground awaiting burial at the cemetery. The crude boxes were not airtight, and the stench was obnoxious six blocks away; residents in the area had trouble sleeping. Dr. George N. MacDonnell, the director of public health for Miami, issued orders that no more bodies from the Keys were to be brought into the city of Miami.

Positive identification of the bodies was considered essential so that the next of kin could be notified and a death certificate issued. Veterans Administration regulations required incontrovertible proof that a veteran had died before insurance proceeds could be paid to the beneficiary. Accordingly, as bodies were recovered personal effects were placed in a brown paper bag upon which was written a serial number. The same number was written on a tag affixed to the body. In many cases identification was made on the basis of personal items found on the bodies such as discharge papers, ID cards, or engraved belt buckles, rings, and bracelets.

Some corpses were naked and had become so bloated that their features were distorted to the point of making them unrecognizable. The task of trying to identify them fell to fingerprint experts. Identification specialists with the Miami Police Department toiled all day Thursday in the hot sun at Snake Creek and Windley Key, immersed in an atmosphere so foul-smelling it seemed to have substance. They went from corpse to corpse, brushing aside the flies that covered the body, gently grasping the swollen fingers, applying ink, and then pressing a paper card to the dead tissue to lift the prints. By early evening the flesh was coming off the fingertips before the print could be obtained. They were about to give up and return to the mainland when one fingerprint expert discovered that slipping the victim's finger skin over his own gloved finger often allow the prints to be taken.

The collection of bodies became more difficult as time passed. Some bodies were so decomposed that the only way they could be handled was to roll them up and stuff them into a bag. Body parts and entrails were raked and shoveled as if so much yard waste. Even when a body was found intact, by the time it was extricated from brush or debris workers were often handling just the torso. It was not unusual for swollen stomachs and intestines to explode, splattering putrid, sticky, gelatinous material onto the exposed skin and clothing of the recovery team. At least one worker was sent back to the mainland in a state of shock after such an experience.

The obvious potential of disease from decomposing bodies prompted some recovery personnel on Upper Matecumbe Key to cremate fifty-six bodies on their own initiative before orders came down from the Veterans Administration (VA) in Washington and from the Florida governor's personal representative that no more bodies were to be burned. The order was issued even though the State of Florida health officer strongly advocated cremation to protect the public health. Hemingway, who had seen first-hand the poor condition of the bodies, was astounded that such an order was issued and that the president's plan was to transport what amounted to boxes of putrefaction all the way to Arlington.

Washington officials never publicly stated a reason for their opposition to on-site cremation, although it was supposed that the VA wanted more time to try to identify as many of the bodies as possible. Governor Sholtz's personal representative said that the governor wanted to tour the Keys before making the decision. The Miami undertakers thought the dead should be given funerals and not treated like rubbish, stacked in a heap, and burned.

Sholtz flew down to Lower Matecumbe Thursday afternoon and met with health and Florida ERA officials amid the stench of eighty-nine bodies lined up at the ferry slip. That night he met with federal, state, and Red Cross officials for two hours at the McAllister Hotel in Miami to define the roles and responsibilities of the organizations involved in the recovery work. All parties agreed to the following assignment of roles and responsibilities.

That the Florida Emergency Relief Administration should be responsible, effective Friday morning, September 6, for the removal of all bodies from the keys, that the Red Cross at their request should be responsible for the relief of all civilians, that the National Guard should be assigned to police duty to prevent persons entering the keys at either end to guard property and to maintain order, that Sheriffs Coleman and Thompson, of Dade and Monroe Counties, respectively, would direct the activities of the three organizations and would clear all questions arising between the organizations.

At 1 a.m., when the meeting concluded, it was agreed that an attempt would be made to assemble five hundred men by 6 a. m. and take them to locations in the Keys where the largest number of casualties had occurred. This plan was carried out, and by Friday afternoon there were approximately eight hundred men involved in recovering bodies from various parts of the Keys and Florida Bay.

The governor's order notwithstanding, Eddie Williams's body was recorded as having been cremated on September 6 in his automobile. His daughter Elizabeth recalled that the cremation of her father was difficult for the family:

They told mother they cremated him—they just burned the car. But, two weeks later, a friend of Mother's and Daddy's went back to make sure that everything had been destroyed, and he found that the body had been only partially burned, and that is what hurt so bad. In fact, the man that went back and found Daddy's body had a nervous breakdown over it.

My uncle Roy went down and put Daddy's remains in a box after they cremated him again. He took them back up to Tavernier, and Aunt Ellie and Ed Lowe's wife had property there, and she said that we could bury Daddy's remains there. Grandpa had been married before and had had three children by his first wife. Her casket had washed up from the little cemetery on Matecumbe and so they took that casket and put Daddy's remains in it and took it up to Uncle Ed's property and buried them there.

Grandma and Grandpa never knew that Daddy had been cremated; the family kept it quiet because it would have upset them so bad.

With the augmented workforce combing the mangroves and waters of the islands, bodies began to accumulate to the point that Henry Hansen, the state health officer, and Col. George Ijams, the personal representative of President Roosevelt, both urged Governor Sholtz to authorize the burning of corpses. On Friday night, the governor issued the following statement: "It is to be regretted that the request of the President cannot be complied with, but the interests of public health make it necessary to dispose of the bodies immediately."

On Saturday, there were 1,200 men engaged in recovering bodies and creating mounds of decomposing corpses and body parts. In accordance with the governor's order, the horrific piles were covered with wood debris, doused with oil, and set ablaze. The first official cremations were attended by solemn ceremonies. Prior to the application of a torch to the pyre, Protestant, Catholic, and Jewish rites were administered, followed by the firing of rifles by an honor guard of National Guardsmen. Most of the cremations thereafter were less formal and considerably more efficient.

Bodies in situations that made extraction impractical were burned where the individual lay. On the islands in Florida Bay, some bodies were buried and some were burned. In all cases, attempts were made to identify each corpse before disposing of it, and the data were meticulously recorded. The information was consolidated on a chart showing the locations where bodies were found, their age/name/hometown if known, whether they were a veteran or civilian, and whether the body was cremated or buried.

As soon as he had his family settled, Edney Parker returned to the Keys to assist with the identification of the dead and to perform his duties as constable. He found the remnants of the cottage on which he and his family had floated out to sea and back. On the one piece of the kitchen wall that remained upright was the bag of coffee grounds his daughter had hung on a nail just before the cottage disintegrated.

In a manuscript prepared in 1951 by Henry Reno entitled "Islamorado" with the byline "by Capt. Edney Parker as told to Henry Reno," Edney recalled a run-in he had with the National Guard while trying to help a friend:

I had a little trouble with Carter, an officer of the National Guard when I went to what was left of my house one day for something. He talked around about martial law but I got what I wanted and I didn't feel like talking to him that day.

The next day I found Ed Albury's wife and child's bodies and told Philbrick [funeral home director in Miami] to send down a metal casket for them, and I was helping Ed put them in when Carter came along. He started talking about orders that the dead were to be cremated. Ed took off with a hatchet. Freshly sharpened, the hatchet was. I got Ed away from Carter and pulled my pistol.

"If you give me anymore trouble," I told Carter, "I'm going to shoot you full of holes. And I'm not going to report it to anybody. I'm burning 88 bodies at Islamorado [sic] this morning. I am in charge of the cremation. I will throw you on there and burn you and nobody will know the difference."

Carter went off up to Tavernier and complained to Doc Lowe [justice of the peace], and Doc told him, "Edney is a constable down there, and a constable has the same authority in his district that the sheriff has. I advise you to do like he says."

We didn't have anymore trouble with the National Guard.

Recovering bodies was terrible work, hard physically and emotionally. As constable, Edney had previous experience handling corpses, but as a man who had fathered twelve children, even he had his limits:

I could take out the bodies of dead men, alright. At Camp Five we found 39 dead stacked by the water in a heap like you stack cordwood. But I came on a pool where five children were drowned. There was a little fellow floating face down, and I took him out.

"Why, your mama just dressed you," I said, and I broke and cried.

Mass cremations occurred on Plantation Key, Upper Matecumbe Key, and Lower Matecumbe Key. The day after the governor authorized cremations, nineteen identified dead veterans and nineteen unidentified bodies were burned on Plantation Key at Snake Creek. On Lower Matecumbe about one mile northeast of the ferry slip, the bodies of two women, fourteen veterans, and Louis Cruze, the ferry engineer, were burned.

From September 8 through 16, sixteen funeral pyres set ablaze on Lower Matecumbe Key consumed the bodies of fifty-two veterans; on Upper Matecumbe Key, four cremations involving thirty-six bodies took place. The final mass cremation in which eight bodies were burned occurred on Lower Matecumbe Key. The last cremation took place on Lower Matecumbe Key on November 15.

Notification of the next of kin of deceased veterans was greatly facilitated by the recovery of an index file from the wreckage of the Matecumbe Hotel. Most people learned who was dead and who had survived from the newspapers, which during the week following the storm published lists of victims and survivors almost daily. For many families it was a period of excruciating anguish, especially when loved ones would be reported as survivors in an early list and then classified as a victim in a later list.

The people who had the roughest time emotionally were the kin and friends of people who were listed as missing. At first there was hope that they would be found alive. As time passed and nothing was heard about the missing person, hope faded and was replaced by a disquieting need for closure. Such was the case of the Knowles, Russell, Pepper, and Grooms families.

A week after the hurricane struck the Keys, a unit of the Biloxi Mississippi Coast Guard was probing the southern shore of the Everglades in the vicinity of Flamingo, a small fishing village just north of the Oyster Keys. Heading east, they followed the coast past the drainage canal and around the point where the shoreline turns straight north. They soon came upon what appeared to be a body lying up on the beach. As the burial detail approached they could see it was actually two bodies, a young woman holding a small baby, both prostrate, both dead. The sand from the water to the bodies had been pushed around in repetitive patterns much like turtles make with their flippers when coming ashore, clear signs that the woman had used her last bit of strength to crawl across the sand while clinging to the baby. The men removed a gold ring from the woman's finger and buried the two bodies on the beach. Their report was submitted along with the ring to the commanding officer of the Coast Guard cutter *Nemesis*.

About two weeks later a letter arrived in Tavernier addressed to Mr. Charles C. Albury, Principal, Matecumbe Graded School, Islamorada, Florida. In the letter, Lt. Cmdr. L. H. Baker reported finding the unidentified body of a young woman near Flamingo, and that "a small gold ring was found on the body which bore the initials 'M. G. S.' date 1932 on the seal of the ring, and on the inside of the ring, the initials 'R. H.' were engraved. This ring was manufactured by Stephan Lane Folger, 180 Broadway, New York City, and by writing him we have learned that in 1932, you ordered three identical rings for Matacumbe [sic] Graded School, Islamorada." The letter went on to request Albury's assistance in identifying the owner of the ring.

Charles "Prof" Albury has been teaching school in the Upper Keys for five years. He teaches grades four through eight, while Gladys Pinder teaches the lower grades at the school in Rock Harbor, and Ferran Pinder teaches grades one through eight in Islamorada. They all survived the hurricane, but the school building did not. As principal, Prof. Albury is still trying to develop a plan for reestablishing the Matecumbe Graded School. He has no idea how many of the seventy-five students who were enrolled for the school year that started the day after Labor Day have been killed, how many of the survivors will return to the Keys, and when they might come back.

He does know that the Coast Guard has misread one of the engraved initials on the ring they found; they are not "R. H.," but "R. K." He writes back that he did indeed order rings for three people in 1932, and that two of the people are living in Key West. The ring they recovered belonged to Mrs. Andrew J. Booth, the pumper's wife and postmaster John Russell's niece.

Ruth Knowles Booth and her two-month-old baby had been swept into Florida Bay toward the northeast. How long they were in the water before they reached that lonely beach twenty miles away from their house on Upper Matecumbe is not known, but the crawl marks across the sand mutely testify that she was alive when she arrived there and of the heroic effort she made to save her child. Her husband did not make it off the island but became trapped in debris and drowned. He was cremated on Upper Matecumbe.

At first Bascom and Rosalie Grooms were not too concerned that they did not hear from their daughter, Rosalind, the day after the hurricane made landfall in the Upper Keys because the telephone and telegraph wires were down and there was no way that either she or George Pepper could communicate with them. On Wednesday some communications were restored, but the traffic was high and it would not have been too difficult to rationalize that they would certainly make contact the next day. On Thursday September 5, Bascom Grooms Sr. received a series of telegrams indicating that there was no sign of Rosalind.

Some reports said that she and George Pepper were seen with Mr. and Mrs. Dumas at the Caribbee Colony before the storm surge hit. A wire from Mrs. Ed Butters of the Matecumbe Hotel said she believes George and Rosalind were lost as they attempted to leave Lower Matecumbe. A report from V. Stanton of radio station WIOD reported that George Pepper's body has been found, and then that George and Rosalind had been seen at Caribbee Colony, but that area was severely damaged and no trace of them has been found.

Still other reports from Gulf Life Insurance personnel who are in the Upper Keys say they cannot locate the couple. The next day an article appears on the front page of the *Key West Citizen* with the headline "GROOMS NOW HAS BUT LITTLE HOPE FOR DAUGHTER." It concludes by saying: "Rosalind Grooms Palmer and George Pepper are two of the most popular members of the younger set in Key West. Their many friends are saddened by the adverse reports."

On Sunday, the director of the WPA in Miami wires Bascom that he believes Rosalind's body has been found. Bascom wires back a request that the body be flown to Key West to confirm identification. The body apparently was determined not to be Rosalind's.

On September 18, an article appeared in the *Key West Citizen* with the headline "SEARCHNG PARTY BELIEVED TO HAVE LOCATED CAR IN WHICH MISS GROOMS WAS LOST DURING RECENT HURRICANE." Dr. and Mrs. Julio DePoo, along with Fernando Camus and four others from Key West were at the demolished site of Camp Five when they received a report that a submerged car had been found in the water between Upper Matecumbe Key and Lower Matecumbe Key. Their party includes a diver who investigates and reports that the car is a Dodge sedan resting on the bottom with its roof about a foot below the surface of the water, three hundred yards from the east end of Lower Matecumbe. The windows were fully up and the doors locked; there was a hole in the canvas roof of the car. Inside were found a pair of white slippers the same size that

Rosalind wore, a new pair of men's shoes, a pair of sunglasses, papers with Ben Davis's name on them, and a bundle of mail addressed to veterans. No bodies were found. Davis later confirmed that it was indeed his car.

A theory begins to circulate that George and Rosalind were in the car when the fill blew out. Being good swimmers, as the car sank they kicked off their shoes and exited the car via the hole cut in the canvas top of the car.

On Wednesday night, September 18, one of the boats that had been searching the outlying islands for bodies in Florida Bay puts into Snake Creek. On Monday they were at Coon Key, about twelve miles north northwest of where the fill between Upper Matecumbe and Lower Matecumbe used to be. The body of a young woman was found on the beach covered with seaweed. She had no hair on her head and all her clothing except for her brassiere was gone.

She is one of eleven bodies found by the search party as they worked the mud flats and small islands of the bay. Most of the bodies were in such an advanced state of deterioration that they were doused with gasoline and burned where they were found, but the girl's body was not badly decomposed and they brought it with them to Snake Creek. Alice Lowe, the wife of justice of the peace E. R. ("Doc") Lowe, views the body and says she is positive it is Rosalind Grooms Palmer. Early the next morning, a telegram is sent to Key West to that effect.

Previous reports of the recovery of Rosalind's body have proved false so to spare the Grooms family additional grief Dr. H. C. Galey, Rosalind's doctor; Dr. Armando Cobo, her dentist; and A. F. Ayala, a close friend of the Grooms family leave on Luther Pinder's speedboat the *Boca Chica* to inspect the body. At Snake Creek the body is placed aboard the motor launch *Sailfish*. The two boats meet at the ferry slip on No Name Key. Using his dental records, Dr. Cobo makes a positive identification; Rosalind has been found. Her body is transferred to the *Boca Chica* and taken to Key West.

When the speedboat arrives in Key West, Rosalie asks for the brassiere to be sent to her. Rosalind was very particular when it came to her bra and only wore a certain brand. The brassiere convinces Rosalie that this is indeed her child. Dr. Galey tells Rosalie that he believes Rosalind died instantly without suffering.

On Sunday, September 22, funeral services are held at the Lopez Funeral Home in Key West with the Reverend A. W. Dimmick of St. Paul's Episcopal Church officiating. Rosalind is laid to rest in the Boyer plot at the Key West cemetery.

The Individual Record of Burial lists the cause of death as accidental drowning; however, the medical examiner told Bascom Sr. that no water was found in her lungs and that she died of exposure. Because the body was not badly decomposed when found, her brother believed Rosalind survived for many days after the storm, marooned on the small key. She must have heard the motors of passing search planes and launches off in the distance; Snake Creek was only eleven miles southeast of where she was found. Without clothes to protect her from mosquitoes, she may have wrapped herself in seaweed and waited for help to come.

Although the funeral brought closure for the Grooms family, the Pepper family in Titusville did not have that benefit. When they did not hear from their son during the day after the storm struck, they became greatly concerned. On the second day after the storm's passage, George Pepper's brother John W. (Cecil) Pepper drove down to the Keys to see if he could find his brother. Cecil looked at body after body until he became so sick he had to go back to Miami. On Thursday, John Good (George's boss) notified the family by telegram that "ALL INDICATIONS POINT GEORGE KILLED IN HURRICANE. AM DOING ALL POSSIBLE TO FIND BODY. WILL WIRE YOU DIRECT IMMEDIATELY ANYTHING ELSE DEFINITE."

On Friday, September 6, a list of dead and missing people appears in the *Miami Herald* and includes an entry simply stating "George Pepper, nephew of Claude Pepper, former state senator," without any indication as to whether he was dead or missing. The waiting becomes too much for the family, and later that day George's parents, his other brother John Daniel Jr., his sister Woodrow, and two of his friends leave Titusville by automobile and attempt to drive down to Snake Creek.

At Homestead they learn that the National Guard is strictly limiting access to the Keys to rescue personnel because of the deteriorating bodies. They turn around and go back to Miami and stay with Cecil for a day while they try without success to get information about George. The group returns to Titusville with nothing but sad hearts. At some point, Claude Pepper went down to the Keys and met with Florida ERA officials.

The only thing the politician learns is that George's body has not been found.

On October 10, 1935, a small boat scouting for storm victims enters Madeira Bay on the southern coast of the Everglades. The body of a young man is found and identified as George Pepper. He is buried along the shore and a note is made of the name, date, location, and method of disposition. The information becomes part of the record listing victims and the disposition of bodies.

For some inexplicable reason, neither Claude Pepper nor any other member of the Pepper family is informed of the body's recovery. There is no mention of it in the media. The Grooms family is not informed. Friends and family in Titusville, Key West, and Tallahassee are unaware that George has been found. This situation persists for decades even though the disposition of George Pepper's body appears in the record of the congressional committee that holds hearings on the hurricane in the spring of 1936.

Woodrow Pepper finally learns of her brother's fate in 1978, when Cecil Wright, a former student of hers, reads *Man in the Everglades* by Charlton W. Tebeau. On page 135, Tebeau states, "George Pepper was buried at Madeira Bay." Wright sends his former elementary school teacher a copy of the book with a note saying this may be her brother. George's cousin Frank Pepper and Rosalind's brother Bascom Grooms Jr. both said that they never had heard that the body had been found.

Once the cremations on the Keys had been completed and the threat of plague removed, people began to wander back to the islands to salvage belongings and to see what was left of their homes and businesses. There was not much.

Assessing the Damage

In October 1935 the U.S. Army Corps of Engineers office in Miami Beach prepared a chart that showed the path of the hurricane across Florida Bay, the direction of the wind at various stages, the maximum height of the water across the FEC Railway right-of-way, the location and extent of washouts, and a tabulation of damage done to the line (track destroyed, ballast lost, and fill removed). The Corps of Engineers established the south end of the "Limits of Storm Damage" about 4½ miles northeast of Marathon near the east end of Key Vaca. The northern limit was set two miles northeast of Tavernier on Key Largo.

Some damage did occur beyond these limits, particularly in the Marathon area. For example, the Parrish family lost their business/home located near Marathon. William and Mary Parrish, five daughters, and son had moved to Marathon in 1927 and built a fish house and home on Boot Key, which is located adjacent to the lower half of Key Vaca on the ocean side. On Labor Day, they had staying with them a Key West attorney, Raymond Lord, and his wife, daughter, and a friend. After 8 p.m. the wind was blowing from the northwest and for a period of several hours varied over a range of 70–100 mph. High tides floated railroad ties and other heavy timbers from a Florida East Coast Railway storage area at Marathon. The northwest wind blew the lumber across Knight Key Harbor and down the canal over which the Parrish fish house and home was constructed on pilings.

The heavy timbers pushed by wind-driven waves became battering rams that pounded against the pilings, shaking the building. The Parrishes and their guests realized the danger and went to the Sombrero Fishing Lodge, where they safely weathered the remainder of the storm; however, their fish house and home collapsed and were a total loss.

There were some casualties in the Marathon area. After the storm had passed, Parrish telegraphed a report to Chief Deputy Bernard Waite at Key West that Ferris Farrington had been found dead in his boat after the storm passed. Farrington was one of six commercial fishermen who lived aboard their boats in the waters off Marathon.

On Key Vaca, the island where Marathon is located, Norberg Thompson of Key West owned a fish house and small residence. Henry Cates and Hemming Lilja, two shark fishermen employed by Thompson as caretakers of the facilities, were on the premises during the hurricane. Little damage was done to the residence, but the fish house was extensivey damaged. Built on a man-made spit and surrounded on three sides by attached docks, the roof was partially blown off and the docks ripped loose by the wind and tide. Cates was able to save himself by hanging onto a railroad tie. Lilja was struck by a heavy timber and died.

A dredge belonging to the Florida East Coast Railway was anchored in a bight on the bay side near Marathon when the storm struck. The wind and tide pushed it up onto the shore about three blocks. Many people in the area lost their boats that night.

On Grassy Key, about 9½ miles northeast of Marathon and within the Corps of Engineers storm damage limits, the Florida East Coast Railway had living quarters for a maintenance crew. There was one white family named Favis; the remainder were black. The Favis family, section gang foreman Davis, and most of the section gang went to Marathon and survived. A man named "Foots" and Jim Ashe, his wife, and child remained on Grassy Key and drowned. All the buildings except for half of the Favis house were washed into the sea.

Much of the railroad track between Grassy Key and Long Key was washed off the roadbed and deposited on the south side of the right-of-way. This indicates the surge in this location came from Florida Bay. The graceful concrete spans of the Long Key viaduct remained intact.

At Long Key, all of the Florida East Coast Railway facilities including the train station, yacht dock, fish camp lodge and cabins, repair crew quarters, and materials storage area were destroyed. Twenty people were on the island during the hurricane; all survived with only minor injuries.

The Corps of Engineers' plot of storm surge height begins at the middle of Long Key, where the water reached sixteen feet above mean sea level, about eight feet above the top of the railroad track, which was laid on an embankment.

At Craig between Long Key and Lower Matecumbe Key, the top of the track was slightly more than eighteen feet above mean sea level. The storm water reached a height of sixteen feet, but waves superimposed on top of the surge came over the track. R. W. Craig's home, store, post office, and marina were wrecked. The bridge tender's home was partially destroyed. On the bay side, Ivor Olson's boat remained anchored on a makeshift marine railway. Although six adults and five children were on the tiny island during the hurricane, no loss of life occurred. R. W. Craig was one of the few people with places on the Keys who carried hurricane insurance.

At the southwest end of Lower Matecumbe, the stormwater reached eighteen feet above mean sea level or about eight feet above the railroad tracks. Veterans Camp Three, Bradford's store and restaurant, and the Corslan fish house were destroyed; the ferry *Monroe County* was washed up onto the north side of the railroad embankment; and the track was ripped off the roadbed and deposited on the bay side of the right-of-way. Just northeast of the veterans camp, two large trenches running northwest to southeast were cut across the face of the island. The easternmost gouge was over a half mile wide and five feet deep. At Veterans Camp Five on the northeast end of Lower Matecumbe, the stormwater was 9½ feet deep over the ground; Camp Five was erased.

The 2.16-mile water gap between Lower Matecumbe Key and Upper Matecumbe Key that had been closed with fill for over twenty-five years was blasted away, and the natural channels that existed before the railroad was built were restored. All that remained was a small island of core material about midway across. The deepest channel was cut to a depth of ten feet below mean sea level.

Indian Key, a quarter mile east of the northeast end of Lower Matecumbe, was swept clean; however, one of the heavy glass panes from the Alligator Reef lighthouse five miles to the southeast was found intact on the island. Leon Coulter and William Hanlan, who elected to stay on the island after receiving airdropped warnings of the approaching hurricane, perished. In contrast, Lignumvitae Key, two miles north of the northeast end of Lower Matecumbe on the bay side, showed little effect from the storm surge.

Top: The Caribbee Colony before the hurricane struck (HMSF). *Bottom*: The site was swept clean by winds of 200+ mph and the storm surge. (FPC)

The Alligator Reef lighthouse was the first occupied place to experience the storm surge. Being poised on the edge of the reef, the steel structure took the full brunt of the wind and water. The men at the lighthouse survived, but they were stranded; their motorboat that had been locked in its davits on the light's tower was washed across Hawk Channel and found on the remains of the fill between Lower Matecumbe Key and Upper Matecumbe Key.

Henry Haskins, the district assistant superintendent of lighthouses, after visiting Alligator Reef aboard the lighthouse tender *Ivy*, was impressed by the concentration of the storm's destructive power. Tennessee Reef light, eleven miles to the southwest of Alligator Reef, and Molasses Reef light, seventeen miles to the northeast, were virtually unscathed. Haskins reported that at Alligator Reef the destruction was extensive: "Every glass in the lantern was broken and the heavy 'first order' lens was completely demolished. Balconies were washed away, boats swept from the davits and the entire illuminating apparatus put out of commission." The lighthouse service installed an acetylene-powered lamp and had the Alligator Reef light functioning again as a navigational aid within four days after Labor Day.

At the southwest end of Upper Matecumbe Key where the highway crossed over the railroad track, the Caribbee Colony had occupied the shore on the ocean side. The tourist camp that George Merrick had built—the place where Mozelle Williams had tantalized tourists with her cooking, where Liz and Evelyn Williams had locked all the toilet stalls from the inside, and where many good times were had dancing under the stars—was "swept away as though a mowing machine had passed over it," according to the Florida ERA damage assessment survey team.

Forty-six-year-old J. Wade Dumas, who operated the camp with his wife, was washed into Florida Bay; his body was found on Twin Key three weeks later. His wife, Marie Polk Dumas, is believed to have been one of the many unidentified corpses that were cremated. Of twenty-six people said to have been at the Caribbee Colony when the hurricane struck, only four were reported to have survived.

The damage survey report prepared by the Florida ERA contained this comment about Upper Matecumbe Key:

There is not one house standing where before the storm was a beautiful sand beach with thousands of cocoanut trees and quite a number of nice residences along the shore line and also some nice residences along Highway #4 in this area.

The only things left standing on this particular section of key called Matecumbe are cisterns that were embedded in solid rock and parts of wrecked cars that were rolled over and over and evidently several hundred feet from where they originally stood. There are bathtubs, sinks and other heavy household things such as stoves, iron cabinets lying all around about 150 to 200 feet from where they originally stood.

The only two houses that were standing on this key are along the highway. Both of these, it is understood, were owned by a Mr. [Berlin] Felton. They were a small residence and a filling station [Rustic Inn] right to the side of the residence. These two places are practically total wrecks and they are still standing. The other place is the Matecumbe Hotel. The whole upper structure of this well built hotel is blown off and the bottom story to the south is practically all blown to pieces. This place of business is beyond repair although it is still standing.

Braime Pinder's fine house, the Russell families' homes, Eddie Carey's house and cottages, the place where Edna and Edney Parker raised eleven of their twelve children, all were now nothing but wreckage and debris mixed with sand.

At the northeast end of Upper Matecumbe Key, the half-mile fill connecting the island to Windley Key had disappeared, taking with it Eddie Williams's boat and the house he had completed six months earlier. The Ingrahams' home and all who were in it were washed away. Mary Louise Ingraham would never get to use her hard-earned two-year diploma.

The low parts of Windley Key were swept clean by the storm surge. Veterans Camp One and the hospital building were demolished.

At Snake Creek, the fill approaches to the concrete abutments of the trestle were washed out, and the trestle itself was nowhere to be seen. Large sections of the highway bridge decking had been stripped off, leaving the pilings standing naked in the swirling water.

Before the storm there had not been much on Plantation Key except cultivated fields, a few houses, and a rock quarry worked by the veterans. Now there was nothing but stripped groves, withered trees, and water-filled pits. Twenty-eight people reported to have taken refuge in a "hurricane-proof" house located on the island survived. An eight-year-old boy was swept out of the house, but he saved himself by clinging to the railroad track. William Alexander Tyree and two of his five children died when their rented house collapsed. His wife, Dolly, and their youngest son, Gerald (7), were in Miami on Labor Day. Billy and Louise Tyree, sixteen-year-old twins who occasionally performed at the Tavernier theater on talent nights, survived by clinging to trees. Their sisters Myrtle (11) and Maybelle (14) were killed.

On the southwest end of Key Largo at Tavernier, the Corps of Engineers determined that the storm surge at the train station was 15.2 feet above mean sea level; about six feet above ground level. This was near the northeastern limit of storm damage. Some houses were moved off their foundations. E. R. "Doc" Lowe and his family tried to ride out the storm at their house, but a sidewall began to collapse, and they took shelter in a nearby cottage. Doc Lowe suffered a head injury, but others in the party came through with only minor scratches. According to newspaper accounts, about half the buildings in Tavernier were damaged, most by the wind.

An interesting racial incident occurred at Tavernier during the hurricane. Clarence "Pop" Alexander and other blacks in Tavernier took refuge in a sturdy building next to the grocery store and theater. While the wind was roaring outside, a white man came in and told them they would have to leave so the white people could use the building. Alexander and the other blacks went out into the storm and found a safe haven in a nearby boxcar on a siding. As the building the whites were in (the one from which the blacks had been ejected) began to lose its roof, the whites fled and joined the blacks in the boxcar. Survival overcame segregation!

From the standpoint of financial cost, there is no question that the Florida East Coast Railway had the greatest losses. The railroad's Key West Extension had been in operation for over twenty-five years. During that time the system had experienced numerous hurricanes and the repair crews on the Florida Keys line had developed a routine for checking and repairing storm damage. When warnings were received that adverse weather was in the offing, repair kits and supplies were made ready and each department that would be involved in recovery operations moved into a stand-by mode. The first indication that damage had occurred was always the same; the telegraph lines between stations would cease to function. This enabled the general location of the damaged area to be determined. When the storm abated, the repair crews—one from the north and one from the south—began working toward each other, removing debris from the track and making repairs where necessary. Except where very substantial damage was involved, this protocol usually resulted in service being restored within a few hours.

After the Labor Day hurricane, as the repair crews probed from the north and south, it quickly became apparent that catastrophic damage had been sustained. On September 6, 1935, the *Miami Daily News* reported, "Wrecking crews that had been sent to the keys, it was learned, have been withdrawn and sent to their own divisions, lending strength to reports circulating for many months that the F.E.C. planned abandonment of that line, possibly replacing it with a bus service."

Over a 39.4-mile segment from just north of Tavernier to the north end of Key Vaca, 30.2 miles of track were destroyed, including four miles of steel rails that just disappeared. Two miles of track were found at Cape Sable, twenty miles across Florida Bay. Nineteen miles of track now lay beside its roadbed, some of which was still attached to its ties and twisted in a spiral. About sixteen miles of track were moved from one to ten feet off center.

Along the main line, 33.6 miles of ballast were blown away. Some ballast was found on the catwalk around the top of the lighthouse at Alligator Reef, five miles from the nearest track. Almost 660,000 cubic yards of fill were gone; if this amount of fill were placed in a container having a base the size of a football field, it would be almost forty stories high.

In addition to the track, roadbeds, fills, and trestles, damage was done to buildings (stations, offices, storerooms, houses), floating equipment (boats, dredges), and telegraph lines. The Florida East Coast Railway estimated its losses at $500,000.

The railroad moved quickly to construct facilities to enable the restoration of railroad car ferry service to Cuba. The FEC Railway determined that the best location for this facility was Port Everglades. To speed construction, the huge steel apron that bridges the gap at the ferry dock between the ship and shore was removed from the Key West facility and installed at Port Everglades. By October 21, 1935, the FEC Railway had restored railroad car ferry service to Cuba, bypassing Key West.

From the standpoint of functionality, the Key West Extension had become two local railways; one from Homestead to Tavernier, and the other from Key West to Marathon. Neither of the truncated lines was capable of producing nearly enough revenue to cover the cost of their operation. The receivers of the bankrupt railroad estimated the cost to repair the damaged portion of the line and restore rail service to Key West, including rebuilding damaged trestles with steel girder beams on concrete piers, to be $2,940,000.

The Key West Extension had been dragging down the bottom line of the FEC Railway for many years. The concept of Key West as a transshipment center had never fully materialized, having been made unnecessary by the rapid deployment of shipboard refrigeration. The income potential of the line did not justify the cost of its restoration.

The dismal income potential combined with the general deterioration of the line presented a strong argument for abandoning the Key West Extension. Parts of the infrastructure had been submerged in salt water for over twenty-five years, and even components above the waterline, such as steel trestles, were frequently coated with salt-water spray. The corrosive environment, the erosive forces of tides and hurricanes, and the wear and tear of heavy locomotives had taken their toll on the system. As soon as the extent of the storm damage was known, many people began to think the railroad should sell its right-of-way to the government for conversion to a continuous highway to Key West.

The relocation of the Cuban railcar ferry service to Port Everglades, although initially portrayed as a temporary exigency necessitated by the storm, proved to be of great benefit to the FEC Railway. Havana is 230 miles from Port Everglades compared to 92 miles from Key West; the extra distance required twelve to thirteen hours more time at sea to complete. After compensating the railcar ferry company for the added costs, the FEC Railway was earning 30 percent less total freight revenues on its export and import traffic than it was when operating from Key West; however, the longer sea voyage eliminated 172 miles from the trip to northern markets. This savings plus the elimination of charges for maintaining the Key West Extension resulted in the Port Everglades operation becoming more profitable for the Florida East Coast Railway than the Key West arrangement. Once the profitability of the Port Everglades arrangement was firmly established, the fate of the Key West Extension was sealed.

Doc Mayer learned of the plan to restore ferry service at Port Everglades when workmen began disassembling the ferry apron and other equipment at the Key West yard. On September 23, 1935, he wrote to the Shedd Aquarium director, Walter Chute: "Received your wire this morning and have been told by the railroad people of a ferry landing to be put in at Port Everglades. No date has been set for completion, but they say it will require at least thirty days." Mayer added that the weather was hot and the mosquitoes swarming, but most of the specimens aboard the Nautilus were doing nicely except for the shellfish and the small stuff.

On the same day, the weathermen in Jacksonville began watching a developing center of circulation in the Caribbean Sea halfway between Haiti and Venezuela. Over the next five days, the system became a hurricane and moved erratically, eventually settling in a path headed toward the Florida Keys. As it raced over Cuba, the hurricane began recurving and by the end of the September 28 was in the Florida Straits off Miami bearing down on Bimini and the northernmost islands of the Bahamas.

At Bimini, fifty miles east of Miami, the maximum winds were estimated to be 120 mph, and the storm surge reached fifteen feet. Half the dwellings on the small islands were damaged, and fourteen people were killed. Miami, being on the left-hand side of the hurricane's path, experienced maximum winds of only 40 mph.

On September 29, Doc Mayer wired Chute: "ANOTHER BLOW HERE YESTERDAY WATER CHALKY WITH SURGE HAVE FISH ON CAR NO NEWS OF MOVEMENT SLIP FULL OF WEED BUT NOTHING IN IT MAY BE ABLE TO PUT FISH OVERBOARD IN MORNING AM BROKE WIRE FUNDS ALSO SEND DELCO FUSES WITH PUMP PARTS= MAX MAYER."

The Nautilus had been parked beside a slip at the Trumbo Point yard for over a month. Essential equipment installed in the custom-built Pullman car was beginning to fail, and the supply of fuses and other consumables was running low. The team had collected about two thousand specimens, and somehow they had to be kept alive and as healthy as possible so they could survive the rigors of the 1,750-mile trip to Chicago.

The problem was that the Nautilus was only designed to transport fish on trips that would last no more than four to five days. The water in the tanks and tubs could be aerated, but there were no provisions for filtering waste, which is why specimens were not fed while being transported.

To overcome this problem, the crew built special caged tanks that could be lowered into the slip to flush the waste with fresh seawater. For the fish that could not be moved from the car, hoses were dropped over the side, and seawater was pumped into the tanks with the overflow drained to the slip.

The delay in departure was hard on the equipment, men, and their fish. The living quarters were cramped, not designed for an extended stay, and the uncertainty of when they would leave the island was stressful. The specimens were manifesting stress as well, with the smaller fish eating each other, the large barracuda threatening the grunts and snappers. A large yellow fin grouper so persistently menaced other fish that they jumped out of the tank. On October 2, Mayer wrote to his boss and confided: "Between storms, broken machinery and indefinite moving orders, I don't know what to expect next. . . . The crew are all well, but just a little anxious for some action."

Each day, trips were made to catch food for the specimens. To keep busy and replenish expired stock, the collection team made several trips to the Eastern Dry Rocks on the reef and collected large pieces of coral and numerous small fish. Tarpon still eluded Mayer. Then one day about the third week of October, as they walked along the top of an exposed reef during low tide, the team found two small tarpon trapped in a tidal pool.

It was a nice present for the beleaguered Mayer, but his elation was short-lived for the collection had acquired a parasitic marine flatworm that first resides in a fish's gills and then spreads over the eyes and the rest of the body. Epibdella produces infections that are usually fatal to the host. The elimination of the parasite is simple; give the infected fish a daily bath in freshwater, which kills the worms.

The problem facing Mayer and his team was that the Florida East Coast Railway terminal at Key West had been supplied with freshwater brought down from the mainland in huge cypress tanks carried on flatbed cars. With the railroad track destroyed, this supply had been cut off since Labor Day, and the freshwater stored at the yard was running very low. Each "bath" would require about three hundred gallons of freshwater. The town of Key West relied entirely on rainwater stored in cisterns for household use; there was no large reservoir from which quantities of potable water could be drawn for bathing the fish.

In a letter to Chute dated October 21, Mayer wrote: "I am doing what I can to save them but lack of fresh water makes it difficult to give them a daily bath. . . . I am bathing the fishes and drying out the cars in hopes that this will get rid of the eggs. I will give them all a freshwater bath before loading as it does not seem to harm the fishes. We are catching rainwater, 'our only means of supply,' from the deck of the Cobb. No rain, No water!" The *Governor Cobb* is a 290-foot steamship that runs between Key West and Havana as part of the FEC Railway's New York–Havana package.

On Wednesday, October 30, Mayer notifies Chute that he had been told they are scheduled to leave for Port Everglades on Sunday. As the team begins making preparations for the trip, another storm forms northeast of Bermuda and begins moving west toward Cape Hatteras. Incredibly, on the first night of November, the hurricane turns ninety degrees and heads south directly toward the Bahamas. On Saturday and Sunday, it steadfastly maintains its southerly heading, closing on the Bahamas; the railcar ferry is held in port. On November 4, as it cuts across the Bahamas, the hurricane curves to the west and makes a beeline for the Miami area.

Around midnight, the center passes right over Miami, placing the Port Everglades/Fort Lauderdale area in the most destructive quadrant of the Category 1 hurricane. Winds of 74–95 mph with heavy wave action assail the area; 5 people are killed, 115 sustain injuries, and $5.5 million worth of damage is done to property in the Miami area before the storm moves across the Everglades and enters the Gulf of Mexico.

Fortunately, damage done to the FEC Railway's Port Everglades facility is minimal, but the result is yet another delay in the removal of the Nautilus to the mainland. As soon as the weather clears, the ferry arrives at Key West and loads the Nautilus, her weary crew, and the collection they have labored so long and hard to protect.

On Wednesday, November 6, the director of the Shedd Aquarium receives a telegram sent from the Western Union office in Fort Lauderdale that reads: "Will arrive Chicago Seminole Saturday morning. All well. Fair load. M. V. Mayer." After hitching a ride with the Atlantic Coast Line train Seminole, the Nautilus rolls to a stop in Chicago on November 9, 1935.

Assigning the Blame

The Weather Bureau reported that the Labor Day Hurricane resulted in total property losses of $6 million, with most of it occurring in the Florida Keys. This included the damage to the railroad and the loss of houses, buildings, boats, groves, and businesses.

The loss of life on the Florida Keys was very heavy. The exact number of fatalities will never be known because many of the bodies were not recovered, and there is no way of determining how many tourists or visitors were on the islands. In the case of the veterans, the Department of Veterans Affairs used the Florida ERA August 1935 payroll for the camps in the Keys to determine that there were 132 missing or unidentified dead veterans (see table 20.1). When added to the identified dead, the total number of veterans dead or missing and presumed dead is 260.

Two lists of civilian dead were documented in the record of a congressional committee looking into the disaster. One list was completed in February 1936 by the coroner of the Upper Keys, E. R. "Doc" Lowe. The other list was compiled in November 1935 by E. U. Woodard assisted by Lt. J. C. Mathison of the U.S. Coast and Geodetic Survey and A. P. Bilobrough of the American Legion. While both documents contain over 160 names, they are not all the same names. A reconciliation of the two lists indicates 182 civilians were determined to be dead or missing and presumed dead at the time the reports were completed.

Doc Lowe knew everybody who lived on the Upper Keys. When he finished separating the tourists and visitors from the residents, he realized 60 percent of the people who had resided on Plantation Key, Windley Key, Upper Matecumbe Key, and elsewhere in the ninth precinct had perished in the hurricane. He added a footnote to his report that read:

Table 20.1 Veteran Victims of the 1935 Labor Day Hurricane

Veterans On August 1935 Payroll[a]	696
Adjustment for Vet Killed in August[b]	-1
Veterans Assigned to Camps 9/2/1935[c]	695
Living—Confirmed After Hurricane	-435
Total Dead/Missing	260
Dead—Identity Confirmed	-128
Missing and Unidentified Dead	132

Source: U. S. Congress, House Of Representatives, Report No. 2899, 74th Cong., 2nd sess., May 29, 1936, 5.

[a] Letter from Frank T. Hines, administrator, Veterans Affairs Department, dated May 4, 1936, to Hon. John E. Rankin, chairman, World War Veterans' Legislation, House of Representatives, Washington, D.C. (U.S. Congress, Florida Hurricane Disaster Hearings, 74th Cong., 2nd sess., 1936, 390).

[b] One veteran was killed by a train several days before the hurricane.

[c] The report cited above lists the total number of veterans as 690. This is believed to be a typographical error since the related itemized numbers in the report add up to 695.

"Note—There were 270 civilian population living in the ninth precinct. The known dead from this precinct is civilians, 163."

According to the administrator of the Florida ERA, Conrad Von Hyning, bodies continued to be found as they surfaced or were discovered in more remote areas of Florida Bay and its coastline. From November 19, 1935, to March 1, 1936, search teams recovered an additional 62 bodies. On April 28, 1936, he reported that a total of 485 bodies had been recovered that were attributable to the storm. Of these, 257 were classified as veterans, and 228 were civilians. Given the state of decay of bodies found months later, it is quite possible that three of them could have been misclassified as civilians. Making this adjustment brings the Florida ERA count of veteran deaths into agreement with that of the Department of Veteran Affairs. The bodies were disposed of as shown in table 20.2.

The loss of 485 lives was not a new record for a hurricane in Florida. On September 16, 1928, a hurricane killed over 1,800 people when it passed by Lake Okeechobee. From a national perspective, the concern was not so much the number as who some of the victims were. As the drama of the *Dixie* passengers' rescue and the cremation of the bodies on the Keys subsided, the media turned their full attention to the fact that hundreds of men who had served their country and had been under the care of the government lost their lives through no fault of their own. Someone and/

Table 20.2 Disposition of Recovered Bodies

	Veterans	Civilians	Total
Bodies shipped to relatives	9	5	14
Cremated on the Florida Keys	168	130	298
Woodlawn Cemetery (Fla. ERA plot)	80	29	109
Woodlawn Cemetery (Private plot)	—	15	15
Homestead Cemetery	—	10	10
Key West Cemetery	—	3	3
Dania Cemetery	—	3	3
Cemeteries on the Florida Keys	—	11	11
Buried at remote locations on Keys	—	22	22
Total	257	228	485

Source: U.S. Congress, House of Representatives, *Report No. 2899*, 74th Cong., 2nd sess., May 29, 1936, 332.

or some agency should be held accountable for these people perishing in the hurricane. There were two primary targets: the Weather Bureau, for not giving adequate warnings; and the veterans camp administrators, for not taking timely action to evacuate the veterans.

As soon as reports of the death and destruction in the Keys reached President Roosevelt's staff, the knee-jerk reaction of blame avoidance rippled through the federal government. The president's aides quickly came to the conclusion that the administration needed to take a pro-active stance with regard to the veterans in the Keys and to determine if there was any culpability. From his home in Hyde Park, New York, Roosevelt instructed Harry Hopkins, the Federal ERA administrator, and General Frank Hines, the administrator of Veterans Affairs, to coordinate the federal effort to aid the survivors of the veterans camps in the Keys and to see that veterans who had been killed were buried with dignity and military honors. They were also ordered to make an "immediate and thorough" investigation.

Hopkins held a press conference on September 5, 1935 in Washington, D.C. to announce the actions taken by the president including the investigation. During the conference, Hopkins—whose office provided federal oversight of the veterans camps program—was asked why the veterans weren't evacuated before the storm struck. Hopkins replied, "I don't think anyone reading the weather reports—and I have been reading them— would necessarily have evacuated those people." The first volley had been fired at the Weather Bureau.

On the same day, the American Legion announced that it was going to conduct its own "complete, unbiased, and impartial" investigation into the conditions that existed at the veterans camps prior to the hurricane and the events that led to the deaths of the veterans. The national commander, Frank Belgrano, designated Howard P. McFarlan of Tampa to conduct the inquiry. That night at a wrestling show sponsored by the American Legion in Lake Worth, Florida, the local American Legion post commander was cheered by hundreds when he announced that the American Legion would not stop until a thorough investigation had been conducted.

On Friday, September 6, the investigation ordered by the president commenced when Aubrey W. Williams, representing the Federal ERA, and Col. George E. Ijams, the VA representative, arrived in Miami. At 2 p.m. they took off in a Coast Guard seaplane, making an aerial tour of the Keys that had been impacted by the hurricane. Ijams was then landed at Lower Matecumbe and Williams was taken to Upper Matecumbe. At 6 p.m. they were back in Miami and went into conference with Governor Sholtz and representatives of the relief organizations. By September 8 a report comprised of 4⅓ pages had been prepared, reviewed by the VA and Federal ERA, and delivered to the president. The report by Williams and Ijams concluded with the following statement:

> After weighing all of the evidence obtained in as orderly and careful an investigation as it has been possible to make up to this point, it is impossible for us to reach the conclusion that there has been negligence or mistaken judgement on the part of those charged with the responsibility for the safety of the men engaged on the Keys projects. To our mind, the catastrophe must be characterized "as an act of God" and was by its very nature beyond the power of man or instruments at his disposal to foresee sufficiently far enough in advance to permit the taking of adequate precautions capable of preventing the death and desolation which occurred.

Critics promptly labeled the hastily conducted investigation a whitewash.

When the meteorologist-in-charge of the Jacksonville Weather Bureau, Walter Bennett, picked up his copy of the *Jacksonville Journal* on September 7 and read the editorial, he found the local paper placing much of the blame on the wording of the Weather Bureau's advisories. The editors of the paper wrote: "There may have been no error whatever in the storm warnings, but they could have been made far more definite. There is too much of a stilted and formal nature about the usual bulletins. It should be remembered that these bulletins are put out for the information of the general public." The editorial went on to say that the warnings would have been more useful if they had told how many miles the storm center was from the coast of Florida, what time it was expected to reach the coast, and where it was expected to hit the coast if its direction did not change. "Why not?" the paper asked; "Why such severe brevity in a matter so vital?"

Bennett told the newspapers, "We did the best we could with available reports and personnel," and then referred the media to headquarters in Washington. There, the acting chief of the Weather Bureau, Charles Clark, said, "from our advisories and forecasts, apparently ample notice was given of the danger and approach of this hurricane." Admiral Cary T. Grayson of the Red Cross backed him up and said the Weather Bureau's forecasts were so excellent they allowed the Red Cross to make preparations in advance for their relief work.

The same day that the stinging editorial appeared in the *Jacksonville Journal*, the governor of Florida implied the remoteness of the Weather Bureau hurricane center in Jacksonville was part of the problem. As he was preparing to leave Miami and return to Tallahassee, Governor Dave Sholtz said: "At the first opportunity I shall recommend to Washington the discontinuance of the recently reorganized method of gathering storm data at Jacksonville, 400 miles north and merely using the Miami office as a loud speaker for hurricane bulletins. I shall insist that Miami be given a primary weather bureau with adequate personnel and equipment."

Among the critics of the Williams/Ijams investigation was the Greater Ministerial Association of Miami, which considered the report a blatant attempt to shift the blame for human foibles to God, and said so in a letter to President Roosevelt dated September 10, 1935: "We regard Mr. Williams' statement that this catastrophe was an 'act of God' and that all was done that was humanly possible as a deliberate attempt to whitewash known facts, ignore the inefficiency and irresponsibility of those in charge, and to appear to be a complete investigation, whereas it is known that statements and facts contrary to this report were ascertained by these investigators and known by them and not included in their report." Of particular concern to the association was the wording of Weather Bureau advisories, which, in their belief, were misleading due to the failure of the weathermen to use all the information available to them.

When Walter Bennett's twenty-four-year-old son, Charles E. Bennett, read that the ministers were criticizing the way the Weather Bureau had handled the hurricane, he took it as a personal attack on his father and felt compelled to act. With the ink on his law diploma from the University of Florida just over a year old, Charles fired off a letter on September 13 unbeknownst to his father, intimating that the group had succumbed to the nonstop barrage of blame propaganda in the media and demanding that the association disclose to him immediately the exact concerns that prompted them to take such unusual action.

Everett Smith, minister of the First Christian Church in Miami and chairman of the special committee appointed by the association for the purpose of presenting a petition to President Roosevelt, promptly responded that the request for an impartial investigation was not influenced by propaganda, but by concerns that observation data and "barometer readings throughout the Florida Keys from Miami to Key West" were not properly considered by the Weather Bureau.

Walter Bennett did not appreciate his son stepping into his professional arena uninvited. When he learned of the exchange between Charles and the Reverend Smith, he sent the following letter to the pastor that summarizes the position of the Jacksonville hurricane center regarding the advisories and warnings issued by that office.

Weather Bureau Office, Jacksonville, Fla.
Oct. 1, 1935
Rev. E. S. Smith
First Christian Church
Miami, Fla.
Dear Mr. Smith:

My son, without my knowledge, wrote you regarding the rather unusual action of the Miami Ministerial Association in condemnation of the Weather Bureau. Being familiar with the work of the Weather Bureau, and interested and active in church work, as teacher of the large Co-Ed class of the Riverside Avenue Christian Church, he was rather surprised at the action of your Association.

As you know an investigation was made by the FERA of the FERA, the Railroad and Weather Bureau, and all three organizations were absolved of blame. An investigation has been made by the Weather Bureau of the Weather Bureau, and the warnings declared by our Acting Chief to have been ample and sufficient. No investigation has been made by the Weather Bureau of the FERA, and is not likely to be made. The local official of the FERA here has admitted that the advices issued should have been sufficient. The high officials of the FERA hastened to make charges against the Weather Bureau, but they have withdrawn those charges. The Weather Bureau has not made charges against the FERA. All testimony, including much not made public has been taken to Washington, and what will be done with it I do not know. Personally, I would like to see all the facts published.

Storm warnings were ordered morning of September 1st from Ft. Pierce to Ft. Myers, and were continued morning of the 2nd. On the morning of the 2nd the barometer at Miami was 29.80, and on the north coast of Cuba 29.65 apparently indicating that the center of disturbance was nearer Cuba. This disturbance passed through the Bahama Islands with little indications of any severity. The lowest barometer reported prior to noon of the 2nd was 29.46 (a very moderate depression) and the highest wind 34 miles per hour. About 1 p.m. of the second our first reports came in of falling barometer and increasing wind at Alligator Reef and from Long Key, and the first reports of rising tide. Hurricane warnings were promptly ordered for the Florida Keys.

We maintain that if the storm warnings were not considered sufficient for actual evacuation, they certainly should have been sufficient for preparations to be made to evacuate, by having train ready. Storm warnings were ordered 36 hours in advance of storm winds, and hurricane warnings at least 8 hours ahead of arrival of storm center.

It should be remembered that Meteorology is not an exact science and probably never will be. It is impossible to tell very far in advance just exactly where the storm center will reach land, and just exactly how severe it will be. Neither is medicine an exact science. When you call in a doctor, he may, or may not be able to diagnose the case perfectly. Nor is the science of government and of law. We do not always elect the best men to office, and many of the acts of legislature and even of Congress are unconstitutional, although most of our law makers are lawyers. I think you will also admit that theology is not an exact science, for theologians differ greatly even on what might be considered fundamentals. Even ministers do not always exemplify perfectly the ideals set forth by the Master in the Sermon on the Mount.

Respectfully,

Walter J. Bennett

On September 8 at his home in Key West, Ernest Hemingway sat down and wrote an article describing in graphic terms the grisly sights he had seen on his recent trip to the Keys. Fuming over the horrible deaths suffered by the veterans, he wrote, "Who sent them down to the Florida Keys and left them there in hurricane months?" The inflammatory article entitled "Who Murdered the Vets?" was submitted to *New Masses*, a dissident periodical described as "fusing art, reportage, and revolution together into a highly readable package." During the economic upheaval of the Great Depression, such publications enjoyed a wider audience in America than they did during good times.

Appearing in print on September 17, 1935, Hemingway's piece was widely quoted in newspapers and magazines. Just the title alone was enough to incite the former soldiers who were meeting in New Orleans at the Veterans of Foreign Wars Thirty-sixth National Encampment. They promptly passed a resolution demanding a federal investigation. Less than a week later at the Seventeenth National Convention of American Legion in St. Louis, overwhelmingly endorsed their leaders' initiative in starting their own investigation.

At about the same time the Hemingway article was published, the state attorney general of Florida, Ambrose Worley, delivered a report containing a summary of his own four-day investigation to Governor Sholtz. Worley found there was no basis for the filing of indictments or recommendations of indictments regarding the storm-related deaths and injuries that occurred on the Florida Keys. The VFW's commander-in-chief, James E. Van Zandt, promptly labeled it another whitewash.

The American Legion began its previously announced investigation of the disaster in October 1935. Major Quimby Melton, the editor and publisher of the *Griffin (Ga.) Daily Times*, was appointed chairman of the investigative committee. Other members were the national vice commander of the American Legion, Dr. W. E. Whitlock of High Springs, Florida, and Catesby Jones of Selma, Alabama, executive committeeman of that state.

The tenor of the investigation can be gauged by the conduct of the inquiry at Key West. The threesome arrived in Key West on October 12 after an overnight cruise from Tampa aboard the steamship *Cuba*. They proceeded directly to the auditorium of the Key West High School. In his opening remarks that Saturday morning, the chairman made it clear this was not an investigation to find out what went wrong and how such future disasters could be avoided or moderated. Major Quimby said bluntly, "We are interested solely and wholly in investigating conditions before and during the storm, and if possible determine who, if anybody, was responsible for the deaths."

The commander of Arthur Sawyer Post 28 of Key West, J. J. Treavor, then testified as "to the general conditions understood to prevail on the keys" prior to the hurricane. Arthur Brown, a veteran from New York who was working as a timekeeper at Camp Three, told the committee that the deaths of many of the veterans could have been avoided if they could have used the camps' trucks to leave the islands. They were told to wait for the train, he said. When the committee asked Brown about discipline at the camps, he responded, "there was absolutely no discipline."

G. S. Kennedy, the meteorologist-in-charge of the Key West Weather Bureau, testified that he had warned the director of the camps, Ray Sheldon, on Sunday morning that "it looks pretty bad." At that time, the Weather Bureau was saying that the storm was expected to pass between Key West and Havana. Major William Albury told the committee of his suspicion that the surviving veterans at Camp Three were pilfering the pockets of the dead when he arrived with a detachment of guardsmen from Key West. Next, administrators of the Florida Veterans Work Program said that funds had been exhausted and the veterans would have been moved off the Keys within a week or two if the hurricane had not intervened. One official said he had relayed instructions from the program director in Tallahassee to Ray Sheldon "to watch the situation closely and take no chances." He added that Sheldon seemed "very confident." By early evening, when the committee closed the Key West hearing, the finger of blame was being pointed toward Ray Sheldon, who was not present to defend himself. The next afternoon the committee flew to Miami to continue hearings there on Monday.

The American Legion investigative committee completed their hearings and submitted their report to the national commander, Ray Murphy, who sent the report to President Roosevelt on November 2. Roosevelt forwarded copies for review by the heads of Veterans Affairs and the Federal ERA. Neither the American Legion nor the government released the report to the general public.

Gary Dean Best, author of *FDR and the Bonus Marchers*, said in his book he could not find copies of the report in the archives of the VA, Federal ERA, or among the Roosevelt papers at Hyde Park. The American Legion has steadfastly refused requests for a copy of the report. Based on his research, Best believes that the American Legion investigation "absolved the FERA and the Florida ERA of guilt in the matter." He reasons that the American Legion report was not released when it was forwarded to the president because the bill to pay the bonuses to the veterans was due to come before the next session of Congress and the American Legion deemed it unwise to release the report at such a sensitive time. Why the report was not released in later years remains a mystery.

According to J. Hardin Peterson, a member of the House of Representatives from Florida, the digest of the minutes of the American Legion's national executive committee meeting on November 1, 1935, at Indianapolis listed five recommendations made by the special investigating committee chaired by Major Quimby Melton:

1. A congressional investigation to fix the blame, if any, on the party or parties responsible for the loss of life.
2. That any further "rehabilitation" program among veterans be directed by the Veterans Administration.
3. That the facilities of the Weather Bureau be extended so that it can operate more efficiently in the future.
4. That a regiment of engineers be stationed at or near Miami during the "hurricane" season.
5. That those parties whose relief work was outstanding be properly cited for their activities.

Howard McFarlan, the attorney from Tampa who conducted the American Legion's first review of the hurricane disaster, was the first to recommend a congressional hearing. He concluded that such a hearing was the only way to get at the facts and made this recommendation to the American Legion national executive committee in September 1935:

No investigation conducted unofficially, as the investigation by the F.E.R.A. and the investigation which I have made on behalf of the American Legion, has the power to summon witnesses, to place them under oath, and to searchingly go into the facts. An investigation conducted by the State's attorney of Dade County is handicapped by the fact that he represents an authority of limited jurisdiction. If the whole picture is to be gone into and any investigation which develops all of the facts is had it must be a body not limited by territorial lines, and have power to bring before it all persons who may have any information, whoever they may be and wherever they may be. The only body which I know having such powers is the Congress of the United States, and if it be desired to go further into this matter and to come to a conclusion based upon all the facts, which will be received as a just verdict by the people of this country, including the veterans, it seems to me that the only way to arrive at that result is through a congressional investigation.

The opportunity for congressional review came on January 3, 1936, when Representative John E. Rankin (Mississippi) introduced H.R. 9486, a bill entitled, "A bill for the relief of widows, children, and dependent parents of World War veterans who died as the result of the Florida hurricane at Windley Island and Matecumbe Keys, September 2, 1935." When the bill came before the Committee on World War Veterans' Legislation, which Rankin chaired, he called for a hearing. On March 26, 1936, the hearing opened at Washington, D.C.

This was a formal proceeding with subpoenaed witnesses, sworn testimony, and full transcript. The chairman and fourteen other members were Democrats, five members were Republicans, and one member was affiliated with the Progressive Party.

Critics have characterized the hearing as a political sham staged by Rankin to absolve the Roosevelt administration of blame and to so thoroughly vet the issues that the Republicans could not use the catastrophe in the Keys against the Democrats in the next election. Regardless of the motive, the hearing provided a venue for airing issues that were of concern to the general public, such as the wording of Weather Bureau advisories, and gave the agencies involved an opportunity to explain the difficulties they were facing and why things were done the way they were done. Sufficient time had elapsed that the emotional intensity of the event had subsided, and the defensive reflex of the bureaucrats had relaxed somewhat. The Weather Bureau saw the hearing as an opportunity to lobby for more funding and did so with vigor.

The people who testified were not figureheads put up to throw a punch or take a hit; they were knowledgeable people with relevant information, and the members of the committee asked probing questions of them. Those making appearances before the committee included congressmen from Florida, key federal and state administrators, veterans camp staff, and survivors of the hurricane.

Testimony was taken for more than a month, producing a printed record of over five hundred pages. Maps and charts were produced that showed such things as where the storm was located when the Weather Bureau issued each advisory and the sites where victims were found after the hurricane's passage. Never before had the actions of those involved with a hurricane been so thoroughly reviewed and documented.

On May 29, 1936, the committee issued its report with the majority (fifteen Democrats and two Republicans) recommending passage of the bill. The report supported the actions of the Roosevelt administration declaring that the federal government was trying to help the unemployed veterans by assigning them to a state project, and that they were sent to the Keys because of the availability of employment and the fact that it afforded favorable working conditions.

The report also addressed the question of who was to blame for not extracting the veterans before the hurricane struck. The majority of the committee found that no one was to blame, stating: "The evidence clearly shows that the tidal wave was entirely unexpected and that it was impossible to even anticipate the hurricane with sufficient time to insure safety of those concerned, including resident women and children, and that in view of the tidal wave accompanying the hurricane resulting in a depth of water reaching 17 feet, it was impossible to save the persons involved."

The Weather Bureau did an admirable job of presenting its case and was

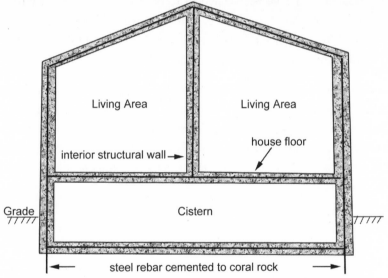

Top: As part of the recovery program, the Red Cross and the Florida ERA built on Upper Matecumbe Key, Plantation Key, and at Tavernier twenty-eight "hurricane-proof" houses. They ranged in size from 1 to 5 bedrooms. (FPC)

Bottom: Cross section of a "hurricane-proof" house showing structural concept. The foundations of these homes were concrete cisterns dug and cemented into the coral rock. Concrete was poured over a cage made of reinforcing steel bars (rebar) so that the cistern, floors, walls, and roof became a single structural unit. Designed to withstand any conceivable hurricane, some of the homes were weakened from within when rust formed on the rebar and cracked the concrete. (author)

rewarded with a recommendation for increased funding. The congressional committee reported, "It was also found that the Weather Bureau had done all that was possible within the limitations of their facilities, but it is believed that an increased appropriation should be made available for the Bureau in order that more adequate safeguards may be established to avoid a recurrence of a similar disaster."

The three dissenting members, Edith Nourse Rogers (Republican), Harry Sauthoff (Republican), and Charles F. Risk (Progressive Party), issued a minority report that included the following comment:

> There is no doubt in our minds that while it would be impossible to place blame for the terrible loss of life, yet the evidence shows a surprising lack of judgment on the part of those responsible for the welfare of the men under their charge. Many blunders were made.
>
> This hurricane has been called an act of God. God may be held responsible for this storm, but He cannot be blamed for leaving these men in the path of the storm, nor can He be blamed for depriving them of their only available method of leaving.

The congressional hearing and all of the investigations and inquiries preceding it had a common point of agreement; no one was found to be criminally or otherwise negligent with regard to their actions related to the Labor Day Hurricane. H.R. 9486 was passed. More importantly, the veterans' bonus bill was also passed and signed by the president. The Bonus Army faded away.

Endings and Beginnings

With their camps on the Florida Keys destroyed, the 435 surviving veterans were dispersed to a variety of locations. More than a third (164) were sent to Civilian Conservation Corps (CCC) camps. Another 154 left the program after being compensated for the loss of their belongings and signing a legally binding settlement in which they agreed not to sue the government. Six veterans simply walked away. Eighteen men were sent home, and another 83 men were sent to the homes of friends or relatives. Seven of the veterans were deemed to have skills of value to the Cross Florida Canal project and were sent to Kissimmee. Two veterans went to the Jacksonville offices of the Florida ERA, and one was sent to the Augusta Insane Asylum.

For many of the civilians who had lived on the Upper Keys prior to the hurricane, there was nothing left to return to once the bodies had been removed. Their lime groves had been reduced to twisted sticks, the topsoil stripped off their gardens, their boats destroyed, homes and businesses smashed, and most if not all of their personal possessions had been washed away. The folks who had been there during the real estate boom in the twenties knew that what was left, the land, had value. Edney Parker's son-in-law Jack Ryder, a realtor, said: "Sure I'm going back. Eighty per cent of the former residents who survived are going back." John A. Russell, his brother Clifton, Edney Parker, Alonzo Cothron, Berlin Felton, Brammie Pinder, and others went back and began rebuilding.

Johnny Russell had been banged up a bit in the storm but as soon as the bodies had been removed, he and his sixteen-year-old son, Bernard, returned to Upper Matecumbe. They lived in a tent on the beach while they built a new wooden post office.

O. D. King and his wife's brother, Charles Carter, went back and helped

Top: The Rustic Inn was extensively damaged by the Labor Day Hurricane (FPC). *Bottom*: By 1938, both the inn and adjacent foliage had recovered. (MDPL)

Berlin Felton restore the Rustic Inn to working order. At first living conditions were primitive, and just getting materials to the islands was a challenge; however, some material was salvaged and some equipment, such as cars and trucks, was put in operating condition with some tinkering. As soon as the Rustic Inn was habitable, Betty King joined her husband, and the inn was busy supplying the workmen with good meals.

Eddie Sweeting returned to the island and reopened his grocery store after repairing the two-story building with materials provided by the Florida ERA. His father-in-law, Edney Parker, continued to serve as constable, commuting from Perrine, north of Homestead on the mainland, where his family was staying. The Red Cross and the Florida ERA built the Parker family a concrete, "hurricane-proof" home. After a year away from Upper Matecumbe, Edna and the children were able to move back.

A total of twenty-eight "hurricane-proof" homes were constructed by the Red Cross and the Florida ERA for displaced families; nineteen were built on Upper Matecumbe Key, seven on Plantation Key, and two at Tavernier. The houses were sized to the needs of the families they were to accommodate and had one to five bedrooms. The foundation of these houses was a concrete cistern dug and cemented into the coral rock. Concrete was poured over a cage made of reinforcing steel bars and mesh so that the floors, walls, and roof became one solid unit.

With walls a foot thick, the design was almost strong enough to withstand a direct hit by an artillery shell; however, some of the houses, including the Parkers', had a defect. The contractor used salt water instead of freshwater to mix the concrete. The reinforcing steel cage was submerged in a salt-water bath as the concrete was poured and hardened around it. This caused the steel bars to rust and expand, creating internal pressure that cracked the concrete. Edney Parker's daughter Fay said they were not in their house very long before cracks appeared in the walls and floors, and chunks of concrete began to fall off the ceilings.

Some people who returned to the Upper Keys found it difficult to begin anew. Betty and O. D. King operated the patched-up Rustic Inn for a while, but O. D. began to drink again, and the business began to suffer. O. D. then tried to operate a small grocery store. His alcohol abuse continued, and that effort failed. He finally left Betty in the late 1930s and died penniless on the streets of Chattanooga, Tennessee. Betty went back to Miami and for many years managed the cafeteria at the Miami International Airport. She never remarried.

There were some residents of the Upper Keys who survived the hurricane and did not return because there was nothing left for them in the Keys now but bad memories. For Mozelle Williams and her three children, the outlook was bleak. Her husband was dead, their house, car, boat, and even the very land where Eddie had built their house were gone. They had no insurance and no savings to fall back on. Mozelle did own a small piece of vacant property in Tampa that she had inherited.

After a week at Eddie's parents' home in Miami, Mozelle Williams took her children, and her niece and nephew, to Tampa on the train so that the four oldest could get back to school. They stayed at her brother's home. Dan Law remained hospitalized in Miami, and his wife stayed with him.

The Red Cross built Mozelle a small home on her property in Tampa. Her daughter Elizabeth recalled: "Mama went to work in a cigar box factory, and Evelyn and I took care of the baby [their brother Bobby]. She was gone from sunup to sundown." Mozelle knew it was not a good situation; her girls were missing school, and she was barely able to earn enough to buy food.

Perhaps out of desperation, she married a man who had three children. Mozelle stayed home and took care of the six children. About the end of 1937, her husband was laid off and the family moved to Jacksonville. They had to move several more times because the husband mistreated the children and the neighbors would call the authorities. For Evelyn and Elizabeth, life had become one nightmare after another. The daughters of Eddie Williams escaped their depressing family situation by marrying very young. Eventually Elizabeth and Evelyn found stable relationships and dedicated their lives to providing their children with the goodness of life they had been denied.

The Labor Day Hurricane was a factor in several marriages. Nine weeks after Rosalind Grooms Palmer's funeral, the engagement of her widower, Lt. j.g. George Goldston Palmer, to Frances Kirk of Charleston, South Carolina, was announced. They married and had two children. He remained in the navy and had a distinguished career, receiving numerous medals and commendations for his service during World War II and the Korean War, including the Navy Cross and Silver Star. In 1959, he retired with the rank of rear admiral after 29½ years of active service.

The woman who single-handedly held down the city room of the *Miami Daily News* on that stormy night in 1935 married the man who was responsible for bringing her back to Miami in time for the hurricane. Helen Theresa Eucharis O'Flaherty Lennehan years later stated that she did not accept his proposal in order to get a shorter byline, but as Helen Muir she wrote extensively in newspapers and books about South Florida. Her book, *Miami USA*, is one of her best-known works. She died in Coconut Grove in 2006 at the age of ninety-five.

Her colleague Jane Wood became disillusioned with social work during the days following the hurricane. In her autobiography, she wrote: "The days and weeks that followed that hurricane were a disgrace to Miami and south Florida. Neighbor failed neighbor; organized relief failed." The experience, "this catharsis of death and disgust" as she referred to it, caused her to leave social work. She became a copy girl at the *Miami Herald*, where she met Henry Reno. He was a seasoned reporter almost twelve years her senior, but his love of nature and sensitivity appealed to her.

Jane was about to leave the *Herald* to pursue a master's degree at Columbia when Henry mentioned that he was going to the Keys to do some crawfishing. She talked him into taking her along. While he skin-dived for the crawfish (Florida lobster), she sat in Henry's boat, the *Vagabond*, tending the catch and sipping whiskey he had brought along to take the chill off diving. By the time they returned to port, the liquor and hot sun had taken their toll, and she passed out. He took her to his home and put her to bed. When she opened her eyes, he had a delicious crawfish supper ready. From then on, Henry Reno's days as a bachelor were numbered. Henry and Jane were married on July 20, 1937, and went to Key West for their honeymoon. One of their four children, Janet, became the first woman to serve as attorney general of the United States.

As soon as she was able, Leone Carter Barr, who rode out the hurricane on a shelf in the Rustic Inn clutching her son, went to work and became the office manager of the Fix-It Plumbing Company in Coral Gables, where her brother John was employed as a plumber. Leone was still married, but did not live with her husband and was scrimping to accumulate enough money to pay for a divorce.

To save the cost of child care, her sister Betty King kept Leone's son with her after she and her husband reopened the Rustic Inn. On Friday afternoons, Leone went down to Upper Matecumbe Key and stayed with her son for the weekend. It was always a rough time emotionally when she had to leave him. "Those days were hard days for me," said Leone.

O. D. King's friend Gilbert Thompson arranged transportation for Leone with various neighbors going to the mainland. One regular driver was John Franklin Carey, Eddie Carey's son. Franklin was a carpenter and made frequent trips to the mainland for lumber and hardware. Leone was terribly shy and Franklin was a quiet man, but as traveling companions the two discovered they had a lot in common. In 1936, her brother John paid for her divorce, which became final on June 1. Ten days later, Leone and Franklin were married, and she moved to Upper Matecumbe Key.

Leone and Franklin Carey remained in the Florida Keys for almost forty years. After he retired in 1971, they moved to Ocala, where their son and his family were living. "He was a good and loving man," Leone said of Franklin. Leone outlived both Franklin and her son; she was ninety-five years old when she died in October 2006.

In 1935, when Franklin's mother Clara Carey returned to Upper Matecumbe, there was nothing left of her home. With materials furnished by the Red Cross and labor provided by the WPA, she had a new house built away from the beach near the Rustic Inn. Five years after the hurricane, she married her longtime friend Johnny Russell, the postmaster who had also lost his spouse in the storm. Johnny Russell was appointed postmaster of Islamorada in 1909 and remained in that position until he died in 1954, at which time his brother and faithful assistant Clifton replaced him.

Mrs. George W. (Ellen) Curry of Key West, Cyril Lowe's grandmother, lost three daughters, a grandson, and a great-grandson when the storm surge demolished Brammie Pinder's house. Her daughters Winnie Curry, Ruby Baker, and Cyril's mother, Mamie Pinder, were killed as was Frank Harvey Lowe, Cyril and Carolyn Lowe's son. Winnie's and Ruby's bodies were found soon after the hurricane and were cremated at Upper Matecumbe during the recovery operations. The bodies of Mamie and her grandson Frank were found a month after the storm and were buried together on October 10, 1935, in the Pinder family's cemetery on Upper Matecumbe.

Ruby Baker's son, William (Billy) F. Baker, was holding her when the storm surge buried them under the wreckage of the house. His mother died next to him as he lay trapped in the debris with a crushed arm and leg as well as other injuries. Unable to receive timely medical treatment, his left leg became infected with gangrene. He was taken to Jackson Memorial Hospital in Miami where his leg was amputated on Sunday, September 15, 1935. The surgery was not in time to prevent the spread of the infection, and he died two days later. He was buried at Key West.

Carolyn and Cyril Lowe, who lost their only son when the twenty-three-month-old baby was wrenched from his father's arms by the on-rushing water, moved back to Key West, where Cyril went to work at the navy yard. They had four more children—all girls, two of whom died at childbirth. When she was interviewed in 1997, Carolyn was justly proud of her twenty-nine grandchildren and great-grandchildren.

At Islamorada a memorial was built in 1937 between the railroad right-of-way and the highway to honor victims of the Labor Day Hurricane. Faced with coral rock quarried on the Keys and built at a cost of $12,000, the impressive monument consists of a 65' × 20' porch with a dais on the back side topped by an 18-foot-high obelisk.

On November 14, 1937, Fay Marie Parker was given the honor of pulling the cord that undraped the obelisk and revealed the large bronze plaque that reads: "DEDICATED TO THE MEMORY OF THE CIVILIANS AND THE WAR VETERANS WHOSE LIVES WERE LOST IN THE HURRICANE OF SEPTEMBER SECOND 1935." Fay was nine years old at the time. In a photograph taken at the event, she is wearing a long white gown with a large schooner bonnet. "The Miami Herald reporter brought it [the gown and bonnet] to the ceremony and insisted I wear it," she recalled. As the crowd of five thousand people watched, she gave the cord an extra hard yank; she was mad at Doc Lowe. "He took my seat on the podium even though it had my name on a piece of paper taped to it!" she said, sounding still a little put off about it seventy years later.

R. W. Craig returned to the tiny man-made island over which the center of the hurricane had passed. He built a new store and gas station at the west end of the key. One piece of memorabilia from the storm that he delighted in showing tourists was a coconut that had been impaled on a piece of two-by-four thrust by the wind. For many decades "Poor Old Craig's" Pure gas station signaled the halfway point for travelers making the Key West/Miami trip on the Overseas Highway.

Wilbur Jones, who was trapped in a boxcar at Islamorada and almost drowned as the storm surge came ashore, graduated from the Wharton School of Finance and became a successful estate planner and financial consultant. He served as chairman of the Florida State Road Department during the mid-1950s under Governor Leroy Collins and is credited with introducing computer-assisted design technology and other innovations for planning Florida's highway systems. He also oversaw the planning related to locating a portion of the state's first interstate highway. Now in his mid-nineties, he remains an active advocate of highway beautification.

The destruction of a major portion of the Florida East Coast Railway

Top: Fay Marie Parker pulls the cord to unveil the monument to victims of the 1935 Labor Day hurricane. *Bottom*: The monument was constructed between the former FEC Railway right-of-way and the highway. Edney Parker said the only thing wrong with it was that the palm trees were shown blowing in the wrong direction. (FPC)

Key West Extension at first seemed to be a cruel blow to the wobbly economic recovery of the Florida Keys; however, with rail service terminated, construction of a continuous highway to Key West became a priority. The two ferries that had been undergoing repairs when the hurricane struck were placed in operation as soon as possible to cover the original water gaps and the new ones created by the storm's destruction of bridges and fills.

During 1935 and 1936, Monroe County and the State of Florida worked to acquire the railroad right-of-way of the Key West Extension from the Florida East Coast Railway. After some negotiations, a deal was worked out whereby all fixtures and embedded equipment including the trestles and viaducts were acquired from the Florida East Coast Railway for $640,000 when they abandoned the line. A $600,000 loan combined with a $3.6 million federal grant from the Public Works Administration enabled construction of the road to proceed.

Work on the highway began under the direction of B. M. Duncan in the summer of 1937. At Tavernier Creek, Snake Creek, and Whale Harbor, concrete bridges on timber pilings were quickly erected, providing vehicular access down to Upper Matecumbe Key. Using the existing railroad trestles and viaducts as understructures to support the roadway, the highway was extended down to Marathon by the fall of 1937.

West of Marathon, the Seven Mile Bridge and the Bahia Honda Bridge presented significant challenges. Because of its length, construction of the Seven Mile Bridge took a lot of time and materials, but was otherwise straightforward. The crossing at Bahia Honda consisted of a series of trestles that enclosed the track in steel boxes too narrow for a highway. In order to get the width required for two lanes of vehicular traffic, Duncan had his crews build ramps at both ends so that the roadway ran up over the tops of the box trestles. The road surface at its maximum height towered above the water as tall as a six-story building.

To expedite completion and keep the project within the limited funds available, the old highway was used wherever it existed. New road was built on the railroad right-of-way between Lower Matecumbe Key and Grassy Key and from Knights Key to Big Pine Key. Consequently, the highway followed a zigzag route down the Keys. On March 29, 1938, the continuous highway was opened to the general public.

As circuitous as it was, the road was hailed as a godsend by the traveling public and the business establishment. During World War II, Key West became a strategic military center with navy and army bases. At its peak, fifteen thousand servicemen were stationed on the island. To provide logistical support, the federal government revamped the highway to follow the more direct railroad route from Florida City to Key West. At the same time, a pipeline to carry freshwater from the mainland to the Island City was installed parallel to the highway. The highway and pipeline provided the basic infrastructure that made the Florida Keys accessible and habitable, and enabled the development that occurred in later decades.

Early in 1938, before the highway to Key West was opened to the public, sixteen-year-old Bascom Grooms Jr. became the first person not involved in the construction of the road to travel on a rubber-tired vehicle from Key West to the mainland without taking a ferry. He was issued a special pass by B. M. Duncan that allowed him to travel over the highway while it was still under construction. The trip from Key West to Miami by motor scooter took 7½ hours.

Bascom and Rosalind's father, Bascom Grooms Sr., became the president of the Key West Electric Company in 1937. Six years later, the company was sold to the City of Key West, and he retired after thirty-five years of service. He died in June 1973 at the age of ninety-seven. His wife, Rosalie, Harry Boyer's daughter, passed away eighteen months later.

Just as his father had done in 1913, Bascom Jr. married the daughter of the official-in-charge of the Key West weather station in 1942. Geraldine Kennedy was the daughter of Harry Boyer's successor, Gerald Kennedy. After Geraldine's death in April 1962, Bascom Jr. married Mary Louisa Porter, whose grandfather, Dr. J. Y. Porter, was credited with eliminating Harry Boyer's nemesis, yellow fever, from the state of Florida.

The Key West Weather Bureau occupied the building the Department of Agriculture had constructed at the corner of Eaton and Front streets in 1903 for a total of forty-five years (it was unoccupied for two years due to damage caused by hurricanes). In 1950, the Weather Bureau moved to the Federal Building located at the corner of Simonton and Caroline streets. As of this writing, the building on Front Street where Harry Boyer's children were married and where his funeral was held continues in service as an inn even though it is over a hundred years old. It would not be surprising to hear that a friendly spirit wearing a green eyeshade has been observed tapping on the wall where the barometer used to hang.

Although not publicized, the hurricane center at Jacksonville was Grady Norton's operation. While the entire station was under the general direction of the meteorologist-in-charge, Walter Bennett, Norton was responsible for managing hurricane operations, including tracking and the issuing of advisories.

Norton's assistant, Gordon Dunn, admitted many years later while reminiscing about the 1935 hurricane that there were problems with the advisories. In an article by Robert Burpee that appeared in the September 1988 issue of *Weather and Forecasting*, Dunn was quoted as saying: "Although the warnings for the Labor Day hurricane were far from timely, they were as accurate as the observations would allow. Grady and I did not realize the intensity of the approaching hurricane." The Weather Bureau had steadfastly maintained that "timely and generally accurate advices" were issued by the Jacksonville forecast center.

Grady Norton went down to the Keys soon after the storm's passage and saw the carnage firsthand: "I went to the Keys and saw CCC boys bring decaying bodies out of the mangrove swamps and cremate them. I didn't think any of this could be blamed on my warnings, but I never wanted to see it happen again."

The Weather Bureau continued to develop new equipment and forecasting techniques. In 1937, the radiosonde, an instrumentation and telemetry package small enough to be lifted by a weather balloon up to fifty thousand feet, began to be used. The radiosondes allowed upper-level conditions to be reliably and regularly observed. By 1944, Grady Norton had developed a theory that the winds aloft rather than winds at the surface steer hurricanes and determine where they will go. He became renowned for his predictions of hurricane behavior. Due in part to his prediction and communication skills, the average number of deaths from a major hurricane striking the United States dropped from five hundred to five during his tenure as senior hurricane forecaster.

In 1943, the hurricane center was moved from Jacksonville to Miami. Grady Norton became the meteorologist-in-charge (MIC) of the Miami weather bureau and established a joint hurricane-warning service consisting of the Weather Bureau, Air Corps, and U.S. Navy. He served as MIC of the Miami office until his death in 1954. His long-time friend Gordon Dunn succeeded him.

The 1935 hurricane season remains one of the most freakish on record. Only five storms were classified as hurricanes by the Weather Bureau that year, but they ranged from the first Category 5 hurricane to make landfall in the United States to others described by the meteorologist Willis Hurd as "peculiarly erratic in general direction of movement." While hurricanes were not officially named in 1935, three of the five storms did acquire monikers. In addition to the "Labor Day Hurricane," there were the "Hairpin Hurricane" and the "Yankee Clipper Hurricane."

The "Hairpin Hurricane" was so named because it formed in the western Caribbean Sea north of the Panama Canal, moved northeast toward the western end of Cuba, then made an almost 180-degree turn and moved toward Honduras. According to Ivan Tannehill, it "produced one of the major disasters of West Indian history." Over two thousand people were killed in Haiti, Honduras, and at sea. Property damage in Jamaica was estimated at $2 million.

As if to emphasize the devilish nature of the season, at Halloween a hurricane of most unusual behavior formed northeast of Bermuda. After moving west until just off the Carolinas, the storm made a sharp turn to the south and traveled off the east coast of the United States directly to the northern Bahamas. Known as the "Yankee Clipper" because it came down from the north, the storm then veered to the west and crossed over Miami and moved into the Gulf of Mexico where it made a U-turn before dissipating just west of St. Petersburg, Florida. Nineteen people were killed, including five in Miami; 115 people were injured. Property loss in Miami and vicinity was estimated at $5.5 million.

The two tropical cyclones that did not acquire nicknames, the first and third hurricanes of the season, could have been called the "Newfoundland Twins." The first storm was tracked from August 18 to August 25. It formed in the North Atlantic Ocean far to the east of Puerto Rico, and followed a path shaped like a reversed letter S, passing east of the Bahamas, then recurving toward the northeast, passing west of Bermuda before turning again, and making landfall in Newfoundland, where it expired. Much damage was done to the fishing fleets, and approximately fifty fishermen were killed on the Grand Banks.

The third hurricane of the season formed on September 23 in the Caribbean Sea and followed a more extended, but similar path as the first storm, passing over Bimini in the Bahamas before making landfall on Newfoundland's coast at the same location where the first hurricane had made landfall about six weeks before. In Cuba, thirty-five were killed and approximately five hundred injured. In Bimini, fourteen people were killed when a fifteen-foot storm surge swept the islands.

Hairpin turns, hurricanes moving toward the Equator instead of away from it, tropical cyclones that killed and maimed thousands while destroying infrastructure that had withstood the test of many previous storms—the weathermen at Jacksonville and many other people were glad to see the 1935 season come to an end.

Walter Bennett remained in charge of the Jacksonville Weather Bureau until he retired at age seventy in 1949. His son Charles E. Bennett, who had impetuously reacted to the Greater Miami Ministerial Association's criticism of the Weather Bureau's handling of the Labor Day Hurricane, subsequently entered politics and served in the Florida legislature in 1941 and then enlisted in the army. A decorated combat veteran of World War II, he was elected to the Eighty-first Congress and served continuously in the U.S. House of Representatives for forty-four years (1949–93).

After the *Dixie*'s return to New York, the ship was overhauled at the Todd Dry Dock Company's facilities in Brooklyn at a cost of $468,000. Substantial modifications were made to the liner including the installation of additional bulkheads, a more streamlined rudder, and a contra propeller. The interior of the ship's passenger accommodations, lounges, and recreational areas was completely redone. A modern hard-liquor bar replaced the soft drink bar that had been installed when the ship was built during Prohibition. A swimming pool was added on the upper poop deck.

On December 17, 1935, the *Dixie* returned to her berth at the foot of Bienville Street in New Orleans to resume her regular run to New York City every third Saturday. Before departing, the Morgan Line hosted a reunion for the passengers who had been aboard the liner when it was stranded in the Florida Keys three months earlier. Of the 231 passengers on the ill-fated voyage, 124 attended enjoying a sumptuous meal with Commodore Sundstrom and a tour of the renovated ship.

The improvements made to the *Dixie* could not overcome the changing attitudes of the traveling public. The Great Depression had made people more cost-conscious and destination-minded; time spent in transit was now viewed as subtracting from vacation time rather than as part of the vacation. With airlines becoming more convenient and competitive, and affordable automobiles and an extensive highway system providing maximum travel flexibility, leisurely cruises on luxury liners lost their appeal. Passenger loads declined sharply. As the 1930s came to an end, the *Dixie* and similar ships were no longer profitable to operate. In March 1940, the liner was sold to the U.S. Navy and converted to a destroyer tender, the USS *Alcor*. The ship was cut up for scrap in 1950.

The *Leise Maersk* safely completed her trip to Ethiopia and continued in tramp service. During World War II, while sailing under the British flag three hundred miles off the northwest coast of Ireland, the freighter was torpedoed. She was one of eleven ships sunk on November 23, 1940, by the German submarine U-100. The *Leise Maersk's* master and sixteen members of the crew went down with the vessel.

Although it no longer went to the Florida Keys, the Shedd Aquarium's collection car Nautilus continued to make trips across the nation. After the United States entered World War II, the Nautilus evacuated almost 250 fish from Marineland when the aquarium attraction near St. Augustine, Florida was forced to close as the result of declining tourism due to gas rationing.

The Atlantic tarpon Dr. Max Mayer and his crew captured on the Nautilus's last trip to Key West were the first of their kind to be displayed in a public aquarium. In 1959, one of the fish sustained injuries to her body and eyes when she became spooked and jumped out her tank. The tarpon made a remarkable recovery, but her vision was obscured to the point of only being able to distinguish light from darkness. From then on she was known as Deadeye.

After the accident, Deadeye would bump into other fish and occasionally collide with some of the rock pieces in the exhibit. Over the years she adapted and was able to navigate by relying on her lateral lines, sensory organs along a fish's head and sides that detect vibrations. She became so good at this that most visitors to the exhibit were unaware she was blind until this was mentioned during feeding presentations. When Deadeye's story was told—how she survived the terrible hurricane and was found on the reef, the difficult trip to the aquarium, her accident and loss of vision, and her remarkable adaptation to her disability—the audience was always impressed.

Deadeye was only three feet long, small for an Atlantic tarpon. By 1998, some of her large scales were missing and her tail was a bit tattered, but the "little fish that could" remained a featured animal of the Caribbean exhibit, and many people, especially the schoolchildren in the Chicago area, knew who Deadeye was. In October 1998, within a month of the sixty-third anniversary of her arrival at the Shedd, Deadeye became wedged between some pieces of artificial coral and fatally wounded herself as she tried to wriggle free.

At the time of her death Deadeye was more than just the oldest Atlantic tarpon in a zoological collection; she had become a symbol of the will to survive and the courage to overcome hardship no matter how severe. In that respect, she had a lot in common with many of the people who endured the Labor Day Hurricane of 1935.

Epilogue

Liz and Evelyn dried their tears. We had been so immersed in the past that several hours of the present had slipped by unnoticed. The women regained their composure and even looked refreshed—as if the bringing forth of trying memories had a cathartic effect. Liz's face brightened as she said, "Now who's ready for some key lime pie?" She did not wait for an answer; she knew no one would refuse. As we sat around the dining room table enjoying the pie, she asked, "Do you think it can happen as bad again?"

Unfortunately, the answer is yes, and such an event has the potential to be much worse in terms of the number of casualties and the amount of property damage. The 1935 census reported that Lower Matecumbe, Upper Matecumbe, Windley Key, and Plantation Key had 284 residents not counting the veterans. Now incorporated as "Islamorada—Village of Islands," these islands were reported to have 6,846 residents in the 2000 census. Similar growth has occurred on most of the other keys where there is substantial privately owned land. Emergency-management personnel estimate that during hurricane season there are approximately eighty thousand people on the islands including Key West who could be in harm's way.

Evacuation has been estimated to require up to thirty-six hours. The Labor Day Hurricane went from a Category 1 hurricane to a Category 5 during the thirty-six hours preceding its landfall at Craig. In a similar situation of rapid intensification, by the time the seriousness of the threat and the probable landfall location can be determined with any certainty, there may not be enough time to execute a full evacuation.

Moving people to the mainland does not guarantee their safety. A very slight change in direction could cause a storm to veer north of the Keys and strike the South Florida peninsula. The worst-case scenario would be for an evacuation to be ordered and for a hurricane to catch hundreds of people out on the road.

Hurricanes have always been a hazard that comes with living in the Florida Keys and other coastal areas. An appreciation that their behavior is not always predictable and an understanding of how they inflict damage and injury are essential to making the right decisions when a storm threatens. In this context, the experiences of the people of the Upper Florida Keys during the 1935 Labor Day Hurricane should never be forgotten.

Exhibits

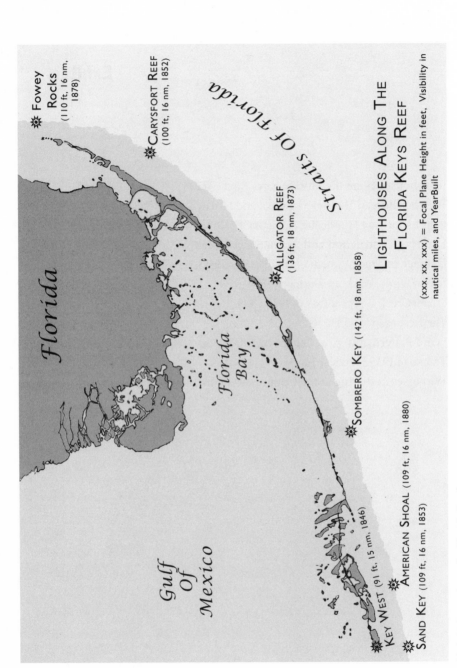

Lighthouses along the Florida Reef.

Within the image:

FOWEY ROCKS (110 ft, 16 nm, 1878)

CARYSFORT REEF (100 ft, 16 nm, 1852)

Straits of Florida

ALLIGATOR REEF (136 ft, 18 nm, 1873)

SOMBRERO KEY (142 ft, 18 nm, 1858)

Florida

Florida Bay

Gulf of Mexico

AMERICAN SHOAL (109 ft, 16 nm, 1880)

KEY WEST (91 ft, 15 nm, 1846)

SAND KEY (109 ft, 16 nm, 1853)

LIGHTHOUSES ALONG THE FLORIDA KEYS REEF

(xxx, xx, xxx) = Focal Plane Height in feet, Visibility in nautical miles, and YearBuilt

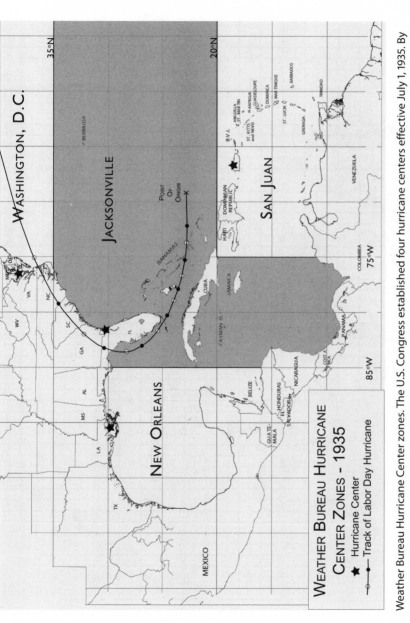

Weather Bureau Hurricane Center zones. The U.S. Congress established four hurricane centers effective July 1, 1935. By federal statute, the centers monitored specific zones of the Atlantic Ocean, Caribbean Sea, and Gulf of Mexico. The Labor Day Hurricane originated in the Jacksonville zone and entered the Washington, D.C., zone just before leaving the U.S. east coast on 9/6/1935. (Adapted from a chart in U.S. Congress, House of Representatives, *Florida Hurricane Disaster Hearings*, 74th Cong., 2nd sess.)

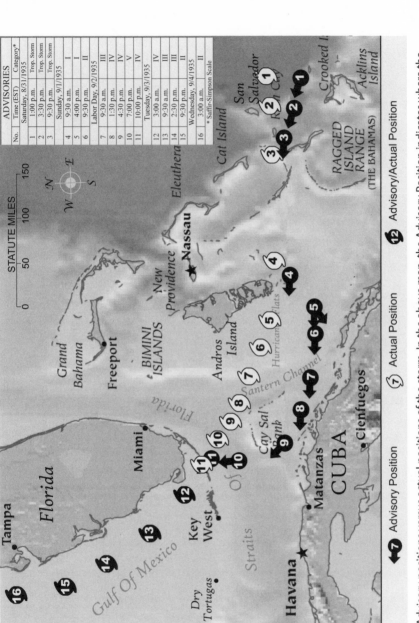

ADVISORIES		
No.	Time (EST)	Category*
	Saturday, 8/31/1935	
1	1:00 p.m.	Trop. Storm
2	3:30 p.m.	Trop. Storm
3	9:30 p.m.	Trop. Storm
	Sunday, 9/1/1935	
4	9:30 a.m.	I
5	4:00 p.m.	I
6	9:30 p.m.	II
	Labor Day, 9/2/1935	
7	9:30 a.m.	III
8	1:30 p.m.	IV
9	4:30 p.m.	IV
10	7:00 p.m.	V
11	10:00 p.m.	IV
	Tuesday, 9/3/1935	
12	3:00 a.m.	IV
13	9:30 a.m.	III
14	2:30 p.m.	III
15	9:30 p.m.	II
	Wednesday, 9/4/1935	
16	3:00 a.m.	II
* Saffir-Simpson Scale		

Advisory Position

Actual Position

Advisory/Actual Position

Advisory positions versus actual positions of the storm. In the above map, the Advisory Position indicates where the Weather Bureau believed the storm's center was located based on the data received while the storm was in progress; the Actual Position indicates where the center of the storm was located as determined later using all observation data, including that received after the storm's passage. (Data source: National Weather Service archives and chart of storm positions in U.S. Congress, House of Representatives, *Florida Hurricane Disaster Hearings*, 74th Cong., 2nd sess.)

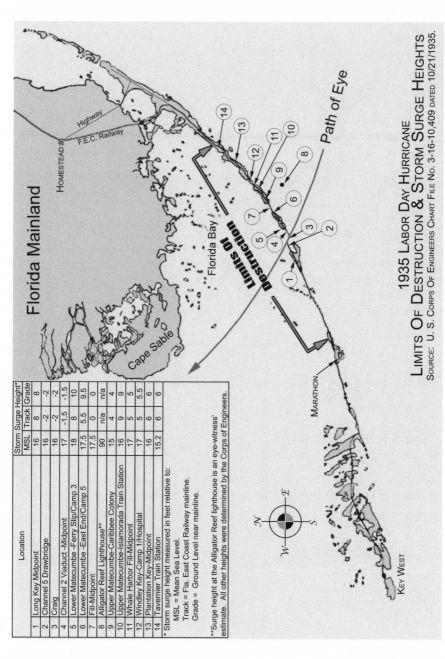

Florida Mainland

	Location	Storm Surge Height*		
		MSL	Track	Grade
1	Long Key Midpoint	16	8	8
2	Channel 5 Drawbridge	16	-2	-2
3	Craig	16	-2	-2
4	Channel 2 Viaduct -Midpoint	17	-1.5	-1.5
5	Lower Matecumbe -Ferry Slip/Camp 3	18	8	10
6	Lower Matecumbe -East End/Camp 5	17.5	5.5	9.5
7	Fill-Midpoint	17.5	0	0
8	Alligator Reef Lighthouse**	90	n/a	n/a
9	Upper Matecumbe-Caribbee Colony	15	4	4
10	Upper Matecumbe-Islamorada Train Station	16	9	9
11	Whale Harbor Fill-Midpoint	17	5	5
12	Windley Key-Camp 1/Hospital	17	5	5.5
13	Plantation Key-Midpoint	16	6	6
14	Tavernier Train Station	15.2	6	6

* Storm surge height measured in feet relative to:
MSL = Mean Sea Level.
Track = Fla. East Coast Railway mainline.
Grade = Ground Level near mainline.

**Surge height at the Alligator Reef lighthouse is an eye-witness'
estimate. All other heights were determined by the Corps of Engineers.

HOMESTEAD #

Highway

F.E.C. Railway

Limits of Destruction

Florida Bay

Cape Sable

Path of Eye

MARATHON

KEY WEST

N E W S

1935 LABOR DAY HURRICANE
LIMITS OF DESTRUCTION & STORM SURGE HEIGHTS
SOURCE: U. S. CORPS OF ENGINEERS CHART FILE NO. 3-16-10,409 DATED 10/21/1935.

Limits of destruction and storm surge heights. The height of the storm surge is shown above relative to sea level, the top of the mainline railroad track, and the natural ground level (grade).

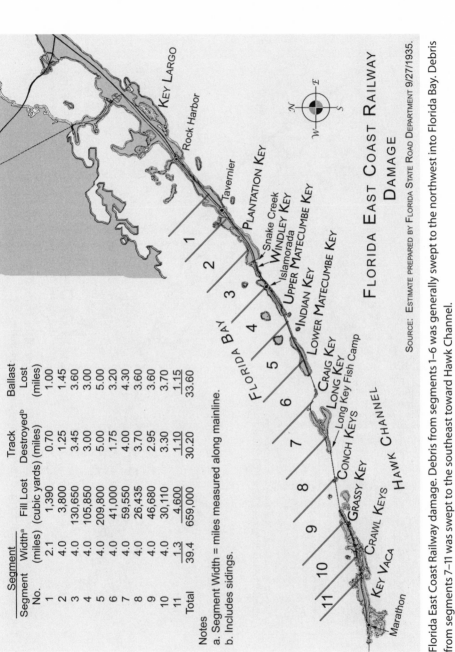

| Segment | | Fill Lost | Track | Ballast |
Segment No.	Width[a] (miles)	(cubic yards)	Destroyed[b] (miles)	Lost (miles)
1	2.1	1,390	0.70	1.00
2	4.0	3,800	1.25	1.45
3	4.0	130,650	3.45	3.60
4	4.0	105,850	3.00	3.00
5	4.0	209,800	5.00	5.00
6	4.0	41,000	1.75	3.20
7	4.0	59,550	4.00	4.30
8	4.0	26,435	3.70	3.60
9	4.0	46,680	2.95	3.60
10	4.0	30,110	3.30	3.70
11	1.3	4,600	1.10	1.15
Total	39.4	659,000	30.20	33.60

Notes
a. Segment Width = miles measured along mainline.
b. Includes sidings.

FLORIDA EAST COAST RAILWAY
DAMAGE

SOURCE: ESTIMATE PREPARED BY FLORIDA STATE ROAD DEPARTMENT 9/27/1935.

Florida East Coast Railway damage. Debris from segments 1–6 was generally swept to the northwest into Florida Bay. Debris from segments 7–11 was swept to the southeast toward Hawk Channel.

STORM SURGE WASHOUT DAMAGE

Source: U. S. Corps Of Engineers Chart File No. 3-16-10,409 dated 10/21/1935.

The 2,700 foot solid fill between Upper Matecumbe Key and Windley Key where Eddie Williams had just built his home was removed below the water line except for a small mound in the middle. The natural channels were restored.

The highway bridge and rail-road trestle at Snake Creek were washed out. The solid fill approaches to the trestle were removed leaving the concrete abutments standing naked. Camp 1 and the FERA hospital were swept away.

The 2.16 mile solid fill between Lower Matecumbe and Upper Matecumbe was demolished. An island of the fill's core remained on the large bank near the middle of the fill. The natural channels were restored; the one nearest Lower Matecumbe Key was gouged out to a depth of 10' below mean sea level. Veterans Camp 5 on the east end of Lower Matecumbe Key and the Caribee Colony on the west end of Upper Matecumbe Key were swept away.

Lower Matecumbe was the only key to have trenches cut through the face of the island. Two cuts, five feet deep, occurred on the west half of the key. The easternmost gouge was almost 1/2 mile wide. All structures at the west end of the island were destroyed or badly damaged. Most of Veterans Camp 3 was swept away.

Veterans Camp 1

Caribee Colony

Veterans Camp 5

Veterans Camp 3

STATUTE MILES

Storm surge washout damage.

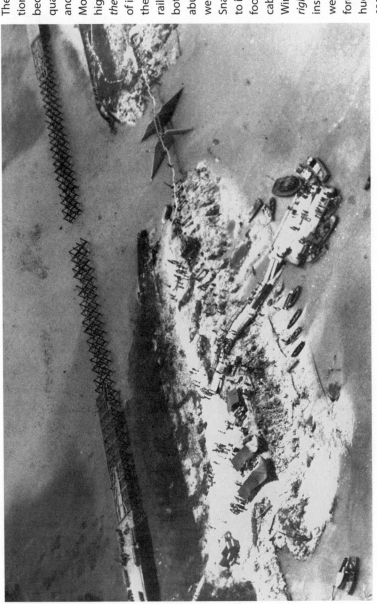

The west end of Plantation Key at Snake Creek became the field headquarters for the rescue and recovery operations. Most of the wooden highway bridge (*top of the photo*) was stripped of its decking, exposing the understructure. The railroad fill leading up to both sides of the concrete abutments and the trestle were washed away as Snake Creek was restored to its natural width. The footbridge of planks and cable strung across to Windley Key (*extreme right*) had not been installed when survivors were evacuated. In the foreground, small craft huddle around a large section of the highway deck that is being used as a dock. September 6, 1935. (Wilkinson)

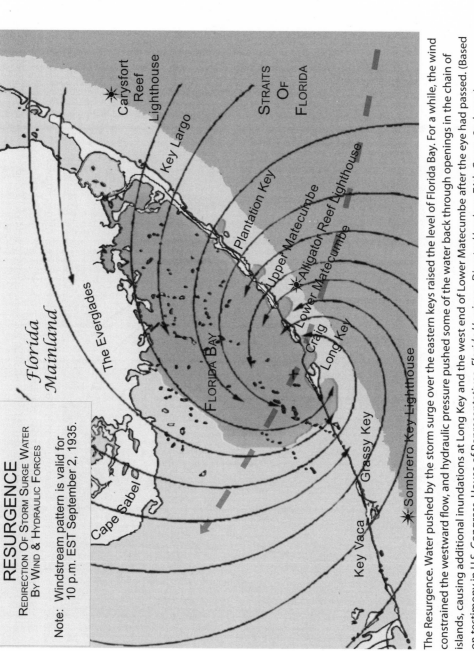

RESURGENCE
REDIRECTION OF STORM SURGE WATER
BY WIND & HYDRAULIC FORCES

Note: Windstream pattern is valid for
10 p.m. EST September 2, 1935.

Florida
Mainland

The Everglades

Cape Sable

FLORIDA BAY

Key Vaca

Grassy Key

Long Key

Craig

Lower Matecumbe

Alligator Reef Lighthouse

Upper Matecumbe

Plantation Key

Key Largo

Carysfort
Reef
Lighthouse

STRAITS
OF
FLORIDA

Sombrero Key Lighthouse

The Resurgence. Water pushed by the storm surge over the eastern keys raised the level of Florida Bay. For a while, the wind constrained the westward flow, and hydraulic pressure pushed some of the water back through openings in the chain of islands, causing additional inundations at Long Key and the west end of Lower Matecumbe after the eye had passed. (Based on testimony in U.S. Congress, House of Representatives, *Florida Hurricane Disaster Hearings*, 74th Cong., 2nd sess.)

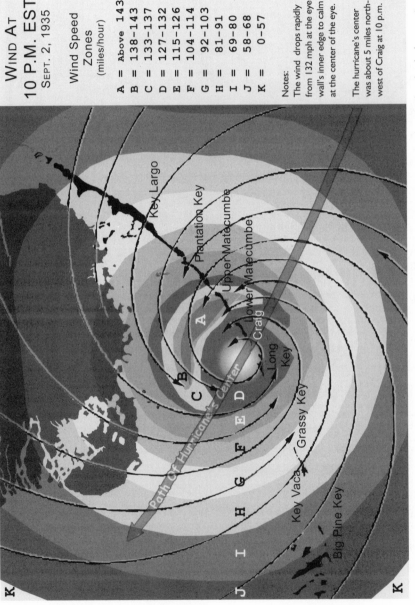

Wind At 10 P.M. EST
Sept. 2, 1935

Wind Speed
Zones
(miles/hour)

A = Above 143
B = 138-143
C = 133-137
D = 127-132
E = 115-126
F = 104-114
G = 92-103
H = 81-91
I = 69-80
J = 58-68
K = 0-57

Notes:
The wind drops rapidly from 132 mph at the eye wall's inner edge to calm at the center of the eye.

The hurricane's center was about 5 miles northwest of Craig at 10 p.m.

Wind at 10 p.m. EST. The direction of the wind is shown by the windstreams (curved ragged arrows). The shaded zones indicate the wind speed in miles per hour at points along the windstreams. At 10 p.m. the highest winds were concentrated in zone A. (Adapted from: S. H. Houston and M.D. Powell, M.D., 2003. Surface wind fields for Florida Bay hurricanes. *Journal of Coastal Research*, 19(3), 503–13.)

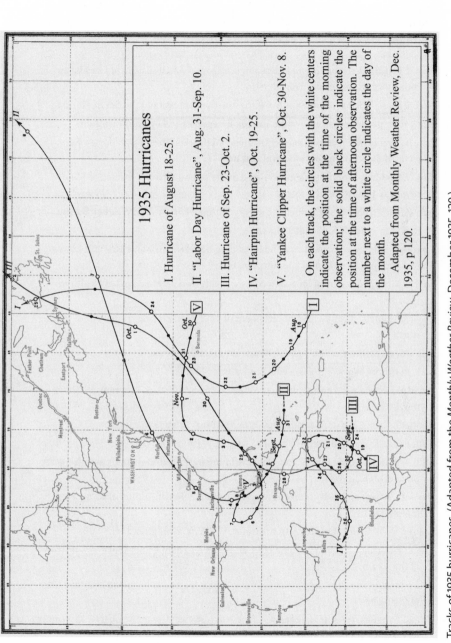

Tracks of 1935 hurricanes. (Adapted from the *Monthly Weather Review*, December 1935, 120.)

Witnesses Testifying at the Congressional Hearing

The following people gave testimony to the U.S. Congress, House Committee on World War Veterans' Legislation, H.R. 9486, House of Representatives, 74th Cong., 2nd sess. The hearing was held in Washington, D.C. Testimony was received from March 26, 1936, to May 6, 1936. As listed in the record of the hearing:

Hon. J. Hardin Peterson, member of Congress from the first district of Florida and sponsor of the bill under consideration

Hon. J. Mark Wilcox, representative of the fourth congressional district of Florida

Julius F. Stone, administrator of the Florida Emergency Relief Administration

Conrad Van Hyning, commissioner of Social Welfare in Florida and Florida Emergency Relief Administration administrator

Ray W. Sheldon, superintendent in charge of the veterans' camps located at Matecumbe; a survivor of the storm

Ivan R. Tannehill, assistant chief of the Forecasting Division, U.S. Weather Bureau

W. R. Gregg, chief, U.S. Weather Bureau

Charles P. Albury, captain of ferry boat running between No Name Key and Lower Matecumbe; a survivor of the storm

Dr. J. T. Googe, director of local and county health work, State Board of Health in Florida

H. G. McKenzie, businessman and resident of Tavernier, Florida; a survivor of the storm

F. B. Ghent, director of the Federal Works Program in Florida

E. A. Pynchon, Works Progress administrator for Florida

David W. Kennamer, central office investigator, Veterans' Work Program, Washington, D.C.

George E. Ijams, assistant administrator of Veterans' Affairs, Washington, D.C.

Gen. Frank T. Hines, director, Veterans' Affairs, Washington, D.C.

M. E. Gilfond, Florida Emergency Relief Administration administrator and the WPA director in Key West

Harry B. Wirin, assistant counsel, Federal Emergency Relief Administration, Washington, D.C.

Aubrey W. Williams, Deputy Administrator, W.P.A., Washington, D.C.

Joseph F. Fecteau, Veteran Assigned to Camp 5 as Assistant Timekeeper; A Survivor of the Storm.

S. C. Cutler, works director for the veterans' camps located at Matecumbe; a survivor of the storm

Harold Langlois, veteran assigned to Camp 1 as a stonecutter at the quarry on Windly Key; a survivor of the storm

Mrs. Laura Van Ness, a survivor of the storm and widow of Benjamin Van Ness, a veteran assigned to Camp 1

Selected Bibliography

The most important sources of information for this book were the firsthand recollections of survivors and others involved with the hurricane. In addition to providing their recollections, they also made available materials from family papers and albums.

The following is a very abbreviated listing of works researched for this book. A comprehensive listing of sources in hard copy and in electronic (pdf) form is available at the Florida History Department of the Monroe County May Hill Russell Library, 700 Fleming Street, Key West, Fla., 33040.

Best, Gary Dean. *FDR and the Bonus Marchers, 1933–1935*. New York: Praeger, 1992.

Brady, Doris L. *The Last Train from Key West*. Published by the author, 1995. Available at the State Library of Florida, Tallahassee.

Browne, Jefferson Beale. *Key West: The Old and the New*. St. Augustine, Fla.: Record Co., 1912.

Chandler, David Leon. *Henry Flagler: The Astonishing Life and Times of the Visionary Robber Baron Who Founded Florida*. New York: Macmillan, 1986.

Chapin, George M. *Key West Extension of the Florida East Coast Railway: "The Overseas Railroad."* Issued by Overseas Railroad Extension Celebration Committee of Key West. St. Augustine, Fla.: Record Co., 1912.

Dean, Love. *Lighthouses of the Florida Keys*. Key West: Historic Florida Keys Foundation, 1992.

Douglas, Marjory Stoneman. *Hurricane*. New York: Rinehart, 1958.

Dunn, Gordon E., and Banner I. Miller. *Atlantic Hurricanes*. Baton Rouge: Louisiana State University Press, 1964.

Eyster, Jeanne, and Irving Eyster. *Islamorada and More*. Marathon, Fla.: Pigeon Key Foundation, 1997.

Fernald, Edward A., and Elizabeth D. Purdum, eds. *Atlas of Florida*. Gainesville: University Press of Florida, 1996.

Florida Dept. of Agriculture. Sixth Census of the State of Florida—1935. Tallahassee: Florida Dept. of Agriculture, 1935.

Gallagher, Dan. *Florida's Great Ocean Railway*. Sarasota, Fla.: Pineapple Press, 2003.

Hemingway, Ernest. *Ernest Hemingway, Selected Letters, 1917–1961*. Edited by Carlos Baker. New York: Scribner, 1981.

Hofsommer, Donovan L. *The Southern Pacific, 1901–1985*. College Station: Texas A&M University Press, 1986.

Lane, Ed, ed. *Florida's Geological History and Geological Resources*. Tallahassee: Florida Geological Survey, 1994.

Larson, Erik. *Isaac's Storm: A Man, a Time, and the Deadliest Hurricane in History*. New York: Crown, 1999.

Lovering, Frank W. *A Hurricane Between*. St. Augustine, Fla.: Published by the author, 1946.

McLendon, James. *Papa: Hemingway in Key West*. 1972. Rev. ed. Key West: Langley Press, 1990.

Miles, Perry Lester. *Fallen Leaves: Memories of an Old Soldier*. Berkeley, Calif.: Wuerth, 1961.

Muir, Helen. *Miami, U.S.A.* New York: Holt, 1953.

Parks, Pat. *The Railroad That Died at Sea: The Florida East Coast's Key West Extension*. Brattleboro, Vt.: S. Greene Press, 1968.

Pepper, Claude Denson, with Hays Gorey. *Pepper, Eyewitness to a Century*. San Diego: Harcourt Brace Jovanovich, 1987.

Reno, Jane Wood. *The Hell with Politics: The Life and Writings of Jane Wood Reno*. Edited by George Hurchalla. Atlanta: Peachtree, 1994.

Rubert, Frank R., and Kenneth Campbell. "Geology and Man." Chapter 4 in *Florida's Geological History and Geological Resources*, compiled and edited by Ed Lane. Tallahassee: Florida Geological Survey, 1994.

Simpson, Lois. *The Island Of Key Largo, Florida—1872–1983*. Mayfield, Ky.: Mayfield Printing, 1983.

Smiley, Nixon. *Knights of the Fourth Estate: The Story of the* Miami Herald. Miami: E. A. Seemann, 1974.

Steen, Murphy J. F. *Twenty-five Years a U.S. Border Patrolman*. Dallas: Royal, 1958.

Tannehill, Ivan Ray. *Hurricanes, Their Nature and History, Particularly Those of the West Indies and the Southern Coasts of the United States*. Princeton, N.J.: Princeton University Press, 1956.

U.S. Congress. House of Representatives. *Florida Hurricane Disaster Hearings: Committee on World War Veterans' Legislation, H.R. 9486*. 74th Cong., 2nd sess., 1936.

———. *Report No. 2899*. 74th Cong., 2nd sess., May 29, 1936.

Viele, John. *The Florida Keys: A History of the Pioneers*. Sarasota, Fla.: Pineapple Press, 1996.

———. *The Florida Keys*. Vol. 3, *The Wreckers*. Sarasota, Fla.: Pineapple Press, 2001.

Whitnah, Donald R. *A History of the United States Weather Bureau*. Urbana: University of Illinois Press, 1961.

Wilkinson, Jerry. "History of Craig Key." *History Talk from the Upper Keys* 39 (Spring 2007). Publication of the Historical Preservation Society of the Upper Keys. Key Largo, Fla.

Windhorn, Stan, and Wright Langley. *Yesterday's Florida Keys*. Miami: E. A. Seemann, 1974.

Illustration Credits

All maps and exhibits were prepared by the author.

Index

investigative report, 292, 293. *See also* Emergency Relief Administration, Florida's

Federal Shipbuilding and Dry Dock Company, 85

Felton, Berlin, 303

FERA. *See* Federal Emergency Relief Administration

ferry: bridge-building versus, 32–33, *33*, 311; Cuban railcar service relocation, 285; Havana–New Orleans, 262; landing, *xiv, xv*; Lower Matecumbe Key west end, 57–58, *59*, 195; *Monroe County* (ferry), 91–92, 94–95, 97–98, 195–96, 239–41, *240*, 241; from No Name Key, 57–58, *59*; repaired, 310; slip, *xiii*

fingerprint specialist, 266

fire balls, 186, 200

first-aid supplies, 229

fishing industry, 8, 30, 58

fish, tropical, 232

Flagler, Henry, 10

"floater," 264

Florida Bay, *xiii, xv, 322*; bodies harvested at, 269; bridge-building plan, 32–33, *33*, 311; Labor Day hurricane route, *196*; redirection of storm surge, *329*

Florida City, *xiii*

Florida East Coast (FEC) Railway, *xiii, xiv*; damage to, 261–62, 283–85, *326*; headquarters of, *xvi*; before the hurricane, 3; rescue train ordered/assembled, 126–28; right-of-way purchased from, 311; track, *325*; volunteers from, 266; "Y" table at Homestead, 134–35, *135*

Florida Emergency Relief Administration. *See* Emergency Relief Administration

Florida Keys, *xii, xiii*; bridge-building on, 32–33, *33*, 311; cemeteries on, 291; Craig Key, *xiii, xiv*; Dinner Key, *xiii*, 237; Garden Key, 108; Grassy Key, *xiii, 329*; Indian Key, *xiii*, 100, 279; Jewfish Key, *xiv*; Key Largo, *xiii*, 52, 140, 165–66, 283, *329*; Key Vaca, 278, *329*; Labor Day hurricane route, *196*; lighthouses along, *323*; Lignum Vitae Key, *xiii, xiv, xv*; Long Key, *xiii, xiv, 196*, 198, 234, *325, 329*; Long Key fish camp, *xiii, xiv*, 143, 250; loss of life estimates, 289–90; Lower Matecumbe Key, 57–58, *59*, 195; No Name Key, *xiii*, 57–58, *59*, 242; Plantation

Key, *xiii, xv, 60*, 219, 221–23, *325*; Sand Key, 109–10; smuggling in, 66; Sombrero Key, *329*; Upper Keys, 44, 170, 239; veterans relocated to, 43–44; Wilson Key, *xvii, xviii*; Windley Key, *xiii, xv, xviii*, 63, 140–43, *141*, 175–77, 223, 249, 282, *325, 326*. *See also* Key West; Lower Matecumbe Key

Florida Mainland, *329*

Florida State Board of Health, 264, 269

Florida State College for Women (FSCW), 26, 113

Florida Straits: *Dixie's* route through, 92–94, *93*; hurricane entering, 131; storm moving toward, 89–90, 108–10

Fokker Flying Life Boat, 243–45

Folds, Dennis, 84

food finding, 226–27, 250. *See also* water

forecasting, history of, 5–6, 15–17

Fort Jefferson National Monument, 109

Fowey Rocks, *322*

Frankenfield, H. C., 6

Freeport, *324*

Freeze, Bill, 218–19, 221

French Reef, 253, 261

French Shoal, 166; *Dixie* on, 165–67, 258–60

Fresnel lens, 164

FSCW. *See* Florida State College for Women

fuel/cargo oil, 77, 261

Fulwood, C. A., 54–55

Gaddis, P. L., 98, 104, 127

Gainesville, Florida, 44–45, 73

Gale, George, 85, 214

Galveston, Texas, 16, 17

Gamble, J. E., 172–74

gangrene, 67

Garden Key, 108

George Washington University, 18, 20

Ghent, Fred, 50, 97, 124–25, 332

Gibson Inn, 90

Gilbert (sponger), 138, *196*

Gilfond, M. E., 332

Golden Gate Bridge, San Francisco, 32

Goluboff, Grisha, 94

Good, John, 37, 50, 97; in storm surge, 171–72

Googe, J. T., 264, 332

Goulds, *xiii*

Governor Cobb (steamship), 288

grade (ground level near mainline), *325*

Modello, *xiii*

Molasses Reef lighthouse, 281

Monroe County (ferry), 91–92, 94–95, 97–98,
138; Coast Guard arrival, 241; as shelter,
195–96; after storm, 239–41, *240*

Moon, influence of, 168–69

Moore, James, 241

Morgan Shipping Line, 258–60. See also
Dixie; Southern Pacific

Morro Castle (excursion ship), 258, 259

Mortensen, Richard, 144–45, 165, 257, 261. See
also *Leise Maersk* (freighter)

mosquitoes, 10–11, 265, 286

motor pool inventory, 56, *56*

MSL. *See* mean sea level

Mudd, Samuel, 108

Muir, Helen, *163,* 202–5, 306

Murray, Karlie, 54–55

Mussolini, Benito, 77–78, 261

Naranja, *xiii*

Nassau, *324*

National Guard, 230, 242, 266, 268, 269–70

National Oceanographic and Atmospheric
Administration (NOAA), 2

Nautilus (custom-built railroad car), 230–32,
231, 250, 261, 286–88, 316

Naval Academy, Annapolis, Maryland, 27

Naval Radio Station, 16–17, 76–77. *See also*
U.S. Navy

Nemesis, 271

Ness, Benny Van. *See* Van Ness, Benjamin

New Deal, 15

Newfoundland, 314

New Masses (periodical), 296

New Orleans, 85–86; Havana–New Orleans
ferry, 262; hurricane-warning center, 16;
prior to hurricane, 3; on Weather Bureau
teletype circuit, 17

New Orleans Zone, *323*

New Providence, Bahamas, *324*

New York City, 260

Nielsen, Torges, 84

NOAA. *See* National Oceanographic and
Atmospheric Administration

Nobel, Isidore, 94

No Name Key, *xiii,* 242; ferry from, 57–58, *59*

Norton, Grady, 18–19, *20,* 23, 120, *162,* 312–13

nurses, 229, 241

ocean waves: Category 5, 143–44; height of
surge, 175; resurgence, 194, 198–99, 200,
201; sea bottom versus, 168, *168*

Odense Steel Shipyard Ltd., Denmark, 77

oil, cargo and fuel: dangers posed by, 77, 261

Old Quarry, xviii

Olivette (steamer), 12

Olson, C. B., 238–39

Olson, Dorothy, 115–16

Olson, Ivor "Ollie": boat, *xiv, 115,* 115–16

Olson, R. W., 279

Overseas Highway Bridge Corporation,
32–33, *33*

Palatka, Florida, 44, 73

Palmer, George, Sr., 27

Palmer, George Goldston, 27, 306

Palmer, Mary Keith, 27

Palmer, Rosalind Grooms, 24–27, 78–79, 80–81,
97, 118, 132, 133, *151, 152*; body found, 273–74

palm trees, 214, 224

Panama, 242

Pan American Airlines, 238

Pandora, 214, 253, 256

papaya tree, 68

Parker, Edney, 51, 165, 180, 250, *251,* 269–70,
303, 304–5; house of, *xvi,* 184–86

Parker, Etta, 51, *251*

Parker, Fay Marie, 227, 250, *251,* 309, *310*

Parker family, *63,* 184–86, 200–201, *251,* 305

Parrish family, 277–78

Paschalls, Stephen, 47

Peacock, Doris, 90

Peggy (fishing boat), *63, 64,* 69–70

Pensacola, Florida, 17

Pepper, Claude Denson, 34–35, *155*

Pepper, George Truett, 34–38, *44,* 50, 52,
78, 81, 97, 118, 132, 133, *152, 153, 154*; body
found, 273, 275–76

Pepper family, 271, 275–76

Perdomo, Felipe, 196

Perdue, Sam, 172–74

Perrine, *xiii*

Pervis, Jones, 139, 164

Peterson, J. Hardin, 298, 332

Pierson, Virgil, 212–13, 252

Pilar, 211

Pinder, Braime, *xvi,* 182–83, 303

Pinder, Charley, 227

Pinder, Edna, 180

Pinder, John, 65

Pinder, Mary "Mamie," 182, 308

pineapple cannery, 30

Plantation Key, *xiii, xv,* 219; population distribution, *60;* storm surge heights, *325;* survivors at, 221–23

Platano, 208, 211–12, 253

Plummer, Ira, *20*

Police Department, Miami, 266

Poock, Fred, 50, 53

Pooser, A. I., 126–27, 132

population distribution (Craig to Tavernier), *61, 62;* racial categories, *60*

Port Arthur: on Weather Bureau teletype circuit, 17

Porter, J. Y., 9, 312

Porter, Mary Louise, 312

Port Everglades, 285–86

Presidential Advisory Board, 16

Princeton, *xiii*

Public Works Administration (PWA), 34

Pueblo (tanker), 129, 131; without engines, 143–44

Puerto Rico, 314, *323;* Labor Day thunderstorms north of, 22; San Juan hurricane-warning center, 16, 21

Pullman Car Works, Chicago, 232

Pumper's House, *xv*

Purvis, Jones A., 112

PWA. *See* Public Works Administration

Pynchon, E. A., 332

Quattlebaum, Harold, *20*

racial segregation: Gainesville veterans, 44–45, 73; population distribution, 60, *60*

radio antenna. *See* antenna system, radio

Radio Club, Miami Amateur, 230

Radio Direction Finding Station, 208, 212

Radiomarine Corporation station WOE, 206–7

Radio Station, Key West, 16–17, 76

Ragged Island Range, *324*

railroad embankment: water approaching top of, 140, 143

railroad mile marker, *xvi, xviii*

Rankin, John E., 299–300

Ransom, L. D., 252

RD-4 Dolphin, 100, *101*

Reaper, 253

Rebecca Shoal, 109

Red Cross, 229, 230, 241, 267–68, 305, 306, 308; house, *301*

Reed, Walter, 10

reefs, 168, *168;* sensitive environment of, 261

refrigeration, shipboard, 30

Relief, 257–58

relief camps (war veterans), *40,* 41–45

Reno, Henry, *160,* 221–22, 269, 307

Reno, Janet, 307

rescue and recovery: coordination of organizations, 267–68; *Dixie,* 252–58; headquarters for, *328;* Homestead's, 235–36; launching ramp for, 229; radio for, 229–30; trucks, 242; volunteers, 228, 242. *See also* American Legion; *Leise Maersk* (freighter); Red Cross; special train

rescue train, 134–35, *135;* headmaster, 127–28, 129, 140, 172–74; hoisting gin cable versus, 140–43, *141;* at Key Largo, 140; snagged at Windley Key, *141,* 142–43; after storm surge, 215–17, *216;* storm surge over, 171–75. *See also* train

resurgence, 194, 200; barometric readings, 201; Duane on, 198–99

Rhoads, N. B. "Dusty," 10

Riverside Hospital, 247

Robertson, Glenn, 50

Rockdale, *xiii*

Rock Harbor, *xiii*

Rogers, Will, 146

Rommel, Edward, 145–46

Roosevelt, Franklin Delano, 42, 43, 74, 251, 259, 263, 291, 294, 298; on cremation, 269; New Deal, 15

Royal Palms Hotel, 242

Russell, Bernard, 189–91, 303

Russell, Emma, 189–91

Russell, John A., *xvii,* 5, 189, 303, 308

Russell, T. F., 176

Russell, Walter, 138, 196

Russell family, 189–91, 271

Rustic Inn, *xv, xvi,* 50–51, 53, 57, 106, 111, 186–87; back in business, 303–5; *Dixie* and *Leise Maersk* survivors at, 234; opening of, 56; survivors at, 223–24

Ryder, Jack, 183–84, 303

Thomas Neil Knowles is a fourth-generation native of Key West who enjoys writing about the history of the Florida Keys and Key West. He recently retired from Florida State University.